Table of Contents

Title Page — 7

CHAPTER 1 — 8

Introduction — 8

E-BOOK HAS COLOR PHOTOS — 8

FOR THE BEGINNER — 8

SAVE SERIOUS MONEY — 9

THE DREADED FLAT TIRE — 9

INSTALLING NEW TIRES — 10

WHEEL BALANCING — 10

YOU CAN EARN MONEY WITH THIS BOOK — 10

DON'T BELIEVE THE DEALER'S HYPE — 11

CAUTION—RIM DAMAGE — 11

FREE TIRES — 12

EXCEPTIONS TO THE DO-IT-YOURSELF RULE — 14

YOU CAN'T TRUST YOUR TIRE INSTALLER ANYMORE — 14

HOW MUCH KNOWLEDGE WILL YOU RECEIVE? — 15

WHAT ABOUT THOSE HUGE 230+ SIZE REAR TIRES? — 15

HOW THIS BOOK WORKS — 16

QUICK REFERENCE GUIDE IS INCLUDED — 16

UNDERSTANDING PHOTO FIGURE NUMBERING — 16

BEFORE WE BEGIN — 16

CHAPTER 2 — 16

Description of Tools Needed — 16

MINIMUM TOOLS NEEDED — 16

TIRE CHANGING MACHINES — 17

TIRE MOUNT/DEMOUNT BARS — 18

TIRE MOUNTING LUBRICANTS — 19

NO TIRE CHANGING MACHINE — 20

HOW TO USE THIS BOOK — 22

WATCH TIRE CHANGING — 23

THE PROBLEM WITH INTERNET VIDEOS — 23

THE PROBLEM WITH SPOKE WIRE WHEELS	24
SPOKE WHEEL FLAT PREVENTION	24
CAST WHEELS ARE BEST	25
WORKSHEET	26
MOTORCYCLE JACK FRAME LIFT	26
AIR COMPRESSOR - SHOP STYLE	30
THE SHORTCUT METHOD USING FEWER TOOLS	31
DEALING WITH FRUSTRATION	32
ORIENTATION	33
SPOKE RIM & MAG WHEELS	33
TOOLS FOR FRONT WHEEL	33
TORQUE SPECIFICATIONS FOR YOUR BIKE	34
FRONT WHEEL TORQUE SPECIFICATIONS	34
REAR WHEEL TORQUE SPECIFICATIONS	34
TOOLS FOR REAR WHEEL	34
TOOLS TO CHANGE TIRES	34
THREAD LOCKING COMPOUNDS	35
EXAMINE WHEEL WHILE ON BIKE	35
BEFORE REMOVING WHEEL: MARK ITS ROTATION	36
BUYING TIRES FOR YOUR MOTORCYCLE	36

CHAPTER 3   36

Front Wheel Removal From Motorcycle	36
FRONT WHEEL REMOVAL	37
LIFTING THE BIKE ON THE JACK	38

CHAPTER 4   42

Removing Tire From The Rim	42
REMOVING TIRE FROM THE RIM	42
WHEEL SUPPORT	42
WOOD BLOCKS	43
REMOVE VALVE CAP AND VALVE STEM CORE	44
BEAD BREAKER - BUYING ONE	46

BEAD BREAKING	46
USING THE BEAD BREAKER	48
RIM PROTECTORS	49
REMOVING TOP SIDE OF THE TIRE	50
TIRE LUBRICANTS	50
REMOVING TOP BEAD OF TIRE FROM RIM	51
REMOVING OPPOSITE LOWER SIDE OF TIRE	53
REPLACING VALVE STEM	55
BUYING NEW WHEELS	55

CHAPTER 5   55

Installing Tire On The Rim - Tire Irons	55
INSTALLING THE NEW FRONT TIRE	55
CLEANING THE RIM	55
LUBRICATING THE TIRE	57
TIRE SIZE - THE CORRECT SIZE	58
TIRE SIZE FOR MY BIKE	59
ADVICE BEFORE WE INSTALL THE TIRE	59
TRADE SECRETS	60
TIRE IRON BITES	61
LUBE THE TIRE & RIM	61
WHEEL ROTATION DIRECTION	63
INSTALLING LOWER SIDE OF TIRE TO RIM	64
INSTALLING UPPER SIDE OF TIRE TO RIM	70

CHAPTER 6   77

End Point Tire Installation Problems	77
PROBLEMS INSTALLING TIRE	77
TROUBLESOME WALKING TIRE BEAD	79
C-CLAMP USE ON TIRE AND RIM	79

CHAPTER 7   82

Inflation of Tire	82

PRESSURE GAUGE CALIBRATION	82
ADDING AIR TO THE NEW TIRE	83
BOUNCING THE TIRE ON THE RIM	85
TIRE BEAD STARTER STRAP - HOW TO USE	85
TIRE BEAD STARTER STRAP - HOW TO USE	87
TIRE SCUFFING BREAK-IN	89
VALVE STEM & CAPS	89

CHAPTER 8   90

Balancing The Wheel	90
BALANCING THE WHEEL	90
WHEEL WEIGHT STRIPS	96

CHAPTER 9   97

Installing Front Wheel	97
INSTALLING THE FRONT WHEEL	97
ALIGNING FRONT WHEEL TO FORKS	102

CHAPTER 10   104

Removing Rear Wheel	104
REMOVING THE REAR WHEEL	104
INSTALLING REAR WHEEL	105

CHAPTER 11   107

Replace Tire on Spoke Rim	107
HOW TO REPLACE A TUBE TIRE	107
BASIC PROCEDURE - REPLACING INSTALLING TUBE-TYPE TIRE	108
DUNLOP TIRE COMPANY'S SAFETY TAG	110
SAFETY WARNING	110
RUN IN	110

CHAPTER 12   110

Fixing Flat Tires	110
HOW TO FIX A FLAT TIRE ON YOUR MOTORCYCLE	110

HELPING OTHERS IN NEED	110
TUBELESS TIRES ONLY	110
FIX-A-FLAT SYSTEM - HOW TO USE	111
FIX A FLAT USING AEROSOL CAN METHOD	112
DON'T BUY A MOTORCYCLE WITH SPOKE WHEELS	113

CHAPTER 13 114

Tubeless Tire Repair - Mushroom Plug	114
TUBELESS TIRES ONLY - TEMPORARY REPAIRS	114
TWO PLUGS TO FIX FLAT TUBELESS TIRES	115
RUBBER PLUG	115
STRING ROPE PLUG	116
FLAT TIRE - OUT OF TOWN	117
EMERGENCY "TO DO" BREAKDOWN INSTRUCTIONS	117
TIRE REPAIR TOOL KIT	117
PORTABLE AIR COMPRESSOR	118

CHAPTER 14 119

Tubeless Tire Repair - Using Mushroom Plug	119
PLUGGING THE TIRE WITH A RUBBER MUSHROOM PLUG	119
PHOTOS USING MUSHROOM PLUG	122
HOW TO REMOVE A LEAKING RUBBER PLUG	124
CAR & PICK UP TRUCK TIRES	124

CHAPTER 15 125

String Rope - Tubeless Tire Repair	125
PLUGGING THE TIRE WITH STRING ROPE	125

CHAPTER 16 131

Tire Machine - Using Manual Machine	131
BASIC MODEL	131
TIRE MACHINE PROCEDURE - MANUALLY OPERATED	132

CHAPTER 17 147

Tire Information	**147**
TIRE TALK	**147**
AIR PRESSURE MONITORING	**147**
HOW TO SELECT TIRES FOR YOUR MOTORCYCLE	**147**
EXPENSIVE TIRES ARE NOT BETTER	**149**
A FATTER TIRE	**150**
TIRE SIZE NOT TRULY STATED	**150**
OVERSIZED REAR TIRE	**151**
OVERSIZE FRONT WHEEL	**151**
EXTRA SET OF WHEELS	**151**
TRACKING LOG CHART FOR SPARE WHEEL SETS	**152**
MAGAZINE BIAS	**153**

CHAPTER 18 — 153

Quick Reference Guide — **153**

CHAPTER 19 — 153

Questions & Answers	**153**
LAST WORD	**195**
The End	**195**
PHOTOGRAPH INDEX	**195**

Title Page

How To Install Tires On Motorcycles & Fix Flat Tires
Copyright © 2012 and 2013 by James Russell - All Rights Reserved

PRINT VERSION
How To Install Tires On Motorcycles & Fix Flat Tires
ISBN-10: 0-916367-77-0
ISBN-13: 978-0-916367-77-0
Published January 2013

E-BOOK VERSION
How To Install Tires On Motorcycles & Fix Flat Tires
ISBN-10: 0-916367-63-0
ISBN-13: 978-0-916367-63-3
Published December 2012

Dedicated To:
A Word of Biblical Wisdom: "My people are destroyed for lack of knowledge." - Hosea 4:6

Gift To:_____

From:_____

Fig. A. Author On Fat Boy Harley With Big Fat Tires

CHAPTER 1

Introduction

"You Will Love Changing Your Own Tires... I Guarantee It!- James Russell

Have you ever wondered why you must pay money to have somebody fix flats and install new tires on your motorcycle, Trike or ATV? Did it cross your mind you can do it yourself to save a lot of money?

When I was growing up, almost all bikers I knew fixed their own motorcycles, including repairing flat tires and removing old tires and installing new ones on the wheels. As time evolved new riders came on the scene. This odd breed of biker paid to have these routine repairs performed. This is especially true with the big heavy-cruiser riders such as the Harley-Davidson, Victory, BMW, Honda, Yamaha and Triumph owners. Yes, you can change fat tires using only tire irons. See Fig.2-9.

The sport bike (crotch rocket) riders are also now gravitating to this "don't fix it yourself" theme. They don't know how to do it or have been repeatedly told by dealers that tire changing can no longer be performed by the motorcycle owner. Don't believe it! This book will show you how.

E-BOOK HAS COLOR PHOTOS

The print version of this book may or may not have color photos depending on the print run, but is generally a black & white printing. For full-color get the e-book version. The color photos have a sharper resolution in the e-book showing much more detail.

FOR THE BEGINNER

This book is specifically designed for the beginner, the complete novice who has never fixed a flat tire and has never attempted to remove and install new tires on a motorcycle. This book will show you how it is done with simple, inexpensive, easy-to-use basic hand tools.

And Fix Flat Tires

SAVE SERIOUS MONEY

The cost of operating a motorcycle keeps rising. Fuel, insurance, registration, oil and tire changes. Calculate what you are paying for tire changes alone, and this should clearly convince you it is high time to do it yourself. It is not uncommon to pay over five hundred dollars just for a street motorcycle's front and rear tires changed. If you ride a lot, you will go through three to four sets of tires each year! It is ridiculous to have to pay so much money for motorcycle tires. The good news is that you don't have to! Doing it yourself and buying your tires on the Internet will get you better brand name tires at half the dealer's cost or less, with free shipping and no taxes—if tax law and website shipping policies has not changed since this book was published. Regardless, you will still save money doing it yourself. That is a lot of money you can save every year of your life! Add it up.

Tip: Often you will see a motorcycle tire brand being used by most riders on certain motorcycles. I used to believe those tires were the best and that is why most riders buy them. However, I have found this not to be true. It is the tire most dealers and repair shops get the highest profits selling and installing those tires. If you shop around and experiment with different brands of tires you will find superior tires that wear longer and ride even nicer. The majority of riders do not have the best tires on their bikes. Best meaning lower price and higher performance and value for the dollar. See Question #261.

Fig. 1-1 Harley-Davidson Sportster Used In This Book - Location: Frenchman's Lake, California

THE DREADED FLAT TIRE

Fixing a flat tire is a simple procedure with a "fix-a-flat," "rubber plug" or "rope tire repair" tool kit. I will show you how to use these kits and inflate your tires so you will never be stranded again with a flat tire on a lonely road in the back country far away from home where your cell phone does not function. I will also reveal the products that do not work but that are readily sold by motorcycle dealers and accessories shops!

Think about that for a moment. Imagine getting a flat tire from a nail puncture in a remote area far from home. Your cell phone has no reception, and few cars pass by to assist. Those that do wouldn't be much help to you either. They don't know how to fix your tire or call for help quickly because no one's cell phones reach into all the remote places motorcycle riders like to ride in. This book will take away one big misery. Whether you get a flat tire in the middle of nowhere or just a few miles from home, you will be up and running again in about fifteen minutes, less than the time it takes to drink a cup of hot coffee! Never be stranded or call a tow truck again. This alone makes the price of this book worth every penny.

Warning: Fixing a flat tire is only a temporary repair to get you home (or to a motorcycle shop to install a new tire if you are touring far from home). The danger is high; the temporary repair could fail and blow out air quickly, making you lose control. Plug the tire, get home, and install a new tire right away. Remember to ride slowly, no more than 50 miles per hour, so centrifugal force will not cause the repair plug to pull out. No hard braking, bumps or acceleration should be applied to the tire. There's more advice on the websites of the manufacturers that make tire repair products, and many motorcycle magazines often do have helpful articles on this subject.

INSTALLING NEW TIRES

You can buy motorcycle tires cheaply from many competing tire dealers on the Internet. That way you get the "best" tires instead of only what the local dealer recommends—which is rarely the best. Usually it's more prone to wear out quickly so they can get you back faster for repeat business!

The first time you buy a set of tires, the money you save will more than repay you for the price of this book! You will also save money on installation and balancing. Yes, I'll be showing you how easy it is to balance a motorcycle wheel. You will laugh out loud when you see how easy it is to static balance a wheel with a new tire, and you'll scream in anger that dealers charge you extra money for doing it!

Best of all, you will learn to enjoy installing your own tires on your motorcycle—and you will be one step ahead of all the other egotistic riders who try to get one up on you. You know what I'm talking about. Now you can say, "By the way, where do you go to get your tires installed?" When they answer, you can say, "I install my own tires and I balance them myself." Add up the savings you will obtain from buying your own tires and slipping them on yourself. This book will pay for itself like the money-making investment it truly is!

WHEEL BALANCING

I will show you how easy it is to do, so do not become concerned about this mysterious procedure. It really is very easy.

YOU CAN EARN MONEY WITH THIS BOOK

You can change tires for your friends and create for yourself a part-time job. You could also work for a motorcycle shop, installing tires for them during their busy season, or for tire dealers who change tires at motorcycle rallies. Even if you live in an apartment or RV where vehicle repairs are not authorized, you can still do it inside your home if your customers simply bring you the wheels. You can change and balance them on your living room floor. Yes, it is that easy to do. All you need is a couple bath towels and a heavy drop cloth, to protect your rug from stains, along with two 4"×4" wood blocks (Fig. 1-2), three feet long, to rest the wheel on. Then go to work. No rotary tire changing machine is required.

Fig. 1-2 Tire Resting On Wood Blocks.

Tip: You can change tires on top of an old oil drum or on blocks of wood or set the wheel on top of some old motorcycle or car tires, but I say, why not make the commitment and do it right? Purchase a tire changing machine or a tire changing stand. Even if you just use tire irons to change tires, the machine or stand holds the wheel firmly at a good height off the floor and the tire changing machine has a bead breaker too. It would be a shame to change tires on the floor only to find it too difficult to do and you become frustrated and say you will never to do it again. If you search the Internet you may even find some plans on how to make your own tire changing stand. It would not be difficult to create your own system.

Fig. 1-3 shows a Harbor Freight Tools® or Chicago Tools® Brand tire and rim stand. This is perhaps the most economical unit you can buy and it even comes with a powerful bead breaker and is portable. With a drop cloth you could easily use this inside any living room floor for those who do not own or have access to a garage. If you must use indoors I would use it to break the beads on the tire from the rim, use it as a workstation to hold the wheel in position and use tire irons not the rotary mounting bar because there is no way to prevent the device from spinning using the rotary method of mounting tires. This device in Fig. 1-3 is all you need for a tire changing machine.

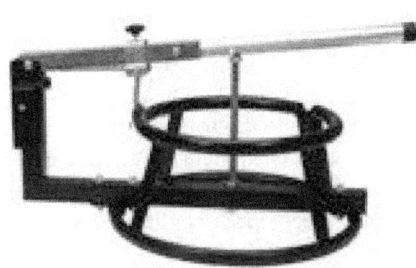

Fig. 1-3 Portable Tire Changing Stand With Bead Breaker

Product: Motion Pro® BeadPro brand tire bead breaker is portable and light in weight designed to be carried in saddlebags and also serve as small tire irons. They appear to be sized for dirt bikes, but magazine reviews say they work on street bikes (sport bikes). This product could be a solution for fixing flat tires on cruiser motorcycles to access the innertube so it can be patched while the wheel is still on the bike. I have not used the product. I am not so certain the small size tire irons will reinstall the tire to the rim and if a cruiser motorcycle will even allow access to the tire to use the tools due to fender clearances. I wish I could have tried them out, but the book is being published and all I could do was get this update. Check Web site for further information: JamesRussellPublishing.com

DON'T BELIEVE THE DEALER'S HYPE

I was shocked to hear motorcycle dealers tell their customers convincing lies that they must use a motorcycle-specific tire changing machine to install tires on the modern motorcycle. They mainly gave the reason of fear: "You'll damage the wheel bearings; scratch, bend and ruin the rim. You can't change these newer tires with tire irons. The rubber won't bend like they used to." They scare you into paying them! They also say, "Today, those big fat rear tires are larger than car tires, and nobody can use a tire iron to remove or install them." Well, even those tire machines can't always install them. Guess what they use to get them onto the rim then? Tire irons! Just like we did in the old days. Imagine that.

Tip: Do not quit with frustration! You can change your own tires on your motorcycle. It seems like a big job when you first do it and it is a big job because you are learning and that discovery process will take longer time than normal. You will make mistakes like letting the tire irons slip out of your hands, lose a nut or bolt momentarily and all sorts of distractions and setbacks will plague you. Bear with it. Push through the hardships and relax knowing the best mechanics all had to go through what you are experiencing. I promise the second time will be easier and it will become exceedingly easier the third time around. There is no need to quit. You can and you will succeed. And the trouble is worth it. Just think of all the money you will save. And it will be nice that you can change tires for all of your biker friends too! Hey, they need to be nice to you or they will lose the free tire service.

CAUTION—RIM DAMAGE

Some soft material rims cannot tolerate tire irons. If your rims are not made of metal and are made of some other soft material (Kevlar® composite wheels are soft fibers in a epoxy glass that can crack), make sure you use a mounting/demount bar that rotates the tire on the rim, not flipping it over the rim like a tire iron does. The forces these two differing methods use are not identical. The tire iron does apply force to the rims in a concentrated manner that could crack or break composite wheels. Check with your manufacturer of the rims to be certain which system they recommend. If you must use a rotary motion mount/demount bar, I will show you how to use one in this book so that you can still change your own tires.

So don't believe the lies many dealers employ to make a buck at your expense. Every tire can be installed on any metal (steel or aluminum or alloy) motorcycle rim by using simple tire irons no matter how big or small those tires may be. How can this be? Look at the wheel. It is just a steel, cast alloy or composite rim. Examine the tire. It is made of rubber. The tire will flex and bend to fold itself onto the rim, that's why. Is it possible to bend a metal rim? Yes, but you will need to use a ton of force to do so, and if you are using too much force, you are doing it wrong! I will show you the right way to do it so you will not bend or scratch your steel, chrome, annodized, polished, painted, composite, billet or alloy rims. As I said before, you should use a mount/demount bar to change tires with composite wheels such as advanced plastic, Kevlar® and carbon fiber construction rims. Tire irons can crack these brittle rims.

I've had many Harley-Davidson employees in many parts of the nation tell me I could never use tire irons on the aluminum alloy wheels of my Softail and Fat Boy. They tell me I'll bend the rim (which can happen if you use excessive brute force with bad technique), break the tire's bead and ruin the tire (which can happen if you use extreme brute force), and other horror stories like the tire falling off the rim and causing a crash—all to prevent me from doing it myself. They will not even sell me the tires or guarantee the tire if I install it myself. I have heard these dealers tell other customers the same things. Little did they know I was a mechanic and have been changing tires myself for many years. I saw through their scam to rake us bikers over the coals and take our hard-earned cash. Do not fall for nonsense scare tactics even if their mechanic is confirming it! If it were true it would be noted in the bike owner manual of the special procedure required to mount tires on the rims.

Tip: The more you learn how to fix your own motorcycle, the more you will realize just how many scare tactics are being used by dealers and repair shops, all designed to get you to give up. A mentality of "let us do it for you or else" is pervasive in the motorcycle world. Few will give advice or be helpful to assist you. In fact, you may even be treated with hostile disrespect. The love of money by the motorcycle repair community is shameful.

I have heard Honda, Kawasaki, Suzuki, Yamaha, Triumph, Victory, BMW, Ducati and other dealers all say the same things to get customers not to change their own tires. And guess what? It works like a charm. Most riders no longer believe that they can change their own tires!

Just ask around. See how many street motorcycle riders you know that actually install their own tires. Most cruiser riders don't. They don't know how and are being told by dealers and repair shops it can't be done. Wrong! You can do it yourself. Even girls can do it! It doesn't require "muscles" to get the job done. Using the right tools (this I will show you) will make the job fast and easy—and I mean really easy.

Tip: Don't go out and buy any tire irons you see at motorcycle parts stores until you read this book. Those stores often do sell useless tools or have good tools mixed with inadequate tools.

FREE TIRES

Yes, you can obtain free tires. Financial stress can be tough on people. The price to pay for new motorcycle tires is expensive so there is a source where you can obtain free tires. Of course, the tires are used, but there can be thousands of good miles left on the tires. If you go to most small motorcycle repair shops you will see a rack of used tires that will be disposed. All you need do is ask and they will likely let you have a set or two or more at no cost to you. After all, they are going to throw them away to a tire disposal firm, so why not let you have them? I have seen tires with an easy 6,000 miles left on them being tossed into the trash racks for disposal.

Danger: Using free used tires can be dangerous as they may have been abused, hit concrete curbs with unseen internal damage. The previous rider may have overloaded the tire delaminating the internal cord bonds. You just don't know, so it is a risk. Many riders who just commute in the city streets at slow speed can often get away with used tires with better results.

How do you know if you have a bad used tire? A tire with broken internal cords will make a lumpy ride in worse case and may not be noticeable at best case. Nobody is going to recommend that you employ used tires on your bike, nobody. You hear of it here in this book because some riders just can't afford to buy new tires. When you are poor you are poor and poverty brings risks the wealthy will never know. I have pur on "used" tires when I was a poor teenager and I had no troubles.

How old of a tire should you use? Check the manufacturing date on the tire. Pass on any tire more than five years old. Most used tires will only be a couple years old.

Free tires can be had, but the clinch is this, the tires are used and there is no way the shop will put them onto your rims due to liability issues, you have to put them on yourself, which this book teaches you how. There is no way you can be certain the tire has a unseen internal broken carcass and could be dangerous until after you put the tires on your motorcycle (you can check the internal and external surface but you can't see within the tire itself to know for sure) and test ride the handling.

A tire with a broken carcass will have a mushy feel and make a thumping, squashing or rapping noise on the pavement. The good news is this, the vast majority of tires being changed are not damaged. The rider, in the spring or fall just wants to slip on a new set of tires for the forthcoming summer months. The key is to seek out small independent motorcycle shops as the major dealers generally will not deal with you (they don't like giving anything away free to nobody).

Tip: Before putting on a used tire you can look for a code that will tell you the date of manufacture of the tire. You don't want to put on a tire that is more than seven (7) years old as the rubber and inner components may be unstable. The code will read like this: 3135. It means the tire was manufactured in the 31st month in the year 2035. As tires age they outgas as they decompose. You can often see evidence of age or brittle exposure to the elements by the hairline cracking on the exterior sidewalls and tread. Select a used tire that has good soft rubber without cracks. Most used tires you will find at motorcycle repair shops will be in nice condition and many will be only one year old or less and nowhere near the wear bar indicators showing there are thousands of good miles left on the tires!

Consider the rider who wants to journey to the motorcycle rallies. He will have a tire that is maybe 40 percent worn down, so he will put on new tires just so he won't have to deal with having to change out tires when on his road trip. Those old tires will be thrown away with 60% tread life left! Ask them to call you when a customer meets this criteria so you can get some good tires for free. You may want to consider giving the dealer a gift or a tip.

As long as you are aware that you are taking a risk of putting used tires of unknown condition on your motorcycle and you gain experience inspecting such tires and evaluating them you can discover a source and method where you do not have to buy new tires.

I know there are skeptics who will condemn this advice, but if you see some of the tires being tossed away you will change your mind. If you happen to know riders who change tires often way before they wear out you can arrange in advance to obtain his used tires.

Yes, there is a risk and the hazard may be slight you could obtain a bad tire that could fail as you ride it, but the same could be said with a brand new tire. There is no way you can know if a fork lift struck the brand new tire carcass during shipping or was crushed under a heavy load with internal damage to the new tire. There is no way you can tell the tire installer ripped your tire's bead, right? He could have ruined your brand new tire and the new tire could fail on you. That is the real world situation. If you choose to put on used tires ride with caution and at slower speeds than you would with new tires just to be safe.

Tip: Many riders buy tires from motorcycle dealers believing they have received a good deal. If they had checked the date code on the tires they may discover they were robbed being sold tires that are old, outdated and maybe not even properly speed and weight rated for the motorcycle. If you do not know about tires (which most riders do not), you can be ripped-off easily by motorcycle dealers selling you goods that are no good. You don't even know if the tire has been put on properly and was not damaged in the process. Most dealers will not let you watch your tires being installed. They don't want you to see what is going on in that back room and maybe you would balk if you saw what was going on. I have seen youngsters putting tires on big bikes and fumbling as they perform their duties. Yes, at the big respectable dealerships and yes, even the Harley-Davidson dealers. For these reasons alone you should be installing your own tires.

Now, for the record, I recommend you buy new tires all of the time. However, I only mention this free tire option for there are people who are riding tires down to the cords and beyond and that is way more dangerous to obtain a blow-out than it is to install a set of used tires with good rubber. Also, it is common practice with cars and pickup trucks that used tires are put on these vehicles. A risk? Yes, but a small one at that. The choice is yours. If you can buy new then by all means do so! If you are financially strapped, and riding on cords and belts showing in the tread area? That is extremely dangerous. Get a used tire with some rubber on the tread and learn to put your own tires on your motorcycle! So what is the bottom line? There is a source to obtain used tires for free for those riders who really can't afford brand new tires.

Note: New tires is always the best way to go. I only include the "free used tire" option here for those who just can't afford to purchase new tires. Installing used tires is a risk only you can decide is acceptable or not. The author recommends that you purchase new tires.

Tip: Excuses are just lame excuses. Riders who don't change their own tires may surprise you with answers such as "I can afford to pay to have it done for me." These same riders often scramble to save a buck. The fact is that they don't know how to change their own tires. Dealers have told them so many lies that they have become totally brainwashed by the motorcycle repair industry monopoly. Most sport bike riders also fall for these lies. Sport bike tires are, next to dirt bike tires, the easiest tires to install. The rubber is soft and flexible and goes onto the rim with hardly any effort at all. I have taken soft tires like these on and off the rims by hand without using any tire irons! When I see a person paying to have their motorcycle tires installed, inside I cry "foul." It is why I wrote this book; to help the biker community save money. They are being robbed.

If you have a sportbike you can get free tires at motorcycle race tracks as tires are discarded with lots of life still left on them.

EXCEPTIONS TO THE DO-IT-YOURSELF RULE

There are exceptional conditions where it is acceptable to have a dealer or repair shop install new tires: (1) when you are traveling and need a new tire because it is worn out, (2) when you get a flat tire when far from home, or (3) if you can get a very good deal. At motorcycle rallies you can often find tire manufacturers offer a deal of buy one, get one free. This is hard to pass up, and it is an excellent deal. I have used it myself many times. Look for special offers like this. These deals come around only once a year, though, and I need three sets of tires each year. At times special deals on the Internet even beat these deals with lower pricing and no shipping costs.

YOU CAN'T TRUST YOUR TIRE INSTALLER ANYMORE

Dunlop Tire Company performed a survey at several motorcycle rallies and detected a high percentage of rear tires to be under inflated. In addition, weight checks of the rear axles of these motorcycles indicated that many tires were loaded beyond maximum capacity. Amazing yet true.

You would think that most riders know best, but we find most riders do wrong best. It means most riders are misinformed or blindly trust their tire installer to do the right thing and are getting improper tire installation! It is now more important than ever to learn to install your own tires so it is performed correctly. I assume tires are being under inflated by design to prematurely wear out the new tire so repeat sales occur sooner for dealers and repair shops. Since most riders today pay to have their tires installed, why then are so many tires under inflated?

Comment: From dealers to aftermarket garages, the motorcycle repair industry has become so corrupted, even car and truck repairs, that I am considering writing a book about how to protect yourself from repair and overbilling scams. I was researching and pricing fuel-injection pump replacement for diesel engines, I found prices over $3,000 but discovered the repair should only cost $1,900 or less. I found shops that will actually do it for that lower price, but most shops bill the higher price. We are certainly being robbed.

This identical pattern of business takes place with tire installers marking up their pricing to exorbitant levels. This is precisely what happens when true competition is wiped out. I mean, if the tire installers commingle a lie telling riders they can't change their own tires and it is believed at truth the competition is totally wiped out and that is the sad condition of the state of affairs it is today.

If you look a the car tire installation system in place where nobody changes their own tires on their cars then why not for motorcycle? Understandably, car tires are heavy and difficult to install for they are much larger, but years ago many people still changed their own tires.

Motorcycle tires are tiny in comparison to car tires and are very easy to install. It just makes no sense to pay those high prices dealers charge to install new tires. It is, in fact, financial insanity.

You can't trust your dealer to give you the best deal. That's not going to happen. You may "think" you are getting a great deal, but I assure you if you changed your own tires you could buy a better handling, longer lasting tire at half-price and not pay any installation fees if you did it yourself. You will pay a premium price for an inferior tire or pay an exorbitant price for a great tire, but you will never get a good deal. Is it really a good deal to have to pay over $500 for two motorcycle tires that may only last 6,000 or 10,000 miles?

I just bought a new Harley-Davidson Sportster 1200 Custom and I found the tires were big 16" donuts on the front and rear. I found quality tires for this new bike for $80 to $98. The dealers and other shops still wanted over $450 to purchase and install. You too will see such awesome savings if you learn to change motorcycle tires. You could even get "free" tires by charging a small labor installation fee to install tires for your friends that will pay for purchasing your tires. And nothing is stopping you from buying the tires on the Internet and marking them up a bit to help you for your time and effort. Add up the savings and now the earnings!

Many riders believe experienced motorcycle mechanics are installing their new tires at the dealership when in fact they hired some kid and taught him how to do it. The mechanic is not changing the oil and swapping out tires, believe me! Shop monkeys are used instead and these chimps make mistakes and don't even know they are making mistakes installing your new tires. They will bend, dent and scratch rims, not clean the rim's tire bead air sealing surfaces, not lube the rim with paste lube, may use rubber destroying lubricants, rip the tire's bead and even split/tear the bead in two and there is no way you will ever know! The tire could come right off the rim without warning! You even believe the wheel is balanced, right? It may not have been balanced. Some dealers just change the tires and take a wait and see attitude to see if anybody comes back complaining about vibration or shimmy. Very few riders return to complain. They save time and money, but remember they billed you for tire balancing!

Can you really trust your dealer/tire installer to give you a good deal? Don't bet on it.

If all goes well there is a somewhat good deal happening at large size motorcycle rallies where the tire manufacturer sponsors a local company of tire installers (a mix of mechanics and apprentices under supervision) offering a 2-for-one tire sale. Of course, you have to purchase the most expensive rear tire and the front tire is given to you free of charge. A tax and a installation fee may apply to remove and install the wheels from your bike. These are not bad deals, but they still will not be your "best" deal for you will clearly pay more for your tires than if you did it yourself, but you will pay less than having a local dealer install your tires. If you are in a pinch for time, look for rally deals like these. The only drawback? It can be a nightmare if anything were to go wrong and it is a weekend and local dealers are closed and parts are needed. Your bike is stranded when you want it most... not a good deal. Since the traveling salesman and van leave it can be hard to get refunds or dispute damages to your bike like scratched and dented paint or chrome. Not a good deal. I have used the rallies to change my tires when I was on the road traveling away from home with good success. But you must be aware of the drawbacks as things can go wrong.

Can you trust your dealer? Yes, you can trust him to open your wallet and drain it dry!

HOW MUCH KNOWLEDGE WILL YOU RECEIVE?

I can promise you when finishing this book you will know more about motorcycle tire changing than 90% of the motorcycle riders on planet earth. You will even know more than most people who change tires at dealerships! How? Because many installers are uneducated, uninformed apprentices and are being taught by mechanics that do it wrong themselves. Imagine that. You won't know everything about motorcycle tires, but you sure will know how to remove and install them.

WHAT ABOUT THOSE HUGE 230+ SIZE REAR TIRES?

You would think that you will need a machine to install these huge 330mm fat tires to the rim, but if you observe these tires being installed at many dealerships the machine will often kick out the mounting bar when trying to get the tire to seat onto the rim. So, they use tire irons to slip the tire onto the rim. So much for that! If they used tire mounting paste instead of liquid lubricant, the tire would slip onto the rim with the tire machine without kicking out the mounting bar! Without tire mounting paste on the tire and the rim's surfaces, including the rim's entire drop center (rim valley) area (Fig. 5-8), the tire can't slip around on the rim. Instead it binds up, stuck to the rim's shoulder and preventing the rubber tire from getting into the optimum position to slip over the rim. There are techniques you can use described herein to install these big wide tires including tall custom 27" front tires.

Fig. 1-4 Reveals Trick of the Trade

Tip: Sometimes you need to push your knee into the tire, directly opposite from where you are having trouble mounting the tire. This forces the tire's bead to slip down into the drop center (deep rim valley) of the rim and releases the binding of the tire where you are experiencing trouble, releasing slack and letting the tire flip over the rim. Yes, you can easily change those big, fat tires with tire irons!

The big tires often are easier to install than some of the skinny 21-inch tires, but they all go on quite easily if you follow the procedures I give in this book. Though I have a tire changing machine I still prefer to just use my tire irons to mount and dismount tires. It is easy and fun to do!

HOW THIS BOOK WORKS

At first we will be "talking" tires, tools and equipment with some photos shown to help you get familiar with the tools and procedures. This may feel awkward at first, but is necessary as there is much to learn. Sometimes it may feel we are not operating in a logical order and sometimes we are and not. Just read and absorb the knowledge for now. Later, you will see how it all fits together. Yes, there is some duplication in the book. It must happen! Without duplication a important event or procedure will be missed. I rather repeat a previous procedure than risk leaving it out and suddenly you don't know what to do when something goes awry. Bear with me on this, okay? This book is for the first-time beginner, it is not a shop manual for experienced mechanics.

QUICK REFERENCE GUIDE IS INCLUDED

I have included a handy Quick Reference Guide that once you have finished reading this book you can jump to the Quick Reference Guide for rapid instructions on how to remove or install a tire without having to read all the explanations given in the book. See Chapter 18.

UNDERSTANDING PHOTO FIGURE NUMBERING

Example: Fig. 2-1. The first number is the Chapter number, in this case is Chapter 2, and the last number is the rising numerical order meaning it is the first photo in Chapter 2. At the end of the book I have included a Photo Index to make it easy to cross-reference and locate certain photographs.

BEFORE WE BEGIN

You should read the Questions & Answers section in this book before you begin wrenching just so you can expand your knowledge about tires, balancing wheels and tire fitment and installation problems that arise. It is then advisable to simply read the entire book casually to get a general idea and feel of what is actually going on when installing tires and fixing flats. Only then will you have not only a good knowledge but also the rising confidence to actually perform the job. Knowledge develops confidence.

CHAPTER 2

Description of Tools Needed

MINIMUM TOOLS NEEDED

You may be surprised at this, but you need very few specialized tools to fix flat tires, remove, install and balance your tires. I list the parts and tools you will need, and thankfully they are very affordable to purchase or make on your own. Everything should cost you well below $100, and it may be half that amount. But even if it did cost you more money due to inflation, the money you save by fixing your own flats and buying and installing your own tires will always let you come out ahead financially. You keep on saving money every time you change tires for the rest of your life!

And Fix Flat Tires

Fig. 2-1 No-Mar Machine & Helping Hand Clamped To Rim

TIRE CHANGING MACHINES

Most everybody is using tire changing machines these days, and so can you! For approximately $300 you can buy a manual tire changer that will last a lifetime. However, you don't really need one. And even if you do buy one, you'll still need to use those tire irons once in a while. So you may as well forgo spending money buying a machine unless you just want one or you plan on changing a lot of tires as a business. This book will show you how to remove and mount tires on a machine. With this book you will learn both the manual tire iron and machine process. You can buy a manual or automatic machine depending on your true needs and desires. Many motorcycle shops still use the manually operated Coats® brand, the No-Mar® brand, or the made-in-China, discount-tool-store manual tire changing machines. None of these require electricity or compressed air to operate, and all of them work just fine.

Fig. 2-2 is the No-Mar® brand manual tire changer the author owns and used for this book. It is designed to be bolted down to a concrete floor. They also make a unit that is entirely portable and attaches to the hitch on a pick-up truck. That would be handy for those who not only travel, but live in apartments where vehicle maintenance work is prohibited on the property.

Fig. 2-2 No-Mar Manual Tire Changer System

Tip: No matter how fat they may be, a tire changing machine is not required for motorcycle tires. You can even change car and pickup truck tires with long tire irons, only it will wear you out if you do it all day long—like at a commercial tire installation shop. The point is that there's no need to buy a tire changing machine unless you are going to be changing tires for a living.

Fig. 2-3 shows a tire mounted to the No-Mar® tire changer. That clamping device is called a "helping hand" and you can see that it is actually pushing down on the edge of the tire deep into the rim. This device is mighty helpful to have! But if you do not have one you can use a tire iron to do the same thing. More on this later.

This book shows you the No-Mar® brand (NoMarTireChanger.com). It is specifically designed for motorcycles and is also designed never to scratch or mar metal or carbon fiber rims. To use the other types of tire changers, you can drape a rag over the metal parts that grip the rim or use a plastic tip or wrap electrical tape over the metal end on the mount/demount bar. See Fig. 16-13 shows a Coats® brand mount/demount bar with plastic rim protectors on each end held on with electrical tape..

Tip: The best cruiser motorcycle tire to buy is the tire that lasts longest and cost least. Keep searching the Internet for tire sales and read the customer reviews to see how long the tires actually do last on similar motorcycles as yours. Keep in mind many riders do ride hard and with a passenger, but at least you will gain a starting point to base your buying evaluations. Just because your bike comes with a certain brand of tire does not mean it is the best tire money can buy. There are often much better tires and deals to be had.

TIRE MOUNT/DEMOUNT BARS

Fig. 2-3 No-Mar® Mount/Demount Bar With Side Handle

Fig. 2-3 reveals the rotary method of removing and installing tires that machines use. The mount/demount bar rotates around a central vertical bar that forces the tire to fold over the wheel rim. The side handle helps the operator stabilize and guide force applied to do the job. Fig. 2-4 is a Coats® brand mount/demount bar with plastic end caps to prevent scratching rims. The plastic slip-on rim savers are taped on with electrical tape because they often fall off during use. Both bars work just fine. The Coats bar has an advantage edge as it has a low profile and has lots of leverage to mount tight-fitting tires. If you do not have a mounting bar go with the Coats despite that it may cost more it will never break and will certainly serve you admirably for the rest of your life.

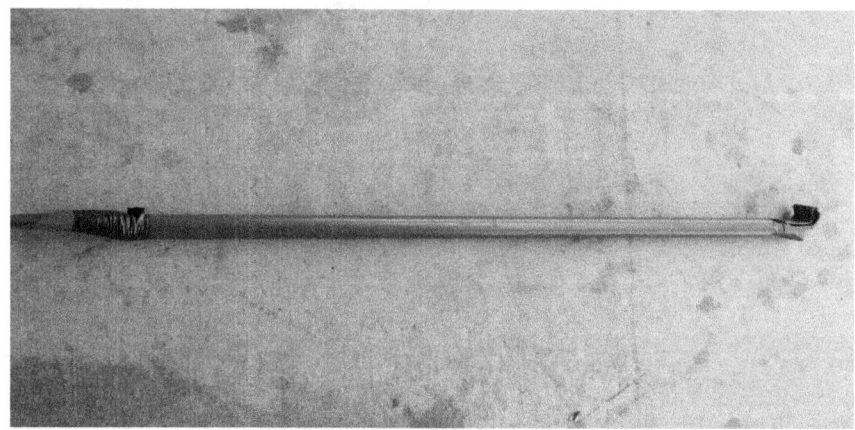

Fig. 2-4 Coats® Brand Mount/Demount Bar

Fig 2-4 shows the Coats® mount/demount bar with protective plastic ends so rims will not be scratched. I use electrical tape to hold the plastic tips in position. The flat end on the left is to remove tires and the curved tip on the right is to install tires.

You may be wondering why I have two different mount/demount bars. The Coats® brand in Fig. 2-4 is a solid rod of steel and the No-Mar® shown in Fig. 2-3 is hollow steel with an assist handle. Both work just fine, but on some tires and rims that give me resistance I like to switch to the Coats bar when mounting difficult tires. And I will switch to tire irons for the very tough jobs. Ultimately all you need are tire irons to change motorcycle tires no matter how tall or wide those tires may be. I suggest you begin and learn using tire irons and later if you want go buy a tire mounting machine that a uses rotary mount/demount bar so be it.

TIRE MOUNTING LUBRICANTS

I like No-Mar's machine, and I like their tire lube paste and I do appreciate using Tyre Lube® which is a drippy gel that is super slippery and can be purchased by Pro Clean Distribution (www.proclean-racing.com product of the UK and sold in America). Both products clean up easily with plain water. What a difference they make! I still use liquid automotive lubricants but not much as they are a bit too drippy, messy to use and evaporate too quickly. The liquid products do work though if you work fast.

Fig. 2-5 Gel Type Tyre Lube® Brand Is Super Slippery

For motorcycles you just can't get any better than No-Mar® and Tyre Lube® lubricants in my opinion at this time. No-Mar's vegetable-based lubricants worked great, allowing the tire to slip right onto the rim with no mess and no fussing about it and does not evaporate rapidly which I really appreciate. When using other products, I have struggled to get some tires to mount easily. When I use No-Mar® lubricants, the tires slip right on the rim with very little force applied and Tyre Lube® gel is even more slippery to mount tires, but does evaporate a bit quicker than No-Mar® brand. Both are safe to use on all rim materials and are noncorrosive and any spills are easily cleaned with plain water. Try all three products shown in this book and try other new products as they become available. Fig. 5-8 shows the No-Mar® paste. Don't forget they also make an excellent liquid tire lube so buy both types.

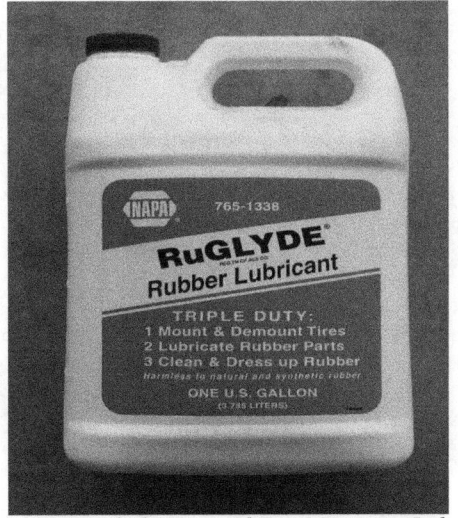

Fig. 2-6 RuGlyde® Liquid Tire Mounting Lubricant

Fig. 2-6 is a liquid tire mounting fluid RuGlyde®. It works, but is messy to use as soapy water. I don't use it as much as I do the paste lubricants, but this is way better than using window cleaner and other destructive products that can ruin rubber and metal rims by far. You can buy this fine product at NAPA automotive stores. Many professional tire installers use this liquid product, but they work faster than the novice, so use paste to install tires especially when learning.

Tip: Tire lubricants also act as a gasket bonding agent that will prevent air leaks from developing between the tire's rubber bead the metal rim. The gel-type paste/grease lubricants work the best. No-Mar® brand is superior in my opinion for motorcycle tires because it does not evaporate before the job is done, even with prolonged delays in tire mounting.

Note: You can install a dry tire to a dry rim without using any tire lubricant, but the job is much harder to do. So, if you find yourself struggling with a tire take a second look to make sure you did not forget to apply tire lubricant to the tire and to the rim. Sometimes being distracted or interrupted will make a novice forget this vital procedure.

NO TIRE CHANGING MACHINE

Should you go out and buy a tire changing machine right away? I say, "No." I believe you should at least try using tire irons once or twice without using any machine. I know of modern motorcycle shops that still use no machine using only tire irons while resting the wheel on two 4 × 4 wood blocks lying on the floor or knee-high work bench. Sometimes I still do it this way because I don't have to bother mounting the wheel into rim clamps on the tire changing machine. Plus, it is still enjoyable to do it the old-fashioned way.

Now after you have performed the tire changing job a few times, you may want to invest money to buy a motorcycle tire changing machine. Why? Because you may say to yourself, "This is a pain in the back bending down all of the time and being on my knees." If this is the case, you may not want to change your own tires again and may want to pay to have it done, which is not a good idea if you want to save a lot of money. If this is the case, you should consider making a wheel stand where you can walk around it without obstruction so you can stand up to do the job.

Cheap Tire Change Machine: A plastic 55-gallon drum filled with water will make a nice tire change stand at the right height and will not scratch rims. You may still want to use wood blocks to support the rim for disk brake rotor can float. You can even drill holes in the top/sides so you can rope down the rim to use tire irons or rotary mount/dismount bar. All you need to buy is a bead breaker and you have a simple tire changing machine.

If you do not have a concrete garage floor, you can dig a hole in dirt outside in your yard, insert a pole, and concrete that into the hole as a mount base for your tire mounting stand. You can contact No-Mar® and buy a nice adapter device that will attach to a trailer hitch on your car or truck. This is great for people who live in areas with rules and restrictions against drilling into concrete or into the earth. No-Mar® also sells a complete tire changing system that mounts to a trailer hitch. Very nice! This unit is portable so you can take it with you on long vacation trips if you are towing your bike to various locations, like when snow birding to the Southern States in the winter.

So, to answer the real question. Try changing the tire without a machine and see that in the worst of conditions it can easily be performed. Then later save up your money and buy a nice tire changing system. If you can't afford the high prices of machines you can buy a tire machine from Chicago Tools (Fig. 2-7). They sell one for less than $200 with the motorcycle attachment (more if inflation bumps up the price, of course).

Note: Make sure you read the "Question & Answer" section at the end of this book before changing tires. There are a lot of tips to help you out to make the job less troublesome.

And Fix Flat Tires

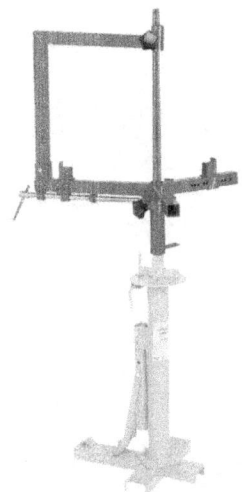

Fig. 2-7 Chicago Tools Manual Tire Changer

The system comes with everything you need to change motorcycle tires, even a wheel balancer and bead breaker. Just remember to stuff cloth rags, rubber or electrical tape over the metal clamps that grip the wheel and wrap the end of the mount/demount bar likewise so you will not scratch the rims. Later on you can sell it and buy a better model if you want to. I have seen motorcycle shops doing a lot of business in tire changing using economy, non-powered, tire changing machines that simply grip the rim and the operator uses a manual rotary mount/demount bar to manually remove and install tires. If they can do it, so can you. There is no need for an automated, hydraulic or compressed air–powered machine.

Fig. 2-8 is a economical and portable tire bead breaker with long leverage handle is perfect for those who do not own a tire changing machine. This bead breaker will make short work of any motorcycle, car or light truck tire's bead. I would lie a carpet over the stand so the metal frame will not scratch the wheel.

Fig. 2-8 Harbor Freight Tools® Brand Tire Bead Breaker

If you plan on going into a sideline business of changing motorcycle tires, you may find yourself getting very busy especially if you discount your prices. Bikers will flood to your door bringing their wheels or the complete motorcycle. In this case you must purchase at least a manually operated tire mounting machine to make the job easier on yourself and to do the job quickly. Motor Sports® brand in Fig. 2-10 will work. Check the Internet for newer devices than shown here in this book.

Check out motorcycle shops and see what sort of tire changing machines they use. Many use brands sold by motorcycle specific tool companies. Some use automotive brands designed for motorcycles. Others use No-Mar® and Coats®.

Fig. 2-9 16" Long-Reach Tire Iron & Rim Protectors

Believe it or not, many shops still use no machine, just tire irons. Once you become proficient changing motorcycle tires with tire irons, you can do the job as fast and easy as a machine. And one more thing; you will always notice that a set of tire irons is hanging on or near the tire changing machines. That's for a good reason—you still need to use them! And that is why some mechanics just don't bother using tire changing machines for motorcycles. The tire iron shown in Fig. 2-9 is a MotionPro® 16" long deeply curved iron. I strongly recommend you buy this brand! You will need 3 but I suggest you purchase 4 of them as the fourth will be a helping hand. See Fig. 5-30. Four rim protectors are installed on the rim so the rim will not be scratched. You can use one, but there is no harm in using more. The string is used to pull the rim protector around the rim when needed and to retrieve it if it were to fall inside the rim.

My advice is to try changing tires without a tire-changing machine a few times. Once you get the hang of it you will find it easy to do.

Fig. 2-10 Motor Sports® Brand Portable Tire Installer With Bead Breaker

The portable rotary style tire change machine in Fig. 2-10 can be used anywhere even inside a living room if need be for those who do not have a garage. To use this machine properly you need to find a way to anchor the base down so it will not rotate on a smooth surface. Outdoors is no problem using long tent spikes driven into the earth or tied to two firm objects. If you can't do this then use the machine as a tire bead breaker and wheel stand to hold the wheel rim then use tire irons to mount and demount tires. Using tire irons applies no rotary forces so the machine will not need to be tied down.

HOW TO USE THIS BOOK

1. Read the entire book first to get a general idea as to what is going on. This is really important, in fact it is mandatory. You need to get familiar with what is going on and the dangers that can arise. Please read the entire book first.
2. Read all of the Questions & Answers at the back of the book as they have helpful tips and make for good reading to increase your

knowledge.
3. Download the Rubber Manufacturers Association information bulletins and read them.
4. Read this book as you change your tires. Follow the procedures and be patient with yourself.
5. Work slowly, take breaks, don't get angry if you have difficulty.
6. Never use brute force when mounting or demounting tires.
7. Visit: JamesRussellPublishing.com for any updates and tips regarding tire changing.

WATCH TIRE CHANGING

Watch how tires are changed. You can see short movie clips on the Internet. Go to an automotive repair shop and watch how they change tires as the principle is the same. You can even ask them to show you how to do it up close. Some shops will not permit this, but many will. They are not as secretive as motorcycle repair shops, who want to keep their customers in the dark. Changing tires and changing engine oil is the core source of income for motorcycle repair shops. It's their bread and butter. They have reasons for not teaching you anything and discouraging you.

Watching will demystify the process. The mechanic first deflates the tire, and then breaks the rubber tire's top and bottom beads away from the rim. Then you'll see the top side of the tire get peeled off the upper rim and then the lower portion of the tire lifted over the upper rim. Then the new tire's lower half slips over the top rim down to the lower inner rim (Fig. 5-20 and the top upper section of the tire goes over the upper rim (Fig. 5-21). Then the valve core is installed and the tire inflated with air.

Note: large, wide tires over 200 mm often must be compressed onto the rim with a strap to spread the tire sidewalls to the rim for an airtight seal and "initially" inflate the tire. And some smaller tires will also need this bead starting strap too! See Fig. 7-4.

Then, when you've seen the tire finally inflated to seat the bead with a loud audible "pop," you will at least know what needs to be performed, how and why and in what order. It will answer many of your questions, and this will make your first few times changing your own tires much easier to do. Take notes as you watch the process. The process of mounting motorcycle tires is essentially the same as the one for automotive tires, minus the fully automatic machine being used and the lack of the use of tire irons. These powered machines use a rotary mount/dismount bar and are powerful.

Your first mission is to go somewhere where you can actually see tires being removed and installed from vehicle rims. A car, pickup truck, and motorcycle are essentially all the same. Take notes on paper as to the process. You may need to go back and see the process one more time in the event you become baffled and confused. The second time clears out the cobwebs.

THE PROBLEM WITH INTERNET VIDEOS

I have never seen a great video on the Internet, though, that fully explains the tire changing or flat tire fixing process and that even includes oil changes, etc. You'll watch a brief movie clip and think, "Gee, that was easy. I can do that." But when you try it yourself, you will soon realize they left out a lot of the tricks of the trade that will guarantee you'll be totally frustrated. They also use rims and tires that are "easy" to install instead of using difficult "real world" situations. Many videos show tire mounting using mount/demount bars and not tire irons to "sell" their mount/demount product, but you often still must resort back to the use of tire irons when things don't go as planned.

For example, they seem to leave out the proper stepping process of the tire irons or tell you what to do when the tire binds and refuses to mount. They do not explain or reveal the true and proper use of tire lubricants and how to use them and where they need to be applied. They use liquid lubes as the automotive industry uses or dangerous corrosive and even explosive household products, but motorcycles should be using paste tire lube especially when using tire irons. They explain nothing about what to do when you try to inflate the tire and it will not inflate. What if you get stuck with a new manufactured mold-deformed tire on a rim that will not hold air? It can be installed, but that Internet film will not help you. They also don't tell you how to prevent "tearing" the tire bead and ruining an expensive tire. They leave out so much I had to write this book to set the record straight.

These videos miss a lot. They make it look easy, but you soon discover that the tire and rim they used are not the same or aren't as tough to install as yours. Another problem with the video is that the images fly by too quickly. A book's photo is captured, in still time and you can actually see with greater detail how the tire iron is actually inserted into the tire and rim and way more knowledge is conveyed. Using this book with a few videos will be valuable to you.

When you are done with this book, you will have just about all of the solutions to every problem in changing motorcycle tires. You will actually know more than many people working for motorcycle dealers changing motorcycle tires! Plus, you will be so proficient you may even want to work part or full-time changing motorcycle tires.

THE PROBLEM WITH SPOKE WIRE WHEELS

If you have a flat tire on a motorcycle with traditional laced, wire (spoke) wheels, the tire can't be fixed on the side of the road or even in an automotive repair or tire shop. Even if you remove the wheel for them, they still may not have the required patches, rubber innertube, the tools, or expertise to do the job. You have to get your bike or wheel to a motorcycle repair shop if yo have the tools to remove your front or rear wheel—or it's time to call a tow truck (if the Fix-A-Flat® system fails, See Fig. 12-3).

The problem with spoke wheels is that they require a rubber innertube, like a bicycle. When you pick up a nail, the tube is punctured or torn and must be patched or replaced. It is easy to do, but there is a big problem. It is almost impossible to get to the tube to patch it. You have to peel the tire from the rim to expose the innertube to patch or replace it. A typical large cruiser motorcycle has saddlebags in the rear and dual disk brakes in the front. There is no way to get tire irons in those tight places while the wheel is still on the axle. Nobody can fix the tire except a motorcycle shop, and they are usually closed on Sunday and Monday and holidays. If you are traveling away from home, you now need to stay in a hotel for two or three days just to get your tire fixed. That is the price you pay for buying a motorcycle with traditional classic style spoke wheels.

People do not realize the total mess they get themselves into by purchasing a motorcycle with tube-type spoke wheels. If you really love the spoke-wheel look, put your money in expensive custom spoke cast (or billet) wheels that are actually tubeless rims with spoke wheel design. The rim spoke holes are mechanically welded or forged or sealed with bonded sealing agents (like vulcanized rubber) so that air cannot escape from the spokes. That way no innertube is required to hold air in the wheel's rim. The wheel now has a true tubeless design. You or any repair shop can fix a flat tire by inserting a plug to inflate your tire and away you go until you can get a new tire installed later. Also, traditional spoke wheels are high maintenance to begin with. They must be kept true, and spokes have a nasty habit of breaking and that requires new lacing and truing. They may look cool, but they are not worth a dime economically and are dangerous. Tubes blow out! Spokes loosen, bend, crack, corrode and break and they need frequent truing even for strong stainless steel wire spokes.

Danger: Disastrous and nasty blowouts can occur with spoke rim tube tires, and these sudden events can toss you right off your motorcycle or run off the road no matter how great of a rider you are. This alone is one good reason to get rid of those spoke wheels. Your life is worth more than looking good with spokes. They are dangerous and hard to repair. Also, if you don't know how to true the wheel—and few riders know how to do that—it's just another expense for you. Spokes loosen up all the time, and they must be tightened in certain sequences or your wheels will hop and wiggle and make for an awful ride that will damage steering and suspension bearings and wear your tires down fast. Enough said.

SPOKE WHEEL FLAT PREVENTION

If you already have spoke wheels, do everything you can to keep from having a flat. Keep good fresh new rubber tires with lots of tread. You can't let them wear down, like you can with cast wheels, or you will lose protection. You should investigate adding some flat tire protection fluid inside the innertube of your tires, like they do with bicycle tires. Use a motorcycle-approved product, though, not a bicycle product (unless there are no alternative product you can buy and you need something that may work).

I have not yet used these tubeless or tube type sealant products, nor do I endorse them. I have heard of the fluids causing a wheel imbalance at highway speeds. They gunk up the internal side of the rims with sticky crud on tubeless tires and could even corrode some alloy or fiber materials, so beware. However, they may work for you, so let's keep an open mind here. New and improved products are always being developed, so keep your eyes open for them. They may work for you. I would certainly try them if you have innertube tires on a motorcycle for added safety protection from sudden a blow-out. I do plan to try out these products and I will submit results on the Website: JamesRussellPublishing.com

And Fix Flat Tires

Fig. 2-11 Slime® Brand Flat Tire Sealant Repair

Tip: Regardless of spoke or cast wheels, do you carry an axle socket with you? Take a look at your wheels. Most motorcycles have a special size socket, usually a large Allen type socket requiring an unusually large Allen wrench. Believe it or not, most repair shops do not have this tool (unless the shop specializes in your brand of bike). Don't learn this the hard way. Purchase and carry this Allen drive bit with you in your saddlebags. If you get a flat tire, anybody can now remove your wheel to fix the flat or change out a tire. Normally the rear tire needs no special tool, but check to make certain. MotionPro.com will have the tool you need. Don't forget a chain/belt adjustment wrench as you may need it for your bike to remove and insert the rear axle. See Fig. 2-13.

Note: At the time of writing this book, an economical system is under development called the "TUbliss Conversion System" by TUbliss.com that when inserted into the tire takes the place of a full-size innertube. It is available now for off-road motorcycles, but is under development for DOT street use. It could be available by the time this book is published. Keep an eye open for any new technology. If the system works it means no more flat tires ever on motorcyles. If this develops it will be mentioned on my Web site.

CAST WHEELS ARE BEST

Anything but spokes are good! Get rid of those spoke wheels and install some good solid wheels. Blowouts are rare on cast (or those expensive custom billet) wheels, and there are of course no spokes to tighten or replace. The nice part is, if you do pick up a nail in your tire, you can fix it right on the spot and drive away in a few minutes as if nothing happened. Fig. 4-3 is a cast wheel. You can see a No-Mar® bead breaker at the 9 o'clock position is breaking free the tire from the rim in Fig. 2-12. Fig. 4-7 reveals how to tie down the rim with rope when using a bead breaker.

Fig. 2-12 Cast Metal Rim Wheel Showing Tire Bead Being Broke Loose

Warning: Cast wheels with tubeless tires may save your life. They rarely "blow out" with a loud explosive "bang" like tube tires do on spoke wheels, causing the tire to instantly deflate and permitting the rider to instantly lose control and crash. When cast wheels with tubeless tires pick up a nail, they usually always let air out slowly, giving you a squish ride and time to pull over without crashing. The cast wheel permits you to plug a flat tire, inflate, and go. This is important in hot or cold weather, in remote areas, or at night in lonely places. Cast wheels are worth every penny. Stay clear of traditional spoke wheels with rubber innertubes.

Tip: Make sure you always carry a small flashlight with spare batteries in your saddlebag. You will need it to repair a flat tire in the dark.

WORKSHEET

For your bike you need to set up a handy worksheet so all the data and tools you need are listed for your quick and easy reference. For this book I am using a cruiser Triumph America motorcycle. For your motorcycle you may need slightly different tools, like different sizes or types of socket wrenches. Normally, your owner's manual will show you which sizes you will need. If not, you may need to perform your own survey while reading the book and write down the nut, bolt and socket sizes you will need. Buying a metric or SAE (Society of Automotive Engineer, American inch scale standard) socket set will be a good starting point. I have included such a place in this chapter in the following pages to use as such a chart.

To measure a larger bolt, you can fit an adjustable wrench on the bolt head and remove it and measure the span distance with a tape measure. That will tell you which socket you will need. Fig. 2-13 is a special large Allen wrench size bit used to remove the front wheel on many metric motorcycles. It is made by MotionPro®. You may or may not need one. Looking at your axle if you see one or both ends require an Allen/Hex socket bit you may need this wrench. The Allen sizes are large and local auto parts stores may not have these larger size Allen's so you need to buy them on motorcycle Websites.

Fig. 2-13 Axle Wrench Multi-Size Socket For Front Wheel

MOTORCYCLE JACK FRAME LIFT

Most riders already have an all-terrain vehicle (ATV) or motorcycle frame lift as shown in Fig. 2-14 and Fig. 2-15.

Fig. 2-14 ATV/Motorcycle Hydraulic Frame Lift

Warning: Make sure once you lift the bike to the desired height that you tie the bike down in such a manner as the bike can not slide off the jack or topple over off of the jack. It will be a disaster if the bike falls off the jack.

Warning for Harley-Davidson Sportster Models: The Sportster model has a very narrow engine cradle compared to most bikes which many new mechanics are not aware of. If you lift the bike with any jack the bike will not just tend to slide off the jack due to being top-heavy unstable, but it will simply lean over and fall down with a devastating crash and it could even land on you. You need to lift the bike slowly to the desired height then immediately tie the bike down to the jack and to the floor or walls of your garage (most riders do not have professional HandyLift® work tables). You can use ratchet-type nylon strap tie downs to do the job. I prefer you tie the bike to your garage wall studs by each end of the fork or handlebar as just tying the bike to the jack as the entire jack could also topple over with the bike. That's why I say to tie the bike to the floor or walls of your garage when it is lifted.

Tip: Make sure you practice with your jack placement under the frame of the motorcycle so you do not crush hoses, pipes or crack engine covers, oil filter, etc. The jack should be on the metal frame to lift a bike on most bikes. With some bikes like the Victory you lift it from the aluminum center seam engine case which I do not like to do, but that is how it is done for there is no steel frame under the engine to lift the bike. You should ask a local motorcycle mechanic the best way to lift your bike and consult your owner manual. You may need to purchase a special adapter to fit on your lift or buy an entirely new lift designed to lift your specific model.

Most large Harley-Davidson's can be lifted with the Simple ATV/Motorcycle style lift shown in Fig. 2-15. Make sure the lift height is low to scoot the lift under the bike as some lifts are just too tall. You can place some blocks of wood under the bike's sidestand and this will give about an inch of height. Make certain the lift is rated to lift the weight of your bike.

Good Advice: To become proficient with lifting motorcycles on jacks it will be worth your effort to practice lifting your bike a few times before you need to change the tires. Lifting a bike with a jack is a separate skill in itself that needs to be leaned. Plus, it is scary to lift a heavy bike on a tiny jack for the very first time. Practice lifting, locking, tying down the bike then untying, unlocking, lowering the bike. You need to get comfortable with this before you begin to change tires. And, never lose your fear of dropping the bike off the jack and it likely will not happen. The moment you "trust" all is well and "forget to check" the jack position under the bike is when danger arises.

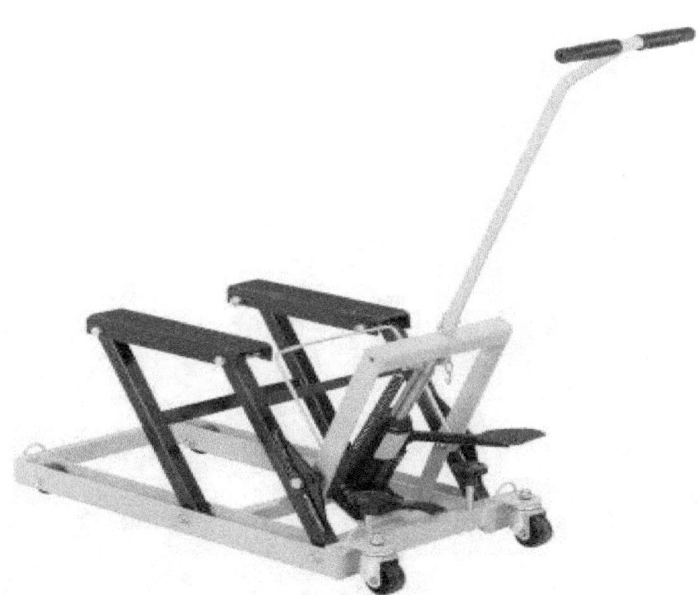

Fig. 2-15 Harbor Freight Tools® Brand ATV/Motorcycle Lift

These ATV style lifts are good if your motorcycle has two exposed, under-the-engine frame rails. The two lift arms are placed under these frame rails to lift the bike off the ground. Believe it or not, the Honda Gold Wing, Victory and classic BMW's have no such frame rails. You need to speak to your dealer and order a "specialized" lift. If you dare to place a typical ATV motorcycle lift on these bikes, the lift arms will be on the aluminum engine cases, exhaust or plastic fairing. It might break them, so don't do it. Use the proper lift for your bike. Ask dealer and repair shops for advice and get second and third opinions before lifting the bike. Read the owner manual or shop manual for advice.

Danger: Fig. 2-16 and Fig. 2-17 shows the ATV/Motorcycle lift arms totally supporting the entire motorcycle frame. Make sure when working the motorcycle does not slip or slide out of position. You should firmly tie the motorcycle down to the lift's frame so both the jack and motorcycle are now one unit and one can't move independently without the other otherwise the bike can fall of the lift unexpectantly. Notice the bike could slip off the lift in any direction, front, rear or sideways. Tie the bike down to the lift and to the floor or walls of the building so the bike can not tilt or slide off of the lift. There are safety latches that must also be engaged so if the hydraulic cylinder were to fail the latches prevents the jack from collapsing. Read the jack's instruction manual and periodically check for loose nuts and bolts so the jack won't suddenly fail.

Fig. 2-16 ATV/Motorcycle Lift Arms Supporting Frame

Fig. 2-17 shows blocks placed under the motorcycle's side stand. Why? This is so you can first tilt the bike upwards just a bit so you can slide the jack under the bike's frame. And for removing the jack too! Both wheels are floating without support and we do not want this unstable rocking condition to exist, so we need to put some wood, plastic or metal supports under both wheels.

Fig. 2-17 ATV/Motorcycle Lifting Entire Bike - Don't Forget To Tie Bike Down

In Fig. 3-4 the motorcycle is completely lifted off the ground and blocks are placed under the front wheel to prevent see-saw movement especially when the heavy rear wheel is removed the blocks can prevent the bike from tilting forward and fall off the jack. The motorcycle should be tied down to the jack with ratcheting tie-down straps (not shown in photo) or with strong metal chains. Also, the back carry-on and saddle bags should be "empty" or removed to not add an unbalanced load condition. This bike is so well balanced I can leave them on and full of items. When removing the front tire move the blocks from the front wheel and relocate them under the rear wheel.

Tip: When you remove the front wheel the bike will want to fall down to the rear wheel like a see-saw. When you remove the rear wheel, but leaving the front wheel on the bike, the unbalance will reverse itself and the bike will want to now fall down to the front.

Caution: Fig. 2-17 shows a bike on a lift with luggage pod and saddlebags. Depending on the bike these items can upset the balance of the bike when on the jack. You may want to remove the items if you find the bike becomes unmanageable when lifted and when a wheel is removed from the bike.

Danger: The moment a wheel is removed from the axle a huge unbalance can occur in causing the bike to want to fall down in a forward or backward motion. This is why we place support under the opposite existing wheel. See Fig 3-4 and Fig. 2-18 shows a scissor lift instead of a wood block. Wiggling the bike can cause the bike to sneakily move ever so slightly and eventually fall off the lift without warning. It will take you by surprise and you had better not be anywhere near that falling bike as it can entrap and crush you. Get into the habit of frequently checking if the bike is moving off the lift arms. The bike will fall over if you become occupied with a troublesome wheel not wanting to install and you keep jostling the bike not realizing the bike is slipping off the jack. Pay attention.

Danger: Do not ever let the motorcycle slip away from the jack or fall over. This can kill or seriously crush or trap you under the bike. Make certain you have a cell phone in your pocket so you can call for help and let somebody know you are working alone in your garage to come check on you if at all possible. Never shake the bike or let it rock side to side in any direction. Work very gently. There is no reason any strong force should be used when removing or installing wheels. Place wood blocks under the bike in case the bike falls from the jack. Even placing a wood block under the rear or front wheel will prevent any seesawing or sudden forward or reverse slippage from the jack.

Danger: If you can avoid an unbalanced lifting situation, do so by all means. If you can use your jack to lift the entire motorcycle off the ground in a perfectly level and balanced manner, all the better. When lifting a motorcycle, tie the motorcycle down to the jack for added stability with nylon straps or steel chains. If you must seesaw the motorcycle, make sure you place wood blocks under the low side and put the motorcycle in gear (if the back wheel is resting down on the floor) to prevent rolling away from the jack. Purchase a quality motorcycle jack that can lift your bike safely. Make sure it has a manual anti-fall locking device in case the hydraulic system fails. If it doesn't and the bike descends on its own, that could crush you or take your fingers and hands . Visit a motorcycle repair shop and ask them to show you how to lift and raise the front and rear wheels independently and safely. Many shops use a full bike lift table and stand, and then use a heavy-duty K&L® (or similar) scissor jack to raise the front, rear wheel or the entire motorcycle off of the lift table.

Note: When working with a jack for the first time it pays to be nervous and aware than be careless and foolish. Get familiar with how the jack operates then try lifting your bike just a few inches then let it down slowly in a controlled manner. Then try again later a bit higher and lock the jack in place with its anti-fall locking device. Progress slowly to higher levels of jack lifting making sure the jack and motorcycle is stable at all levels. Soon you will not be as nervous any more, but always stay careful. Accidents happen, and they always happen quickly and by total surprise.

Tip: Search the Internet under "Motorcycle Lifts USA" to find quality lifts you can trust. If you want to spend more money, look for a lift that has a removable approach ramp and even a removable nose to easily remove and lower wheels from the lift to the floor. Electric/hydraulic or compressed air drive is nice, but you will need a large, high-psi (approximately 125 psi or higher) shop air compressor for these large lifts.

Tip: Torque the axle bolts when the wheel is touching the ground, not when on the jack. It is a good habit to not lose your fear of a bike falling off a jack. It's when you forget and become careless that accidents happen. Also, do not slip in any axle grease. Clean up any spills and remove greasy rags from the work area right away, not later. Make sure the jack's lift arms are not soaked in oil or grease so the bike can slide around and off the jack.

Note: Your Victory motorcycle may not have frame rails. After checking with two dealerships I found it was okay to lift the entire bike from the bottom engine cases and to use wood Carpenter shims on the lift arms to hold balance the bike from the highly raised center case seam. I still never felt comfortable fearing the heavy weight of the bike could crack the engine case. I don't like lifting bikes that have no steel frames under the bike. Some bikes require a special "jig" be applied before the bike can be lifted. So far, Harley-Davidson bikes all have steel frames, while many metric bikes do not.

Another lift I have used, especially when I am traveling in my RV on vacation, is a scissor jack. This is no ordinary scissor jack you find in automotive stores. It is an expensive ($200+) K&L® scissor lift. It is wide, flat, and stable enough to lift an 800-pound motorcycle. Other companies are now making these lifts and selling them at a lower price. I use the lift to raise one end of the bike off the ground to change tires when I am traveling in my RV on long vacations. See Fig. 2-18. A competing company is now offering these scissor jacks at a lower price seen in motorcycle parts catalogs and they are heavy-duty.

Fig. 2-18 K&L® Brand Motorcycle Specific Scissor Jack

At home I use it to lift the detached wheels up toward the axle so I don't expend energy holding up a heavy tire while trying to slip the axle into place. It makes the job much easier, so much easier that you will see all motorcycle repair shops using them as an assistant to lift the wheels into place to align an axle and insert the axle into the frame. Be aware that these scissor lifts are heavy duty, designed to lift motorcycles. This one is rated for 850 lbs. Shop around as there are other companies now making jacks like this and offering them at lower cost.

A much cheaper alternative: if you are going to use the jack to lift "only" the wheels and "not" the entire motorcycle off the ground, you can buy an economic scissor jack at an automotive parts store and weld on a wide bottom and a wide top steel plate. Then it will not flip sideways and will be stable. You do not absolutely need this scissor jack. It is just a tool that makes the job of lifting the wheel easier to do. For years I never used one, but as motorcycle wheels became larger and heavier, it was time to change.

AIR COMPRESSOR - SHOP STYLE

You don't need a large air compressor for inflating new tires on a rim to seat the beads and for final air pressure inflation. A small one that has a two or three gallon reserve tank (with or without an air compressor) is all that you need for home garage use. See Fig. 2-19. Do not confuse this portable shop air compressor with the portable air compressor for fixing flat tires when on the road shown in Fig. 12-1.

Fig. 2-19 Air Compressor 3-Gallon 100 psi

You can find shop compressors everywhere at discount tool stores at low cost. If you are really tight on cash, you can buy a three-gallon portable air tank and have it filled with compressed air at an automotive tire repair garage. The portable air tank will work just fine. If you have no portable air tank or compressor, you can inflate the tire/wheel anywhere that has a source of compressed air. It's better to have an air source close to home so you don't have to run around so much, but I realize we all need to start somewhere and some of us have very little money to get started. Most full-service automotive and motorcycle repair shops, not gas stations, will seat the beads by filling your tires with air.

And Fix Flat Tires

The portable air compressor (See Fig. 12-1) you take on your motorcycle to inflate a flat tire (where the tire's bead is intact) will not work to inflate a tire that has a broken bead wheel's rim. They do not give the burst of air volume needed to inflate the tire to expand against the rim to seat the bead.

Tip: If you get a flat tire pull over and fix it right away. Do not ride, even slowly, for miles as this is how the bead separates from the rim creating a broken bead condition which makes it impossible to fill the tire with air. However, a tow truck may have a portable air tank that could give you a strong burst of air to seat the bead. So, while waiting for a tow truck to arrive, go ahead and plug the flat tire.

THE SHORTCUT METHOD USING FEWER TOOLS

Not everyone can afford to go out and buy all the tools needed to change and balance motorcycle tires. There are some of us who are direly short of cash and need help. So my solution is this. Simply buy the tools you need to remove your wheels from the motorcycle. That will be only a few hand tools, and you may already own them, like a special Allen wrench socket. Then buy the bare minimum of tools needed to remove and install your tires. That will be three tire irons, three rim protectors, a valve core removal tool, and a bead breaker (a steel carpenter's C-clamp works for this if it's large and strong). See Fig. 2-13, Fig 2-20, Fig. 2-21, Fig. 2-22 and Fig. 2-23. You will need more tools than these to service your bike.

Important: Buying tools is a good investment that will save and earn you money.

Note: Using large carpenter's C-clamps to compress a tire's carcass to assist tire installation will work and they are for those who already have these clamps in their tool chest. If you do not have C-clamps don't buy them. Instead, purchase professional tire installation tools designed for the specific purpose like the No-Mar® Helping Hands device or tire irons to drive the tire into the rim's drop-center. You will like the results using the proper tools for the job. It is possible to damage the internal components of a tire using C-Clamps. Buy a bead breaker such as in Fig. 2-8.

Fig. 2-20   Large Metal Carpenter's C-Clamp

Fig. 2-20 shows a 8" Carpenter's C-Clamp that is not recommended as it does not have the squeezing power as the traditional metal 8" C-Clamp operated by a screw, but it will work on small diameter 18 to 21 inch size front tires. Rear tires require much more power to squeeze them to break away from the rim.

You can see in Fig. 2-21 the metal screw clamp is very powerful compressing the tire edges down into the rim's drop center when installing a new tire. You don't need to use a C-clamp, you can tie down a tire iron or two to do the same thing. You can also use the metal screw C-clamp to break the tire beads away from the rim to begin the tire changing process. Later, you can actually employ the C-clamp to also force the tire down into the rim drop-center also shown in Fig. 6-4 that can "sometimes" help free up a stuck tire to the rim, but the method in Fig. 2-21 will do a better job getting tire slack. With the tire not hung up on the rim you can now use your tire irons 180 degrees opposite and the tire's rubber at both ends (C-clamp and at tire irons) can now move and the tire will install.

Fig. 2-21 Large 8" Metal Screw Carpenter's C-Clamp - Use With Gentle Care

Now you can remove and install the tires. More on this later in the section on bead breaking.

But, after installing the new tire, you still must inflate the tire and set the bead into place and balance the tire. Let's assume you have no money to purchase a tire balancer or a bead starting belt. Then find a motorcycle shop that will inflate and balance your wheels for you. You'll still be way ahead financially because of the labor fees saved and the deep discounts you obtained for buying your tires on the Internet. Later, you can buy the rest of the tools you need.

Note: Not all tires require a tire bead starting strap to help seat the tire on the rim to inflate the tire. Your bike may not need one! What else will work? You can use a ratcheting nylon strap, tied down to wrap around the tire, to squeeze it into place against the rim. That will save you about $100 if it works. However, if you can afford it, buy the proper tools for the job so it will go easier every time. Warning: Don't forget to release the strap right away the moment the tire begins to inflate so you will not explode the tire or rim. More on this later.

Note: The term, "drop center" is used in this book, but it can also be described as the "rim valley" or "rim depression" area. In all cases, it is describing the deep concave depression shape of the inner wheel rim. You need to remove the tire to see this drop center. In Fig. 5-1 and Fig. 5-2 you can see the convex depression shape in the center of the rim. This area of the rim is important to know about as it will greatly assist you to install your new tire. It is one of the great secrets of getting tires to slip on to the rim. More on this later in the book.

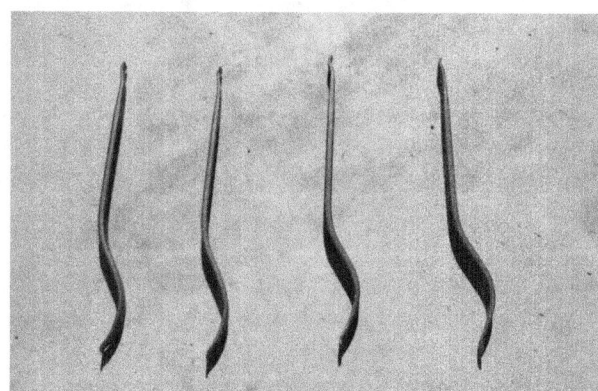

Fig. 2-22 Shows Four 16" Motion Pro® Tire Irons

DEALING WITH FRUSTRATION

Tire changing is easy, once you know how! But to learn how to do it on your bike is going to be miserable and frustrating simply because it is your first time and you have to learn the process. The simplest things may frustrate you the most, like removing the wheels from your motorcycle. I can't show you how to do this on your motorcycle, but it will be somewhat similar to what you will see in this book. You may need to seek advice from your motorcycle dealer, the Internet, owner manual, or a shop manual. You may discover you need a special tool nobody has in town and have to wait until the tool arrives to remove your wheel from the motorcycle.

It is a good idea to first find out by talking to a mechanic what tools you will need to remove your wheels. Once you get the wheels removed from your motorcycle, this book should cover the rest of the details.

You may also become frustrated in mounting your finished wheels back onto your motorcycle. You may have to remove brake calipers, maybe a fender, exhaust pipe muffler, saddlebags, or a fairing component or even buy a special lift to get your motorcycle lifted off the ground. It's the little nuisances that will frustrate you the very first time you try to change tires on a motorcycle. The good news is rest assured once you get past this initial phase of troubles the second time will be a breeze to do. It will help to keep a log instructional book of the sequences so the next time nothing will be a surprise and the job will go easier.

Tip: Control anger. It is expected you will become frustrated at times when learning. Just relax and know that there is a solution to all things. If things get tough it is because you are doing something wrong and you need to learn. It is absolutely normal to become discouraged and upset. Just don't be upset that you are upset. Realize we all had to learn and often it is painful, but once you learn it becomes easy. Trust me, it even becomes fun.

The best way to handle frustration is to keep telling yourself that this is your choice and that this is your way of enjoying yourself by working on your own motorcycle. Every motorcycle mechanic runs into trouble here and there, and what should go smoothly often will not. When trouble arises take in stride. All things are fixable.

Another frustration that must be avoided at all costs is losing expensive parts. Get some magnetic parts bowls, and don't forget to use them! I recently placed my axle bolt nut on the carpet near my rear wheel and when I installed the wheel I couldn't find the axle nut. I looked everywhere, and I became terribly angry at myself. It was a weekend, the motorcycle shops were closed, and they likely wouldn't even have one on hand. That meant I couldn't ride the bike until a replacement nut arrived days or even weeks later if back-ordered. I eventually did find the nut after much toil and grief. What was worse is that I had been using the magnetic bowls for all the items on this job, except for this one item that I thought I would not lose. It took me an hour of misery to find that nut! Where was it? It was still in the socket wrench! Don't laugh, it was hidden inside the socket.

If you are exceptionally prone to lose parts, consider having a supply of replacements on hand. It is better than being frustrated looking for that one nut or bolt and holding up the entire job.

Tip: Listen to the cling! When a nut or bolt, drops it will make a clinging noise and that is where the item usually stops, or close by. The part will bounce, roll and spin until it hits something. Use a flashlight or magnet to locate the culprit. Always use a magnetic parts tray to store nuts and bolts.

ORIENTATION

When you read in this book the word right or left it is as sitting on the bike. So if you are standing in front of the motorcycle and you are instructed to remove the left axle nut, it will be, in your current view standing in front of the bike, the right axle nut.

SPOKE RIM & MAG WHEELS

There's no different procedure installing tires if you have wire spokes or cast (including alloy, pressed steel, riveted, solid, carbon fiber or billet aluminum wheels). The mounting and balancing is essentially identical except the tube tire has a tube and a rim band and maybe a rim clamp to install. See Fig. 11-1. However, fixing flat tires with cast wheels is easy, and fixing them with spoke wheels is more involved as the tube must be removed to be replaced, but you can install all tires with simple tire irons.

TOOLS FOR FRONT WHEEL

(This is for the Triumph America Motorcycle, some tools you will need are listed. Depending on your specific model motorcycle you may need alternate tools. Drive adapters allow you to use a 1/2" drive to a 3/8" socket, or to use a 3/8" drive to a 1/2" socket, you may need both.)
Hex 6mm, 12mm, and MotionPro® 24mm hex tool, see Fig. 2-13.
3/8" socket drive.
Phillips and flat screwdriver.
1/2" size torque wrench.
1" socket (optional) or 8"-long adjustable wrench.
3/8" drive 12mm socket for brake caliper bolts.

3/8" drive 6mm hex bit (Allan) for the fork pinch bolts.
3/8" socket drive extension..
Shop rags (rolls of paper towels).
Socket drive adapters 1/2" to 3/8" and a 3/8" to 1/2".
Magnetic parts bowl so you won't lose parts and tools.

_____
_____
_____

TORQUE SPECIFICATIONS FOR YOUR BIKE

Find out how much torque is required for the items below for your bike. You can do this later if you want to upon final assembly. Torque specification is how much pressure or force must you apply to properly tighten a nut or bolt measured in inch-pounds, foot-pounds, or Newton meters. The latter is a metric rating. With a torque wrench the nut or bolt will be tightened properly. Make sure you lightly lubricate the threads with oil or grease before you torque them down. Thread-locking fluids normally are not used on nuts and bolts when changing motorcycle tires, but you would use them on frame and engine parts and disk brake calipers.

FRONT WHEEL TORQUE SPECIFICATIONS

Front Axle: _____
Front Fork Pinch Bolts: _____
Front Brake Caliper Bolts: _____

_____
_____
_____

REAR WHEEL TORQUE SPECIFICATIONS

Rear Axle Nut Bolt: _____
Rear Brake Caliper Bolts: _____

_____
_____
_____

Note: You will need to purchase two sizes of torque wrenches. One that reads in inch-pounds (a 3/8" size) and one that reads in foot-pounds (a 1/2" size). The 3/8" drive size torque wrench has a limited scale to handle small nuts and bolts like fork pinch bolts and brake caliper bolts. The large 1/2" drive torque wrench handles larger size nuts and bolts like for axles and sprocket bolts. See Fig. 3-1.

TOOLS FOR REAR WHEEL

(This is for the Triumph America Motorcycle, some tools you will need are listed. Only two adjustable wrenches may be needed. Your specific model motorcycle may need different tools. Sockets can be 1/2" or 3/8" with a 1/2" to 3/8" socket adapter, but the former is preferred as these socket sizes are large in size).

Scissor jack: K&L brand is shown in Fig 2-18.
1/2" socket drive breaker bar.
22mm socket or 8"-long adjustable wrench for axle bolt.
24mm socket or 8"-long adjustable wrench for removable axle nut.
8"-long adjustable wrench or 8mm open-end or box wrench for drive chain or belt adjustments.
1/2" size torque wrench.
Rubber mallet.

_____
_____
_____

TOOLS TO CHANGE TIRES

And Fix Flat Tires

Three or four MotionPro® long S-curve tire irons; see Fig. 5-6 (you may need to use four irons for tires over 200 mm wide as an extra helping hand. See Fig. 2-22).
Three to four rim protectors Fig. 4-11 and Fig. 4-12.
Hand cleaner.
Shop rags.
Two 4"×4" wood blocks cut at least 4" longer than your largest size wheel's rim diameter (Fig. 4-1, Fig. 4-2).
One valve core removal tool Fig. 2-23.
Compressed air source: portable tank or shop compressor. Fig. 2-19.
Spare valve cores Fig. 2-23.
Large C-clamp or motorcycle bead breaker. See Fig. 2-8, Fig. 2-10, Fig. 2-12, Fig. 2-20 and Fig. 2-21.
Tire inflation trigger and pressure gauge with air hose; see Fig. 7-4.
Safety goggles or safety glasses.
Tire rim lube liquid and paste.
Wood carpenter's shims 8" long (to spread disk brake pads apart in the caliper) Fig. 3-5.

Note: Also see tools required for front wheel. There are other inexpensive tools or items not listed above you will need and they will be shown later in the book. Most are common tools or devices like two 4" wood blocks and a tire bead starting belt which may be pricey at around $100 but there are other methods you can try before you buy.

Fig. 2-23 Photo of Schrader Valve Core & Tool

The Schrader valve is the tiny device below in Fig. 2-23 that is used to seal, add or remove air from a tire and it resides permanently inside the valve stem. The tool above will install, remove and even repair damaged threads in the valve core's hole in the rim or innertube's valve stem.

THREAD LOCKING COMPOUNDS

You may notice that in this book we do not use red or blue thread-locking sealant on bolt threads. That's because we are using a torque wrench to tighten the bolt properly. However, you can use thread locking compounds if you wish. Red is for permanent and blue is for temporary installations. To remove easily a bolt that has been red thread locked, you need to heat the bolt up with a propane torch or a heat gun. Keep this in mind if you find a bolt on your bike very difficult to remove. Check with your dealer if any bolts on your bike require thread locking. Most bikes don't need the red thread lock when changing tires unless you are changing the belt pulley or chain sprocket or disk brake rotors. You can use blue thread lock on anything you wish. It is just an anti-vibration glue to prevent a bolt from loosening. Use blue color threadlock on brake caliper bolt threads.

Note: If you find a bolt difficult to loosen make certain while facing the bolt's head you turn it counterclockwise to loosen it and clockwise to tighten it. On some engine sprockets and clutches there will be a left-hand thread which will be the opposite of what was described above. Thankfully, these "lefties" are rare in tire changing situations, but just in case you need to know as your specific bike just may be one of them.

EXAMINE WHEEL WHILE ON BIKE

You may want to take a digital photograph of the front and back wheel on both sides of your motorcycle so you can reference how the finished wheel should look. When assembling the wheel components it is amazing what you can forget.

Example: You need to install the speedometer hub, and it's not going on easily. You think you have it on right, but you aren't certain. By looking at the photograph, you can see that it isn't sitting flush with an air gap near the wheel's hub and still is not installed properly. It's the little things like this that can frustrate you when learning, especially the first or second time.

BEFORE REMOVING WHEEL: MARK ITS ROTATION

Important: Use a MagicMarker® to mark a directional arrow in the direction of the front and rear wheel rotation. Mark it anywhere on the wheel or the disk brake rotor hub area near the axle (not on the disk brake contact patch on the rotor). Especially mark the front wheel if you have dual disk brakes (see Fig. 2-24). This will make it easier to know which direction to put the tire on. You can use chalk, ink or even electrical tape in the shape of an arrow. On my own bikes I use a prick punch to permanently mark the wheel with an arrow. If you don't do this, especially with a wheel with two disk brake rotors, you will be hard pressed to figure out which way to mount the front tire on the rim because the wheel looks perfectly equal on both sides, yet cannot or should not be installed backward. Mark the front and back wheels right now on your motorcycle. Left or right side does not matter, as long as you have an arrow marked on the rim or disk brake. See Fig. 2-24. The new tire already has an arrow embedded into its sidewall from the factory. Do this wheel marking now! Use a white or yellow crayon, paint, ink marker, just do it.

Note: Always mark the rim not the tire. It is okay to also mark the tire's rotation on the tire as long as you have marked the rim too. You will understand the reasoning behind this the first time you forget to mark the rim for you will now have a trying time figuring out which direction to fit the tire on the rim. On my personal bike, I etch the arrow permanently on the rim so I always know which way the wheel is rotating without second thought. I suggest you do the same, but for now you can use a Magic Marker® as shown in Fig. 2-24 and also see Fig. 5-9.

Fig. 2-24 Rotation Arrows Marked on Rim

Tip: What if you install the wheel backwards so it is rotating in the wrong direction? You could ride the bike in town at low speed, but it would not be wise to ride the bike at highway speed. The tire is designed to be operated only in the proper direction and it could be dangerous to ride at speed on a tire mounted in reverse rotation especially when braking. If you install it backwards just redo the tire installation job. It is very easy to make this mistake, so don't feel bad if you do. That is why I recommend making permanent indentations to mark wheel rotation direction. The back wheel often does not need to be marked. The chain sprocket, shaft drive gear, or belt pulley clearly indicates only one way the wheel should be installed, making it easy to determine your tire rotation. If you are not certain now is the time to examine the wheel assembly and rotation. Put the bike on a lift and gently rotate the wheels being careful to not get your fingers in the way of any drive component like spokes, chain and sprockets and do not rock the bike in anyway.

Tip: Be aware after you perform a tire change you must pump up the front and rear brake prior to lowering the bike down off the jack and even after cleaning the disk with rubbing alcohol the brakes will not function well until you use them about a dozen times or more.

BUYING TIRES FOR YOUR MOTORCYCLE

Please read Chapter 17, "How To Select Tires For Your Motorcycle" for advice on how to choose tires for your motorcycle. Also, the Question & Answers section in this book (Chapter 19) has a lot of advice you need to read. When you have finished reading those two chapters come back here.

CHAPTER 3

Front Wheel Removal From Motorcycle

And Fix Flat Tires

FRONT WHEEL REMOVAL

Before you remove the wheel I want you to mark your rim with an arrow showing the normal direction of wheel rotation. You can use paint, crayon or even electrical tape shaped like an arrow. Mark the rim, not the tire. You will need to have this rotation information when installing the new tire. Do it right now so you do not forget later. Mark the rim! See Fig. 2-24 for marking the wheel rotation on the rim. Leave the bike on its sidestand for now.

Special Instructions: Don't lift the bike yet with the ATV/Motorcycle jack. We will do that in the next section titled: "Lifting The Bike On The Jack."

Now is the right time to loosen the front wheel axle nut. In most cases you will loosen it buy turning it counter clockwise when facing the nut. In Fig. 3-2 notice both front forks on the Triumph motorcycle has four pinch bolts, two on each fork. All must be loosened (very loose), but not removed. Two wrenches are used to loosen the axle bolt. One on the left holds the axle so it will not spin and the wrench on the right downward force is applied to loosen the axle nut. The special metric adapter that was shown in Fig. 2-13 is shown inserted in the right fork leg in the photo Fig. 3-3.

Caution: If you try to loosen or tighten axles with the bike lifted on a jack the bike will or can tip or slide off the jack and fall down. This can cause severe personal injury, entrapment and or death. Always tie the motorcycle down to the jack and to the garage sidewalls or foundation anchor bolts so the bike can not slide off the jack. You can use long and short ratcheting tie-down straps to do this. I use the long tie-downs attached to the bike's handlebars or fork tubes and snug them to the garage foundation anchor bolts and this prevents the bike from sliding, twisting or tipping over off the jack. Then I tie the bike's frame on the left and right side down to the jack itself. But you must also insert a scissor jack or blocks under the opposite wheel so the bike will not see-saw and fall off the jack. I suggest doing a lot of practice lifting and lowering and securing your motorcycle if this is new to you. You can not afford to make mistakes using jacking procedures. Take all precautions so bike can not come off the jack and you'll be okay.

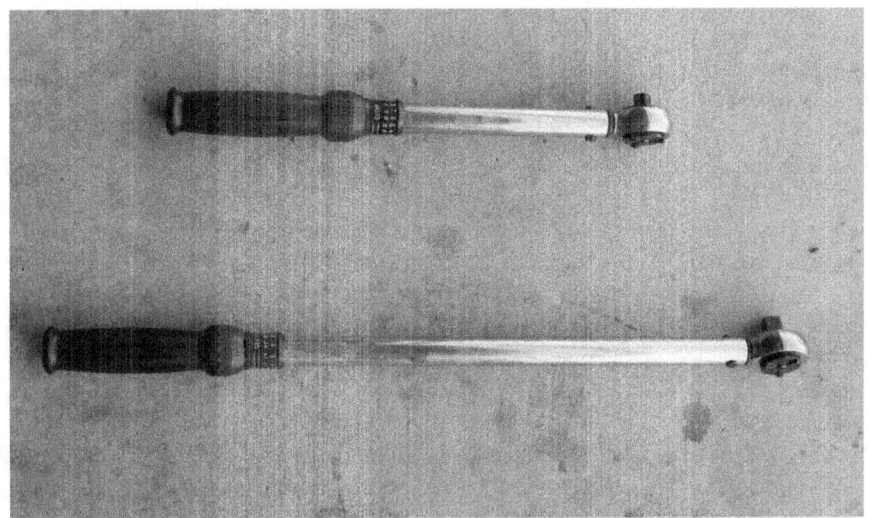

Fig. 3-1 Torque Wrenches - Click Type 3/8" & 1/2" Sizes

Fig. 3-1 reveals a smaller size 3/8" torque wrench and a larger 1/2" torque wrench. You will need both. You can't just put a socket adapter on the large one to omit the smaller one as the scale will not read down to the small torque values as the smaller torque wrench will.

Fig. 3-1 shows the click type torque wrench. You can use the analog dial, digital or bar type. They all work. You may still need two torque wrenches to measure tiny inch pounds (3/8" size wrench) and larger foot pounds (1/2" wrench). Expensive does not mean best. You can get by with cheap torque wrenches as long as they are close in calibration and most all are. When working on motorcycle frames a economical torque wrench is just fine. When working on the engine you need the best as the engine components demand precise spot-on accuracy and the click types shown in Fig. 3-1 are fine for precision engine work.

Note: You can if you wish lift the bike by turning the jack screw with a wrench if you are using a wide motorcycle scissor jack. (You can also use the ATV/Motorcycle lift.) I use a 1" socket, but don't lift the bike all the way yet. Just get it off the side stand with both wheels still in full contact with the ground. This will level the bike and make it easier to work on. The bike should not feel wobbly or want to fall over in this position.

Using the 6mm hex on a 3/8" drive, loosen but do not remove (turn counterclockwise) the four Allen head pinch bolts, two on the left fork and two on the right forks. They should be loose so they are no longer pinching the fork tube. See Fig. 3-2.

Fig. 3-2 Pinch Bolts To Loosen On Front Fork

Then, with the 12mm hex, turn the axle bolt counterclockwise from the right fork and remove the bolt from the axle sliding it out from the right fork leg (some bikes may need to slide out from the opposite left fork leg). See Fig. 3-2.

Note: Check to see if you need to remove the disk brake caliper, speedometer drive cable, or any wiring before removing your wheel. On the Triumph America/Speedmaster models of motorcycle, I like to remove the speedometer cable and remove the disk brake caliper. Why? The plastic cable insert to the speedometer drive gear on the front wheel easily cracks and is expensive to replace. And it's difficult to install the speedometer drive gear hub to the wheel with the cable attached, since the hub keeps pulling away from the gear spline. Other motorcycle brands don't use speedometer cables to the front wheel.

In Fig. 3-3 you can see a "spacer" or "spool" between the fork and the wheel hub. Note that some wheels will have one or two per axle usually one on each side of the axle. Sometimes you need to spread the front fork or the rear swing arm a tiny bit with a long screwdriver as leverage to slip the spacers into position. They fall out easily once the axle is removed and are a tad troublesome to get back into position when reinserting the axle. Patience is required. Only gentle persuasion force is required, never brute force.

Tip: Depending on your motorcycle some bikes only have pinch bolts on one fork and others may have them on both forks. You should loosen the main axle nut first then loosen the pinch bolts. This way the pinch bolts are "pinching" the axle so the axle won't rotate when loosening the main axle nut.

Warning: Do not let the bike slip off the jack. Don't use force on anything to upset the motorcycle balance. Be gentle and always vigilant. Tell someone to check up on you often when working alone with a motorcycle on a lift. Be safe.

Read the "warning" paragraphs below before proceeding with the following procedure.

LIFTING THE BIKE ON THE JACK

Fig. 3-3 Loosening Front Axle Nut

Put the transmission in first gear so the bike won't roll backwards when you position the jack under the frame and lift the front of the bike. Position the jack or jack arms under the frame, ahead of the oil filter (on a Triumph twin motorcycle, about three inches). We only want the front of the bike to rise off the ground, not the back wheel like a seesaw, but without the seesawing motion, leaving the rear wheel on the ground. See Fig. 3-4 that is showing how to lift the rear wheel only off the ground with blocks under the tire. You will do the same except you will be lifting and blocking the front wheel instead of what is shown in Fig. 3-4.

By shifting the jack just a tiny bit forward under the bike's frame rails it will lift the front wheel only. In both cases, you must install blocks under the raised wheel. Only when you are ready to drop the wheel away from the bike will the blocks be removed.

Note: When using the ATV/Motorcycle jack we normally tie the bike down to the jack, but when using a motorcycle-specific scissor jack the bike is normally not tied down to the jack. It should be, but there are no welded loops on the jack to tie to. That is why you see mechanics using scissor jacks without tying the bike down to the jack. The bike is tied down to the HandyLift® or to anchors to the concrete floor or building walls.

Tip: I did not meet anyone who had Kenda brand tires, so I tried them and found out they were super economical and long wearing cruiser tires. It pays to take a chance and try out lower price brands. You may be in for a pleasant surprise. Shinko is another brand of tire company that has lower prices and riders are discovering they work very well for the price. I found excellent Bridgestone brand tires for my Victory motorcycle and both tires including shipping charges was only $200. I could have overpaid that amount just for one rear tire with other big name brands easily. The tires gave me 8,000 miles. Not bad for a big bike on rough, burning hot summer desert roads. Of course, I could get better miles, but the cost of the tires doubles and I won't get 16,000 miles on those expensive tires. A high price is never a guarantee the tire is superior, it just means you paid more than you should have for that tire and you made a tire dealer happy to sell it to you. Keep in mind tires are DOT approved to be safe, so don't get lured into marketing hype as all tires must meet the Department of Transportation safety standard as so stamped on the tire's sidewall.

How To Install Tires on Motorcycles

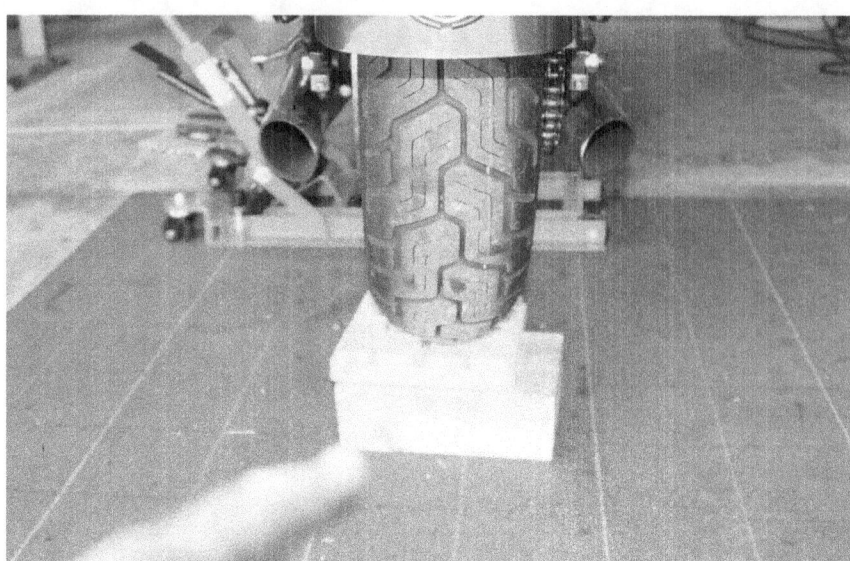

Fig. 3-4 Wood or Plastic Blocks Supports Under Wheel

If the rear wheel rises off the ground, lower the bike then re-position the lift a bit rearward or put a block of wood under the rear tire. See Fig. 3-4.   It is okay to not tilt the bike and just totally 100% raise the bike as shown in Fig. 2-16 and Fig. 2-17.

Note: You can lift the entire bike off the ground if you wish as long as the bike is stable, tied down to the lift so the bike will not slide off the lift. Practice jack-lifting for it is a skill to be learned to performed safely.

Caution: Pay attention to the forces you are making on the entire motorcycle. When you are removing or installing wheels it is easy to forget the bike is on a jack and it can slowly be inching itself off the jack then suddenly it falls over without warning and no way to stop it. Do not make any jarring motions to the motorcycle. Keep checking the jack is still under the frame and has not moved position. And if you think a bike will not fall over even when using a expensive motorcycle-specific table lift like HandyLift® devices dealers and repair shops use think again, the bikes can and do fall off usually wrecking the motorcycle even more severely due to the tall height falling. Operator error and failing to tie down the bike is the major cause for accidents.

Lift the bike on the jack, slowly. Make sure it does not fall over. Raise the front of the bike until the front wheel is 2" off the ground or so, only as high as needed for the tire to clear the front fender when the axle is removed. The front wheel must now be off the pavement, and the rear wheel should still be on the ground. If not, you can position some blocks under the rear wheel to stop or reduce any seesaw motion that can make the bike unstable and slip off of the jack. See Fig. 3-4.

With axle nut removed turn the axle using the 24mm hex tool in any direction and the axle will start to slip out from the right side on a Triumph. If not, raise the bike up a little bit more or push the axle out gently from the left side, but not with your finger—to avoid pinching it if the wheel suddenly drops down. Remove the axle completely. Your bike's procedure may differ a bit, but it should be similar even if it is a Harley-Davidson or some other brand the only difference will be the number of pinch bolts on the fork, sizes of wrenches to use and the direction the axle slides out from the forks.

Warning: If you did not place blocks under the rear wheel the bike could unbalance and seesaw violently backwards and bounce away from the jack and fall over when you remove the front wheel. When you are working on a motorcycle suspended on a lift, always remember the bike is unstable and could fall over if you use too much force tightening bolts, wiggling or removing the wheel, etc. Always periodically check to see if the bike has shifted from the jack. The bike can creep over time by your gentle movements of the bike then suddenly slip away and fall down. When you use a jack it is always a good idea to place some blocks under the bike so that if the jack fails the bike will not fall down. Make certain to use the manual safety stop/brake device on the ATV/Motorcycle jack in case the hydraulic system fails. Work slow, keep your eyes open for danger, and be safe. Accidents happen, but we don't ever want one to happen when a motorcycle is lifted in the air for any reason. It will not be a bad thing to stop once in a while and ask, "Is this safe? Will the bike fall over?" Perform a safety inspection to make sure all is well. Fear is a good thing. It is one of my greatest fears of having the motorcycle fall off the jack, so I am extra vigilant all of the time to ensure it does not happen. I rather bore you with repetition to insure your safety.

Caution: Not dealing with frustration can be hazardous. It takes your mind away from the job at hand, and you become absent-minded forgetting the safety factor of the job at hand. When you become frustrated for any reason, you need to stop and take a short break and wind down. Being angry when working with machinery is a recipe for disaster. Now go back and read again the above paragraph, "Lifting the Bike on the Jack."

Now raise the bike two inches higher. This should be enough to drop the wheel downward. First remove the right axle spacer spool, then the speedometer should wiggle free and drop away. Raise the bike so the wheel rolls straight out from under the front fender. Note how the disk brake rotor just slides away from the two disk pads in the caliper. The rotor will go back in the same way. However, removing the disk caliper beforehand makes the removal and install much easier to do.

Do not touch the brake lever at all, or the pads will close. If this happens, gently use a thick tapered piece of wood (carpenter's shim; see Fig. 3-5) to put side pressure against the pads.

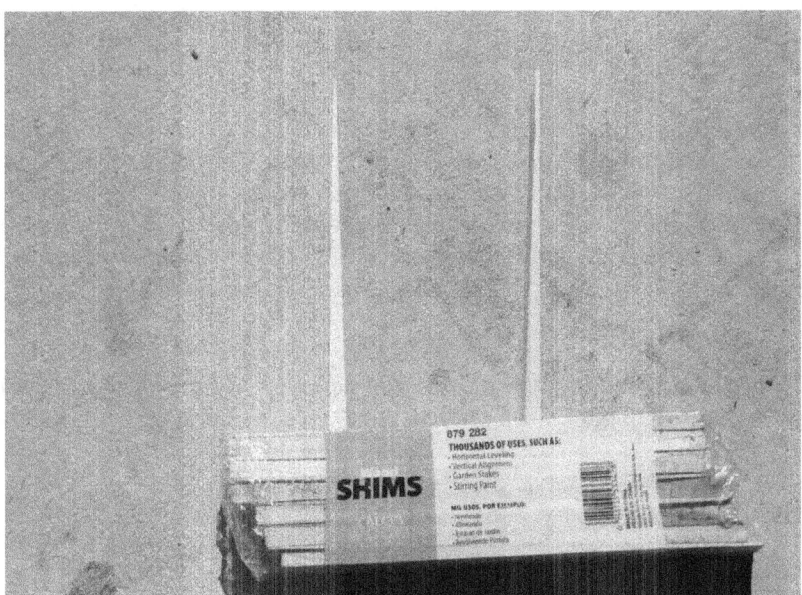

Fig. 3-5 Carpenter's Wood Shim used to Spread Caliper Brake Pads

Then push them away from each other, being careful not to gouge up the pads. You can use a thick flat screwdriver blade, but they will gouge the soft disk brake pads if you are not very careful (I don't recommend it). The pads are actually quite fragile and crush with ease. A single groove won't hurt a disk brake pad, but if you crumble a huge chunk from the pad (the size of a dime or more) you should renew both pads. You can, if you wish, make a wood brace to place between the brake lever and handlebar and tape it in place with electrical tape so the clutch lever will not be accidentally be pressed. Use the Carpenter's wood shims! You may need to snap the shim in two at some point as they will be too long to fit into the caliper between the brake pads.

Note: New brake pads are always thicker than the worn pads being replaced. When installing new pads, it is a normal requirement to separate the new pads from each other. Otherwise the rotor can't slip in between the pads when installing the wheel. When you remove the old pads, this is the time to clean the caliper pistons with soap and water and a soft nylon brush (never use brake cleaner or a metal brush; these will destroy caliper piston seals). Then push (expand) the caliper pistons into the caliper with a tapered block of wood. If you don't clean the exterior caliper pistons first, grit will enter the piston cylinder and cause hydraulic leaks due to cylinder wall and piston surface scratches. Stop pushing the pistons when the caliper pistons are flush with the caliper housing. Then install your new pads into the caliper. Generally you only need 6 or 7 mm of space between the brake pads for the 5mm disk brake rotor to slip between the pads.

You can use these shims to also spread apart axle components to slip in wheel spacing spools or even to create a guide to adjust headlights. Just adjust the headlight where you want it, insert the wedge shim (if it fits) then tighten the headlight. As the headlight adjusting bolt tightens the head lamp will compress against the shim preventing a drop or rise in the head lamp. The wood shims can be used as crush points between the lift and the frame or aluminum engine if needed. I use them on the Victory motorcycles as otherwise the bike can't be lifted squarely with a flat jack, that crankcase seam gets in the way, so shimming on both sides of the seam permits the bike to be lifted evenly without tipping. Your bike may need some shims too for jack placement.

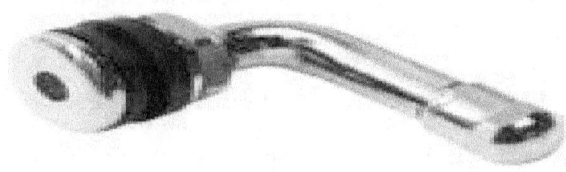

Fig. 3-6 Valve Stem With Valve Cap, Bolt-In Type

The valve stem cap (at right side of Fig.3- 6) holds air in the event the inner valve core fails and leaks air. It is a secondary backup device. You normally do not need to replace these external valve stem caps each time you change tires, but once each year should be fine. Replacements should be compatible with the air pressure monitoring system you may have installed on your wheels. Plastic is fine, metal caps are better. They are installed snugly hand-tight. Do not over tighten them or use a wrench of any kind to tighten them, but you can use a wrench to remove them as the caps internal rubber O-ring or gasket may bond to the valve stem. If the bond required using a wrench to remove the valve stem cap replace the valve cap with a new one as the sealing internal O-ring is likely damaged and will not hold air.

Note: Plastic valve caps are okay, but they can become brittle. Metal caps are much stronger to seal air in the event the valve core failed, but they can rust. Caps are cheap. Replace them once every three years or less.

CHAPTER 4

Removing Tire From The Rim

REMOVING TIRE FROM THE RIM

The wheel is now ready to be placed into position so we can remove the tire.

I will show you how to do the job with tire irons, then later with a tire changing machine. You will learn both methods. And believe it or not, I usually do not use the expensive tire changing machine to change my tires, I just use tire irons because it is faster and easier. So, you do not need to spend a lot of money to change your tires and that includes all Harley-Davidson and other brands of big cruiser motorcycles. Yes, even those big fat wide custom bike 250mm size tires, they go off and on the rim with tire irons.

WHEEL SUPPORT

You can place your wheel with the disk brake side facing down on 4"-×-4" wood blocks cut slightly longer than the diameter of your rims. Usually the front wheel rim is the longer than the rear wheel so measure and cut about 4" longer than the width of the front wheel. See Fig. 1-D.

And Fix Flat Tires

Fig. 4-1 Wood Blocks To Support Wheel

WOOD BLOCKS

If the disk can float without touching any hard surface, it won't be damaged. You don't want any pressure to be applied on the disk brake rotor. See Fig. 4-18 as the disk brake rotor is facing downward and floating in mid-air. Your wheel may have two disk brake rotors. Generally there is no need to remove one or both of the disk brake rotors to change a tire as the tire irons or mounting bar will not get in the way. The same for the rear wheel there is no reason to remove the chain drive sprocket or belt pulley. However, if the chain drive sprocket has a habit of falling out of the hub, then remove the sprocket when changing tires.

Fig. 4-2 Wood Blocks Floating Tire Reveals Blocks Are Long Enough to Use

Fig. 4-3 Harley-Davidson Wheel Floating on Two 4"x4" Wood Blocks

Okay, Fig. 4-3 does not show the tire attached to the rim, but you can see if the wheel were so positioned the disk brake rotor would be floating above the floor so it could not be scratched or warped. Also, you should wrap the wood blocks with towels to soak up any spills and to prevent marring of the rim. Chrome and alloy rims won't mar against wood but some rims might. Placing a drop cloth under this assembly will prevent degreaser and tire lubricant stains to carpet or concrete.

Note: On many bikes it is not practical to remove the rear wheel sprocket or drive pulley from the wheel for they are bolted into the wheel hub and new bolts need to be reinserted. In this case, just try positioning the brake rotor down and remove/install the tire. If that does not work, then flip the wheel over. And if for some strange reason you still find a rotor disk or pulley is getting in the way you will need to remove one or the other so the tire irons can function properly. Or use a rotary mount/demount bar to remove/install the tire.

You can obtain old tires at no cost at any tire store or motorcycle shop to support your wheel off of the ground. I don't like using old tires because they are too soft and wobbly. I like the rim to be on a non-movable surface. You may eventually construct a box of wood with a hole in the middle for the disk brake rotor to enter and with the wood frame supporting the wheel while you mount and demount the tire. For now, using the wood blocks lying on a hard surface is probably best for rock-solid stability and ease of construction. You can create your own design.

Yes, you can stack a couple of old motorcycle tires upon each other to raise the wheel off the ground instead of using wood blocks, but the tires flex and wobble. Strap the tires together with rope, large zip ties, duct tape, or electrical tape. This may make the job more comfortable for you to do. You can use old car or truck tires as they are thicker and more stable. Old rubber tires are nice as they prevent the wheel from rotating when you are working on the rim and they are flexible and will not scratch the wheel. Just make a system that works for you.

Note: Your bike may have a drive belt pulley. You don't have to remove the pulley unless you feel in the process of handling the tire it will fall out and hit the floor and be damaged. Some bikes pulley's are slip fit into the wheel and others are bolted to the wheel. To remove a pulley is like removing a sprocket you just pull upward on it. If stuck, spray some liquid tire lubricant where the pulley seats into the wheel hub, rock it and pull it straight out. Some can be stuck in there good. If so, odds are it won't fall out so leave it be.

REMOVE VALVE CAP AND VALVE STEM CORE

Before you can remove the valve core you must first remove the screwed on plastic or metal valve cap on the end of the valve stem. See Fig. 3-6. Turn it counter clockwise to remove it. When replacing valve caps with newer ones make sure they are compatible with any tire pressure monitoring system you may have.

Warning: When removing a valve core to release air pressure, always close your eyes and wear safety glasses or goggles. Otherwise debris or a valve core may strike your eyes at missile speed. Valve cores can escape from your finger and fly like tiny bullets with enough force to easily blind you! See Fig. 4-5. Also, close your eyes and move away as the air blast from the tire can be fierce and throw dust and grit and even the inner tire's valve core straight into your face. It is like a rocket blasting a bullet so beware. It won't hurt your fingers, so keep your fingers over the valve stem as air first releases so you can catch the valve core.

Remove the valve cap. Insert the valve core remover's slotted end into the valve core on your wheel's rim. Gently turn counterclockwise until you hear air coming out. Then stop turning the tool and let the air bleed out slowly. You can do it faster, but I don't want you to see the compressed air shoot the core and the tool out at you like a bullet. You don't want anything flying into your eyes or your valve core lost. (And remember to wear safety goggles.) When the air has been let out, you can remove the valve core completely and set it aside in a parts bowl.

Fig. 4-4 Valve Core Removal Tool Slotted End On Top - Multi-Purpose Tool

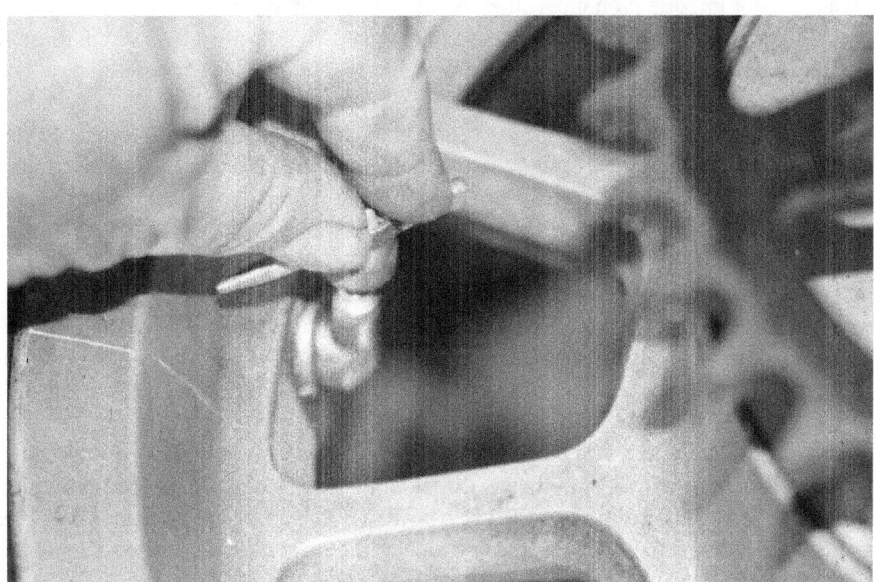
Fig. 4-5 Using Tool To Remove Valve Core

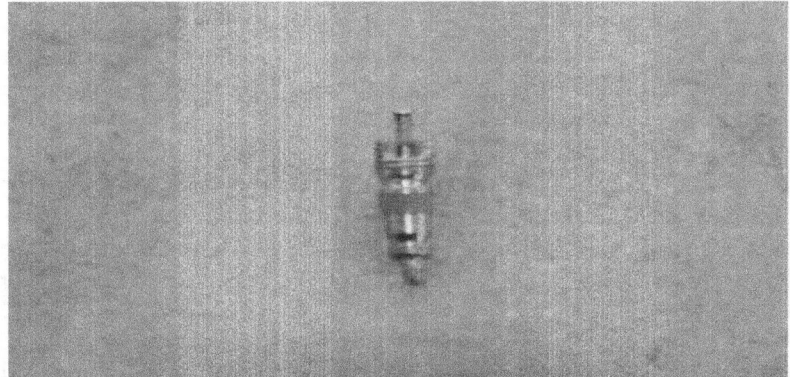
Fig. 4-6 Valve Core Is Often Called A Schrader Core or American Valve

How To Install Tires on Motorcycles
BEAD BREAKER - BUYING ONE

Believe it or not, there is a company that actually makes a small tire bead breaker and tire install kit small enough to fit in your motorcycle saddlebags. Contact BestRestProducts.com and seek information on their Bead BrakR® system and other motorcycle tire changing tools. Their tool won't work on solid cast wheels. There must be some spokes or thin webbing in the rim.

Another company that makes a portable bead breaker is Stopngo.com that can be used on solid wheels, but it is limited to tire size. It will work on tires up to 160 mm wide, but this tool should break any tough bead with great ease. So will the Tyrepliers® (made by ExtremeOutback.com) that will break the bead on tires up to 6.75" wide, though it cannot accommodate 8" cruiser rims with 240mm rear tires. It too cannot be used with solid wheels.

MotionPro.com makes a chisel-like device called the "Bead Popper" that will work on any type of rim or any size tire and can be carried with you in your saddlebags, but it does require more manual force to use. A heavy hammer is needed to operate this tool and if you slip by accident you could ruin a rim. I would not use this for street bikes. The heavy-duty shop floor stand tire bead breaker with high-leverage action sold by JC Whitney™ accommodates small and wide tires, but it isn't touring portable. It is meant for use in the home garage or repair shop.

When you see the simple design of a tire bead breaker you may want to design and make your own that will work for your bike. Any welding metal fabrication shop can make one for you. Also, ask motorcycle mechanics in your area for suggestions as they may know of the newest and best tools available that are not listed in this book. As crazy as it may sound, a large vise will also do the trick. Anything that will compress and squeeze the tire away from the rim will work. A metal screw-type carpenter's C-clamp will work. See Fig. 2-21 and Fig. 4-9.

Tip: Portability of a tire breaker is not important on most street bikes. The portable devices are usually needed by adventure touring and dirt bike riders who are out in the back roads far from any sort of service. All flats must be fixed in these remote and extreme locations. As a street rider, you only need to carry a tire plug kit and a portable air compressor (12-volt electric or manual air pump) (See Fig. 12-1) unless you have spoke wheels and are riding with a passenger. Then you should consider a portable tire bead breaker and the tools required to remove a front or rear wheel to stuff in your saddlebag so that any automotive service station can help you patch a leaking innertube. They can lift the bike, but they may not have the tools to remove the wheel(s). Many automotive shops do not have Allen wrenches larger than 14mm. Your bike may have a 17 or even a hefty 24mm Allen axle on your bike. Once they get the wheel off most, but not all mechanics, can fix a tube motorcycle tire.

The manual and automatic tire changing machines all come with integrated bead breakers that will handle any motorcycle tire. You may want to resort to a large steel carpenter's C-clamp. It will work like the Stopngo.com tool but can be used on larger tires. If you can't find a tire bead breaker that will work, most tire changing facilities can break the bead for you on both sides of the wheel. Make sure they don't scratch your rims! Tell them to use a cloth rag on any surface with wheel, hub or rim contact points.

Tip: Before you buy a bead breaker, make sure it will work with the tires you will be changing now and in the future. Find one that works with an immense leverage of force. A cruiser's tire bead is stuck onto the rim like a super-powerful glue and is impressively difficult to break from the rim, especially the first break of the tire's bead. My tire changing machine has a breaker bar over 4 feet long, and I still have to put big grunt force to break the bead. This task is one of the most difficult to do, so a good tool is your best investment.

BEAD BREAKING

You can use a large C-clamp to break that stubborn bead. The bead must be broken on both sides. "Broken" doesn't mean we are breaking anything—it just means separating the bond of the tire from the rim. You should buy a bead breaker designed for motorcycle tires. If you have no money to buy any tool, then any truly biker-friendly and cooperative tire or motorcycle repair shop can break the bead for you.

To break the bead, you are simply going to squeeze the tire together near the rim. Do not squeeze the rim. The tire is amazingly stuck on the rim like a powerful bonded glue, and it takes a lot of force to get that tire to pop free. Once you break one side of the bead, the other side breaks loose with much less pressure. Both sides of the tire must be broken free. You know the tire's beads are totally broken when you can easily rotate the tire on the rim. The tire will move easily and may actually feel loose or floppy on the rim.

Warning: Make sure the disk brake rotors are fully floating in air and are not in contact with the ground or any other hard or soft surface. When bead breaking force is applied to a tire the rim will want to move or sink if resting on rubber tires. Watch and make sure the disk brake rotor never touches anything so it will not crack or bend. It takes very little pressure to warp a rotor.

Tip: When you place your tire and rim down on the 4"×4" wood blocks you will need to apply a lot of force to one segment of the tire on the rim. This can make the other side of the rim want to leap into the air. To stop this, just wrap-tie the rim and tire down to the wood blocks with 1/8" nylon rope (not string), and keep a knee or foot on the opposite end where you are trying to break the bead. After the bead is broken you can remove the ropes. See Fig. 4-7.

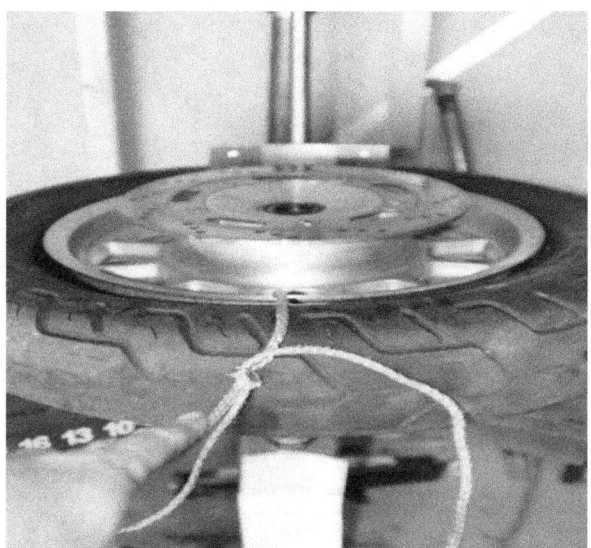

Fig. 4-7 Tying Down Rim With Rope & Setting The Bead Breaker On Tire.

You will find purchasing a nice small tire changing machine will be an investment in saving money and time. Yes, you can get by without one. The choice is yours to make. Fig. 4-7 shows the No-Mar® brand tire changing machine with its high-leverage knife-edge style bead breaker ready to depress the tire away from the rim. It breaks the bead with ease. I tied the wheel down with 1/4" nylon rope to the tire changing machine so the wheel will not flip or fall off the machine when the bead breaker is pressing down at the opposite end. Most tire changers use their hand or knee, but I still like to use the rope. This way I can just concentrate on breaking the bead and not have to balance the wheel with my body to keep it from flipping over or sliding off the machine.

Bead Confusion? When the word bead is used it can mean a tire bead or a rim bead. Fig. 5-3 shows a tire bead. There is another bead on the opposite side of the tire. The tire bead meets and fits to the rim bead to create a very tight air seal and creates a powerful grip to bind the tire to the rim. Fig. 16-16 shows a upper rim bead and Fig. 16-17 shows a rim lower bead surface. The word rim is often used for the word wheel.

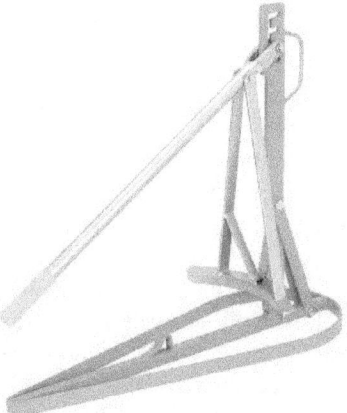

Fig. 4-8 Bead Breaker For Tire - Powerful, Portable & Inexpensive

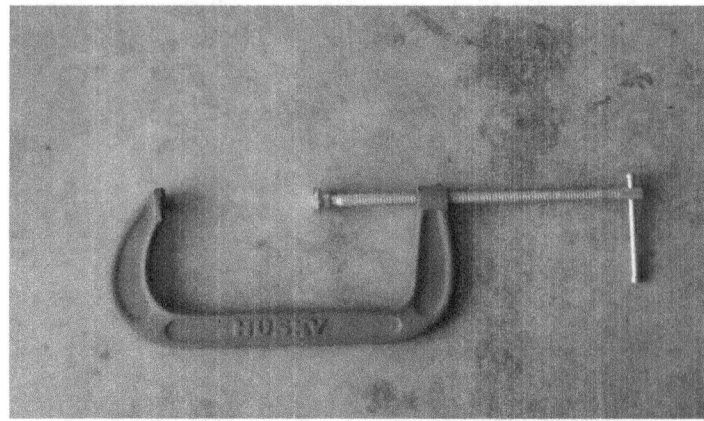

Fig. 4-9 Carpenter's C-Clamp - 8" Size - Cast Iron or Steel

Fig. 4-10 Bead Breaker Breaking A Tire Bead - No-Mar® Tire Changer

USING THE BEAD BREAKER

 Note: Before removing a tire read the owner manual or aftermarket instruction sheet to determine if any special procedure is required so you will not ruin any internal air pressure monitor sensors.   After you remove the tire from the rim it would be a good time to change any batteries in wireless monitoring systems.

 Using the bead breaker is easy. All air must be deflated from the tire with the valve core removed. As you squeeze the tire close to where it meets the rim, you separate the outer edge of the tire's sidewall from the inner edge of the rim. That causes the tire to break away from the rim. It is important not to crush the rim! See Fig. 4-10. So install the bead breaker only on the rubber tire surface, never let one end of the bead breaker creep or slip away to contact the rim. Other than this, the bead breaking tools are easy to use, but the bead is going to be very hard to break most of the time. Some bead breakers will squeeze both ends of the tire simultaneously, adjacent to the rim (the top and bottom), or just squeeze one side of the tire (the top side only).

 Warning: Before you use any bead breaker, make sure that the wheel's rim is supported underneath on two wood blocks (or on a tire changing machine's rim clamps) so that the wheel, hub and disk brake rotor is floating in mid-air. This will prevent parts from cracking under the great force needed to break the bead. Also assume the wheel may slip and fall down, so make sure it is tied down (See Fig. 4-7 and cloth rags are used (if needed) to prevent any scratching of the rims.

 Follow the instructions that came with the bead breaker. If you use a screw-type carpenter's C-clamp (Fig. 4-9), make sure it is of strong steel construction (not plastic or aluminum) and the clamp ends are only pinching the rubber tire near the rim, not on the rim.

And Fix Flat Tires

Tighten the C-clamp until you hear a loud "pop" and the tire's rubber becomes loose and falls away from the rim.

Remove the C-clamp and turn the tire and wheel over and break the bead again, if need be, on the opposite side. You will know the tire is broken from the rim when you can see the tire is no longer bonded to the rim and the tire is loose on the rim. You may have to break the bead 180 degrees opposite from each other to get the entire rubber tire broken away from the rim.

Can you stand on the tire to break the bead instead of using a bead breaker tool? Yes, on a dirt bike you can. Dirt bike tires have much less bond to the rims than street bike tires do. Most sport bikes also have tire flexible sidewalls that break away easily, but some brands and styles do not. A cruiser motorcycle will need a tire bead breaker. Cruisers have very stiff sidewalls to carry the immense weight of the bike. The bond to the rim is incredibly severe, making bead breaking very tough, if not impossible, without using the right tools. Investing in a good bead breaker tool will make the tire changing job so much easier to do.

Tip: All of the warnings you see in this book will all become common sense to you later on. I need to warn the "beginner" so costly and dangerous mistakes will not happen.

RIM PROTECTORS

I use three and sometimes four rim protectors. They slip over the rim to protect the soft rim from being marred or scratched by the steel tire irons. The strings on the rim protectors just make it easier to pull and slide them around the rim and to remove them when the tire mount is finished. You will need to move them as needed. How many should you use? As many as you want. You can use one, but two will be better. Sometime I dip the entire tips of the tire irons in liquid plastic instead or wrap the tire iron tip with electrical tape. Then you don't need to use any rim protectors. If the plastic or tape wears off, just coat them again. See Fig. 2-4 and Fig. 5-6.

Tip: A nylon rim protector that mounts to the rim in Fig. 4-11 will last much longer than plastic or rubber ones. K&L® nylon brand is what I use. They come with ropes. The rim protector is not used with a rotary mount/dismount bar, it is only used with tire irons. These rim protectors do break so buy about eight of them. You may need to use four rim protectors per wheel. Yes, you can use just one and slide it around the rim as needed, two is even better and three and four better still.

Fig. 4-11 Rim Protectors Made of Nylon Are Very Strong

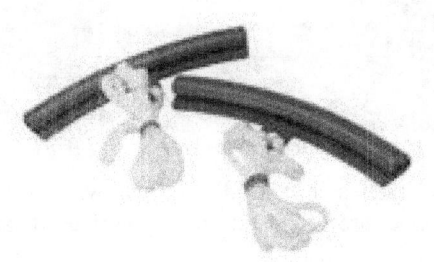

Fig. 4-12 Rim Protectors With Rope - Use On Metal Rims

Fig. 4-12 shows a pair of rim protectors with rope. You snap the rim protector on the outward edge of the rim and use the rope to pull and slide the rim protector along the rim circumference as needed. Problem is, they can get stuck and are difficult to move at times so I use four of them mounted to the rim so I always have one nearby where I am working. You only use these rim protectors when using tire irons. They prevent the tire iron from scratching expensive metal rims.

Note: Just because a rim protector is used so it will not scratch composite wheels (synthetic fiber wheels like advanced plastic, carbon fiber or Kevlar®® rims) you should not be using tire irons to work on composite rims. Use the rotary method of installing tires, not tire irons or the composite material can crack, chip or break.

REMOVING TOP SIDE OF THE TIRE

When the beads are broken and the tire is loose on both sides of the rim, we must use the tire lubricant. Normally, a liquid lubricant (Fig. 2-6) is used to remove tires because the process is faster as it penetrates and dries quickly. Spray or swab the liquid liberally on the tire where the tire meets the rim. I like to use paste lubricant on the face of the tire. This way the tire comes right off with much less resistance. See Fig. 4-13 and Fig. 4-14 for two brands of paste tire installation lubricant. Using just liquid lubricant is okay to remove a tire from a rim.

Warning: Do not use soap and water for even dish washing liquid and window cleaners can attack the metal or composite rim and corrode it. Never use any sort of lubricating oil as it will dissolve your rubber tires!

Yes, you can use liquid tire lubricant to demount and install tires just be aware that you must work fast as the lubricant evaporates quickly. I strongly advise that you use the tire lubricating procedure outlined in this book when working with tire irons and manually operated tire machines. Pneumatic (air driven) machines only need (in most cases) liquid tire lube.

TIRE LUBRICANTS

The great secret to tire changing, especially installing the tire on the rim, is using the proper lubricant (and depressing the tire into the rim's drop-center). Yes, some people use window cleaner but is not recommended. It evaporates a bit too fast, but if you are quick it will work. I don't use it as it is ammonia based and it will corrode rims. There are two lubricants you need to know about. We will be using both types of lube in this book.

Liquid Lubricant: For tire removal use the liquid lube as shown in Fig. 2-6. It is a soapy water mix specially blended to make the tire slip off the rim with great ease. No-Mar® makes a nice blend of this lubricant. You can also buy liquid tire mounting lubricant at auto supply stores, but once you use No-Mar® you will want to stay with the best.

Fig. 4-13 Paste Lubricant No-Mar Brand Works Very Nicely

Danger: Never use dish washing liquid or soap and water or window cleaner when installing tires. Be aware that using non-approved products like this can actually deteriorate the rubber tire and metal rim as you ride! It can also cause a devastating delamination failure in composite rims causing a crash.

Tip: Read the Question & Answer section in the back of this book for it has a lot of advice and knowledge including many tips and tricks of the trade along with troubleshooting tips. It also makes for good reading to enhance your overall wisdom regarding motorcycles and tires.

Fig. 4-14 Tyre Lube® Brand Gel Lubricant Is Very Slippery

Tip: Never use axle grease or lubricating oil or water to mount a tire to a rim. These products will absolutely create a dangerous condition of wheel slipping and rapid tire deterioration. Water based products will upset tire pressures as the water vaporizes, condenses or freezes upon temperature changes. Get into the habit of using the proper product designed for the job at hand.

Solid Lubricant Paste Grease: This special tire formula is for mounting the tire to the rim. It is absolutely critical to use this grease if you wish to be successful when using tire irons or a machine. Nothing works better than tire mounting grease! It is super slippery, stays put, and evaporates very slowly and will not harm rubber. No-Mar® makes this product.

Yes, you can lubricate the bead area of the tire and the rim with liquid or paste lube. However, a light coating of lubricant is all that is needed.

REMOVING TOP BEAD OF TIRE FROM RIM

Note: Write down the size of the tire you are removing from the rim and make sure before you install a new tire that the tire will properly fit that rim. The previous owner of a used bike may have installed the wrong size tire on your rim, so don't assume what you remove should be the tire that goes back on. Consult the owner manual and look at the rim data stamped on the inner rim for sizing determination (if available and if readable) as your wheels may now be aftermarket rims for all you know.

Front Rim Data: _____.
Rear Rim Data: _____.

Place the wheel on a protected surface like wood blocks or use some other method of your choosing as long as the tire and rim are off the floor and disk brake rotor is floating high and protected from coming into contact with anything.

Note: Go to Chapter 16 and see how to use a machine to remove/install a tire because the photographs reveal tire to rim details that you may find helpful. We are using tire irons in this section of the book.

Fig. 4-15 Rim Protectors - Inserting Two To Four

Insert four rim protectors with an external string attached to the rim protector so you can pull it around the rim as you work as shown in Fig. 4-15 and 4-16 shows two rim protectors installed. The other two are nearby.

Note: Which end of the tire iron to use? Generally, you use the shallow curve end of the tire iron to remove tires and the steep curve end to install tires. Fig. 4-16 shows the shallow curved tip being used to dismount a tire from the rim. Of course, you can use the deeply curved portion to do the job, but it will be more inconvenient as the deep curve just gets in the way preventing you from working with ease.

Tire Iron Orientation: To remove a tire from the rim insert tire iron with the small curved end facing so the tiny "lip" will "hook" onto the tire so it can be pulled up and over the rim. That tiny curve at the end of the tire iron is concave so the tire's shoulder willl sit in that concave portion of the tire iron. This is how to orient the tire iron when inserting it between the rim protector and tire. When installing the tire you just use the deeply curved end of the tire iron with the tiny concave end lip facing down so it grabs the rim, not the tire. Practice with this orientation so it becomes familiar.

Fig. 4-16 Inserting First Tire Iron

Spray or swipe liquid tire lubricant at tire and rim faces 360-degrees all around the rim where the tire meets the rim.

Insert a tire iron as shown in Fig. 4-16 using the shallow curved end of the iron and pull the tire's edge over the rim and hold the tire iron in that position. Now insert another tire iron next to the first about six inches away and pull the tire over from the rim as shown in Fig. 4-17. This is easy to do. Now take out the first tire iron and do the same thing until the top side of the tire comes off of the rim.

Note: The deeply curved end of the tire iron is for installing the tire, the shallow end is for removing a tire. However, there is no law telling that you must abide by this formula. Use the correct ends and the job will go easier. Fig. 4-16 shows four rim protectors are in use. Always keep the working end of your tire iron on top of the rim protector and you will not scratch your rims. See Fig. 4-17.

Fig. 4-17 Both Tire Irons Inserted Over Rim Protectors

Let's assume you run into a problem of taking a bite of tire as shown in Fig. 4-16 and as you move around the rim taking off more rubber you notice the tire is self-installing itself nearby. To stop this just insert another tire iron at that troublesome location and pull the tire over the rim then tie the tire iron down in that position. The tire will not self-install again so you can go to work removing the tire's top edge over the rim. See Fig. 5-24 and Fig. 5-27 for an example of tying down tire irons to prevent the tire from walking (and in this photo in Fig. 5-24 showing a method of forcing the tire down into the rim's drop-center when installing a new tire. It is rare to have a tire self-install itself when removing it from the rim, but it can happen on some tires. I mention this just in case you come upon any tire walking problems you will have the solution. Tire walking definitely happens a lot when installing tires, especially the upper portion of the tire.

You should have completed removing the top side of tire from the top rim. It is time to remove the bottom side of the tire from the rim which will remove entirely the tire from the rim.

REMOVING OPPOSITE LOWER SIDE OF TIRE

Don't flip the wheel over—leave it as is. Lift the lower bottom edge of the tire with your left hand. Insert the shallow curved end of the tire iron with your right hand so you can get the bottom section of the tire's lip (edge) to rise upward to contact the top of the upper metal rim. Insert another tire iron's thin shallow end as shown in Fig. 4-18 and pull downward making sure you still are using the rim protector. The bottom tire's edge is now being forced to rise over the top rim, just like we did earlier. Same procedure: nothing new here at all. See? You already know how to do it!

We are just doing the same thing, but we are now pulling the bottom side of the tire over the top rim surface.

Insert the shallow end of the long tire iron down to grab the edge of the tire. It will likely now be deep down into the rim. Just get it hooked and bend it upwards and over the rim, using the tire iron as leverage. Keep the tire iron leverage point on the rim protector. It may take a bit of effort to get this first bite. Often the tire will slip away from the tire iron. This happens once in a while. Just keep on trying—the lip of the tire will come out. Use liquid tire lube if needed.

Fig. 4-18 Starting To Remove Upper Bead on Tire

Leave the first tire iron in that position and slip another iron just to the right or left of that iron and take another bite of rubber. Use this same technique alternately with two tire irons. Just work the tire irons along with the rim protectors in place under the tire irons to get that bottom lip over the top edge of the wheel's rim. The entire tire will then just come right off, in most cases without even using any tire lubricant. When tire looks like Fig. 4-19 you can just pull the tire off the rim by hand.

What if you do run into resistance? Spray some liquid tire lube on the tire's edge and the inside lip of the rim where the tire is meeting frictional resistance with the metal rim.

Note: This procedure of removing the bottom side of the tire from the rim is so easy to do many mechanics just pull up on the tire and it comes right off the rim. You may want to try it after inserting a couple tire irons and see what happens. If not, just walk the tire irons around the rim until the tire comes off. See Fig. 4-19 how to use the tire iron to flip the tire's lower bead up and over the rim's top edge. Once you lift just one portion like this you can usually just pull up on the tire and it will come right off the rim by hand.

Fig. 4-19 Lifting Lower Tire Bead Over Upper Rim Removes Tire From Rim

If the tire is big, cold, wide, and stiff and you can't lift it with your hand, you can drive a tire iron down to the bottom edge of the tire to lift the tire upwards to get things started as shown in Fig. 4-19. In most cases you can do the job without using the tire iron. You can use three or four tire irons instead of just two. On some larger tires you will need four of them as the rubber is just very thick and stiff to move with only one or two irons. And the more irons you use, and the smaller the bites of rubber taken, the less force is applied to the rim—and that's a good thing. Removing the old tire is easier than installing a new tire.

REPLACING VALVE STEM

You need not replace the valve stem on your tubeless rim each time you change tires, but you can if you want to. I change mine once every five years as they do not dry out and crack where I live, but your experience may be different so inspect them and replace if you feel so inclined.

There are two types of valve stems. Use the proper one that came with your bike. You can interchange them if you install the proper size.

Pull-Through: These are like automotive valve stems as they are made of solid rubber and you pull them through the rim to install them into the rim. To replace these you must purchase the entire valve stem. These stems usually only come in straight angle configuration. I have no photo as they are so common. Just look at your car rims and you will see solid rubber pull-through valve stems. To remove you just push or pull it out of the rim. To install you do the reverse. It is okay to lubricate the rubber valve stem so it will insert and be removed easier with less chance of tearing the rubber especially when inserting a new one into the rim use tire lube.

Bolt-In: These are threaded metal stems that bolt into the rim sealing with rubber washers or a special rubber grommet. Easy to replace the rubber grommet, but you may find they are not sold separately and you will need to replace the entire valve stem which will be more expensive than the pull through type. The bolt-in type of valve stem is nice as you can purchase angled stems that make checking air pressure and filling the tire with air easier. Fig. 3-6 is a bolt on valve stem. To install, the nut on the valve stem is first removed, the stem inserted into the rim and the nut then inserted and tightened snugly. Do not overtighten.

Caution: Make sure when you install new valve stems that they are of the proper size for the rim hole and are not installed in any rim-clamp holes on tube-type rims. You should mark any rim-clamp holes with paint so you won't make mistakes. Tubeless tires will not have rim clamp holes in the rim unless it was used for drag racing. If you need to see what rim clamps look like on rims go to a dirt bike dealer and look at the wheels on the dirt bikes on the showroom floor. See Fig. 11-1.

BUYING NEW WHEELS

Before you buy new wheels (not tires) make sure you get a good low discounted price if possible, shop around for the very best price. Make sure the drive pulley/sprocket and disk brake rotors will fit the wheel and your brake calipers including the wheel bearings and axle and spools and spacers for clearance issues.

My advice when shopping for new wheels is to check first with the manufacturer of the motorcycle for they will have the wheel that will fit everything perfectly with no regrets. It will be a simple wheel swap out. I especially like Harley-Davidson motor company as they have so many accessories for their bikes that fit wonderfully. I bought two custom chrome Fat-X wheels from Harley-Davidson for my 1200 Sportster Custom and I got both wheels, bearing kits, pulley and two disk rotors all for about $1300 (see Fig. 4-3). Just one wheel alone by some well-advertised custom wheel manufactures would have cost me $1400 to $1700, yes just for one bare wheel. Chapter 5 gives advice on buying tires.

CHAPTER 5

Installing Tire On The Rim - Tire Irons

Note: Before cleaning the rim check for any sensors fixed to the wheel that may need to be covered up with duct tape or some other protective media so grit and cleaning fluids do not touch the sensors.

Caution: Inspect the rim for any cracks, dents, depressions, spalling, flaking, rusting, oxidation. Have your wheel rims checked by a professional rim repair firm if you detect problems or just buy new wheels.

INSTALLING THE NEW FRONT TIRE

CLEANING THE RIM

First clean the rims with a soft abrasive pad like they use for cleaning Teflon® coated pots and pans. See Fig. 5-1 as it shows the cleaned rim surface void of all black rubber spotting. Fingers also touching the lower bead surface area of the rim. There is a upper and lower bead surface. Both must be clean.

How To Install Tires on Motorcycles

Fig. 5-1 Cleaning Lower Bead Edge of Rim

Note: Do not use sandpaper or use small grinding grit wheels to clean rubber from the rims. Use a Scotchbrite® pad as shown in Fig. 5-1. They don't scratch pots and pans and they won't abrade the rim surface beads. They can also polish out tiny dents and scratches too in the rim where the rubber meets the rim's bead surface area. The illustration shows the abrasive side is cleaning the sensitive bead area with ease. Fig. 16-16 shows a slightly dirty rim with tire rubber stuck to the rim that should be removed especially if it is found on both shoulders and the upper and lower curved bead surfaces of the rim. Dirt or rubber on the bead surface can create air leaks and affect tire performance.

If you look at the wheel in Fig. 5-1 you can see the center is concave by design to assist in mounting tires to the rim, it is the drop-center. The shinny top part of the rim above the drop center is the bead where the tire seals air in the tire. We don't want any dirt or scratches here at all. The abrasive pad is polishing the lower rim bead area. If you come upon a dirty wheel due to old age, the bead surface areas should be cleaned as shown. Fig. 5-2 shows the precise lower edge of the bead area.

What is a bead? It is the portion of the tire and the rim that contact each other and make a firm attachment to each other. It is accomplished with compressed air forcing the tire outward against the beads to seal air and bond the tire to the rim. This force is so powerful that even when you let the air out of the tire you need to use a powerful squeezing force to "pop" this rubber to metal bond apart. If you get a flat tire the weight of the bike can, but not always, pop the bead and the tire will wobble badly with possible loss of control. Usually rear tires with passenger weight tend to pop the bead when going flat due to the large amount of weight on the rear wheel, but today's stronger tires tend to resist this tire separation from the rim.

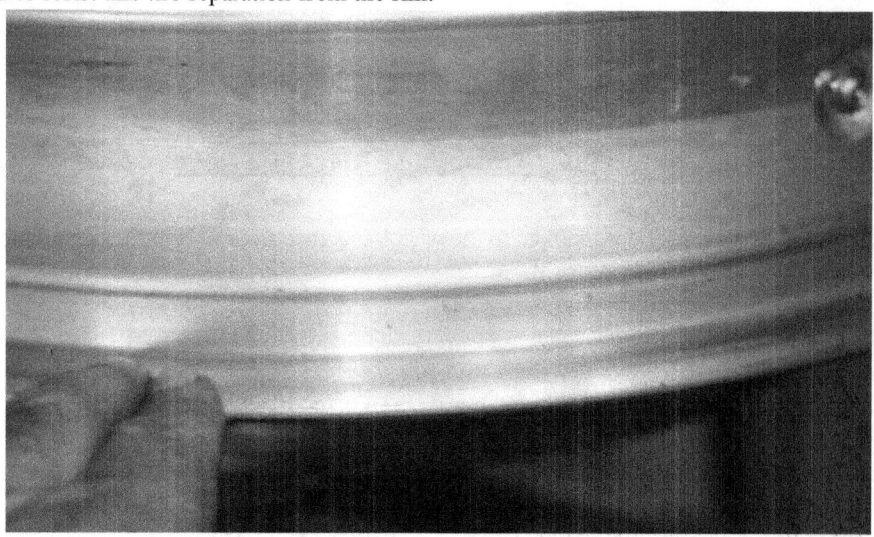

Fig. 5-2 Lube The Cleaned Lower Rim Bead Surface

These Scotchbrite® non-scratching pads bought in supermarkets work great and can be used dry or with degreaser to get the job done quickly. Look for where there is residual black rubber stuck to the rims. This is where the tire seats (beads) to the rim and seals air, so we want it to be clean. Many shops do not even bother to clean the rims, and you are paying for good service and not getting it. People ride down the road and thousands of miles later get a flat tire from a slow leak and wonder why. Now you know.

Set two or three rim protectors onto the rim if they are not still in place. Look at your tire. There will be a dot on the tire in white, yellow, red, or another color. This is the balance mark. Just line it up with the valve stem. We will do this final alignment later after you install the tire onto the rim, but you need to get that mark aligned to the valve stem now as some tires will not rotate later. When the tire is not inflated but has its bead set, the tire will rotate on the rim with ease on some rims, but not all. You may have to break the bead again and rotate the tire's balance mark or just forget about it and balance the wheel and tire assembly. Don't worry, it will still balance perfectly.

Tip: Is installing an inflexible tire giving you trouble to flip over the rim? You even hear the tiny tearing noise that the tire's bead is ripping? Stop! Push down on the top of the tire from the opposite side of where you are working so the tire is pushed down into the drop center of the rim. This allows the tire's rubber to decompress and relax, and then the tire irons can stretch and flip the tire over the rim. This is one of the secrets of tire changing that dealers won't tell their customers so they will discover how difficult tire changing can truly be. If you know this drop center trick you'll find tire changing is easy to do after all. Also, don't forget to add more liquid or paste tire lube to help the tire move around the rim. Lubricating is important—but believe it or not, once you know how to install motorcycle tires you can actually put them on without using any lubricant whatsoever. However, I always use lubricant and tire manufacturers also recommend that you do. The tire lubricants can create a tacky seal to help the tire bead to the rim tightly.

Always inspect the rim bead surface for any foreign material dirt and look for scratches that can create an air leak. The bead should be nice and polished as shown in Fig. 5-2. When you inspect your wheels for the first time you will be horrified to see how filthy dirty those wheel bead surfaces will be. Why? It is because dealers often do not clean the rim before installing a new tire. Amazing, but true. They just slap on a new tire and hope it works and most tires do. If one does not work? They blame it on the tire, not themselves. You really do need to learn how to change your own tires. Most riders are being cheated by tire installers in many ways and paying through the nose for the privilege of being robbed. Let the brutal truth be known. But worse, a dirty wheel can cause a sudden deflation of air and cause a crash. I wonder how many riders have crashed due to tire retailer/installer malpractice?

LUBRICATING THE TIRE

Fig. 5-3 shows the smooth dimpled area of the tire bead that will be inserted into the wheel rim. This smooth area is the sealing and gripping bead of the tire where it seals the air inside the tubeless tire. Do not scrape, scratch, rip or cut this smooth area. Some tire installers do not lube this area, but you should, at least a little with paste tire lubricant for the lube acts like bonding agent to help make a nice air-tight seal. Lube with paste lube all around on both sides of the tire's bead area, top and bottom sides. If you do not have paste lube then use liquid tire lube. Paste will not evaporate quickly giving you much more time to work and it makes the installation job much easier to do. No lube is used for racing tires at the track as there is no time for the lubricant to dry and tire can slip on the rim. This book only covers "street use" and not racing.

One-hundred miles of riding should be enough for tire lubricant to have set up, until then, do not do burn-outs or use hard acceleration as the tire can slip around the rim. This still may not bother a tubeless tire much, but a tube tire can rip the innertube in half.

Fig. 5-3 Lubricating Curved Bead Section of Tire

Fig. 5-4 shows the inside or underside edge of the tire. Lubricate the entire inside surface as shown. Some mechanics do not lube the bottom side of the tire because the lower edge of the tire goes on the rim so easily lube is not needed on the inside edges, but go ahead and lube both sides. We don't want any trouble to surface for the beginner.

Fig. 5-4 Lube the Flat Inside Edge of Tire's Bead

Fig. 5-5 shows the edge of the tire. This flat stiff surface is where the tire irons will do their work to pull the tire over the rim. Lubricate the tire's edge all around the tire on both sides of the tire with paste tire lubricant.

Fig. 5-5 Tire Bead's Face - Lubrication Are.

Once the entire tire edge and face of the tire is lubed as shown in Fig. 5-3, Fig. 5-4 and Fig. 5-5 insert two or four rim protectors onto the rim as appears in Fig 5-17 showing four rim protectors installed on the rim. Do not place tire on the rim just yet.

Note: Use paste tire lubricant as shown in Fig. 5-3, Fig. 5-4 and Fig. 5-5 on both sides of the tire all around the entire 360 degree surface of the tire. Just lube the entire surfaces as shown despite the fact many installers just lube certain points needed, I do not want to get too technical in this book.

TIRE SIZE - THE CORRECT SIZE

Before you install a new tire you need to determine the proper size tire for your motorcycle and even the proper type of tire. This information is in this book and in the Question & Answer section. For now here's the basics.

1. Look at the tire you removed. It will have three sets of numbers looking like this: 180/90/18. Just buy a new tire that has the same dimensions as your old tire and you should be okay.
2. Buy a "cruiser" tire for cruiser motorcycle. Buy a "sport" tire for a sport bike. Buy a "adventure" tire for an adventure style motorcycle. Buy a "dirt" knobby tire for a dirt bike. There are different brands within each category.
3. Even step #1 could be the wrong tire for your bike. Check the owner manual and/or the sticker on the frame indicating correct tire

size.

4. Even step #3 could be wrong if someone changed the rim size of the wheel. So, check the rim.

5. Odds are favorable that step #1 will pan out okay since the tire was used with success. Just double check in case an error has been made and the wrong tire has been installed on the rim from a prior installer or owner.

6. The back tire will usually be a different and larger size than the front tire. This is normal, but should not be hitting any frame, body or driveline parts.

7. Check with the dealer who sells the model bike. They can tell you which style tire to buy if you have stock wheels installed on the bike.

8. The rubber compound of a cruiser tire and a sport bike tire are of two extremes and there are sport-touring blends of tires that supply a bit of both road adhesion benefits. A cruiser motorcycle should stay with cruiser tires and you should look for maximum mileage. A more expensive tire never means the best tire, not in this industry, as retail price is no true reflection of value.

9. The physical size of the tire often determines the price you pay for replacing tires. Many cruiser riders are finding out the big fat rear tires are too costly and wear out quickly. Live with it, sell the bike or install a smaller wheel and tire is a cure for belt and chain driven bikes. Larger tires cost more and smaller tires cost less. That is the rule. Yes, you can change tire size within 10 millimeters wider in most all cases without running into clearance problems. You can change the name brands of tires in most all cases especially if you are getting poor mileage life on a cruiser tire. Sport bikes usually get low milage due to the soft rubber compounds they use.

10. Speed rating and load rating can be important to some riders. Most tires are rated to handle legal freeway speed and above. Be realistic, you do not need a tire rated for 180 mph for street use. To buy a racing tire like that is just wasting your money and it will wear out terribly fast too. If you ride two-up (with a passenger) are personally over 225 lbs in weight or have heavy luggage get a tire that can handle the load.

11. Shop and learn. Get yourself a few large motorcycle parts catalogs. At the time of writing this book DennisKirk.com is one example. There are others. In the tire section you can see lots of different tires and prices along with many photos of tire components to become familiar with. You can learn a lot from these catalogs and everything you learn will save you money. Here you can compare tires, sizes, price, features, company branding, style, fitment advice, wheel parts and accessories and tools.

TIRE SIZE FOR MY BIKE

Write down the Motorcycle, Tire Size, Price, Mfg. and Model and Where to Buy the tire for your bike below. Up to four bikes can be used here.

Example: Harley Sportster, Front 130/90/16 - $90. Rear 150/80/16 - $110 Mitchelin™ Commander II®, best prices at: DennisKirk.com also Competition Accessories.com and Amazon.com

#1. _____
_____.
#2. _____
_____.
#3. _____
_____.
#4. _____
_____.

ADVICE BEFORE WE INSTALL THE TIRE

Warning: Rim Bending and Injury: This is going to be a tough beginning, as a lot of rubber will resist your efforts. Use caution so that the metal tire irons do not slip away from the rim and you gash your knuckles. Go slowly at first so you can get the feel of things. Don't use so much force that you bend the rim. The trick is to apply force smoothly and gently in a controlled manner with some force, but always seeing the rubber folding and moving upward and over the rim. If anything binds up and the rubber is not moving at all, just stop and reposition the tire irons again somewhere else and start over. If you remember this trick, you will never bend a rim.

Note: If you do bend a rim? You can have a professional rim repair shop hammer or press it out on tube type rims. On tubeless it is not a good idea for safety reasons unless you go to a specialty shop equipped to straighten tubeless rims. Yes, they can be fixed, so you will not ruin your rims. Even cracks can be fixed. Always remember when using tire irons to see rubber moving or stop applying pressure. With time and experience you will know when too much pressure is being applied. Make sure when things bind up the tire is not hanging up on the shoulder or bead area of the rim 180 degrees from where you are working, but the tire is actually depressed down into the rim's drop center. More instructions on this later will be given in detail.

Tip: In this book I say to use a lot of tire lubricant. I say this so the beginner will have a much easier time removing and installing the tire on the rim. As you gain experience changing tires, you will learn that it is better to use less lubricant. Generally the reason is this. Using too much solid tire lube may make the tire slip along the rim as heavy engine torque or strong braking is applied. So, when learning, use as much tire lube as you feel is required. Just drive with care with the new tires for two days. I use a lot of tire lube as I want my tires to come off and go on with great ease. For this reason I use a soap-based lubricant made specifically for changing rubber tires that have no harsh chemicals and evaporates with a tackiness like glue.

Note: You normally do not need to apply tire lube to rim protectors as they are slippery as is, but you can if the tire is giving you trouble from tight friction upon the rim protectors and giving you trouble.

When replacing tires renue both front and rear simultaneiously. The reason being the worn rear tire may be cupped or a worn rear profile upset just enough to create vibration due to the mix-match of a new tire up front. Some riders only change the rear tire as they obtain a 2 to 1 replacement ratio (meaning the front tire lasts two times longer than the rear). This method is okay as long as handling problems do not occur.

Important: Read Chapter 17 before continuing beyond this point. It explains more advice on selecting new tires. The Question & Answers section also give tire selection advice. Place a bookmark here and come back to this page later.

TRADE SECRETS

Actually trade secrets have already been revealed so lets take a second peek at them. When working with thick and stubborn rubber tires, work the tire iron lever slowly so as to allow the thick rubber time to adjust its position, stretch, and flex. If you apply too much pressure all at once, the rubber can't move and you will bind up the tool, forcing way too much pressure on the rim. That's how rims get bent! Another trick of the trade is to work on tires that are warm, not cold. Cold rubber will not flex and if too cold (like near freezing temperatures) may not even be capable of being installed. Place the new tires outside in the sun so they can heat up in the summertime.

In cold weather, store the tire in the house and then bring it to the garage when you need it. Yes, you can use a hair dryer to heat the tire. A heat gun, though, will internally overheat and melt the tire so don't use it. So try to schedule tire mounting and demounting inside a warm area or in warmer weather outdoors. You must also take small bites of rubber with your tire irons (Fig. 5-28) to pull over the metal rim. Taking too large a bite will just make the job hard if not impossible to do and risk bending your rim if you try to use excessive force. Taking very small bites of rubber is one of the great secrets when using tire irons to change tires. And make sure you can see or feel rubber moving as you apply force to a tire iron.

Also, let us not forget tire lubricant. Use paste lube. It doesn't evaporate as quickly as liquid lube will, giving you more time to slip and slide the tire on the rim. Using a paste tire lubricant on the face of the tire's edge, all around the circumference of the tire, will make the tire almost want to leap over the rim, especially at the very end, where the going gets tough. It's the same when installing the tire—the tire will flip right on to the rim easily. Remember this whenever a tire is tough to remove or painfully stubborn to install. Lubricate it!

Keep these secrets in mind whenever you get a tough tire! Another secret is long-leveraged, highly contoured 16 inch long curved tire irons as shown in Fig. 5-6. Short, straight, stubby tire irons that are used for bicycles and dirt bikes will not cut it for cruiser and street bike tires. Those long tire irons is another key to success. You should have three of them, but four is best as the extra 4th one is often used as a helping hand and sometimes you just need more than two.

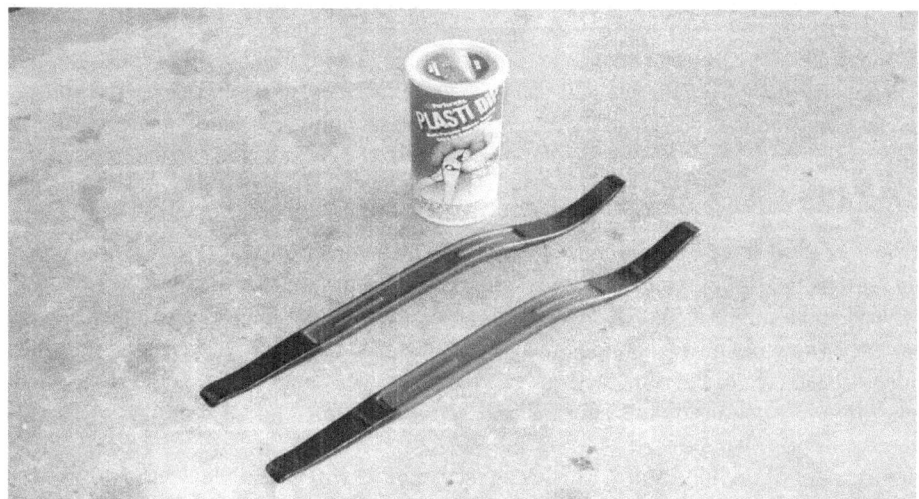

Fig. 5-6 Tire Irons - Highly Curved 16" Long.

In Fig. 5-6 there are two long tire irons with very deeply curved surfaces. These are made by Motion Pro® and they work great. The shallow curved end on the left is for removing tire from the rim and the deeply curved end on the right is for installing the tire to the rim as they dive deeply into the rubber and give a nice leverage due to the deep bend in the steel. You can coat the ends in liquid Plasti Dip® which will paint a think rubber coating on the tire irons. The coating won't last long, but it will reduce rim scratching if you have no rim protectors. You will need four of these long tire irons until you become proficient to use only two or three. You can use two of these long tire irons as your working irons and use two shorter and cheaper tire irons to use as tire drop-center holders that keep the tire down into the rim and to prevent tire "walking" out of the rim when installing a new tire (Fig. 5-27). I say just buy four of the 16" irons and be done with it. When you drop one iron (and you will drop them) you can grab the spare and keep on working.

TIRE IRON BITES

Work the tire irons around, taking small bites of rubber at a time. How small is a bite? It can be as tiny as the width of the tire iron itself or as large as 3", depending on the resistance you feel on the tire iron and the ease at which the rubber is flexing. Every tire will be different. Remember, small bites are always better. Move the rim protectors as needed so there is no metal to metal contact to scratch your rims. See how it is done in the photos. When the entire top bead of the tire is now draping over the rim, this first half of the job is done. We now have to get the bottom section of the tire over the top side of the rim.

Note: Yes, your tire irons will not bite at times. They will slip, and the bead will fall back down into the rim. This "missing" is normal and to be expected, especially when it is your first time mounting and demounting tires. Be patient. Work very slowly and learn. Take smaller bites and you will see less slipping. Make sure your tire irons are not too lubed up. They will slip if they aren't dry. The tire should be lubed liberally, or the tire irons will miss and slip away from stubborn rubber that will not flex or slide away from the metal rim.

The tire's edges, if lubed, will slide the rubber over the rim with less flexing and folding of the rubber tire. This means there will be less friction and effort with much less fighting the tire and a much enjoyable procedure to get the tire off or on a rim. Many people do not realize the importance of proper tire lubricating and struggle like mad to change their tires! If you lube the tires and the rim in the right places, the job will not be a struggle. It will be easy to do, no matter how fat or stiff that tire's sidewall is! I will give you more advice on this later when we install the tire.

Note: Do not believe the rant and rave that cruiser motorcycles have such stiff and thick sidewalls you can't install them with tire irons without bending the rims. Not true!

Note: When I mention "metal rim," the term also applies to composite rims or any sort of high-technology rim unless specifically stated otherwise, but keep in mind a composite rim is anything non-metallic or space age material and tire irons and certain tire lubricants may not be used on these wheels. Read the owner manual regarding the treatment of composite rims when mounting, dismounting tires and cleaning such wheels. They are often fragile and will crack easily. I would not use tire irons on these wheels.

Troubleshooting Tip: If you hear any tearing or ripping sound of rubber when installing a tire with tire irons, you are doing three things wrong. First, you are trying to take too much of a bite of rubber. Ease up and take a small bite and use more tire irons. Each tire iron inserted makes the job go easier. Second, either you are not using enough tire lubricant or you have lubed the tire and rim in the wrong places. You need to lube the tire's entire edge, including the entire metal rim, and the entire rim's center drop section area. Then the tire's edges can slip and slide with ease into the drop center when you're getting the last section of the tire's edge to flip over the rim. Third, push the tire down with your hand 180 degrees opposite from where you are having trouble. Then, with your knee in the same area, push the center of the tire's tread inward into the drop center of the rim (if you can). This will cause the rubber at the tight end giving you trouble, which is the opposite end, to loosen up and flip over the rim with your tire irons. When installing a new tire and you can't get the last bit of rubber over the rim the problem is 180 degrees opposite where you are working. The tire is not in the drop center area of the rim preventing the tire to install. More on this later.

Okay, let us now lube the rim and the tire and install the tire.

LUBE THE TIRE & RIM

The new tire should now be lubed with paste lubricant as described in the previous section of this book. Now we must lubricate the rim, yes, the rim!

Note: This is another trick of the trade that is often not revealed in videos found on the Internet that if you fail to perform can make installing some tires impossible to install onto the rim and is a major reason why people fail on their first attempt to change the tires on their motorcycle.

Fig. 5-7 Lube the Rim's Two Bead Edges

First, lube the rim's internal lip edge bead areas as shown in Fig. 5-7 that reveals the lower edge, but you must also lube the upper edge. Lube it all around including the wide drop center section of the rim too, as shown in Fig. 5-8. It is okay to use paste lubricant on the entire inner surface of the rim as shown in Fig. 5-8. Also, lubricate the two shoulders too on the rim. The narrow flat rim shoulders are above and below my fingers as shown in Fig. 5-8. Paste lubricant should be used on rim and tire when installing a tire.

I know professional installers will call this a waste of time and lubricant, but for beginners it is best to just lube the entire inner rim surface until they obtain a better grasp as to which portions of the wheel needs lubricating and which portions do not. Plus, when a wheel or tire moves out of position through error the novice does not know what to do next to establish the lube point locations once again.

A jar of No-Mar® tire paste lubricant is sitting on top the wheel's hub in Fig. 5-8. You can use a lot of this lubricant without much worry of doing harm. As you gain installation experience you can use less lubricant and apply it only in specific locations on the rim where resistance is expected. However, a beginner should follow the instruction in this book and use the lubricant on all areas as described to reduce difficulties from arising.

Fig. 5-8 Lubricating Drop Center Of Rim With Paste Lube

Use the paste lubricant, which won't evaporate rapidly like a liquid lube will. Lube the tire's inside edge where it must slip and slide over the rim as shown in Fig. 5-8.

Note: Lube the rim's drop center and the flat shoulder risen area all the way to the bead area and all the way around the tire. Yes, lube the entire internal metal area as shown in Fig. 5-8. This may be overkill for the professional tire installer, but for the beginner it is essential. Use as much as you want, but a thin layer is all that is needed. With your finger if you feel lubricant on the rim that is sufficient, globs of paste is not required, just a thin film. No dry spots, lube every portion of the internal surface, but try not let any paste lubricant enter the air hole at the valve stem. If lube plugs the air vent hole you can easily unplug it with compressed air.

Tip: You don't really need to lube it all the way around, but for your first time this way keeps things simple. Normally, I install the tire by hand as far as I can without lube, then lube the remaining portions of the tire and rim. We are still going to be lubricating the bead seating section of the rim where the tire seals itself to the rim. However, we are lubricating just above that, near and just below the visible section of the rim, the raised shoulders, that final edge where the tire must slip over the rim. Confusing? Don't worry about it, just lube the entire inner surface of the rim and forget about it.

Some tire installers fear lubricating the bead surfaces of the rim and tire, but it is good if you do lubricate the bead sealing area on a tubeless tire; the lube will dry up over time and actually help bead the tire to the rim. The Rubber Manufactures Association recommends it. Just don't try pulling any burnouts or wheelies or deep high-speed cornering—the tire will rotate on the rim with the lube there! Study the tire and rim, and you will see how the tire fits onto a rim and seals itself. It is okay to lightly lube the actual tire bead surface area. I discuss this further in the Questions & Answers section. You can, after you install the tire before inflating it wipe away tire lube from the bead surfaces if you will be racing the bike somewhat, but remember, a new tire also needs to be broken in and driven hard for the first 100 miles.

What you will not see or understand at first is that when installing a new tire on a rim that tire must at various times slide upon the internal rim surfaces. If the rim were not lubricated the high friction of the rubber tire will bind up on the rim and create a nasty end point situation where the tire is hung up entirely over the rim and will not install as shown in Fig. 5-28.

Note: A professional can install a tire on a rim without any lubricant, but lubricant is a requirement according to the Rubber Manufacturers Association for it is a bonding agent that enhances the tire and rim grip and seals air leaks at the bead surfaces.

WHEEL ROTATION DIRECTION

Before mounting the tire, you must know the direction of wheel rotation. The tire will have an arrow on it indicating the direction of travel. If you forgot to mark your wheel, take your rim back to your motorcycle and place it near the front forks. On the Triumph America model with a single disk brake, the brake rotor should be on the left side. Mark the wheel with an arrow showing the normal direction of travel. You can use electrical tape strips to form an arrow shape, paint or a crayon. If you have a dual disk brake bike, then the location of the spacer spools or speedometer or some other item can show how the wheel is supposed to go back onto the motorcycle. You can use white chalk or a lead pencil to mark an arrow on the disk brake rotor on the hub area. It is important to mark the front wheel, so do it now in a permanent way so you will not run into problems of putting the wheel on the wrong way ever again on this bike. See Fig. 2-24 and Fig. 5-9 for marking wheel rotation on motorcycle rims.

Fig. 5-9 Wheel Rotation Mark

The chrome Harley-Davidson rim shines so brightly in Fig. 5-9 that you can't easily see the black arrow placed on the outer edge of the rim at the 1 o'clock position. It is pointing to the right telling us the wheel is to rotate in that direction. Use a pencil, magic marker or engrave the arrow somewhere on the disk brake rotor near the axle not on the disk area wheels the brake pads ride on the disk rotor.

Fig. 5-10 Tire Rotation Indicator Embossed by Tire Manufacturer

Fig. 5-10 shows the arrow on the tire installed by the tire manufacturer. When you lay the tire on top of the rim check that the tire rotation is facing in the direction you marked the rim. The reason is the tire is designed to run in only one direction due to braking or acceleration forces placed on the tire. The tire's bead is the smooth concave section of the tire below the arrow mark in 5-10. The very flat inner edge of the tire is where tire mounting tools are used. Tools should never contact the actual sealing bead surface of the tire. It is okay and recommended to lubricate both the bead, and underside edge of the tire when installing a new tire. Make sure you are using a dedicated tire lubricant and not lubricating oil or window glass cleaner, etc.

You only need to apply enough lubricant to create a slippery surface, the excess can be wiped away with a clean rag. Later, wipe your finger around the tire and if you encounter friction resistance lube that area so the finger glides along with ease around the entire circumference of the tire.

INSTALLING LOWER SIDE OF TIRE TO RIM

Notice how the tire is placed squarely on the rim in Fig. 5-13 with the arrow pointing in the proper direction of rotation in relation to the wheel. Notice also how the tire is mounted in an awkward slanted downward position, see Fig. 5-14. Notice the rim protectors in place in Fig 5-11. We install the rim protectors after the lower portion of the tire is already installed or prior to.

Fig. 5-11 Tire Position Prior to Mounting to Rim

Position the rim with the disk rotor facing upward toward you. It can be facing down, but it does not really matter. In this book you notice the disk brake rotor is facing up in some photos and facing down in others.   However, if you find installing the tire is difficult using tire irons as the brake disk rotor or drive pulley gets in the way you may need to remove the pulley or brake rotor, one or the other, not both. But keep in mind this would be a rare situation or when installing a very wide tire. Most all street bikes can mount and dismount tires with the brake rotors in place including any sprockets/pulleys.

Tip: Tire arrow may be on the top and rim arrow on the bottom unseen. That's okay as long as the tire is still rotating in the same direction as the rim's arrow direction.

Now lay the tire on the rim as you see in Fig. 5-11. Check the tire rotation mark to make sure it matches the mark you made on the rim. We want the tire to rotate properly in the same direction the rim rotates.

Fig. 5-12 Yellow Dot

Look for that round dot paint mark on the tire. See Fig. 5-12. It is usually white or yellow and sometimes can be red. For now, look for the white or yellow dot and turn the tire until it is aligned with the rim's valve stem. This is the tire's lightest section so it helps you later balance the tire with less wheel weights when you align the dot to the valve stem which is the heavy spot on the rim (usually, or should be, but not always the case).

Don't be surprised to discover that the embossed arrow and the ink dot marking will be on the bottom side of the wheel where you can't easily see them. Just copy these markings on the top side of the tire to make it easier on yourself. The ink dot must be directly opposite for it is a balancing mark to be positioned adjacent to the valve stem. The ink dot is the lightest segment of the tire so it is placed at the heaviest section of the rim, usually the valve stem.

Some wheels are so heavy they may be heaviest not near the valve stem. What do you do? Check the balance of your wheel and mark it where it is the heaviest point then align the new tire's ink dot to that wheel mark instead of the valve stem.

If you press your hand on one end of the tire it will sink down into the rim's drop center. Try it at the 6 o'clock position so the tire looks like Fig. 5-14.

Caution: You can use a lot of bare hand force drive the tire down and over the rim, just be prepared the tire can suddenly slip into position and you could strain your wrist. I use reasonable force and resort to the tire irons to avoid injury.

Fig. 5-13 Place Tire on Rim as Shown Tilted Downward at 6 O'clock Position

   Just by pushing the tire down with reasonable force using both hands the tire will install itself 1/2 way just by hand pressure alone, but as you can see in Fig. 5-13 and Fig. 5-14 it will bind up. In this case the lower lip bead of the tire is riding high over the top edge of the rim at 12 o'clock position. It will only take one or two tire irons to gently lift that tire's edge over the rim shown in Fig. 5-15 and Fig. 5-16. The lower bead of the tire installs amazingly easy. It is the top bead that will give you grief, but I will show you tricks of the trade to make that job easy. Notice in both photos you see rim protectors on the top edge of the rim. You can and should put some rim protectors on the lower edge of the rim to prevent the tools from scratching the lower rim's edge.

Fig. 5-14 Installing Tire By Hand - Lower Edge Of Tire - Side View

   In Fig. 5-13 I have placed the 6 o'clock section of the tire way down into the upper rim as if I already have half of it installed by hand just by pushing down on the tire. Note the 12 o'clock position is up and not down over the rim. Do not let the upper bead section of the tire drop down into the drop center, it needs to still be high above the upper part of the rim as shown. We are only installing the lower section of the tire over the top part of the rim. Use both hands to push the tire downward. It should now look like Fig. 5-16, the top bead is floating high above the top edge of the rim all the way around. Fig. 5-14 shows at 12 o'clock the lower edge of the tire is still not yet over the top edge of the rim. Use tire irons if need be, but it should go on by hand. My hand is pushing the tire down into the rim's drop center to ease the installation.

   Fig. 5-14 shows the bottom lip of the tire being driven down over the top lip of the metal rim. At the 12 o'clock position you can clearly see the tire's bottom edge riding above the top edge of the rim. Use both hands. We are only installing the bottom edge of the tire over the wheel's top rim. Don't try to do both sides of the tire.

Note: Take a good look at Fig. 5-14. Where my hand is in the photo you can see how the tire is being forced downward and the tire's edge is sinking into the wheel's deep drop center area. This is the precise effect we want to achieve when using a helping hand device at the end point stage. I also want you to now realize just how easy the tire installed onto the rim. Remember this when we get to the end point of tire installation.

If you can't push the tire down all the way by hand you may need to employ rim protectors and a tire iron to shove the tire over the rim as shown in Fig. 5-15.

Notice in Fig. 5-15 how I placed one tire iron. The left I will use first and then the right. Then I'll work clockwise all around the rim, putting the bottom edge of the tire onto the rim first. You can work counterclockwise if you prefer. Large tire iron bites are okay as shown in Fig. 5-15.

Important Instruction: To install the lower bead of the tire over the top section of the rim you can use the shallow curved end of the tire iron as not much leverage or angle is required. See Fig. 5-16.

In Fig. 5-14 you can rotate the tire by hand to assist getting the tire over the rim, but I do not do this because if you rotate the tire you are also moving the balance mark on the tire far away from the valve stem. You can then reset the balance mark with ease, but I just don't bother using the rotation method. I just push down and use a tire iron to fit the tire over the rim as shown in Fig. 5-15.

Fig 5-15 shows the bottom installed and the top of the tire now resting on the rim. It's just dying to go on.

How To Install Tires on Motorcycles

Fig. 5-16 Bottom Edge of New Tire Folding Over Upper Rim on Harley-Davidson Wheel

Fig 5-17 shows the rim protectors installed before the lower edge of the tire is installed. You can install them at any time you wish. You can wait to install them whenever you plan to use a tire iron. Notice white rim rotation mark on wheel spoke at 7 o'clock position.

Insert your four rim protectors. When you gain experience you can use just one or two. Insert your tire iron where the tire is still hanging over the top of the rim and flip the tire over using the tire iron. As long as the tire is in the drop center area of the rim in Fig. 5-16 it will flip over the rim with great ease. You don't even need to use a tire iron. Try pushing the top side of the tire down with your hands and the tire will install just from hand pressure. If not, use the tire iron.

Fig. 5-17 Harley-Davidson Rim with White Nylon Rim Protectors Snapped Onto Upper Rim Edge

Fig. 5-20 shows a good view of the tire iron digging down to the tire's lower edge and flipping it down and over the lower edge of the rim. Notice how the disk brake rotor never gets in the way as the tire irons are working away from the disk rotor. The wheel is a Harley-Davidson which are easiest tires of all to install.

Fig. 5-18   Bottom Lip of Tire Going Over Top of Rim

Fig. 5-18 shows the top side of the tire when pressed down by hand at the 6 o'clock position the tire will actually install itself by hand half-way. Fig. 5-19 shows a Harley-Davidson wheel doing the same thing. I show both the Triumph and the fat 16" Harley-Davidson wheel to dispel any myths that Harley-Davidson tires are impossible or harder to install tires than other motorcycle rims. Actually, the Harley-Davidson is the most easiest of all to install. Why? Because H-D rims have really deep drop-centers in the rim which is just absolutely fabulous for installing tires on rims. Don't let people and dealers fool you. You can change your own tires regardless of the motorcycle you ride! With this book you'll be laughing all the way to the bank. You won't be fooled again!

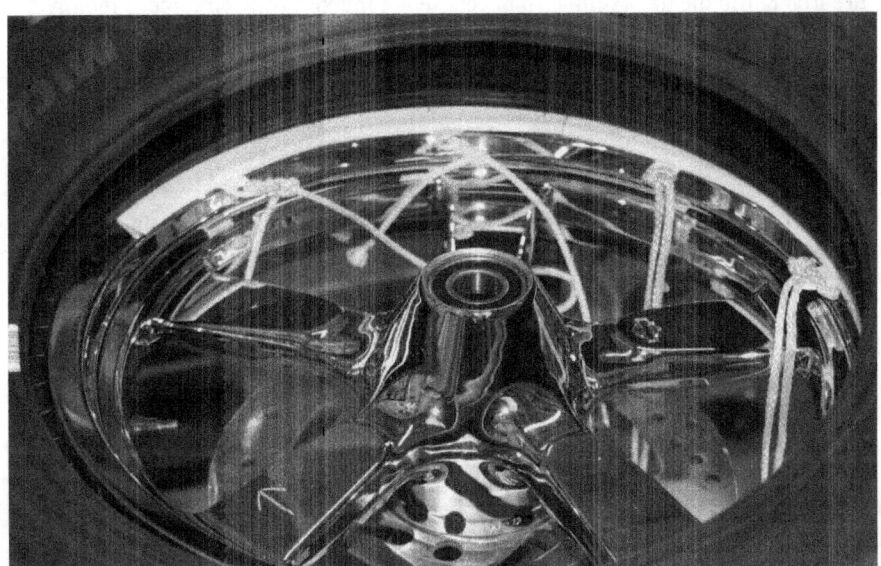
Fig. 5-19 Harley-Davidson 16" Wheel Tire 1/2 Way Installed by Hand

Fig. 5-16 Shows the bottom edge of the tire going over the rim as in Fig. 5-18. It will take hardly no effort at all to install the lower tire bead over the rim. Notice how the rim protector prevents the tire iron from rotating on the rim that can create scratches. The tire in Fig. 5-16 and Fig. 5-19 is a Mitchelin Commander II which is a seriously wonderful tire all cruiser riders should experience. Keep your eye open to try the new technology tires that are introduced to the market. In the future even the Commander II tire will be improved or replaced by a superior tire design. Tires just keep getting better and better. If you ride a sport bike read a sportbike magazine for tire advice and product reviews.

In Fig. 5-18 I took both my hands and pushed down on the 6 o'clock section of the tire and look, it is already going on. You should be able to actually install the bottom bead edge of the tire entirely by hand. If not, use a tire iron as in Fig. 5-16 to flip it over the rim.

Tip: When using tire irons you do not flip the wheel over to install the tire, but you do have the option of flipping the wheel over if you wish. If the tire is extremely wide you may need to install the lower side of the tire so you can work the tire's bead, but this would be for those big 330+mm size tires. I do flip the wheel over if I can't by hand push the lower tire bead all the way onto the rim on certain stubborn thick and stiff cruiser tires. Keep this in mind in case you do come upon a stiff tire or a rim with a very shallow drop center. By flipping the wheel over you can use the tire irons conventionally as shown in Fig. 5-20 top side instead of a bottom side view as shown in Fig. 5-16. Flipping the wheel over is a rare situation though. You should have no trouble, but if you do that is the fix. You'll understand this once you come upon a very, very wide tire that custom bikes usually have.

Fig. 5-20 Bottom Edge of New Tire Folding Over Upper Rim on Harley-Davidson Wheel

Fig. 5-21 shows the end point of installing the lower bead of the tire over the top side of the rim. The tire iron was used for illustration as you can usually just push the tire on by hand, but if you can't for some reason, use the tire iron as shown. We are using the shallow curved end of the tire iron to flip the tire over the rim because not much leveraged force is required.

Now that the lower section of the tire is installed we now have to install the top side of the tire over the upper section of the rim. This is where most people who try to change their own tires fail. Don't worry, you won't fail this time! You will learn the proper method and the tricks of the trade.

INSTALLING UPPER SIDE OF TIRE TO RIM

Important Instruction: This is where you want to flip the tire iron and use the extreme curved angle end to work the tire over the rim. This is the upper side of the tire going over the rim for final installation and where the going gets tough for those who do not know proper motorcycle tire installation procedure.

If a tire starts walking (lifting up off the rim Fig. 5-28), just insert another tire iron at that spot where the tire is walking and hold it down into that position with your knee or with a rope and go back to work.

Notice in Fig. 5-29 the small bites of rubber I am now taking with the tire irons. This is so we do not rip the tire and ruin it. This is one of the little secrets. Take tiny little bites, even smaller than shown if necessary. If you hear stretching rubber, that is sometimes okay, but you should hear very little of it because it means the rubber is tearing. No tearing is the goal. If you hear too much, it means the tire is being overstretched and being ripped and destroyed.

As long as you keep working the tire on the rim with little one-inch bites, you will be just fine. If not, something is wrong. Stop. Also, taking large bites just makes the job harder. You have to force too much rubber to roll over the rim, and too large a bite will make everything bind up and grind to a halt. If you apply more pressure, you will rip the tire's bead or bend a rim. Remember, tire lubricant overcomes rubber resistance so the tire will slip over the rim, but small bites are required.

Tip: When using tire irons or a mount/demount bar to install a tire, turn off any music or radio station and listen to the tire. If you hear a slight tearing noise you are using too much force. Once the tire is installed, you can turn the music or talk radio back on.

Towards the end the tire is going to look like it will never go onto the rim, as in Fig. 5-21. A lot of tight rubber is overlapping the rim. And, it is possible at the 1 o'clock position the tire may start walking, uninstalling itself, so watch for it. Insert a tire iron and tie it down at that spot if need be.

Fig. 5-21 End Stage of Mounting Tire to Rim

Yes it will install, but you have to take little bites of the tire irons, walking them slowly onward inch by inch, and then suddenly the tire will just flip over the metal rim.

What if the last remaining section of rubber is stubborn? It just will not go onto the rim and is overhanging excessively and binding up and will not fold over the rim? Push your knee into the opposite side of the center of the tire 180 degrees from where you are working and gently use tire iron force to push tire over and into the rim. This knee pressure, if strong enough to push the rubber tread inward or downward, will release the pressure of the binding rubber and allow the tire to flex when using the tire irons. However, there are tools you can use to do this.

Tip: Keep reading as more tricks of the trade will be explained as we go. And there is more knowledge in the Question & Answer section in this book. Visit: JamesRussellPublishing.com for even more updates and advice on many subjects regarding motorcycles.

Fig. 5-22 Shows Harley-Davidson Wheel & Mitchelin Commander II Tire

Fig. 5-22 is showing the upper tire's bottom lip of the tire's bead being lifted over the top edge of the rim. We are working clockwise from left to right. Note the end of the tire iron is resting on a white nylon rim protector so the metal fulcrum action will not scratch the chrome plated metal rim. The strings are used to pull the rim protectors into the next position as needed. At the 3 o'clock position the tire is rising, uninstalling itself out of the rim (walking) as we work defeating our efforts. Just insert a tire iron at that 3 o'clock position and flip the rubber over and use your knee or tie it down with a rope to keep the tire iron and the rubber tire in position, then continue installing the tire.

Note: Do not let anyone tell you that you can not change Harley-Davidson tires with tire irons. You can!

This is one reason why we lubed the inside drop center area of the wheel's rim: to permit the rubber to slip and slide and flex into position when being installed. The rubber tire's edge can lodge itself and get stuck near the drop center section and bind up the entire works if the drop center is not lubed with paste lubricant. This is one of the secret tricks of the trade you may have never heard of before, but it works like a charm and solves many problems of mounting motorcycle tires onto their rims! And this works on the tire changing machines too.

Important Tip: Even then, using your knee to compress the tread inward may not be enough if the top section of the tire 180 degrees where you are working is hung up on the upper section of the rim holding tightly. You must use your hand or a C-clamp to compress the tire ends together to separate them from the shoulder or rim bead edges or even insert a tire iron at that point and pull the tire down away from the rim so it can drop away and fall into the drop center of the rim (a preferred method I use). Tie a tire iron down with a rope 180 degrees from where you are having trouble, then go back and try again and you will see the rubber tire will now bend, flex and slide once again and the rubber will not be held firmly in place and it will install over the rim.

But before we get to the end stage we need to start installing the upper tire onto the rim. We begin the process the same way as shown in Fig. 5-16 by pushing down on the tire at one point by hand so a portion of the top of the tire falls down into the drop center of the rim. It is easy to get the tire to install itself by hand 75% of the way. You now only need to use tire irons (or rotary bar) on the last 25% of the way.

Now is the time to insert the No-Mar® "helping hand" tool. It is worth every penny to purchase this handy tool, but you can later use a tire iron if you can't afford to purchase one.

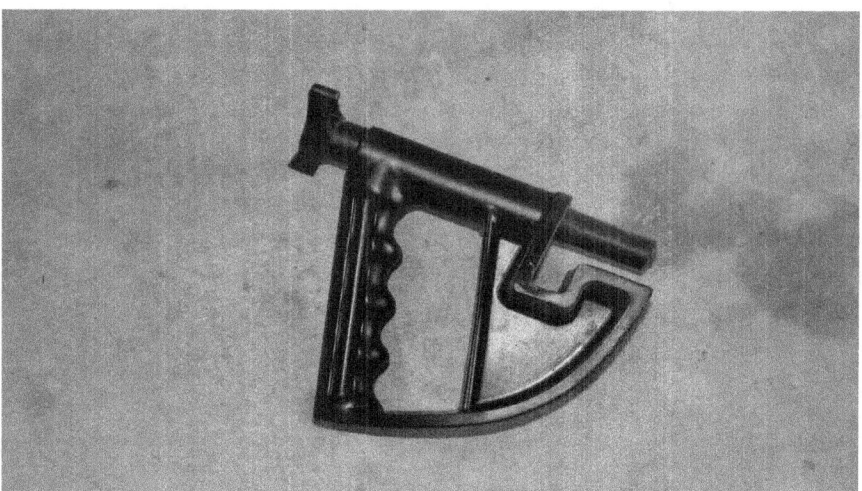

Fig. 5-23   No-Mar ® Helping Hand Tool

Fig. 5-24   No-Mar ® Helping Hand Tool Installed on Victory® Kingpin Wheel

Fig. 5-24 shows a wide 180mm rear tire being installed on a big cruiser Victory motorcycle. Fig. 5-22 shows a Harley-Davidson tire being installed on a Harley-Davidson big fat 16" rim custom chrome 5-spoke cast wheel. Fig. 5-21 is a Triumph America model wheel. The rims and tires are all designed the same way so they can be installed using the same methods and tools. No mystery here! You only need to figure out which size tire to buy that will fit your wheel's rim. If it fits, it mounts.

Tip: When your new tires arrive make sure the retailer delivered the right size tires. Mistakes happen.

Fig. 5-25 Drop-Center Enforcement - Tire Irons Tied Down Forces Tire Into Rim's Drop-Center

As you can see in Fig. 5-24 the No-Mar® helping hand tool is pushing down hard on the top side of the tire forcing it to ride lower than the top bead section of the rim. This is the desired result so when you get to the last end stage of installing the tire this pushed down section will permit the rubber tire to "move" so that tight rubber can flip over the rim. Notice how in Fig. 5-23 revealing the tire being squeezed and pushed down below the shoulder into the rim's drop center. So which should you use? I prefer the No-Mar® brand Helping Hand as shown in Fig. 5-23 and 5-24. And yes, if you need to you can use two of them.

Tip: You can use two No-Mar® helping hand tools, but I have had only to need one to get the toughest and biggest tires installed. If you need to use two then insert them in such a manner as in Fig. 5-25 so the tire is pushed down into the rim drop-center. If you still run into resistance installing the tire try narrowing the devices distance from each other as tire irons shown in the photograph can drive the tire much deeper into the rim's drop-center.

Easy to Install: Fig. 5-24 is an example of changing the big tires on the Victory® brand V-Twin motorcycle. In many cases these larger tires are actually easier to change. So don't believe the hype that large motorcycle tires can't be changed using tire irons or on manually operated tire machines. Yes, tires on Harley-Davidson wheels (Fig. 5-25) are easy to install despite the persistent fear-speak perpetrated by those who aim to make money on preventing riders from changing their own tires!

If you were to install a tire iron and bend it down and hold it in place with a rope it will do the same thing, but the No-Mar® Helping Hand Tool does a good job faster. You just insert it into the rim then remove it after the tire is installed, a very handy tool that works like a dream.

Insert a tire iron near where the rubber is in contact with the rim. I like to work in a clockwise direction, but it does not matter which direction you choose. Don't forget your four rim protectors. You can use one rim protector, but I like to use four as relying on one often gets stuck between the rim and tire and halts progress.

Note: With 2 tire irons tied down in Fig. 5-25 you would begin installing the tire at 9 o'clock position working clockwise. If the tire "walks" out of the rim it will stop at the right side of the tied-down tire iron. With this setup the tire will install easily. As you pull the tire forward with your working tire irons and cover the rim the lower section of the tire will move forward into the rim's drop center freeing up rubber tire slack so the tire will not become stuck/jammed on the rim.

How To Install Tires on Motorcycles

Fig. 5-26 Just Starting To Install Upper Bead of Tire On The Rim

In Fig. 5-26 The tire is already installed from the 6 o'clock and 9 o'clock position. A tire iron is inserted at the 4 o'clock position and the tire is flipped over the rim. Yes, we are working counterclockwise just to show you that you can install your tire clockwise or counterclockwise depending on your choice. Generally you do not alternate working left then right sides, but you can on tires that are stubborn to install. The rule is whatever works, works!

Fig. 5-27 Installing Tire With One Tire Iron

In Fig. 5-27 shows the tire iron will be moving counterclockwise as I install the tire. You will notice the tire iron is taking a huge bite of rubber and the tire is installing with ease. Small bites are only required if a tire gives resistance. Also notice the tire installs with only the use of one tire iron. If you lube the tire and rim with paste tire lubricant you will get many easy installs like this. The rubber in this case was also warm being installed at 85 degrees and that makes the rubber soft and flexible. The same tire, if installed in cooler conditions, may require up to four tire irons due to rubber resistance to stretch, flex and flow.

Notice the top section is riding high in Fig. 5-27. We need to insert a tire iron and flip the last section of the tire over the upper rim. Now the tire will soon be installed on the rim. Notice the overlap of the tire in Fig. 5-27 is not as severe as shown in Fig. 5-29. This is because the tire was pushed down into the rim's drop-center properly.

Important Instruction: When the rubber seems to be giving you increasing resistance now is the time to insert a tire iron where you are working, bend it down so it is facing away from the tire and rim then tire it down with a rope so it holds the tire in that position if you have not used the No-Mar ® Helping Hand Tool (Fig. 5-24) to get the same effect as Fig. 5-25 is doing. This will primarily stop any "walking" of the rubber uninstalling itself as you work. When you get to the end point you will need to install another tire iron 180 degrees opposite, bend it down away from the rim and tire and hold it down with some rope so it will be doing the same job as the helping hand does. See Fig. 5-25, there is no possible way this tire can walk or not install onto the rim. If any tire give you trouble just use this set up as shown in the photograph and the tire is going to install with very little effort. Once you use this method and see how easy it is to install a tire you will be a believer!

When you get to this end point as shown in Fig. 5-28 and Fig. 5-29: You may want to take a break, read this book to get a good understanding of what is taking place in regards to tire walking and how to use the helping hand devices.

Fig. 5-28 Walking Tire Uninstalling Itself

Fig. 5-28 Reveals the method of using a tire iron with rim protectors on a Harley-Davidson wheel. The technique is used on all steel and aluminum alloy wheels except composite (plastic, carbon fiber or other fragile material) rims. But as you work with your tire iron you may notice tire walking uninstalling itself. Watch for this. It is easy to stop, just insert a tire iron and tie it down where the tire is uninstalling and it will stop right there.

Fig. 5-29 End Point - Tire Overlaps Rim

Fig. 5-28 is a perfect example of a tire iron working the tire's top bead over the upper edge of the rim only to see at the very far right the tire is "dismounting" from the rim. To stop the walking you need to insert a tire iron where the tire is dismounting and flip the tire iron down taking a bit of the tire down with it and use your hand, knee, body or rope to hold that tire iron down so the tire can not dismount as you work the other tire iron. Fig. 5-30 is somewhat an example to stop tire walking and to force tire into the rim's drop-center.

We are going to insert that "helping hand" tire iron where the tire is already installed on the rim 180 degrees away from the view as shown in the End Point in Fig. 5-29.

Tip: Fig. 5-29 reveals a problematic end point and it is caused by failing to lubricate or evaporation of lube prior to installation, a rim that has a very shallow drop-center, tire not pushed down into the rim drop-center, a very cold tire temperature and in some cases the tire is too small size for the rim.

Note: The "end point" means there is only a few inches of rubber left to install the tire and that rubber is taught over the rim and will require more tool pressure to force that rubber up and over the rim. Fig. 5-29 reveals the tiny bites of rubber you should use to slowly coax that rubber to move over the rim. Work slowly so you give the rubber time to stretch as you work.

End Point Trouble: If you ever do come upon a very tough to impossible end point you may need to uninstall the tire about six inches from the rim then setup tire irons as shown in Fig. 5-25 because the tire is "locked" onto the rim and not setting low into the rim drop-center and that will create a severe end point that will not install. You can also just insert one tire iron 180 degrees opposite of the end point and pull the tire iron down and tie it down with rope. See Fig. 5-30. Here's two more photos of helping hands at work. See Fig. 1-4 and Fig. 2-1.

Fig. 5-30 Helping Hand Tire Iron

When you get to the end point (Fig. 5-29) now is the time to insert the "helping hand" tire iron as described earlier (Fig. 5-24 or Fig. 5-25. You don't need to use a "helping hand tire iron" if you have earlier inserted the No-Mar ® Helping Hand Tool as shown in Fig. 5-24, so choose and use one or the other, but you can use both.

Fig. 5-31 Helping Hand Tire Irons

Fig. 5-31 shows how two tire irons can be inserted as a helping hand. You may want to use two or more depending on how much rubber needs to be held down in place. The photo also reveals what the tire may look like at the end point requiring tiny bites of rubber to install the tire. There is no rule here. Use as many tire irons as you wish in any locations to get the job done. If you only need one tire iron that is fine, but if more is needed then by all means do so. If the tire won't install due to the rubber binding up over the top rim of the wheel as shown you need to make certain the tire 180 degrees opposite is driven down into the wheel rim drop-center so the rubber at the working tire irons can move forward and fold the tire over the rim. See also Fig. 6-5.

This photo in Fig. 6-1 is also an excellent demonstration of how to take small bites of rubber when using tire irons. Bites can even be smaller than this when the going gets real tough at the end point. Notice how the tire's rubber is getting awfully tight and does not want to flow over the rim to be seated.

Just continue onward little by little until the tire drops down. Take little bites with the tire iron if you feel too much resistance. You won't have to go very far in many cases. The thicker the tire, the more distance your tire irons will need to travel with many tiny bites to get the tire slowly onto the rim. Do not rush. Work the tire irons as if in slow motion to allow time for the rubber to stretch and adjust its position. If you work too fast, everything will just bind up into a stalled stalemate. Use paste tire lube liberally!

But when the going is tough like as shown in Fig. 5-29 you should insert a helping hand 180 degrees away from this troubling end point as shown. And if the going is still too tough? Insert two or even three helping hands and tie them down for it means the tire has not fallen down into the wheel's drop center where the helping hand is located and this causes the binding up at the end point making it difficult to impossible to install the new tire to the rim Fig. 5-25. The helping hand technique is a magical trade secret along with using paste lubricant in the right places on the tire and rim!

Some new automotive automatic tire installers now come with a power ram that forcibly pushes the tire way down deep into the rim's drop center acting as the helping hand. You can see these machines on the Internet video sites like U-Tube or search "Tire Changing Machines" on the Web to get to manufacturers sites. Not all automatic machines have this helping hand ram, most don't as they use brute force to install the tire in a rotary manner. Tire irons do not use a rotary motion as a mount/demount bar so the tire installation procedures are different.

Also, even if you have a manual tire changing machine that installs tires in a rotary fashion you can still run into trouble with the mount/demount bar popping out from the tire and you will then need to resort to using tire irons. Do you really need an expensive tire changing machine? No, not at all.

Remember: Use liquid tire lube to remove tires, paste lube to install tires. Many tire repair shops only use liquid tire lubricant. That's okay, but when you try the paste lube you will become a believer especially when using tire irons or a manually operated tire changing machine.

The next chapter will concentrate on end point tire installation troubles.

CHAPTER 6

End Point Tire Installation Problems

PROBLEMS INSTALLING TIRE

If you still have problems? Then go back and read this book and see which procedure you may have left out. Don't forget to read the many tips and tricks in the Question & Answer section at the back of this book. Maybe you are mounting the tire iron into the rim in the wrong orientation (using the tire iron backwards), forgot to deflate tire and break the tire bead, or applied insufficient lubricant on the tire and rim. Maybe the tire is too cold. Maybe you're taking too large a bite of rubber with tire iron. Maybe you're working too fast. Perhaps you're frustrated, angry, upset, and not thinking straight. If so, take a break.

Fig. 6-1 End Point Problems Begins Here

Take a look at Fig. 6-1 and you will see the tire's rubber is almost going over the rim, but for some reason it is not flexing to fold over the rim and binding up as shown. You can see the very tiny bites being taken with the tire iron on the right slowing working about 1" of tire over the rim. It is getting awfully difficult to even get the tire iron into the rim too and a ripping sound is heard of the rubber. Stop if you hear ripping sounds. You may be working too fast. After every bite, rest so the rubber has time to reposition itself.

Unfortunately this tire in Fig. 6-1 has become so distorted with too much tire overlapping the rim at the 12 o'clock position it will not install. Something is wrong. We need to apply a few tricks of the trade here to get this tire to fold over the rim. Using a "helping hand" device will cure this problem, but you have to had installed it before reaching this end point, so back off the tire bead and remove enough of the tire to install the helping hand or insert a tire iron and tie it down at the 6 o'clock position. This forces the tire to drop in the rim's drop center and like magic the tire will now install with great ease at the end point. Keep reading for more tricks you can use.

When learning, you should take many small breaks. You will make mistakes. So what? We all do! Relax and try again with a more confident stride. Sometimes a break gives the tire's rubber time to stretch just right and make the job go with ease the second time around.

Remove the rim protectors. Count them. If one is missing, it is inside the tire and rim so you need to remove it now. Just reach inside and fish for it as best as you can. There is a tool you can purchase that makes lifting the tire away from the rim so you can reach inside. Great to use with tube tires to gain access to the tube, valve stem or rim locks. It is called the "Tire Tamer" and made by KLSupply.com.

Believe it or not, some tires are just a pain to install due to their construction of materials. The rim may even be to blame for having a profile that prevents the rubber from falling down into the drop center of the rim or worse, not even have a decent drop center to begin with. In cases like these you will have to insert more tire irons where the tire is binding up to get that tire off of the bead seating area of the rim. You don't want a tire to sit in the normal bead section of the rim when installing it. It has to be loose and away from the rim. By forcing the tire down off the rim with tire irons held in place with rope the opposite end of the tire will be able to flex over the rim when you work your tire irons. Take tiny bites of rubber and work slowly. See Fig. 5-28.

Note: Sometimes, you may even need to use three tire irons to install a tire at the last end stage shown in Fig. 6-1, but most of the time only two will be needed as shown in Fig. 5-30.

Tip: Keep in mind just because you have had extreme trouble with your bike and tire do not think you will always have this grievous pain. It just may be your bike's rim design and the choice of tire you are installing. I have had some tires go on ridiculously easy and some brands of tires become devilishly stubborn on the same rim. Odds are, your first time changing tires could be the worse you ever encounter especially because you are not truly yet familiar of what is going on. This is why I encourage you to go watch tires being installed so you can understand the concept of what is happening. Keep in mind, using a rotary method of installing tires like machines use is different than using tire irons, but the final effect is the same.

TROUBLESOME WALKING TIRE BEAD

When a tire is being removed and/or installed (Fig. 5-27) on one end, it may actually fold back upon itself and install itself on the opposite side of the rim or close by where you are working (usually about 45 degrees away). This is normal and it will happen to you. To stop this you simply insert a tire iron at that spot and tie it down with a rope, or place your knee on top of the tire at that point to hold it down, so the tire's rubber will not move anymore at that location. Then go back to work and that problem will cease. If the knee trick won't work, the tire iron most certainly will.

I once worked on a tire when I was a beginner for about fifteen minutes and the tire was coming over the rim, but I kept going around the tire many times. I said to myself, "I feel like I have been here before. Why am I going in circles?" I noticed the tire was installing itself as I was removing it. Each time I took a bite of tire pushing it down over the rim to install it, another equal size bite nearby was being pushed back out of the rim. I was going in circles. You will see this happen, and I guarantee it will happen to you! Watch for it. It happens after you have gotten 75% of the tire onto the rim, then the tire begins to play games with you. It doesn't happen when you take a tire off, just when putting them onto the rim. Read Chapter 5 to resolve tire walking problems.

Tip: Clean the tire and rim of any excess lubricant with a soft dry cloth. Do not use water! It is okay once the tire is installed to inflate it right away if you are using approved tire installation lubricants. If you used forbidden high-content water or ammonia base lubricants or cleaners you should wait until they have evaporated to avoid trapping these corrosive agents inside your rim and tire.

C-CLAMP USE ON TIRE AND RIM

To get the tire to flex when using your tire irons, you may need to use a carpenter's C-clamp to compress the rubber tire. These tools can be used at the final stage of mounting a tire to a rim. Sometimes a tire just gets jammed stuck and will not permit the other parts of the tire to stretch or move freely. Compressing the tire with the C-clamp will let the rubber relax. There are two ways to use the C-clamp. Fig. 6-2 and Fig. 6-3 shows two different types of C-clamp compressing both sides of the sidewalls of the tire. The Screw type is much stronger and recommended.

Note: If you use the "helping hand" devices (Fig. 5-23 and Fig. 5-24 you should not have to use any of these C-clamps except in rare situations. I mention the C-clamps in this book so you can use them if needed now or one day in the future. The day may come that tire construction will be so stiff and strong you may need to use extra devices like these to install them.

Fig. 6-2 Steel Ratcheting C-Clamp

You can use this method to help push the rubber tire down into the drop center area of the rim. Then the rubber is free and will release tension so the final end point bead Fig. 6-1 can flip over the rim.

Fig. 6-3 Steel Screw 8" C-Clamp Compressing Tire Away From Rim

Fig. 6-3 shows the powerful screw type C-clamp compressing the center of the tire. On a tough tire that just refuses to go over the rim, the rubber tire is laying hard and flat over the bead section of the rim shoulder and just won't budge. At the working end point the rubber is so flat and under a stretching stress because it does not want to fold backwards and it can't flex downward into the rim's drop center... it is stuck! See Fig. 6-1. The C-clamp is crushing the tire which is not good for the tire as it could break internal components. A little squeezing is okay, but Fig. 6-3 is not to be exceeded.

The C-clamp compresses the tire so both the upper and lower sections of the tire are forced into the rim drop-center, but even on the toughest of tires you only need to drive the upper side of the tire down into the drop-center to install the tire. That is why the helping hand system works so well.

In Fig. 6-4 the tire has become so embedded onto the rim. Sometimes if you can put your knee in this area (Fig. 6-4) and push inward this bulge will unwind and the tire flips right over the rim easier. You can use a C-clamp to do this too. See Fig. 6-4.

Fig. 6-4 C-Clamp Compressing Out Tire Bulge

If you compress the tire at the bulge it will release the stress so your tire iron can flip the rubber over backwards on to the rim. In most cases you will not need to use these C-clamps, but feel free to do so if it makes the job easier for you to do. You will find that tires with high load rating capacity have the thickest rubber sidewalls and are the most difficult to install on heavy cruiser motorcycles.

Before you buy the C-clamps make sure they have a jaw gap wide enough to fit the width and diameter of your tires, 8" or larger in size (8" works up to a 180mm tire). And before you buy any C-clamps buy an extra tire iron or two as they will take the place of using any C-clamps whatsoever in 99.999% of the time. I recommend four (4) long leverage tire irons (Fig. 5-24) and the No-Mar® helping hand tool (Fig. 5-23).

Always keep in mind that without the tire lubricant needed for the tire to slip about the rim, the tire will become very stubborn to install and may eve refuse to install at all. And the tire should be able to drop down into the drop center of the rim to permit the tire to be installed onto the rim without binding up the rubber like a knot so it can no longer stretch, flex or flow over the rim as shown in Fig. 6-1.

The Miracle: Looking at Fig. 6-1 the rubber is held tightly over the rim and it looks like it will never be able to go over the rim. But if you insert a tire iron 180 degrees away and insert that tire iron into the top portion of the tire and fold the tire iron downward over the tire and hold it there with rope, you will see the miracle happen Fig. 5-23 and/or Fig. 5-24. When you try once more to install the tire you will see all that overhanging rubber suddenly diminish in size and flips right over the rim with less effort.

Note: Before you insert the helping hand tire iron you may need to back off the pressure on the working end tire irons so the helping hand iron can fold the tire down away from the rim. If the rubber is too tight you can't get the helping hand tire iron inserted. You operate this tire iron not to lift the tire from the rim, but as installing the tire and that forces the tire down and away from the upper rim, then you tie the tire iron down in that position with rope.

A tire with a high load capacity and/or with a shallow drop center rim will refuse to drop into the drop center of the rim and will bind up on the rim's shoulder or bead seating area, but with good lubrication and small bites of rubber it will install even without C-clamps or a helping hand device, but barely and with extreme difficulty which could bend your rims or rip the tire's bead. The force is just too much. But to prevent tearing the tire's bead use the C-clamps to make the job easier or use the procedures mentioned in this book for this is the preferred and generally acceptable method anyway.

Fig. 6-4 shows a C-clamp taking compressing a convex bulge in the tire tread. This happens when the tire has nowhere to go because it is hung up on the rim's bead/shoulder area and that occurs with a rim with a shallow drop center. Conditions like this do happen on some bike models making the tire difficult to install. The C-clamp is trying to push the tire tread inward to give up rubber slack so the tire irons can fold the rubber over the opposite side of the rim as in Fig. 5-21.

Experiment with the C-clamp positioning to see which formula works best for your application. You can use both at the same time or just one. You can have both tight or one tight and one looser. You can position the clamps anywhere that you find makes the tire mount on with greater ease. Write down the unique formula you discover for the front and rear tire so you will not forget. When using a metal C-clamp, place a piece of wood on the rim so the C-clamp will not scratch the rim.

Remember: Instead of a C-clamp you can insert a tire iron to hold the tire down with a rope to keep the tire's bead area away from the rim's shoulder.

You can purchase a "Helping Hand" bead clamping device from No-Mar® as shown in Fig. 5-22 as it holds down the tire away from the upper shoulder area of the rim and forces the tire down below the shoulder and down into the drop center shown in Fig. 5-23. All you need is one No-Mar® helping hand device in most cases.

I have used the No-Mar Helping Hand® with good results, but some rubber tires are so tough (with shallow rims) I have had trouble even inserting the No-Mar® Helping Hand on rare events, so if you run into a tough situation like this, just go back and use the tied down tire iron as your helping hand as shown in Fig. 5-24. And don't be afraid to use two or even three tire irons if needed! Tire irons are very thin and even then they can be a bit tough to install between the rim and tire. It will not hurt to place some paste tire lubricant on the tire iron ends in such situations.

See Fig. 6-5 for an example. The left tire iron is being pulled backward then will be tied down and the right tire iron will also be pulled backwards and tied down. Use this technique on stubborn tires!

Fig. 6-5 Inserting Two Helping Hands Tire Irons.

Now you can go back to work with your free tire irons and you will see the rubber will flip right over the rim and the tire will be installed. But if you run into more trouble read the detailed Question & Answer section entirely. You will find the solution there.

Note: Don't forget to remove any rim protectors, nuts, bolts, tools, valve cores, shop rags or whatever may have fallen into the tire and rim before adding air to the tire.

Now that you have the tire installed on the rim remove it from any mounting machine or device and bounce the tire on concrete floor or sidewalk while rotating the wheel like bouncing a basket ball. This helps relieve the stress in the tire to get it into the optimal position on the rim for inflating it with air.

If you just happen to forget to bounce the tire don't worry about it as it is not an absolute requirement in most cases. When the tire inflates it will align itself to the rim. Getting a new tire to inflate can be a challenge!

With the tire inflated check for air leaks on the tire/rim and valve stem area with soapy water solution. Watch for tiny air bubbles indicating a leak.

CHAPTER 7

Inflation of Tire

PRESSURE GAUGE CALIBRATION

Ask a garage if they can check your pressure gauge reading with one or two of their pressure gauge readings. This is so you can know whether your pressure gauge is actually close to being accurate, broken, or way off the mark. Some gages have a calibration screw to reset the gauge pressure indicator needle to zero. The indicator needle should be on zero with no air pressure. Adjust the air supply line pressure to 75% of the dial reading on your gage then test that pressure with a gage that is known to be accurate. The two gage reading should be very close give or take 2 or 3 psi.

Note: When using a off-the-shelf pressure gage as shown in Fig. 7-1 (or any air fill device) you must install the valve core into the valve stem for the air fill tool to work properly. Some mechanics rig the device fill nozzle hose end (where it attaches to the valve stem) so no valve core is required. This also gives huge volume bursts of air that can greatly assist inflating the tire to seat the beads. The valve core is restrictive to the flow of air.   Using the bead starter strap permits you to use off-the-shelf air fill tools.

Danger: There are air burst bead seating devices you can buy, but they are not recommended as one mistake can blow up the tire and rim and maim or kill you.   There are also "explosive" methods to set tire beads that can not only kill you, they can burn your house down. Stay away from such products until they are proven to be safe and become accepted in the industry as standard operating procedure. Any method can be deemed safe if it is perfected, controlled and in competent hands. In the future we may see these devices approved. Who knows? At most they would speed up tire installation procedures.

Fig. 7-1 Dial Pressure Gage With Trigger & Lock-On Fill Connector

Fig. 7-1 reveals the proper pressure air fill device (air chuck) to use. The valve has a trigger to add and stop air flow, a pressure gage and the end that attaches to the valve stem locks on so you do not have to hold it in place.

Danger: Imagine the horrific danger of using a pressure gage that was broken or inaccurate? You could be inflating your tire and rim to "explosive" pressures and the tire and rim could actually explode like a bomb and your defective pressure gage lying to you saying all is well below 40 psi air pressure! Test your gages. Use two gages alternately to double check pressures when in doubt. Another thing you should do is adjust your air pressure supply tank or air supply line to 40psi to reduce the possibility of overpressurizing a tire and rim. Doing this and using an accurate pressure gauge will keep things under control.

ADDING AIR TO THE NEW TIRE

Note: Read the questions and answers at the back of this book for more advice. And if you can't add air to the tire to inflate it you need to read, "Tire Bead Starter Strap - How to Use" in this Chapter. The tire is not conforming to the rim and will not permit inflation.

First, align the tire's balance mark adjacent to the valve stem as shown in Fig 7-2. I know we did this earlier but sometimes the dot moves when mounting the tire to the rim. If the rim was lubed up good as instructed you should be able to grab the tire and with some force applied and rotate the tire on the rim to move the dot to the valve stem, but you will need a tire stand that holds the rim preventing it from turning. If you can't? Don't worry about it, just leave it as is. You can still balance your tire with the dot not aligned properly.

Fig. 7-2 Tire Balance Mark by Valve Stem

Insert the valve core into the valve stem. Do not over tighten it. Just snug with two fingers on the wrench is fine. It has a rubber O-ring seat, so it should not be torqued down too tight. There is no affordable torque wrench tiny enough to measure the torque so just use finger pressure to tighten valve cores as shown in Fig. 7-3. Also see Fig. 2-23, Fig. 3-6, Fig. 4-4, Fig. 4-5 and Fig. 4-6.

Fig. 7-3 Installing Valve Core

With a 2-gallon (or more) air compressor or portable air storage tank, rapidly pump up the tire pressure, but do so in short bursts of air using the fill device shown in Fig. 7-1. Never pump air into a tire in one continuous blast of air. Use a pressure gage as shown in Fig. 7-1 with a valve stem clamp so you do not have to hold the air hose onto the fill valve.

Danger: The proper method if inflating a tire is never to stand next to it. The tire should be in a protective cage and a remote valve used to inflate the tire. In the real world few tire installers use this safety measure.

Wear eye protection then stand back as you fill the tire with air. If the tire will not inflate and you hear a high pitch sound of rushing air noise the tire is leaking air and not inflating the tire. It is leaking from the bottom or on the top of the rim and it is hard to locate the exact area from hearing air noise alone. If leaking on the bottom you will have to lift the tire as you inflate it so the lower part of the tire will be sealing up against the rim. Then it will inflate. If not? Read below, Tire Bead Starter Strap-How to Use.

As you fill the tire with air lift the tire and drop the tire along the rim to try to catch a blast of air from escaping. As you do this the air will be momentarily trapped in the tire forcing the tire to conform to the rim right away and inflate. Of course, this does not always work, but it will most of the time.

Tip: When air is leaking from a rim it emits a high pitch sound of rushing air. When air is properly filling a tire you will hear a hollow sound of air very much like the sound of helium filling a balloon. Listen for these different sounds. When filling a new tire to the rim for the first time short bursts of air does not work. At this phase long, steady flow of air is required as long as you hear the high pitch sound of air escaping from the rim. Only when you hear that hollow sound of air entering the tire then resort to the short burst of air method of inflating the tire.

Note: If you watch car tires being installed on a machine watch the operator make intervention movements with his hands and you will see some of these tactics I mention in this book at work. However, motorcycle rims and tires are not the same as car tires. Yes, the general design appear similar, but motorcycle tires are a bit tricky to install because sheer brute force can not be applied to the rims. Car rims are super thick and strong and a powerful machine can use brute force on car tires without causing damage. Plus, motorcycle rims scratch easily so low air pressure (50psi) tire machine is required.

Tip: If you are using a tire installation machine make sure the tire changing machine's lower rim clamps are completely disengaged holding the wheel's rim to the machine or air will never be able to fill the tire. These rim clamps are unseen and you can easily forget they are preventing the tire from contacting the rim so the tire can never be inflated.

Inflate to the tire pressure noted on the tire in short bursts of air, but do not exceed 40 psi on your inflator's pressure gauge. You will hear a loud pop when the tire's bead seats to the rim. It is a small explosion like a firecracker exploding and it will surprise you and this process is normal. In fact, you want to hear that loud "pop" for it tells you the tire's bead has seated to the rim.

Continue inflating to the recommended tire pressure and let it sit for a few seconds and then let out the air from the tire using the valve core removal tool. Then inflate the tire one more time to recommended tire pressure. This procedure is to insure the tire is properly seated. Some mechanics don't use this procedure, but they should!

Inspect the tire to see if it is fully seated properly around the rim. On most motorcycle street tires you will see a tiny line encircling the tire near the rim. By looking at this line you can see if that line does not waver and the distance from the rim is the same all around the tire. In Fig. 8-5 you can see two lines on the tire just near the bead area of the tire. That lower line should be an equal distance from the rim all the way around concentrically and be visible to your eye. Any wavering of the line means the tire is not seated down properly due to debris on the rim or tire is hanging up due to lack of installation lubricant or under inflation or just plain out of alignment. Deflate, lube with some liquid both beads all around the tire and inflate again to 40 psi. Now you know why I insist on you cleaning the rims and lubricating the rims with paste lube. It solves these problems!

If the line still varies, deflate the tire by removing the valve core, bounce the tire as described below, "Bouncing The Tire On The Rim" and refill with air. In this case you may want to bounce the tire on the rim with air installed in the tire to help nudge the tire into final position. A tiny imbalance in the line usually is not a problem. A wide imbalance means something is stuck between the tire and rim's bead area (old rubber, dirt, bits of cloth) the rim is bent at this location or the tire itself is defective not being perfectly molded when manufactured or damaged in shipment. It is rare to have a tire not align itself to the rim after seating the bead.

Note: Some tires are plain defective and will not set their bead to the rim at all. They usually will not inflate with air. After trying the bead starter strap mentioned below, exchange the tire with a new tire. Most reputable tire manufacturers will exchange the tire for free if it will not inflate. Buy tires with a credit card so you have dispute protection.

BOUNCING THE TIRE ON THE RIM

After you get the tubeless tire onto the rim prior to inflating it with any air it is okay to bounce the tire tread on a hard surface like a concrete floor rotating the tire. It helps to bounce the tire as it moves the rubber beads a bit outward so air can become trapped when inflating the tire. Some installers use a rubber mallet on the tire tread. Don't use a steel or brass hammer as it will ruin the tire.

Tip: Don't forget after you bounce and hammer the tire tread down toward the rim, as you attempt to fill the tire with air, raise and lower the entire tire so the incoming air may capture the tire to permit inflation.

You don't always have to perform this ritual of bouncing and hammering the tire. You can by-pass it and try to inflate the tire right away. If you can't get the tire to inflate use the bounce method first. If it still does not work use the Tire Bead Starter Strap.

TIRE BEAD STARTER STRAP - HOW TO USE

Do not use the tire bead starter strap unless you have to use it. A good many tires inflate and seat the beads without using the strap. It is just the problem tires and rims that require the strap. Also, cooler temperatures makes for stiff rubber and the strap needs to be used to force the tire down on to the rim.

Also, don't confuse the tire bead starter strap with the tire bead breaker as they are two different devices.

Note: the strap is only used on tubeless tires to begin the inflation process. It is not always needed. In warm weather you may or may not need to use the strap. It also depends on the rim and tire shape and even the brand of tires. Some tire brands inflate easier than others. I would list those that were easy, but what works on my rims will not work on yours. For that reason we are all on our own to find out which tires mount the easiest. In Fig. 7-4 you can see the tire bead starter strap crushing the tire inward toward the rim like a constrictor snake. We need to use strong force to compress the tire to the rim to seal out air leaks so the tire can inflate with air. It can be a frustrating process, but it does work.

Fig. 7-4 K&L® Brand Tire Bead Starter Strap

Fig. 7-4 shows the tire strap not riding dead-center on the tire. You need to get the entire strap all around the tire dead-centered so the tire will be squeezed down properly to the rim. Fig. 7-5 shows a strap dead center. Using these devices are a bit tricky and will take practice. Sometimes the tire inflates on first try and other times you feel nothing what you do will ever work to inflate the tire. You have to loosen, move the strap around the tire, tighten and try again. It can be a frustrating procedure, sometimes.

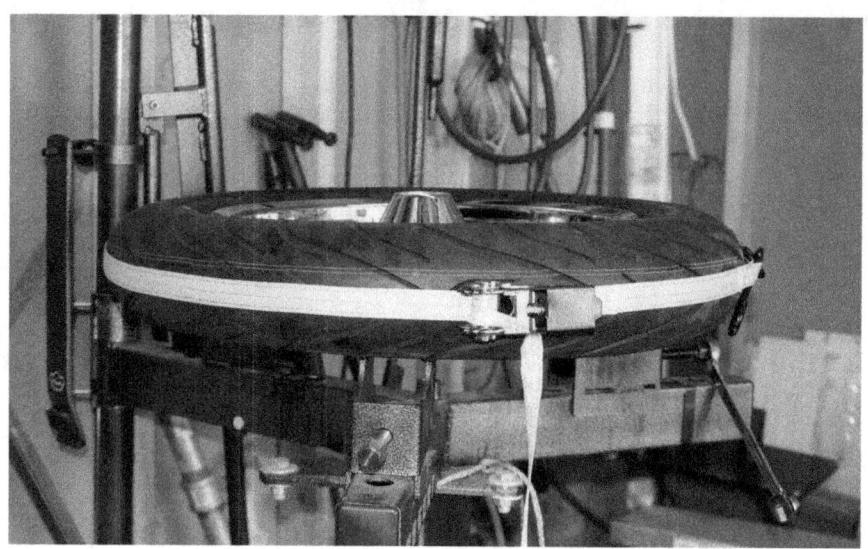

Fig. 7-5 Reveals a Common Ratchet Tie-Down Strap Used to Seat Tire Bead to Rim

Fig. 7-4 shows a professional tire bead starter strap. You may not need to use one, but they can really help sometimes, especially installing stiff street cruiser tires or any tire in cool weather conditions. The belt has three separate heavy-duty ratchets and straps which you assemble around the center tread area of the tire as shown in Fig. 7-5. When you tighten the ratchets equally it squeezes the tire down onto the rim to create a temporary air seal so you can begin to inflate the tire.

Fig. 7-5 shows a "poor man's" method to seat the tire's bead to the rim so the tire can be inflated. Problem is, these general purpose "tie-down" ratcheting nylon straps have weak ratchets so they break because a lot of pressure has to be applied in many cases, crushing pressures to force large wide tires down onto the rim so the tire seats tightly on the rim stopping air leaks when air is applied to inflate the tire. Fig. 7-4 K&L® product is super heavy-duty and well worth the money. However, it won't hurt to try using a typical ratchet tie-down. For this book I tried the cheap ones and sometimes they work and sometimes they just break. If you can't afford the K&L® just buy the strongest you can buy. Truck stops do sell very wide and strong ratchet tie-downs that will not break, but notice the K&L® has three powerful ratchets on one strap to get a concentric compression of the tire to the rim. Using only one ratchet will compress the tire into the shape of an egg and may not work for you, so buy the K&L® Tire Bead Starting Strap.

A tubeless tire with a stiff sidewall construction (mostly cruiser and fat, wide custom bike tires) sometimes will not sufficiently contact the rim when trying to inflate it. When you try to add compressed air to inflate the tire, there is no seal and air just blows out everywhere. Some shops use a large burst of compressed air to overwhelm the air leaks. It works, but if you do not have a large air tank capacity, a high-capacity air hose, and a nozzle that can flow a huge burst of air, you will need to use the bead starter strap or take your tire/wheel to auto tire dealer to inflate it. They will do it for free or for a couple dollars. A motorcycle shop will likely charge you more than you want to pay.

You install the strap around the center tread area and tighten the ratchets. This squeezes the tire tightly against the rim. It has to be cranked down pretty tight too. Yes, the tire will appear crushed to the rim and distorted in some cases. If you search the Internet you can see how this strap works. Also going to K&L's Web site they have a video you can view.

Fig. 7-6 C-Clamp Used to Help Seat Tire Bead For Tire Inflation

Sometimes all you need to do is squeeze the tire at one spot where the air is leaking and a Carpenter's C-Clamp as shown in Fig. 7-6 will do the job. Make sure the clamp touching the rim is protected with wood or other soft material so the rim will not be scratched. Also, don't use too much force so you won't crack or deform the rim. Just a gentle squeeze will do. Problem is with C-clamps if it does not work the first time moving it around the rim likely won't work either and a strap will have to be used to begin the inflation process.

Danger: The Bead Starter Strap can be dangerous to use, so make sure the moment the tire begins to inflate (hearing that hollow sound of air) you remove the strap to prevent an explosion. It would be to your advantage to pay attention when using the strap with no distractions and no music playing. You need to hear the air flowing into the tire. Use short bursts of air and you will see air pressure rise in the chuck's air pressure gage.

TIRE BEAD STARTER STRAP - HOW TO USE

1. Begin assembling the strap segments around the tire's tread. Install the valve core to the valve stem on the rim so the air valve and gage will function as designed.
2. There is a central steel ring and three straps that assist keeping the strap from falling away from the tire and they are adjustable. You don't have to use this feature as it relies on a center post. You can insert your bike's axle shaft into the wheel bearings so the ring can loop it.
3. Start ratcheting each ratchet handle an equal amount until the tire is snug tight against the rim visually.
4. Apply short one second bursts of air. Listen for that deep hollow sound air makes when filling a confined space. This will require prior experience. And simultaneously watch to see if the tire sidewall is filling and expanding every so slightly. You don't want to see a large amount of movement. Stop if your pressure gage reads more than 20 psi. Be careful, it can go to 80psi in a couple seconds due to the strap confining the tire!
5. If you see no tire sidewall expansion and the air pressure gage reads zero the tire bead seater is still not squeezing down tight enough to seal air. You will hear a high pitch sound of air escaping from the rim/tire.
6. Tighten the bead strap even tighter then try to fill with air again. If this fails you will have to start using brute force to crush the tire down. If this still fails? Go to the next step.
7. You need to loosen the strap enough to rotate the strap to a different location. Usually just 6" then try again to fill the tire with air beginning with step #3 or jump to #6. Eventually, even after three more tries of relocating the strap the tire will seal against the rim and inflate. Be patient, be persistent and determined and do not get angry.
8. Take a break if you fail to get the tire to fill with air. Think. Is the rim off the lower rim clamps if you are using a machine? See Fig. 16-18 to see the lower rim clamps are released from the rim. Is there a tire iron still stuck somewhere? How about a rim protector still stuck on the rim? Look for a rag or cloth stuck under the tire's bead edge.
9. Loosen the straps and spray liquid tire lubricant on both sides of the tire bead area and push the tire about 1 inch around the rim. This may help the tire find a better spot and relieve any internal stress in the tire.

10. Something is preventing the rubber tire from compressing down equally on the rim. I find that the problem is often this model of the strap itself. It only has three ratchets and that makes for trouble failing to sink the tire to the rim in equal points. It pinches down the tire at three points making the tire take the shape of a triangle shape. The strap actually needs four to six ratchets to make a more circular shape. This is what to look out for and by rotating the strap to a different location on the tire as in step #7 you find the lucky spot where the tire finally seals to the rim and it begins to inflate.

11. Keep in mind that having the strap too tight on the tire will distort the tire so badly it can not seal due to the triangular shape it has taken. I have often had to just relocate the strap, snug it down, tighten more, tighten a bit more and the tire will begin to inflate. It can be a tricky process and it can be frustrating.

If leaks persist, loosen the strap and relocate and try again. You could try using a wide ratcheting tie-down strap. If that won't work, then invest and buy the proper tool for the job as shown. When the tire has inflated check for air leaks on the tire/rim and valve stem area with soapy water solution. Watch for tiny air bubbles indicating a leak.

Note: make sure when compressing the tire to the rim you have the strap dead center around the tire's tread. If it is off center it can't squeeze the tire properly to the rim and it will leak air. You may also have to use a tire iron to lift any low spots of the tire's bead higher up on the rim's shoulder. If the tire is cold below 50 degrees the rubber may become stubborn and not want to flex and seal air. Warm up the tire with a hair blow drier, bring the tire and wheel into a warm area for a few hours or wait for better weather. Tire's can be stubborn at times. It is the nature of rubber to not flex when cold.

Warning: Make sure you use an "accurate pressure gauge" to inflate the tire so no overpressure dangerous conditions will occur (such as shown in Fig. 7-4). Have it tested. Your air compressor should have an output line pressure gage. Your hand-held gage should be close to what that tank gage reads. There may be a small 5 psi difference and that is okay.

Tip: When using the bead starting strap, you apply about 10 to 20 psi of air pressure until you see the tire is inflating. The moment it begins to inflate, loosen the tire strap, add a little bit of air, loosen the strap again and add some more air, and then remove the strap entirely.

Note: Listen to the air flowing when using a Bead Starter Strap. A sharp high-pitch hiss of air detects an air leak and is not inflating the tire. A low frequency dull, hollow sound of air is filling the tire with air.

Danger: You must pay attention here. You are adding air to the tire and rim and the pressure will climb incredibly fast once the tire begins to inflate. It can overpressure the tire and cause it or the rim to explode like a grenade. Watch your pressure gage and don't go beyond 20psi. Pay attention! Using any strap or bead seating device is "not" recommended by the Rubber Manufactures Association due to the explosion hazard. Use at your own risk. Never leave this device unattended not even to answer the telephone as the air chuck valve could be leaking air into the tire and explode. If you must answer the telephone, remove the air chuck from the valve stem first.

Note: Though the bead starting strap creates a hazard, it can be used safely if you pay attention and in the real world on motorcycle tires we often have no other choice for there is no other tool we can use to get the tire to conform to the rim to get the air seal required to begin the inflation process. Catch 22. I have used them for years and they work just fine. You would have to be reckless to over pressurize the tire and that can happen if you are not paying attention! Do not let anyone interfere with you or interrupt you when using a tire bead starting strap. I even shut off the radio so I can pay close attention to hear the air flow sound and to watch the air pressure gage.

Note: Turn off the noisy radio, air compressor and all other distractions when performing this tire inflation procedure and do not answer the telephone, take delivery of packages, etc. Let nothing distract you.

When the strap is completely removed from the tire, then you can add 40 psi of air to seat the beads in short bursts of air, then lower or add pressure according to your motorcycle specification.

Warning: This procedure of adding no more than 40 psi is very important to prevent a tire or rim explosion.

The key is to strap the tire down tightly to the rim, add some low air pressure just enough to see the tire begin to inflate. You can also hear that familiar hollow sound of air filling the tire like the inside of a balloon. If you see or hear these events stop adding air and loosen the strap. Do this procedure in very small stages, two second bursts of air each. The strap's job is compress the tire tightly to the rim to seal the tire to the rim (to stop air leaking from the rim and tire gap) and direct the air to fill and expand outwards the tire. Once that begins the strap must be removed right away.

Important Procedure: Don't fill the tire with air with the strap in place to no more than 10 or 20 psi of air. It does not take much air pressure to begin the inflating process so loosen the strap, add a small burst of air and if no air is leaking out remove the strap entirely then start inflating the tire in short bursts of air up to 40 psi to seat the beads.

Danger: Don't just loosen the strap, you must completely remove the strap and hang that strap on the wall before you inflate the tire to 40 psi to seat the tire's beads to the rim. Do not forget this!

Note: The correct tire pressure for your motorcycle is not stamped on the tire. It is located on the frame of your bike, and the pressures are usually lower than what is indicated on the tire. If no such sticker exists, then contact the motorcycle manufacturer's dealer for the correct pressures. Also, the rear and front tires often do have different pressures. This air pressure determination generally does not change when you use a different brand of tires than the stock tires that came with the bike.

If the bike's sticker on the frame says to use bias tires, then stay with bias and do not put on radial tires or mix and match between the two. However, I have installed radial tires on a large cruiser motorcycle designed with bias tires and only found a better ride, better miles per gallon, better handling and a better price to buy the tires. You may find the results to be the same or worse.

Nobody wants to go on record saying to deviate from the manufacturer's recommendation for fear of liability. A sport bike may require a more strict adherence to the rules whereas a cruiser motorcycle may not. It is up to you if you want to try out different tires on your motorcycle. If you do drive slow and do not lean hard into turns. Drive with caution for 100 miles to adapt to the new feel and scuff up the smooth tire surfaces. This is true with installing any brand new tire.

This book does not intend to cover advanced riding technique, racing, engineering design, etc. It's just a book on how to install tires and fix flats on cruiser, sport and street legal motorcycles.

TIRE SCUFFING BREAK-IN

A new tire may be slippery due to tire mold release. Use caution when first riding the tire for 100 miles being careful to not lean hard or accelerate/brake in turns. Be aware smooth concrete surfaces may cause slip, slide or fall such as at fueling stations and avoid painted lines and arrows on blacktop roads as they are slippery. You can ride on a gravel road a short distance of even 1/16th mile is enough to take off the mold release and scuff up the tire's surface. Some riders just use sandpaper to rough up the tire a tiny bit. All tires need a short break-in period to allow the tire to better conform to the rim and to the bike and mostly for the rubber tire to relax and find its grip to the road surface. A new tire usually comes with paperwork explaining these things. Whoever was installing your tires is obligated to give you these written safety documents. Did they ever give them to you? Incredibly, many dealers hide this information from their customers to endanger them by their own incompetence and untrustworthiness. Some are even affixed to the tire with glue and still dealers fail to give the safety information to their customers. Believe me, riders have crashed due to not following tire break-in procedures and many dealers are at fault for these accidents. Just one more reason to change your own tires!

For the first 100 miles after installing new motorcycle tires, stay under 65 miles per hour. The rough road surface will scrub the tire and break it in. I usually just drive slowly and let the normal road surface rub away the shiny rubber. Be careful not to ride at high speed and lean deeply on new tires when taking on sharp corners. Do not accelerate at full power or brake hard. Also, this time is required for the tire lubricants to evaporate and become tacky. New tires being developed may not require a break-in period, but assume that one is required unless the manufacturer says otherwise in writing.

VALVE STEM & CAPS

Don't forget to install the plastic or metal valve stem cap! Is metal or plastic better? Both will work just fine, but metal caps will be safer. Just make sure the inner rubber O-ring seal is in good condition so if the Shrader valve were to leak, the valve cap will still hold air and prevent your tire from going flat. See Fig. 3-6. You don't have to replace the valve stem if it is made of metal at each tire change. Only the rubber push-through type are usually replaced at each tire change, once each year or you could go two years before replacement on the rubber pull-through types even in dry desert climates.

How often should you replace the rubber seal on metal valve stems? Once each three years should be fine. But be it known that your tire dealer has likely never changed your valve stem seals. Imagine that. Now on cars and trucks they do, but motorcycle shops usually just skip that maintenance. Why? No money in it. It takes them time to replace a few dollar item so they lose money doing you right. Another good reason to be changing your own tires.

If and when you do install a new rubber gasket seal on a metal valve core to the rim, put a bead of silicone rubber around the nut on the inner rim area being careful not to plug the air hole. You do this for two reasons. Silicone as it hardens will create an additional air seal and act as an anti vibration device to prevent the nut from coming loose.

CHAPTER 8

Balancing The Wheel

BALANCING THE WHEEL

Static balancing a tire and rim is simply letting gravity locate the heavy spot on the rim. You just add a tire/rim weight 180 degrees opposite to counter this out-of-balance condition. Dynamic balancing does the same, but the wheel is rotated at high speed and the machine calculates where and how much weight to be placed to balance the wheel. There is no difference that you will be able to tell using either method. Racing bikes even use the static balance method at the race track so don't be fooled into thinking computerized balancers are superior, but they are only brainless and faster to use and are often wrong giving you an unbalanced wheel!

We are using gravity static balancer in this book. There is another machine called the bubble static balancer. Search the Internet for them. They too are easy to use. You lay the wheel on the device and a bubble in oil tells you if the wheel is blanced. If not, the bubble will float out of the center circle, say at the 4 o'clock position. You would then add wheel weights to the wheel at the 4 o'clock position until the bubble is centered. That's how easy that is. Balancing a wheel is easy to do and no mystery at all.

Tip: Do not be overly concerned about balancing your motorcycle tire/rim. If you look at your wheel, you will see weights already installed. This means that your wheel is already balanced or close to near-perfect balance. What if you see no stick on wheel weights on your rim, or spoke wheel weights are missing or have flown off the rim? Then you will likely need a good degree of balancing. Yet, you likely didn't even realize it!

Note: The device you use to balance the wheel and tire assembly must have a low friction design so just barely touching the wheel with your finger in the device permits the tire to rotate on the axle. You can't do it with the wheel on the bike unless all axle nut pressure is released and disk brake caliper removed and even then you could run into too much friction. The wheel needs to fall from the mild force of gravity to static balance a wheel.

Fig. 8-1 Harley-Davidson Rim on Static Balance Stand

Fig. 8-1 shows a Harley-Davidson wheel to be balanced. Yes, you can balance the rim without the tire, then install the tire and check the balance to make fine adjustments. This procedure of balancing the wheel may or may not have been performed at the factory. You can also forego this step, install the tire and balance afterward. Some heavy cast wheels are so out of balance it can be worth your time to balance the rim without the tire, but do install the sprocket and disk brake rotor too before you balance the rim.

Fig. 8-2 No-Mar® Brand Static Balancing Stand

Note: You can easily build a wheel balancing stand out of wood and use your bike's axle set into V-notches in the wood. There will be some drag from the grease in the wheel hub, but it works. I say why bother when you can get a nice ball bearing unit like in Fig. 8-2 that will serve you well for a lifetime of use.

Fig. 8-2 reveals the No-Mar® brand static tire balancer. You can see it is just a stand with a axle rod sitting on two roller bearings. The axle rod has two black cones that can slide into the wheel's inner bearing races for a snug fit when rotating the wheel. These balancing stands are not expensive to purchase. You can also make one yourself out of wood and cut a V-notch at the top of each riser for the axle to rest upon the top posts. Use your bike's axle as it will fit tightly in the wheel bearings for easy rotation.

Fig. 8-3 shows the wheel and mounted tire on a wheel balancing stand. You can buy a wheel balance support at any motorcycle parts supply, and they are listed in many motorcycle parts catalogs. You can also make one yourself using a steel rod (your bike's axle will work just fine) placed in two V-notches in wood stands, or even place the steel rod in a protective jaw bench vise and slip the hub's wheel bearings over the steel rod. You just want the wheel to rotate easily around the steel rod that will act like an axle. The steel rod need not be perfectly matched to the size of the axle and can be much smaller in diameter.

Fig. 8-3 Wheel Mounted On Low Friction Static Balance Stand

Rotate the 6 o'clock portion of the wheel to the 12 o'clock and let it be. If you wish, you can start with the valve stem down in the 6 o'clock position as this is often, but not always, the heaviest part of the wheel. It does not matter where you start, just perform the above partial rotation of the wheel assembly and see where it stops.

If the wheel is heavy at one spot, it will fall downward and stop at the 6 o'clock position. Grab a 1/4 ounce wheel weight (don't stick it on just yet) and place it at the 12 o'clock position on the top of the tire and use a small strip of duct tape to hold it in place. Repeat the procedure. Add another wheel weight if need be. Keep doing this until you can rotate the wheel and the wheel no longer falls, it just hangs in balance. The weights counter balance the wheel obliterating the heavy areas.

Tip: So you think you get a better wheel balance at a dealership that has a dynamic wheel balancer machine? Well, think again. Most all of those machines are out of calibration and will not even be close to balancing your wheel and when you add in on top of this inexperienced or uneducated operators you are being robbed by the dealer. More people pay for wheel balancing and never get their wheels balanced due to out of calibrated machines. Do it yourself, save money and know it is done right. Many professional racing mechanics still prefer to use the static wheel balancer because it works.

Fig. 8-4 Affixing Temporary Wheel Weight With Duct Tape

Note: You don't have to affix the weight on the side of the wheel as shown in Fig. 8-4. You can place the weight on top the rubber tire itself and hold it in place with Duct Tape. Then once you have the correct position for a good wheel balance just put the weight onto the metal rim and stick it in place permanently. If you have a chain drive or you use cleaning degreasers or high pressure water to clean your rims you should smear some silicone rubber or other clear glue over the weight otherwise the degreaser will slowly break away the glue bond and the wheel weight will eventually fall off.

A minor, slow fall is okay for most cruiser riders. There is no need to get the wheel balance perfectly spot on. Rotate the wheel from many angles. If there is very slow falling or none at all, the wheel is statically balanced. If not? Keep adding and subtracting wheel weights as needed as you repeat the procedure above.

How to rotate wheel? Just move the wheel a few inches to the left or right. Let's use Fig. 8-4 as an example. The wheel has stopped and the wheel weight is as shown at the 12 o'clock position. Just rotate the wheel so the weight is in the 9 or 3 o'clock position and let the wheel go and see where the wheel stops. That is how you rotate the tire. No spinning is required.

Tip: Just remember, the heavy spot will always be where the wheel stops at the 6 o'clock position and the wheel weight will always be placed 180 degrees away which happens to always be at the 12 o'clock position in most all cases, but sometimes more wheel weights may need to be placed elsewhere. It is normal to have wheel weights placed at different sections of a rim. The ideal is to have just one weight on the wheel, but in the real world more weights are often required due to the rim being unbalanced when it was manufactured.

When the wheel is in balance, you can remove the wheel weight from the tire and affix it permanently to the rim. Do this task one wheel weight at a time, being careful to put the weight precisely on the rim where the weight was on the tire. Then check the balance again and make any adjustments as needed. Meaning, add more weights or remove weights if need be.

If you have spoke wheels, there are special wheel weights that clamp around the spoke. You need not stick the weight to these rims, but you can.

Tip: Yes, you can affix the weight to the rim on a spoke wheel with glue. There is no law saying you must use spoke weights on spoke wheels. The benefit of the spoke weight is they clamp on a spoke and will never come unglued and fling off.

On cast rims (no spokes), the wheel weights have a sticky glue to affix the wheel weight to the rim. They can fall off due to cleaning chemicals and high-pressure washes. You can apply Gorilla Glue® instead of the glue that comes on the weight, or you can use silicone rubber to hold the weights to the rim. Racers use duct tape. It works, but it looks bad. If you smear clear silicone rubber over the exterior of the weights where the weight meets the rim, this keeps water and cleaning solvents from dissolving the glue under the weights.

How critical is balancing your tire/rim? Surprisingly, on most bikes manufactured today, the rims are closely balanced (though some are way out of balance) and the tires manufactured are also close to a decent degree of balance (unless the tire is defective from a faulty molding process). It means that in many cases (but not all) you can actually ride away without any balancing weights and you may not feel any vibration or wheel hopping.

Consider also the professional dirt bike racer. He begins with perfectly balanced wheels. Once he hits mud the wheels are out of grossly balance, but the race continues on at high speeds without a hitch.

I am not saying not to balance your tires. What I am getting at is this; that when you do balance your tires they may not need to be perfectly balanced. Just close is usually fine, unless you are riding beyond highway speed limits. The higher speed you ride, the more critical tire/wheel balance will be. Many riders are riding around just fine with unbalanced wheels. Their wheel weights have long ago fallen off, and they don't even realize it. And many times your tire installer forgot to balance your wheels and you'll not even know it. Amazing, but true.

Tip: Once you have balanced your rim with the new tire installed, write down the number of weights and the weight (in ounces) of each. As long as you are not changing to a different brand or model of tire, your wheel/tire may not even need to be rebalanced. Many times I have put on new tires and found the wheel dead on or slightly off balance, and that did not require adding or subtracting any wheel weights.

Tip: If you have placed four 1/4 oz. weights you can supplement those four for a single 1 oz. weight.

It never hurts to balance your wheel and tire spot on to a perfect balance, being diligent to get the assembly as perfect as you can. For most street cruisers it will be a waste of time as long as the balance is off by only a couple ounces or three. I have tested riding new tires intentionally out of balance by four ounces, and I could not see any difference in feel, ride quality, tire wear, braking, etc., at normal highway speeds. All was fine up to 80 miles per hour.

Tip: Some wheels are so out of balance they require an unusually strange amount of heavy weight to get the tire into balance. This is usually due to the rim being out of balance and not the tire. If you look at many motorcycle in new showroom floors you will see some brands and models have a lot of weights while others have very little. The rear wheel often requires more weights than the lighter front wheel.

So if you are balancing your wheel and find you are lacking a few ounces of weight or over weighted by a few ounces, don't sweat it. This is good news for the novice attempting to balance wheels for the first time. Close is close enough. It need not be absolutely perfect unless you ride a sport bike at high speeds and take deep corners. How many people are riding their motorcycles with out of balance wheels? Too many to count! In fact, your wheel goes out of balance each thousand miles you ride. By the time you need a new tire your wheel is out of balance, in most cases not by much, but still it is out of balance.

Important: If you have lost your wheel weights long ago and find you need to keep adding more than four ounces to the wheel to get it balanced, so be it. The only fix is to remove heavy rim material, but that will "weaken" the rim's strength. Don't do it. Just add weights. Make sure the wheel is freely floating on the steel rod or axle when balancing. Any sticking will create friction and will force you to add weights unnecessarily! Some mechanics do not like to use the bike's axle just for this reason and prefer to use a smaller diameter rod.

Warning: If you ride a high-speed, street-class sport bike (exceeding 80 miles per hour) you should attempt to dial in your wheels' balance as close as you can to perfection. You don't need a dynamic balance even if you are competing on a high-speed closed course in professional racing. Keep in mind this book is written for the average street rider. Racing is an entirely specialized and demanding discipline that this book is not intended to explore.

Fig. 8-5 Weight Placed On The Wheel Rim

Fig. 8-5 shows we have cleaned the area where the wheel weight will be attached with rubbing alcohol and we have put three segments of 1/4 oz. weights on the rim. These weights have a sticky foam backing so you just peel off the protective plastic layer and press on to a clean surface and the job is done. However, soap, water, cleaning agents over time can work its way past the foam backing and loosen the bond glue and the wheel weight will fly off. See Fig. 8-6 for caulking the weights.

Note: Applying glue or duct tape to cover the wheel weights does not look nice. But guess what? Hardly nobody notices and if some observant does happen to notice and comment on it, who cares? Really, who cares? The odds are the critic has lost his wheel weights months ago and is not even aware of it. And the odds are even greater this guy does not even know how to change his own tires or balance his own wheels.

Note: Balance weights need not all be installed on the same side of the wheel's rim. If you have to attach six weights put three on each side to better balance the wheel axially so centrifugal force will not lopside the wheel's spin to the left or to the right. It is not critical for street use, but you may want to do this for appearances.

Tip: My new Harley-Davidson came with no wheel weights installed on the front wheel. They simply forgot to install them or the weights fell off during delivery I will never know. I never bothered to complain nor did I rebalance the wheel. I just ran it as is for it never gave me any handling or tire wear problems. Just goes to show you that 99.999% of the time a cruiser motorcycle's wheel out of balance is just not a critical as many people will tell you. If you are working on a customer's bike that is a different story, remove the wheel and balance the wheel. You may need to add a few 1/4 ounce weights.

Speed: The faster you ride the more important wheel balance becomes. Speeds above 70 mph and especially beyond 80 mph wheel imbalance shows its face mainly as a vibration. Sport bikes are more sensitive than cruisers and need a closer balancing because they are lighter and faster. Static balancing is still okay to use.

Fig. 8-6   Gluing Weights To Rim or Caulking Edges

Here in Fig. 8-6 we are applying clear silicone rubber glue all around the wheel weights so chemicals and road grime will not loosen the weight's foam backing glue. You can use any other clear glue to act as a weather seal and help keep the weights from gradually migrating out of position and fall off the wheel. Or you may option to just use no glue at all and rely on the sticky foam tape on the wheel weight. Use whatever system you desire and don't feel guilty about it.

Look at all those wheel weights on the rim in Fig. 8-6 having ten weights. Most people will cry foul and say this procedure is wrong if one must use this many weights on a rim to balance the tire and rim. Problem is, they are wrong. This wheel actually came from the Triumph factory with many wheel weights applied and the back wheel is even worse. Yes, you can use heavier weights. Instead of eight 1/4 ounce you can apply just one 2 ounce weight to the rim. There is no rule or regulations here. Less looks better, but all methods will function okay.

Wheel weights were once made of lead, but now alternative heavy metal so are taking their place. The weights come in strips as shown in Fig. 8-7. You simply snap off the weight from the strip. They come with a sticky foam backing. Start your balancing using 1/4 ounce size weights. After you have balanced the wheel and tire assembly you can then use heavier weights to replace the multiple smaller weights. In Fig. 8-6 there are eight 1/4 ounce weights. You could replace these with just two 1-oz. weights if you prefer. You may have to reposition the two weights so rebalance the wheel before you affix the weights permanently.

Note: Some wheels like that shown in Fig. 8-6 are heavy wheels and much weights are required due to the imbalance condition of the heavy cast wheel. There are eight 1/4 ounce weights shown from the factory. I bet you few to nobody will be questioning your wheel weights. Nobody has ever questioned mine or commented that there are too many weights on the wheel.   Only a mechanic would recognize this anyway and suggest using four 1/2 oz. instead of eight 1/4 oz. weights.

WHEEL WEIGHT STRIPS

Fig. 8-7 reveals a strip of twelve 1/4 ounce wheel weights. You don't apply all of them to a wheel. You first break off four, two or one wheel weights and apply them to the tire or rim temporarily with duct tape as you balance the wheel. This way you can easily move the wheel weights, add or subtract weights. Once the wheel is in balance then you can permanently affix the wheel weight to the wheel as shown in Fig. 8-6. The back of the weights has a sticky foam glue. Just peel off the protective backing and stick the wheel on the rim. But before you do, clean the rim surface with rubbing alcohol and let dry for a few seconds, apply the wheel wieghts and hold them in position firmly for fifteen seconds to create a good bond.

Note: If you have a problem with wheel weights falling off your wheel then you may want to try applying some clear fast-bonding glue to the sticky tape or not use the foam tape at all and just rely on the glue. Bikes with chain drives often lose their wheel weights on the rear wheel because degreaser chemicals and soaps along with high pressure water is used to clean the wheel which dissolves the glue holding the wheel weights in place.

Tip: Don't use any glues on composite wheels such as plastic or carbon fiber. You don't want to harm the finish of the wheel or risk a deterioration of the rim's structural integrity. If you change tire brands the wheel will need to be rebalanced and the weights moved

And Fix Flat Tires

to a new location. Using glue can stain and ruin the good looks of your expensive composite rims.

Fig. 8-7 Strip of 12- 1/4 Ounce Weights.

CHAPTER 9

Installing Front Wheel

INSTALLING THE FRONT WHEEL

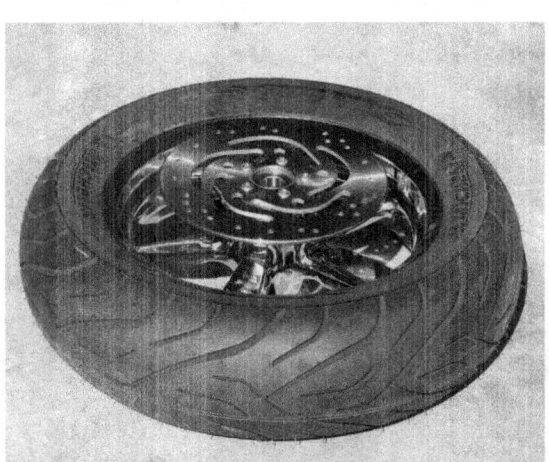

Fig. 9-1 Harley-Davidson 16" Fat Tire Installed on Rim - Job Well Done!

Warning: Make sure once you lift the bike to the desired height that you tie the bike down in such a manner as the bike can not slide off the jack or topple over off of the jack. It will be a disaster if the bike falls off the jack.

That nice looking chrome wheel in Fig. 9-1 is a $1,000 wheel, right? Wrong! That wheel is less than $400 and can be found in the Harley-Davidson parts catalog. You do not have to pay $1,000 for each wheel to get nice looking wheels for your bike.

This chapter reveals installing the front wheel on a Triumph America model motorcycle. It is very similar to many motorcycles in regards to the procedure, but you should use your bike's owner manual or a shop manual for the precise procedure if you feel so inclined, but you may want to try doing it yourself using this book as a general guide.

Fig. 9-2 shows motorcycle-specific axle grease being applied to the front axle shaft, coating it all around with a thin layer. Fig. 9-3 shows grease being applied into the wheel hub and Fig. 9-4 the speedometer drive-plate tabs and spline.

Take a good look at these two tabs and the speedometer hub drive cut-outs (hub is attached to the speedometer cable). These tabs will need to be aligned later when we put the wheel onto the bike. I just want you to see them clearly so installation will be easier for you. Many motorcycle do not use speedometer hubs anymore. However, smearing axle grease inside the hub chamber is still required in most cases. The wheel bearing ball bearings are normally sealed so they can't be lubricated, but if you can see ball bearings go ahead and push some fresh grease into the balls and race area.

Hint: If you see a lot of dirty black grease in an area, this is a hint that you should clean up this old grease. New grease should also be reapplied to this area, as long as it is an "internal" area. External areas are not greased. If you see grease it means it is excess grease flowing out from an internal area. Clean it up so this grease does not spread and flow on to the disk brake rotor. Black smears of grease extending from an axle onto a disk break rotor should never be greased as this is an "external" area.

Fig. 9-2   Lubing The Axle With Axle Grease

Note: You may be wondering what kind of axle grease must be used. Any axle grease will work just fine. Silkolene® is a motorcycle specific brand of grease I like to use. They also have a synthetic oil that Motorcycle Superbike School uses and when I tried it I found the oil was superior. Shifting was smooth, fuel mileage increased along with acceleration and engine longevity was never in question when I inspected the camshaft journals. Check it out.

Fig. 9-3   Lube Added to Wheel Hub Bearing Chamber

Roll the front wheel under the front fender with the disk brake rotor slipping between the two brake pads. Wiggle the wheel a bit to get the rotor between the disk pads. You may also need to lower the bike a bit if you see the left fork tab protruding striking the rotor.

This tab needs to be set below the rotor. See Fig. 9-7 as nothing will line up until it does fall into this shallow depression. You can see this depressed area in Fig. 9-3 and 9-7. Not all bikes will have a fork tab to obstruct an easy installation of the wheel, but most bikes will have a certain unique way of going about it. Just be patient and you will figure it out.

Danger: When lifting a wheel to a bike make certain you are not binding up the wheel or tire to the bike's frame, forks, disks, calipers, fender, etc so the bike is secretly being lifted off the jack. Only the wheel should be moving up or down, in or out. Pay attention here as the lifting is often subtle and your mind and eyes are looking elsewhere. You don't want the bike to fall over!

Trick: When lifting a wheel to the bike I keep this rule in mind. The wheel must lift into final position with little to no restriction. If a tightening is encountered then something is in the way. Stop, lower the wheel a little and try to find the problem, move things around and try again. It can be tricky and it is often a gentle balancing act. Be patient, the wheel will get installed.

Fig. 9-4 Lubing Axle Grease To Speedometer Hub

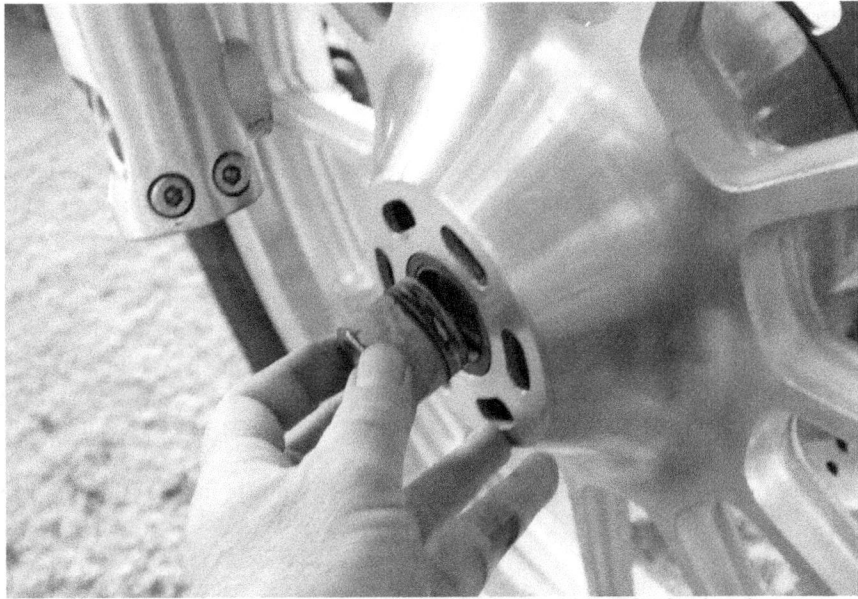

Fig. 9-5 Insert Spool Spacer In Opposite Side Of Wheel Hub

How To Install Tires on Motorcycles

Fig. 9-6 Spool (Spacer) Inserted Into the Wheel

Fig. 9-5 shows a spacer (spool) coated with a thin layer of grease and inserted into the wheel hub. There may be one for each side or just one spool. It is easy to lose these spools as they are dirty and hard to see and they roll away on the floor into hidden areas so store them in a magnetic parts pan or a plastic bowl. If you lose one you must find or replace it. You can't install the wheel without it.

Note: What is a spool or spacer? The spacer is just that, it is a cut of hollow metal tubing to a certain length that positions the wheel in a precise location between the fork tubes (or swing arm for rear wheel). Precise spacing is required to align the brake rotor to the caliper and for wheel alignment. Be aware they are not interchangeable so pay attention where each spacer must be returned. Use a parts bin to hold them so they don't get kicked and they roll away into oblivion or worse you trip on one and fall down. Some wheels only use one spacer while other wheels may require two of different size lengths. You can label them or engrave identifications on them if you wish for easy reinstallation.

Fig. 9-6 reveals a round and hollow spacer is being inserted into the wheel hub on the left (opposite) side of the wheel. Some motorcycle wheels have one on each side and each can be a different size. If you have trouble installing a wheel to the forks make sure these spacers are in the proper location. Position the wheel perfectly so the disk brake rotor enters the brake caliper. You may have installed the spools backwards or in the wrong side of the wheel. Some spools are short and others are long and if inserted wrong will offset the wheel into the wrong position so the brake disk rotor will not enter the slot in the brake caliper. It is possible a spool could have a narrow end to it so examine to see if your spools are narrow/tapered and where they should be oriented to the wheel/forks.

Remember I told you to mark the rotation of the wheel earlier? Now you know why. Slip in the wheel between the forks and check the wheel rotation arrow so the wheel will rotate in the proper direction. This has got to be performed for many reason for the tires to function properly as designed. Read the Question & Answer section for more advice.

Tip: Don't be surprised to find a juggling act is needed to get the front wheel in place (back wheels too). Use a scissor jack under the tire to help you slowly lift the wheel into position. Those spools have a nasty habit of falling out of position. If you run into a ton of trouble here I recommend removing the brake caliper (with the brake line intact) from the fork(s). This will give you more room to maneuver the wheel. You could even use a small diameter concrete rebar as a tool to run ahead of the axle and this will prevent spools from falling out of position.

What is the proper end point position we are seeking? We want the wheel axle hole to line with both fork axle holes so we can slip in the axle.

And Fix Flat Tires

Fig. 9-7 Wheel Insertion Between Forks

Note: Removing a wheel is always easier than installing one. Inserting the wheel can be tricky—you must lift the wheel, insert wheel axle spacers (spools, See Fig. 9-5) and maybe a speedometer hub too, and insert the axle. The problem is that all these parts love to drop away. It can be a balancing act. Use a scissor jack to raise the wheel into position in tiny increments of motion and that will make the job easier. Some bikes have tabs on the forks like the Triumph does in Fig. 9-7, and these tabs will get in the way.

The trick is to make the tabs clear the wheel hub's depressed area before inserting the axle. Removing the brake caliper is also recommended to give you wiggle room. Do not aggressively shake, push, pull, twist or apply up-or-down force. The motorcycle is on a lift, and we don't want it to fall off.

Tip: You can use a jack to lift and lower the entire bike, or to see-saw the bike if you only have one jack. It is not as convenient and easy as using the ATV/Motorcycle Jack (or scissor jack) to lift the bike and using a scissor jack to raise the wheel assembly into position when installing a new tire/wheel on the bike. The jack under the tire makes the job so much easier. You never have to lift the heavy wheel, hold it into position and try to get the axle into position or inserted and jiggle with spacer spools falling out, etc. Two jacks gets the job done pleasantly. See Fig. 9-8. The lift plate is not on the exhaust pipe, but resting on and lifting the unseen frame.

Danger: Always be aware the bike can be forced off the jack silently and slowly if you are lifting a wheel into position and the wheel contacts the motorcycle forks, fender, brake caliper or frame. When you lift a tire into position using a small jack under that wheel, keep your eyes peered on that wheel and the frame. Only the wheel should be rising. If you see the bike's frame rising it means it is raising the bike's frame right off the main ATV/Motorcycle jack. This will let the bike slide in any direction off the main lift. Very dangerous! Work slow, turn off the radio and pay attention to details.

Important Safety Tip: I usually take a brief interruption in the job just to walk around and see if the bike is still on the main jack and any supports under the rear wheel are still in place. It does not hurt to put the motorcycle in 1st gear. If the bike were to roll off the jack it will not roll very far if it is in gear, but it can still fall over. You never want a motorcycle to fall off a main jack/lift device as you can be crushed and the bike could rupture the gas tank and ignite.

Important: Pay attention when a bike is on a lift. Tie the bike down so it can not fall off the lift.

Now align the speedometer drive tabs (if your bike has one) by turning the wheel so the tabs are set top and bottom 11 o'clock and 5 o'clock. Then turn with your finger the speedometer spline in the wheel hub, so they are in the same position, and then insert the speedometer gear into the wheel hub. There will be some trial and error. Don't force anything. It will fall into place with ease when you get it aligned properly, but you may need to practice a bit to do so. When the speedometer is inserted properly, it will not be cocked but will sit flush in the wheel hub. See Fig. 9-4 and Fig. 9-7.

How To Install Tires on Motorcycles

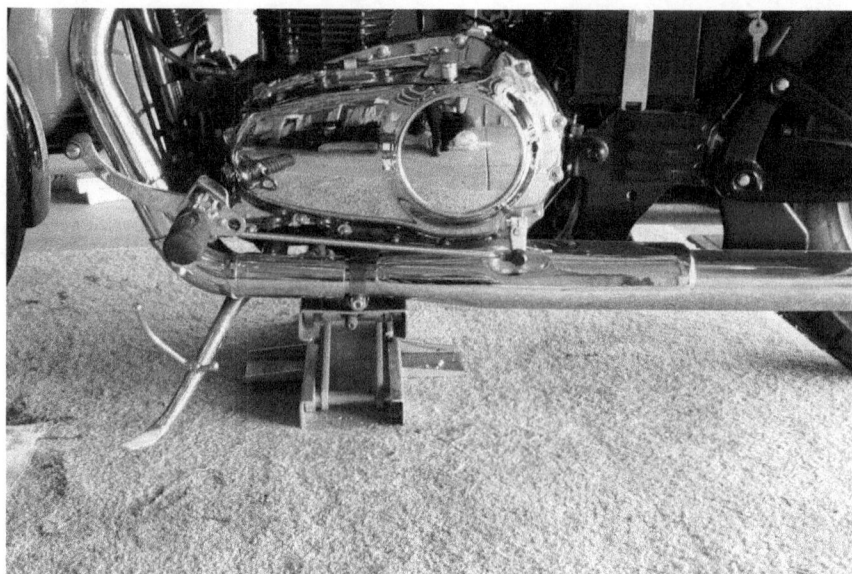
Fig. 9-8 K&L® Brand Scissor Jack Lifting Bike By The Frame

As you try to insert the axle and slightly wiggle the wheel to get the axle to slide into the wheel bearings, don't be surprised to see the speedometer fall out of position. Again, this is a balancing act. Once you get the hang of it, this won't cause you any more problems in the future. You will have trouble if you leave the speedometer cable attached, so disconnect it. It is held in place with a Phillips head screw.

Warning: Make sure the wheel axle is installed and the end nut is spun on at least hand-tight before proceeding to the next step. Remove any wood blocks from under the bike or rear wheel. No need to tighten the pinch bolts or torque the axle yet. Read your owner's or service manual for the wheel removal procedure specific for your motorcycle. If the forks on your bike have older type split-end axle caps install them hand tight so the axle can't fall out from the forks.

Make sure there are no tools under the bike and clean up any oil or grease on the floor or on the wheel and tire. The front tire and wheel install job is now finished.

Fig. 9-9 shows after the axle is inserted through the wheel and forks the end nut is inserted in the left fork and the axle is threaded into this nut.

Danger: After you insert the front axle, the front brake caliper must be installed and torqued to specification. You will also need to pump the brake lever so the brake pads are tight once again on the brake rotor. If the bike is in gear, set the gear shifter to neutral before rolling or starting the bike.

ALIGNING FRONT WHEEL TO FORKS

Now you can lower the bike onto the ground and remove the jack. Sit on the bike, straighten the front wheel, and roll the bike forward. Grab the front brake hard and pump up and down on the bike so the front forks bounce up and down. This helps center the forks to the axle.

If you fail to align the front forks to the axle you can stress the brake pads, warp the brake rotor and caliper brake pad pins including the wheel bearings for early failure. The front forks will track untrue and handling of the bike will suffer. So, if you forget, just loosen the axle nut and fork pinch bolts then bounce the front wheel up and down using a forward rolling motion and jamming on the front brake to "bounce" the forks to align with the axle. Bounce it three times should be enough.

Warning: Taking your bike to a dealer or repair shop for new tires will not guarantee this front wheel alignment to the forks will occur. In many instances it does not happen at all. You may never notice it. Then again, you may hear the brake pads are scuffing with a syncopated sound which can warp the brake disk rotors in less than 1,000 miles ruining the rotors and the pads. Most dealers use parts people or any employee they can grab in the dealership who has been "indoctrinated" to swap tires on motorcycles to do your bike. Forget about an experienced mechanic doing the job. A good reason to learn to change tires yourself. Believe me, you pay dearly for dealer mistakes!

And Fix Flat Tires

Fig. 9-9 Axle End Nut Screws Into Axle On Triumph

With the bike on the extended side stand as shown in Fig. 9-10. Now we can torque the front wheel axle. Set the 1/2" drive torque wrench to 60 Newton meters for the Triumph America (or 25 foot-pounds).

Note: Your bike's torque specifications will be very different. Check your owner's manual, or ask your motorcycle dealer for the torque specs. It is always best that you check with your dealer for "updated torque specifications" as the motorcycle factory frequently makes safety-related changes and are not updated in old service manuals. Even the torque values used in this book may be outdated.

For the Triumph America model motorcycle use the Motion Pro® 24mm hex tool to hold the axle so it will not turn then use a 12mm Hex to tighten by turning clockwise. Stop turning when the torque wrench tells you to stop. The left side of Fig. 9-10 shows the torque wrench with a Hex bit, and the right side shows the special tool Motion Pro® brand Allen wrench. Hex and Allen are interchangeable terms.

Fig. 9-10 Holding The Front Axle With Special Tool

Pinch bolts tighten to 20 Nm (or 185 inch-pounds), all four of them. Use the 6mm hex drive with a torque wrench. There are two Allen pinch bolts on each fork. Fig. 9-11 and Fig. 9-12 shows a 3/8" drive inch-pound torque wrench being used.

How To Install Tires on Motorcycles

Fig. 9-11 Using Torque Wrench To Tighten Front Fork Pinch Bolts

Fig. 9-12 Torque Wrench Tightening Fork Pinch Bolt

CHAPTER 10

Removing Rear Wheel

REMOVING THE REAR WHEEL

I'm not covering in great detail how to remove and install the rear wheel or the new tire. I give you a general itemized list of instructions below. Installing a rear tire is generally the same procedure to install a front tire. All of the tricks and tips apply. In fact, if you run into trouble installing your new rear tire to the rim just follow the front tire instructions. I will give some instructions for installing the rear wheel in the next section.

The rear tire change procedure is the same as the front tire. Your owner's manual or a specific service manual will explain how to remove and install the rear wheel, adjust the chain/belt, etc.

And Fix Flat Tires

Also, do expect to have more trouble installing the new rear wheel tire on the rear wheel rim. The rubber is usually thicker and the tire is often wider. More rubber means more effort required.

Check your owner manual as they often do give tips and advice on how to remove the motorcycle's wheels. If not, a service manual will.

1. Break the axle nut loose while the rear wheel is still on the ground. Some bikes have a cotter pin that must be straightened and removed with pliers before the nut can be turned.
2. Jack up the bike so the rear wheel is off the ground. Place a wood block under the front wheel if needed. Do not let the bike slip, slide, or fall off the jack. Put transmission in first gear.
3. Place a scissor jack under the rear tire, remove the axle, remove the chain or drive belt from the sprocket, and lower the tire to the ground. As long as you drop the wheel straight down and not cocked sideways, the disk brake rotor should not cause concerns. Once the rotor is clear of the brake caliper, you can flip the tire on an angle to slip the tire away from under the rear fender. Note the direction the axle needs to be reinserted. Was the axle nut on the left or the right side of the bike? _____.
4. Remove any wheel hub spacer spools. Place them in a magnetic parts tray along with the axle nut and axle.
5. Demount the old tire and mount the new tire.
6. Clean and grease the axle and insert any spacers back into the wheel hub.

INSTALLING REAR WHEEL

1. Slip the wheel under the rear fender, place drive chain or belt around the sprocket or pulley, lift the wheel by hand or preferably with scissor jack, and slip the disk brake rotor into the caliper, then insert the axle. If the caliper gets in the way, unbolt it from the frame. Threading the axle through the disk brake bracket and spacer spools can be troublesome. Sometimes you even need to use a long screwdriver to slightly spread the swing arm a bit and let the wheel hub axle spools slide into place. Use a scissor jack to align the wheel's hub bearings with the swing arm frame axle holes. Do not shake the wheel too much, as this can cause the bike to slide away from the lift and fall on you. There is no need to apply heavy force up, down, or side to side.
2. You may need to tap the axle gently with a rubber or brass hammer for the axle to slide all the way into place. Don't use heavy force; soft tapping is fine. Heavy hammering can strip the external axle nut threads. If you do accidently strip the thread, any shop can fix it with a pipe thread die. If the axle seems stuck, it is stuck. Parts are still out of alignment. It takes some wiggling of the wheel and simultaneous tapping of the axle sometimes to get things done. When the axle is now exiting the swing arm you can now proceed to step #3.
3. Install the axle nut finger-tight. Do not torque it. Reinstall the brake caliper if you removed it.
4. Adjust the drive chain or belt if necessary.
5. Remove any wood blocks under the bike or front wheel, and then lower the bike to the ground and roll the jack away.
6. Torque the axle nut to specifications, readjust chain or belt if needed, tighten chain/belt adjuster bolts and their locknuts.
7. Pump up the foot brake lever to set the brake pads to the rotors.
8. Clean up the area. Put transmission in neutral.
9. Make sure there are no tools under the bike, and clean up any oil or grease on the floor or on the wheel and tire. The rear tire and wheel install job is now finished.

Fig. 10-1 shows the view from the rear of a Triumph America with rear wheel removed. Note the brake caliper hanging on left. The caliper should be supported and not hung as damage to the brake line could occur. You will find many mechanics ignoring this rule when they work on your bike. You can see the inner swing arm brake caliper metal location tab on the left swing arm. See also Fig. 10-2.

Fig. 10-2 shows a welded metal protrusion on the left swing arm called a "tab". The brake caliper has a slot in it that must slide fully into this tab. You will need to shake and wiggle the wheel gently to do this (don't let the bike fall off the jack). Binding can occur as you lift the rear wheel with a scissor jack as the caliper wants to jam and this happens on many bikes. There is a formula, a series of steps that must be completed to get everything back into alignment. When I did my Victory motorcycle tire install and the rear wheel was terribly tricky to get the wheel back into position. I had to lift the wheel, tilt the caliper at an angle, lift the wheel a bit more and finally everything lined up.

An experienced mechanic figures out these things, but even for mechanics the first time is a "learning experience." My advice is to write down the installation formula when you discover it as best you can so the next time the job will be easier to do. Don't rely on your memory, you will forget and have to figure it out all over again.

Fig. 10-1   View of Triumph Rear Wheel Removed

Fig. 10-2   Swing Arm Frame Brake Caliper Tab

Fig. 10-3   Brake Caliper Inserted Into Swing Arm Tab

In this case, the Triumph motorcycle's rear brake caliper assembly must first be installed in this slot and tab as shown in Fig. 10-3. Be aware as you insert the wheel under the fender to align the axle holes this caliper plate will often fall out of position. If it does it will prevent the axle holes to line up.

Note: Learn to install brake pads on your motorcycle. Go to: JamesRussellPublishing.com and click on the books section.

Fig. 10-4 Axle Sliding Into Left Swing Arm

Fig. 10-4 reveals the rear axle is inserted into the chain adjuster, swing arm and just through and past the brake caliper bracket. Do this to help keep everything in alignment then insert the wheel spools on both bearing hubs then slowly lift the wheel using a screw jack to align the axle. Slow movements and very little force is the rule when I bike is on a jack.

Tip: If wheel bearing hub spacer spools keep falling out of position as you insert the wheel here's the trick. Take a screwdriver and spread the swing arm away from the spool just a little bit then lift the wheel and this will give you the clearance you need to get the wheel between the swing arms.

Note: There can be many different formulas to install the wheels. I am only giving one example. Your bike will need its own special procedure. In most cases it is a balancing act getting all the components to line up so the axle can slide through the components. Softly tapping the end of the axle with a rubber mallet is a common practice, but if you do it right the axle should just glide into place. When you figure out the unique sequence of events to install your wheel write it down as a formula so the next time it will be easier to do. The first time is always the most frustrating and most difficult and most time consuming. Each time thereafter becomes easier and easier to do. So, be patient and forgiving with yourself for you are learning a new skill. You will make dumb mistakes, stupid errors and that is okay. When I buy a new motorcycle I have the same problems as you do!

CHAPTER 11

Replace Tire on Spoke Rim

HOW TO REPLACE A TUBE TIRE

The procedure is almost the same as for the tubeless tire, with only a few alterations. Yes, you may install a tubeless tire onto a spoke rim as long as you install the correct size tube. The below procedure is good for both street bikes and dirt bikes.

How To Install Tires on Motorcycles

Fig. 11-1 Rim Lock Clamp For Tube Type Tire

The rim clamp shown in Fig. 11-1 is typical. It is a rubber coated horseshoe shape device inserted into the rim, but is left loose then you install the tire's lower bead on the rim using tire irons (or rotary machine mount bar). You then hand tighten the rim clamp nut to lower it just so it is floating above the rim and tire. Powder the innertube with talcum powder, puff the tube up with a smidgen of air, insert the tube and make sure the tube rides on the upper rubber concave section of the rim protector. Install the top bead of the tire on the rim using your tire irons. Bounce the tire on the ground a few times, then inflate the tire to operating pressure. The tire should be concentrically installed to the wheel rim. If not, deflate, bounce tire on a hard surface in different spots and inflate and check concentricity of tire to rim and air pressure again. If all is well, tighten the rim clamps (there can be more than one).

In Fig. 11-1 the black rubber surface of the rim clamp cradles the innertube. It has no desireable effect on the tube. It is rubber coated so as not to abrade the tube and that is all. The gray plastic area on the sides of the rim clam squeezes the tire down to the rim locking the into place with the rim. This rim clamp only shows one nut on the bolt. Some will have two nuts. The lower nut tightens the rim clam and the upper nut acts as a locknut when tightened against the lower nut.

Note: Many street motorcycles with spoke and cast wheels do not have rim clamps. These devices are designed to prevent the tire from rotating on the rim when ridden hard such as for racing purposes. The cast wheel can have them for drag racing to lock the tire to the rim. Spoke rims need them to prevent the tire from rotating on the rim for the tire will drag the innertube along with it and the valve stem will be torn right off the rim causing a rapid and dangerous blow-down deflation of the tire. Dirt bikes most always have rim clamps.

Don't forget to read the Question & Answer section as more tips and advice are given.

What is a rim-band? It is a continuous wide band of rubber like a rubber band then encircles the drop-center area of the rim covering the spoke nipples so the spoke ends do not puncture the tube. The rim-band has one reinforced hole in it where the tube's valve stem passes through it and the rim. However, never let the spoke threaded ends protrude beyond the nipple threaded ends as they will eventually puncture the rim-band and innertube giving you a flat tire. This can happen if you attempt to true your spoke wheel with the tire still installed on the bike. The rim-band is a one-time use device to be renued each time you replace tires.

BASIC PROCEDURE - REPLACING INSTALLING TUBE-TYPE TIRE

1. Remove wheel from the bike. On a dirt bike, loosen up the rim clamps (Fig. 11-1) on the rim before you do anything. Mark the rim clamp holes on the rim so you can replace them properly and not insert them into the valve stem hole in the rim. When installing a new tire, always install a new tube and a new rim band to cover the spoke end nipples. Always check the size markings on the tube so that the correct tire size appears on the tube to match the tire size. Do not fit tubes in radial motorcycle tires or radials on tube rims requiring tubes unless the tubes bear matching size and radial (R) markings.

2. Remove the locknut(s) on the tube valve stem that is poking out of the rim. Remove the tire and old tube and the inner rubber spoke band inside the rim. Clean the rim from any rust and feel with your finger for any sharp or roughness that needs to be sanded down smooth. Rust under the rubber rim-band is okay as long as no sharp flakes are emitting from the metal that can cut the rim band.

3. Insert the rim clamps, but do not tighten them. Unlike a tubeless tire/rim combination there is no permanent rim-affixed valve stem to replace on the wheel as the tube has its own valve stem. Always replace tube with a new tube of the proper size for the rim and tire you are using. Heavy duty tube is always better.

4. Install a new rubber spoke rim-band inside the rim aligning the rim-band hole with the rim's valve stem hole. Install the lower side of tire to the rim. Slightly inflate new tube so it is puffed up, dust it lightly with Talcum powder, insert the tube into the

rim starting with inserting the tube's valve stem through the rim-band hole, then into the valve stem rim hole (not the rim clamp hole) and spin on the valve stem locknut(s), but do not tighten at this time. Check to see that the tube is not twisted but is round in shape everywhere. If all the rim holes are identical in size? Rim clamps, if two are used will be polar opposite from each other. The one off center will be the tube's valve stem hole.

5. With the lower section of the tire installed and a new tube also installed make sure the innertube is sitting on top of the rim clamps and is not folded under the clamps in any way or the clamp will pinch and ruin the tube. The rim clamp should be riding above the tire bead. You should be able to push the rim clamp up and down about an inch to insure it is not wedged anywhere. Dirt, adventure and drag racing bikes use rim clamps, but cruiser motorcycles usually do not. Rim clamps are usually only found on rear wheels.

6. Lubricate the upper rubber rim-band surface with or Talcum powder after you install it so the tube won't stick to the rim-band and tend to fold the innertube when you install the tube into the tire. Make sure you have the right size tube and the valve stem on the tube. It may be straight or angled so look for this variation. Do not insert a straight valve core into a angled valve core rim hole. You need the correct tube valve stem angle. You can use paste tire lubricant if you have no Talcum powder, but Talcum is best for it keeps the tube lubricated for thousands of miles. This is good for tubes to reduce heat and friction!

Note: How to not pinch a tube with a tire iron? Insert your finger to push the tube away then insert your tire iron. This will keep the tube away from the flipping motion of the tire iron that can grab the tube and cut it. If you can't insert your finger due to the end point being reached mounting the tire try inserting a blunt piece of plastic, cardboard or other soft nonmetallic thin item to nudge the tube away from the tire irons. K&L (KLSupply.com) makes a handy hand tool called the Tire Tamer® specific for saving you time and skinned knuckles when inserting valve stems, rim locks and innertubes. It keeps the tire away from the rim so you can work with greater ease in tight spaces. You don't have to buy one, but it will make the job easier.

7. Install the top bead of the upper side of the tire to the rim. When inserting tire irons, make sure the innertube has a little touch of air in the tube so that the tube will be "puffy." This will help (but not prevent) a tire iron from grabbing on to the tube "pinching" the tube and creating an air leak. Do not inflate the tube with high air pressure. Just a few psi inside the tube will do the trick. We just don't want a flat tube flopping around inside the rim with tire irons poking around to pinch the new tube. Position the tube down into the rim's drop center.

8. Use the same tire iron procedure as installing a tubeless tire on the rim using rim protectors and being careful not to pinch the tube (or use same machine procedure). Make sure the rim clamps have slack and push against the surface of the innertube. When installing the tire near the rim clamp push the rim clamp inward so it will ride above the tire bead. This way once the tire is installed the rim clamp will clamp down on the tire's bead area locking it down in place once it is tightened. It is best to use paste lubricant when installing the tire to the rim.

9. After installing the tire, inflate to the tire's normal operating pressure and spray a soapy water solution on the rim, tire and spoke nipple ends looking for any leaks. Tighten snugly (not too tight) the rim clamp nuts and test for leaks one more time.

10. Deflate the tire completely and then inflate again to normal operating pressure. This is so the innertube will not form folds or wrinkles. Also check to make sure the tire is installed concentric to the rim.

11. Snug down the locknuts on the valve stem.

12. See the wheel balancing section. You do not need to use weights that clamp around a spoke. You can use adhesive weights just as if you had cast wheels. You can see new Harley-Davidson motorcycles with spoke wheels doing this. Of course, clamping the weight to a spoke is best as they do not work loose and fall off especially on dirt bikes.

You just need to use a bit more care to keep your tire irons from pinching the innertube. The same care and attention is required when using a rotary mounting bar to install the tire; the bar can easily grab and pinch the tube. Tire lubricant that smears on the innertube will not hurt anything as long as it is a tire lubricant and not motor oil or any other solvent or cleaner.

Danger: Do not use window cleaner or any other household cleaner to mount tires. It may dry out, crack or eat a hole in the innertube from corrosive deterioration. Make sure you always install new, heavy-duty innertubes (not standard thin-wall) when you change your cruiser motorcycle tires. Tubes do wear and dry out. Keep tires correctly inflated. A tire that is very under-inflated generates a lot of heat, which can lead to a blowout. Always put a new rim band and tube when installing new tires.

Don't feel bad if you pinch a tube. Don't patch it, just throw it away. Even the best tire installers sometimes pinch a tube and when learning, it is the learning process we all had to go through. Don't get mad, don't get angry, it just happens that's all.

DUNLOP TIRE COMPANY'S SAFETY TAG

When you buy a new tire, there should be a tag on the tire giving advice. If not, here's what the tag should say. It is good to review it.

Improper mounting can cause tire explosion and serious injury.
Wear approved eye protection.
Clean and lubricate beads and rims.
Note directional arrows on sidewall if applicable.
Lock assembly on mounting machine or place in safety cage.
Set air hose relief valve at 40 psi.
Use extension gauge and hose with clip-on air chuck.
Stand back with no part of your body within the perimeter of the assembled tire and rim.
Inflate with (valve) core in valve stem.
Never inflate beyond 40 psi to seat beads.
Spin wheel to check bead seating, alignment and clearance.
If the beads do not seat by 40 psi, deflate and repeat the above procedures.

SAFETY WARNING

Always use tires of the same size and construction (radial or bias ply) as the original equipment or replacement.
Always use the same brand and design tires on the front and rear wheels.

Always use specified tires in replacement … refer to the motorcycle owner's manual.

RUN IN

Dealers and tire fitters must warn riders that when new tires are fitted they should not be subjected to sudden acceleration, hard cornering, maximum power, or braking for at least 100 miles. Failure to do so may result in loss of control and serious injury.

CHAPTER 12

Fixing Flat Tires

HOW TO FIX A FLAT TIRE ON YOUR MOTORCYCLE

HELPING OTHERS IN NEED

When you carry a flat-tire repair kit with air compressor, you can help others. Whenever groups ride together, one member should have one at all times. Most importantly, the person with a flat tire may be you—all alone in the middle of nowhere with no means to call for help.

TUBELESS TIRES ONLY

If you purchased a motorcycle with spoke wheels, you are out of luck if it has a rubber innertube. You can't use plugs to fix a flat tire with a tube in the rim. You need a patch or a new innertube, but you can try a fix-a-flat system in a can as in Fig. 12-3. You also need tire irons and space to use them, which many cruiser motorcycles don't have. The only practical solution is to tow the motorcycle, remove the wheels then replace the tube.

What if you have a tube tire? You can try to use a liquid sealant and inflate the tire and hope it works. It likely will if you only have a small nail hole. Ride slowly on surface streets, not on a highway, and get to a repair shop as soon as you can. The innertube and the tire will need to be replaced.

Tip: If the tire has a nail in it, pull it out. If it has a screw head showing, unscrew it. This is so you will do less damage to the tube. But don't do anything yet. Read the next paragraph.

But before you call a tow truck try this. Mark the location where the nail is with tape, paint, fingernail polish or ink. After you have inserted the liquid sealant (Fig. 12-2 or Fig. 12-3), add some air to the tire, rotate the wheel a few times then pull out the nail slowly, rotate the tire three times and add air to the tire to normal operating pressure. Test for leaks near the nail hole. Use water or soda pop. If you have soap, make a soapy mixture and apply it to the nail hole and look for a stream of bubbles. If the bubbles are tiny, you may be able to ride on slowly. The tire sealant may seal even that leak in a few minutes.

Note: You cannot fix a flat tire on a motorcycle if the tire has a gash in the sidewall or a lengthy wound in the tread area. Tire plugs or tube sealant won't work. Nothing will work! But if you have a small round hole, like a nail or screw puncture in the tread area, you can usually fix the tubeless tire temporarily with a plug to get you home or to a repair shop to install a new tire. Keep in mind that even tubeless tires can use products such as in Fig. 12-2 or Fig. 12-3.

A blown innertube cannot be fixed or even patched safely and only small nail holes can be patched on the innertube.

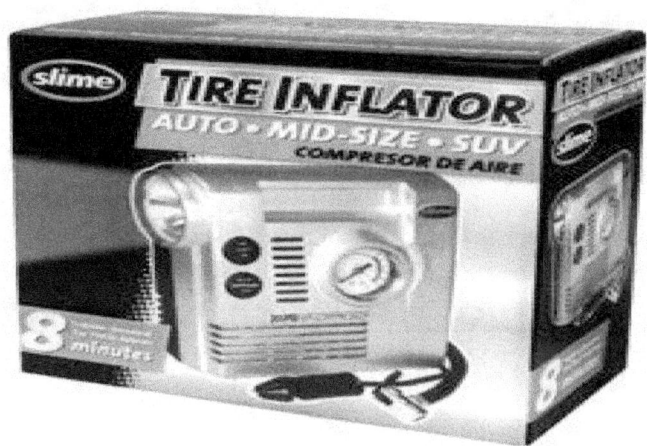

Fig. 12-1 Slime® Brand 12-Volt Portable Air Compressor

As shown in Fig. 12-1 I have used a Slime® brand 12-Vold portable air compressor to bail me out when on the road with a flat tire. Use the motorcycle specific brand or make sure it has a power source that can fit a motorcycle coaxial or SAE power connection to your battery. You can buy power adapters especially where heated clothing is sold. Once you install the leads to the motorcycle battery you can plug in your heated clothing, other electrical devices or the air compressor when needed. I use the coaxial type. The power lead shown in Fig. 12-1 is a cigarette lighter type. You can purchase battery connected adapters for these portable air compressors which is what I like to use. Sometimes they are included in the box. If not, sites like MotorcycleSuperstore.com has them. See Fig. 12-4.

Important: The battery pigtail (positive & negative) connection that will be installed on your motorcycle battery (or whatever system you are using) must have the proper amperage rated fuse between the battery and the air compressor device. Many people use their auxiliary power supply to power their heated clothing that may require 10 amps, but if the tire inflating air compressor needs 15 amps, then change the in-line fuse on the power cord to 15 amps so you are not blowing fuses trying to inflate your tire. You don't deserve that grief. I suggest using the pigtail power supply cord that has the highest amperage to safely handle 15 amps from the battery. Many of these generic power cords only come with a 7.5 amp fuse not even enough current to power heated clothing.

Another reason to purchase the motorcycle air compressor model is it is smaller in size. It is a good idea to buy a air compressor that has a pressure gage on the air compressor. Once when fixing a flat tire while traveling, I found my pressure gage broken. I had to fill the tire using my hand pressure to feel the firmness of the tire's sidewall which will get you down the road, but is not accurate.

FIX-A-FLAT SYSTEM - HOW TO USE

The procedure to fix a flat using aerosol cans as shown in Fig. 12-3 is essentially identical for tube and tubeless tires. There are preventative products you can buy to insert into the tire before you get a flat tire. See Fig. 12-2. If you have tube tires you should use them. Read, Spoke Wheel Flat Prevention. It is optional for tubeless tires as the sealing product can make a sticky mess of the rims and will need to be cleaned when changing tires. The Slime system in Fig. 12-2 is not an aerosol product. You just deflate the tire, inject the contents and use your portable air compressor to reinflate the tire. Insall this product before you get a flat tire, but if you didn't you can do so when you do pick up a nail. You will still need an air compressor with this product to inflate your tire.

Fig. 12-2 Slime® System

But before you do plug a tire or call a tow truck if you have a tubeless tire you could try to fix it with Fix-A-Flat® in Fig. 12-3 or simular product. The can has an explosive sealant or an inert compressed gas, but you should carry a portable motorcycle air compressor with you in case you need to add more air than the can gives you! This fix can work to get you home or to a nearby motorcycle repair shop, as long as the tube is not blown with a large hole. A nail hole should be okay, even a small screw hole. If it works, it will save you time and money. Read the instructions on the can, but this is how it works.

FIX A FLAT USING AEROSOL CAN METHOD

Fig. 12-3 Fix-A-Flat® Aerosol Can Is Portable & Needs No Tools

Warning: Do not use any sealant in a tubeless tire with an internal tire pressure monitoring sensor in the internal area of the rim and tire. Method can be used for tube and tubeless tires and no tools or air compressors are required. Visit: FixaFlat.com as they have lots of tire repair products. The large sizes for light truck tires have lots of air to inflate motorcycle tires with ease. Fig. 12-2 and Fig. 12-3 can be used if they "temporarily" disable air pressure monitor system as long as the monitor is not destroyed and only needs to later be cleaned when the tire is changed.

1. Gently remove the bolt or nail by pulling it straight out, at the same time twisting the nail left and right. See Fig 15-5. If it is a threaded screw, try to work it out by unscrewing it, turning it counterclockwise with a screwdriver or pliers. Pulling or yanking on the penetrating object will rip the tire (or innertube) making a larger hole and the system may not work. These systems work best with small holes in the tire. Fig. 12-5 shows a tire that can not be patched or repaired due to sidewall damage.
2. Move the motorcycle so the valve stem is at the 8 or 4 o'clock position.
3. Remove the valve stem cap on the wheel and insert the hose from the can by screwing it onto the valve stem, turning the valve stem fitting clockwise; some fittings clamp onto the valve stem with a tightening lever on the chuck while others use a threaded knob. Make sure you have a good tight connection with the fitting. Not too tight, just finger-tight.
4. The can must be near the 4 or 8 o'clock position so the sealant will flow first into the tire (or innertube).
5. Push the button on the can to open the valve and put all of the contents into the tire. Some sealant foam may leak, but not too much. Make sure there is no kink in the hose. The tire should inflate. You may still need an air compressor.
6. Rapidly unscrew the hose from the valve stem so as to not lose air pressure.
7. Now rotate the tire by moving the motorcycle slowly. Just a few revolutions, but don't ride off just yet. Look where the nail hole was. Is air escaping from it? If not, you are ready to ride away, slowly, to give the sealant time to gel and seal the leak. Look at the tire. Does it still look flat? Can you squeeze the tire with your hand? If so, you need to add air. Get your portable air compressor (See Fig. 12-1) and fill the tire with air. Put the valve cap on, and you are okay to go. A dab of soapy water or plain water or soda-pop may

be used to test for air leak at the nail hole. Look for tiny bubbles.

8. Drive slowly, get off the freeway, or take side roads if you can. You should stay under 50 miles per hour and be prepared for the tire to go flat again. Sealants can work, but the hole in your innertube may be too large for it to last any distance.

9. Get to a motorcycle repair service and buy a new tube and tire.

10. Consider buying a motorcycle with cast wheels, or install cast wheels now on your current motorcycle so you can fix flat tires easily from now on.

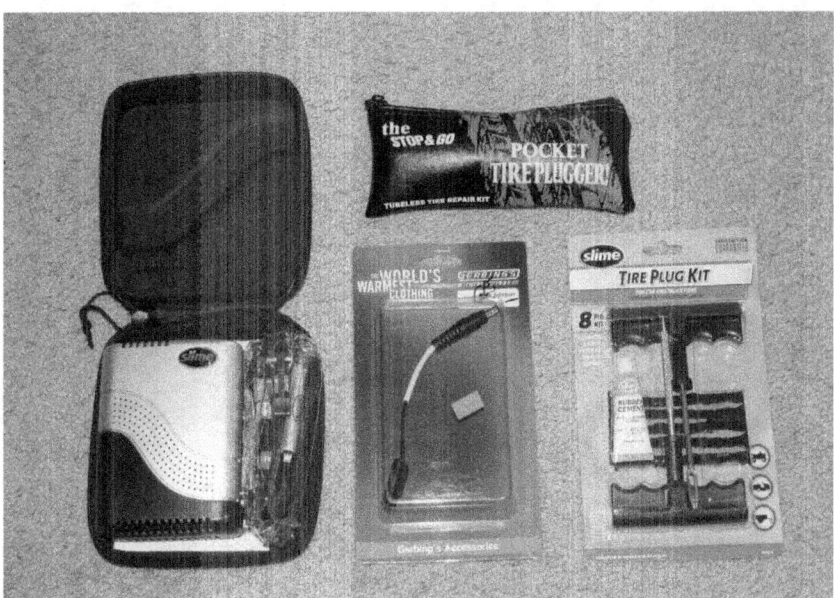

Fig. 12-4 Flat Tire Repair Kit With Electric SAE to Coax Adapter

Look at this simple kit in Fig. 12-4 you can carry with you in your motorcycle saddlebag or inside of a fork tool bag. The Slime® brand air compressor is on the left, center is a Gerbings® brand electrical power adapter SAE female to male Coax to run the compressor from a motorcycle battery. I use this setup if the air compressor requires a SAE (Society of Automotive Engineers) connection and the wires from the bike's battery have a Coax female connection which most riders with heated clothing will have installed on their bike's battery. On the right is a Slime® brand string rope repair plug system and above is a rubber mushroom plug system the, Pocket Tire Plugger®. Perfect for repairing tubeless tires! StopnGo® brand who makes the rubber mushroom plug system also makes string/rope tire repair kits.

Tip: When you install auxiliary wire connections direct to your battery you may want to carry a larger size fuse than 10 amps and install a 15 amp fuse. I have found this stops nuisance fuse blowing when operating heated clothing or the air compressor. At least carry extra 15 and 20 amp fuses in case you need them.

DON'T BUY A MOTORCYCLE WITH SPOKE WHEELS

You can't fix flat tires easily with tube spoke wheels. You can't even call a tow truck to fix the flat for you or tow your bike to an automotive service station. They don't have the know-how or the specialized tools to remove the wheel or tire from the rim. Generally your tube and tire must be fixed by a motorcycle dealer. Good business for them, bad for you. Let this be a lesson learned to always buy a motorcycle with cast or composite wheels. Now if you get a flat tire, any vehicle service station or tire dealer can fix it with a plug, just like they do with car tires. To learn how to purchase a motorcycle, go to JamesRussellPublishing.com for free articles to save you time, money and grief.

Note: If you have spoke wheels, you should always have a tube patch repair kit and a set of tire irons with an air compressor. You may come across a mechanic who knows how to use these tools to fix your leaking innertube. Consider installing cast wheels or the more expensive (but not necessarily better) spoke rims that are permanently sealed inside the rim to accept a tubeless tire without a tube. They are tubeless spoke rims. Carry special tools to remove wheels. Some bikes require a tool like in Fig. 2-13.

Fig. 12-5 Screw In Sidewall Condemns Tire To Trash Heap

Fig. 12-5 shows a tire with a screw penetrating the sidewall of the tire. Sidewalls can not be fixed. You can't plug, patch, glue or do anything to fix a sidewall puncture. In this case, the screw missed going deep into the sidewall and did not penetrate the inner cords, so it seems. Odds are it did and there is no way of knowing for certain so toss this one in the trash.

CHAPTER 13

Tubeless Tire Repair - Mushroom Plug

First we are just going to talk a bit about tire repairing then the actual procedure will be explained in Chapter 14 and Chapter 15 using mushroom and rope/string plugs. Also, the Question & Answer section has additional knowledge and advice.

TUBELESS TIRES ONLY - TEMPORARY REPAIRS

In motorcycles, tire plugging is a temporary repair so you can get to a place where you can install a new tire. The plug will eventually fail if you don't. You could plug it again, but what if it fails and you lose control of the bike and crash? It isn't worth that. Go buy a new tire.

Don't buy those cylinders of compressed CO_2 (or other inert gas) as shown in Fig. 13-1. They may let you down. First, they often freeze up when discharging (when trying to fill your tire), and this refusal to release gas will leave you stranded beside the road in complete frustration for it will not warm up and fill the tire it will stay frozen due to equalized pressure conditions and bleed gas too slowly to be of any good. I had them freeze on me. You see them for sale everywhere leading you to believe they are functional and reliable but they are far from it. Stay away from these devices.

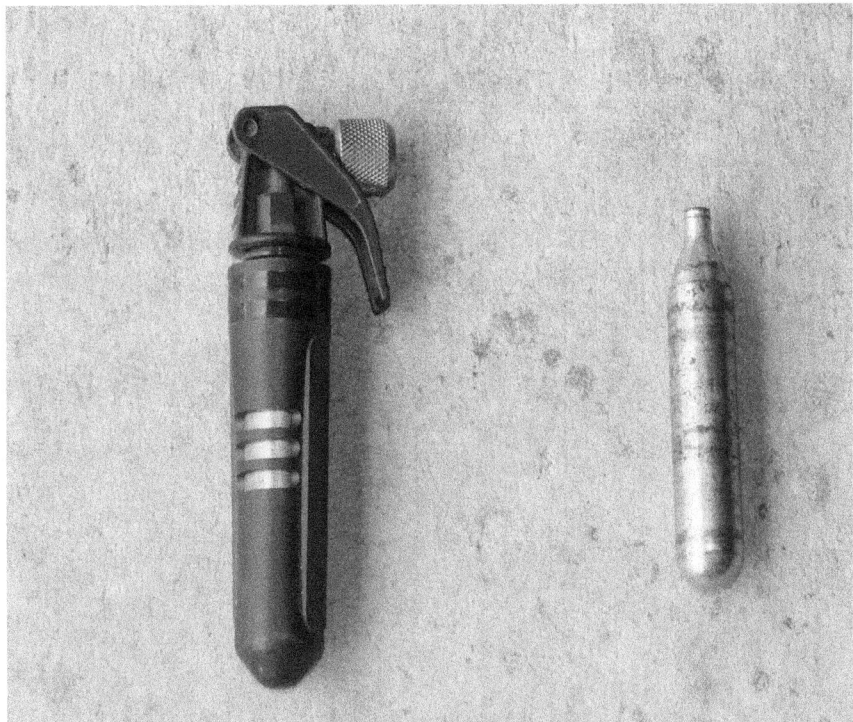

Fig. 13-1. Compressed CO2 Gas Systems Are Unreliable

Secondly, they rarely have enough gas to inflate the average large-size cruiser motorcycle tire. I used them and found they were a total waste of money and will leave you stranded with a flat tire. Plus they can give you a severe case of frostbite in a split second or spray and freeze your eyes to permanent blindness. They are dangerous. They also don't work in some temperature ranges and that causes the icing in the nozzle and valve mechanism freezing up the device. So what can you buy that will work? Read on.

Note: Motorcycle shops that sell these tire inflating CO2 systems are stocking and selling useless and inferior products that may fail when you need them most. A manual or battery powered air compressor will work. Stay away from CO2 systems no matter who tells you otherwise that they work for they freeze up too often to be relied on. I often discover the people selling these CO2 systems have never personally used them! They "assume" they will work. I can tell you from personal experience... they do not work reliably whatsoever, are temperature and altitude sensitive and can freeze up when dispensed leaving you stranded. Why bother? Just carry a portable air compressor with you.

Don't confuse the CO2 cylinders with those large tin can flat tire fix (see Fig. 12-3) you find in auto parts stores that have compressed air (or nitrogen) and have a viscous fluid within to seal flats. These do work, but not as well as using plugs. Keep reading.

TWO PLUGS TO FIX FLAT TUBELESS TIRES

Both the rubber plug and the braided string/rope type of flat-fix products will work. I carry both types on my motorcycle. If one won't work, the other likely will. A rubber plug is fine to plug a nail hole in the tread area, but the string rope can fill larger holes in the tire tread the rubber plug can not fill.

Danger: Plugs, rope or any other plug-type device cannot be used on a tire sidewall. Only the tread surface area can be plugged. Generally if the tire is blown out with a large hole larger than the plug diameter, the tire is ruined and cannot be safely repaired. But multiple string/rope plugs can be used to fill a large hole in emergencies.

RUBBER PLUG

Fig. 13-2 shows the rubber mushroom plug insertion tool. There is an Allen wrench inserted into the tool and I have wrapped some electrical tape on the wrench to act as a depth gage. When the Allen wrench is rotated inward and the tape reaches the tool I know the rubber plug is fully inserted into the tire. You don't have to use this depth gage, but it prevents overtightening of the tool's internal plunger which can ruin the tool's inner threads if you tighten too much. First time and infrequent users will appreciate this depth gage.

Fig. 13-3 reveals the StopnGo® brand kit with a rubber plug (next to the razor knife) designed for motorcycle use. If you are in a pinch and you have no flat tire repair kit, call a tow truck. Any tire repair shop (car, truck or motorcycle) can fix your flat "tubeless" tire with a rubber plug for car tires, but read the note below.

Note: Due to liability and insurance reasons more and more automotive and car tire repair shops will not help you as they are not motorcycle repair shops and if anything would to go wrong they can easily lose in court if sued. All the more reason for you to carry your own flat tire repair kit. See Fig. 12-4. Even tow truck assistance firms that handle emergency roadside repairs may not plug a motorcycle tire. It seems nobody will plug or repair a motorcycle tire these days unless they are a motorcycle dealer or motorcycle repair shop and even they won't do it. So don't rely on your towing insurance to help you out, they will only tow your bike to a motorcycle repair shop. It can mean motel room expenses for you and lost time, ruined appointments and lost wages for you.

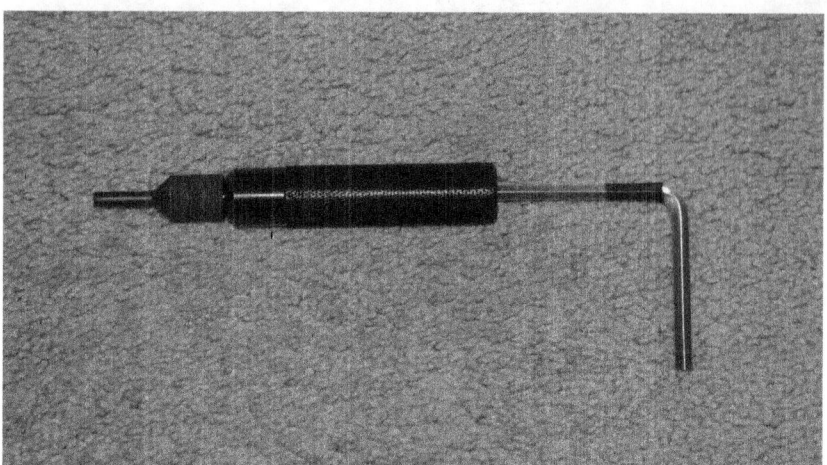

Fig. 13-2 StopnGo® Brand Mushroom Plug Insertion Tool

Caution: Rubber plugs are for tubeless tires only.

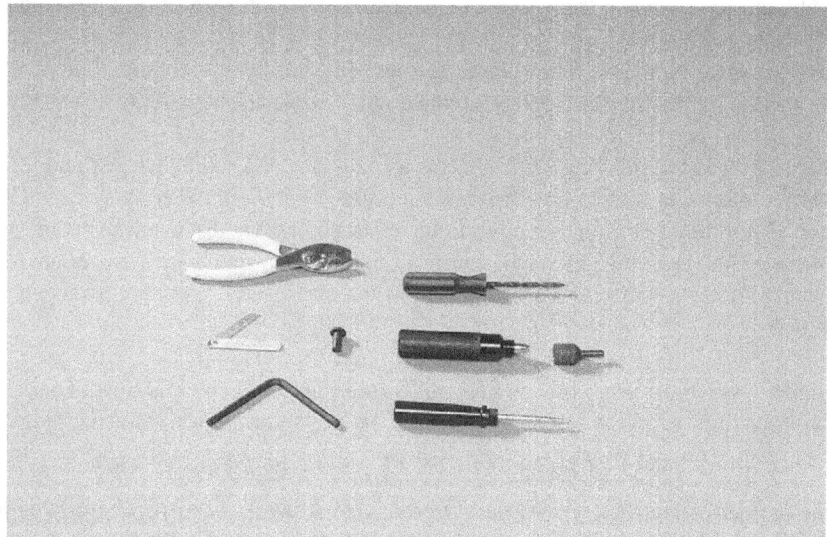

Fig. 13-3 StopnGo® Brand Mushroom Plug Insertion Kit

STRING ROPE PLUG

Fig. 13-4 at the far right in the photograph shows a tube of glue and the treated rope (this rope can be black, red, brown, or any color). Make sure you get the brand of rope specifically made for motorcycles. If you can't find any, the premium vulcanizing type for radial tires is next best. Fig. 15-1 reveals the brown or red tint color rope and this package has no glue because the glue is already impregnated into the rope. Just insert into the tire, trim the exposed edge, fill tire with air and ride away. In reality, the glue is used as a lubricant to help insert the sticky string rope into a high friction rubber tire.

Caution: String/rope plugs are for tubeless tires only.

Warning: Motorcycle tire manufacturers insist that plugging a tire is not safe. The plug can work loose and deflate the tire at any moment without warning, causing you to lose control of the motorcycle. Plugs should only be used as a temporary repair.

Cars use plugs routinely with great reliability. Motorcycles have different loads on the much thinner tires, and the cords inside can act as a saw, cutting the plug in two and may cause the tire to release air from the plug. This is just one reason why plugs should be used for only temporary emergency repair on motorcycles. I have found the rubber plug can last over 1,000 miles before it starts to leak air and the string/rope plugs can last the life of the tire. That is my experience, yours may be different.

FLAT TIRE - OUT OF TOWN

If you have a flat tire and cannot fix it and are way out of town, consider a rental truck with tie-down straps or a car with a trailer hitch and tie-down straps to trailer the disabled motorcycle home. Another option is to have it towed to a secure area—most tow companies have space available—then take a plane, bus, or train home. You can hire a transport company to ship your motorcycle home and motorcycle dealers can help you locate such specialty shipping companies. Some transporting firms are advertised in motorcycle magazines.

Tip: Consider developing a "To-Do" list explaining what to do when you break down and keep it with your vehicle. This way you will know what needs to be done at the moment. When you breakdown your mind will likely race with elements of despair and confusion making things worse than what they are and you can make costly mistakes. Blank lines 7 through 10 is for your own unique listings. It could be your insurance towing service.

EMERGENCY "TO DO" BREAKDOWN INSTRUCTIONS

This list is a handy chart you can photocopy and keep with you. If your vehicle breaks down the mind often becomes overwhelmed as to what to do and thinking is cloudy. Determine now what you should do and fill in the blanks. You'll be glad you had this instruction sheet when you are left stranded and out of town. The American Motorcyclist Association (AMA) has a superior towing insurance that cover for a low price towing for RV, Truck, Car, Motorcycle and you get their free AMA Magazine. They may or may not still have this coverage.

1. Try to fix problem. If you can't, call tow truck. If phone does not work flag down passerby for assistance or wait for a police or other public department vehicle you can hail.
2. Call tow truck and have bike towed to their safe area. If no safe area is provided ask them about another safe area or nearby business that has secure parking that you can use or tow to nearest motorcycle shop or auto repair shop. A police or fire dept. parking lot will also work. Call insurance company for towing/roadside assistance: _____.
3. Find motel room and make arrangements to get bike repaired.
4. If motorcycle can't be fixed while you wait take a bus, train, airplane home or stay in motel longer with a weekly extended stay rate.
5. If you must be home, then get home. Return later to retrieve your bike when it is fixed or consider renting a vehicle to tow trailer the bike home.
6. Use a long distant transport company to deliver your motorcycle to your if distance is great from home. Transport Co.: _____.

Moving Van Firm that can transport a motorcycle: _____.
7. _____.
8. _____.
9. _____.
10. _____.

As you can see breaking down can be expensive, inconvenient and time consuming and if you have spoke wheels with a innertube you will be in trouble if you pick up a nail in your tire if you can't seal that leak with a can of flat tire fix in a can.

However, if you have tubeless tires the air compressor and a plug system (rubber mushroom and string rope) you will avoid the above grief and expense and be on your way in fifteen minutes or less.

TIRE REPAIR TOOL KIT

1. Premium string rope kit or rubber plug kit.
2. Needle-nose pliers or narrow-end Vise-Grip pliers, with teeth
3. Flat and Phillips screwdriver.
4. Portable 12-volt air compressor or hand operated air pump (no CO2 gas).
5. May need SAE to coaxial wiring adapter to run 12V air compressor that is compatible with heated clothing, see Fig. 12-4.
6. Tools to access and remove front and rear tire.
7. Extra glue and tire repair plugs (tubeless tires only).
8. Hand cleaner and sanitizer wipes.
9. Water to drink.
10. Flashlight.

How To Install Tires on Motorcycles

11. Knife.
12. Chalk or white paint to mark nail hole in tire.
13. Chemical hand warmer for cold weather (optional).
14. Two tire irons and tube patch kit (for wire spoke wheel only).
15. Wrench to loosen rim clamp (for wire spoke wheel only, mostly for dirt bikes).
16. Small bar of soap to mix with water to create leak test solution.
17. Water. You can use any liquid such as eyeglass cleaner to mix with the soap to create the leak test solution.

You have to get a complete tire repair kit with everything you need to insert and glue the rope or rubber plug into the tire. Fig. 12-4 has all items in the package ready to go, but the kit is useless if you have no pliers to remove the nail or screw.

If you aren't certain of the tools you need, ask your mechanic for a shopping list. Tell him you need tools to access the front and rear tires, so you can insert a plug to fix a flat tire while traveling. The bare minimum of tools required is all you need.

 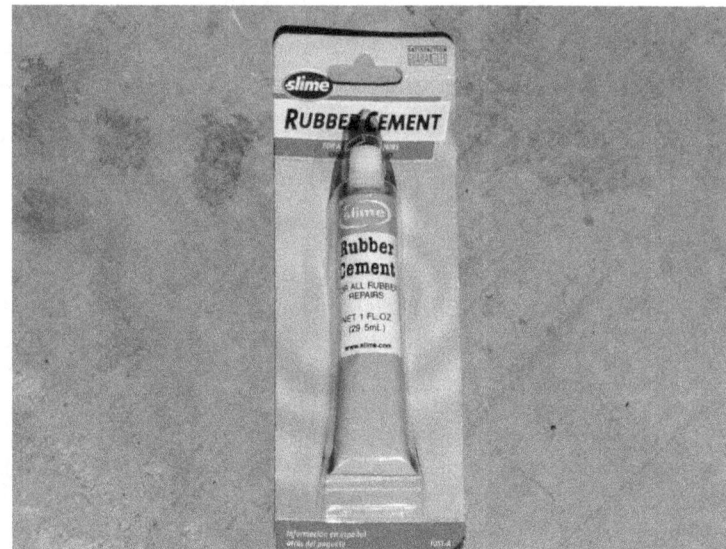

Fig. 13-4 String/Rope Tire Repair Kit With Rubber Cement Glue

Reminder: The kit shown in Fig. 13-4 is useless unless you have a source of compressing air into the flat tire, so do not forget to purchase a 12-volt portable air compressor with needle-nose pliers to get the embedded object out of the tire. And don't forget to pre-install wiring to your motorcycle battery with the proper connectors to run the air compressor before you get a flat tire.

Your fingers will not do the job, and even a screwdriver will not remove a deep nail. You must have needle-nose pliers with serrated teeth. You're still going nowhere unless you have a reliable means to inflate your tire. You need the portable air compressor, as in Fig. 12-4 or a hand-operated pump for bicycle tires (which is not recommended as they are slow to inflate, tiresome and can be difficult to use for motorcycle use, but is better than nothing), I find them tiring slow and miserable to use.

You need tools to remove a fender or saddle bag or muffler to get access to your tire. Front tires are usually easy to get at, but the rear tire on baggers can be a bear to even see the tire. What if you pick up three or more nails? Better have a few plugs and glue on hand. Hand cleaner will make the dirty job easier. And if it is a hot day, the ground will even be hotter where you will be working. You will need water to drink or to cool off any hot tools you will be handling in summertime.

PORTABLE AIR COMPRESSOR

StopnGo.com and Slime.com make portable air compressors powered from the motorcycle battery. They work. Bicycle hand pumps also will do the job, but with exhausting wearied effort. And make sure you can operate the pump in the tight confined areas of your motorcycle. You may discover that you can't pump the hand pump with saddlebags, belt drive and fender in the way. If this is the case, go with the portable 12-volt electric air compressor. See Fig. 12-1 is a compressor with pressure gage and flashlight combined. See Fig. 13-5 for a handy bright light for night repairs. Every rider should have one of these in their tool bag.

And Fix Flat Tires

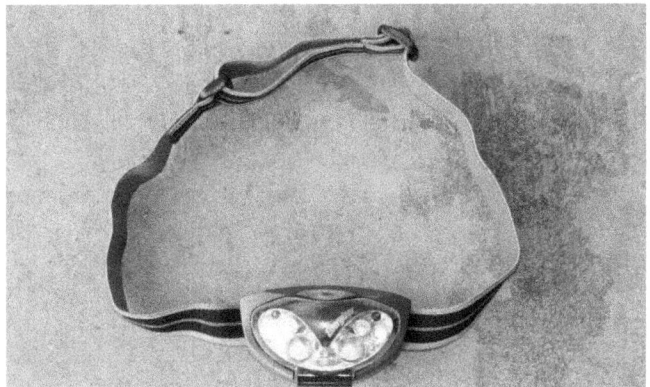

Fig. 13-5 Headlamp LED Flashlight Is Needed At Night

Before you buy a portable 12-volt air compressor (Fig. 12-1 & 12-4), make sure it has the proper inflatable adapter to fit the Schrader (or other unique type) valve on your motorcycle wheel valve stem (or tube valve stem). Are the power cord and air hose long enough to reach your front and rear wheel Schrader valves? Does the power cord have the power cord attachments to connect to your battery? Alligator clips are not practical as many batteries are buried in the motorcycle frame preventing convienent and quick access.

Important: Also make sure the power adapter you use to power the air compressor will fit your auxiliary power supply from your motorcycle battery. Generally this will be a 12-volt Coax or 12-volt SAE automotive type connection.

Look for an SAE-compatible fused line and plug that can be permanently attached to your battery. The SAE plug connects to your portable air compressor. A built-in pressure gauge can be handy on the compressor. Run the motorcycle engine while filling air into the tires so that the motorcycle battery is not taxed and drained, preventing you from starting the motorcycle after you fix your tire. Motorcycle batteries are small, and yours may be near the end of its life which will drain down very rapidly.

Note: New tire repair products are constantly being developed, so do an Internet search for motorcycle tire repair products and check out motorcycle magazines for any new items. But regardless of what is new, keep the old string/rope plugs with you in case the new-fangled device fails. You will find the tried-and-true string/rope type plugs to be the better insurance policy!

CHAPTER 14

Tubeless Tire Repair - Using Mushroom Plug

PLUGGING THE TIRE WITH A RUBBER MUSHROOM PLUG

This is the StopnGo.com tire repair system. It can be used on motorcycle, cars, RV's, pick-up trucks, ATV's, golf carts, and even lawn mower tubeless tires. No rubber cement is needed. Flat tires can be fixed without removing the wheel from vehicle. This system is for emergency repair on motorcycles and not a permanent repair. Install a new tire after you fix your flat tire. The mushroom plug can be, but not always, stronger than the string plugs, as the locking design keeps the rubber plug from blowing out or working loose out of the tire. The mushroom plug insertion tool is easy to use.

Warning: I have used the mushroom plug system on tubeless tires and it works, but at 300 to 1,000 miles the plug may develop a slow leak due to tire flexing upsetting the sealing area. For this reason the tire will slowly deflate overnight. I have also seen the internal mushroom head cut right off from the rubber stem, yet still holding air with the plug's stem still embedded in the tire. While the mushroom plug system works, keep in mind it is for temporary repair only to get you home.

Note: Push or slowly power the motorcycle to a safe location off or on the side of the road. Rotate the wheel's puncture area to an exposed location so the tire repair tool can be inserted and place motorcycle on the side stand with engine off. The Pocket Tire Plugger (a compact tool for tubeless tires) as shown in this book can be ordered from StopnGo.com. With this kit and a portable air compressor, there's no need to call a tow truck.

Buy the Pocket Tire Plugger® and try it out so you will be familiar with its use before you get a flat tire. You need an old spare tire to go through the motions and you can get them for free at any tire shop. The rubber plugs only work on motorcycle tires not car or truck tires due to those tire treads are too thick for the motorcycle plug, but you can purchase longer plugs for car and truck thin tread tires (not all-season tires). Here's how to fix a motorcycle flat tire.

Caution: Rubber plugs are for tubeless tires only.

Note: Before beginning this procedure you should use some white paint to draw a circle around the nail on the rubber tire because after you remove the nail the rubber closes up and can make it hard to find where to insert the mushroom plug.

1. Mark the nail hole with chalk, white paint or some other means. Once the nail or screw is removed it can be hard to see the hole as the rubber closes up on itself. Even a tiny pine needle or twig slightly inserted in the hole can be used in a pinch. Fig. 15-3 and Fig. 15-4 shows tire chalk and chalk mark encircling nail/bolt head on the tire tread. Once you remove the nail/bolt the rubber closes up and can be hard to find where the nail hole is and even more so in dim light, shadow or at night.

2. A nail or bolt can be removed from the tubeless tire with pliers. Just grab and twist it left and pull it straight out. You twist is left in case you can't see if it is a threaded screw. It may require quite a bit of force if the object is bent inside the tire. A screw should be unscrewed (counterclockwise) with a flat blade or Phillips screwdriver or pliers. See Fig. 14-1.

Note. Fig. 14-1 shows general pliers that comes with the StopnGo® kit which is great for grabbing exposed nails. You need to add to your tool kit needle nose pliers as nails can be driven deep or flush with the tire tread and only the needle nose will be able to dig into the rubber to grab hold of the broken nail to remove it. See Fig. 15-5 shows needle nose pliers. If you still can't remove the nail then use the probe tool to drive the nail all the way past the tire into the rim space of the wheel. You should carry a Phillip's head screwdriver to remove screws in the tire.

3. Attach the smooth sharp-pointed probe tool to the nozzle and insert it into the nail hole into the tire. See Fig. 14-2. Use this smooth pointed probe tool to clear the hole of any obstructions. Just slide the tool in and out of the nail hole. There could be a broken piece of metal inside the path where the nail or screw penetrated the tire. It is okay to go all the way with this tool pushing it as deep as it can go.

4. (Optional) Read the "note" below first. Use the rasp tool (the one with very rough and sharp edges on the shaft that looks and feels like a twisted file) in Fig. 14-3. Insert the rasp tool without twisting, and push it in and out of the nail hole two or three times. This roughens up and enlarges the hole so don't overdue it. If you encounter metal, keep rasping until you clear the steel belt inside the tire. Fig. 15-2 and Fig. 15-6 reveals a rasp tool.

Note: The rasp tool does not always need to be used when using smooth, round, rubber plugs as the rasp makes the hole in the tire larger and leaves a jagged surface. After using the probe tool just install the mushroom plug without using the rasp tool when using the mushroom plug for a tighter fit of the plug in the tire. If the nail hole was a tiny brad the rasp tool will make the hole in the tire larger so you can insert the insertion tool and the mushroom plug. Try not to use the rasp tool first. See Fig. 15-2 on left is a typical rasp tool.

5. I have found that rasping the nail hole six to eight times allows the hole to be widened enough to insert the plug tool's nozzle tip into the tire. Anything less and you may struggle, but keep in mind this does make the hole in the tire larger and rougher and this is not good for inserting a smooth round rubber plug.

Note: Try inserting the mushroom plug without rasping and if it does not go inside the tire then rasp until it does. Lubing the tool shaft with a layer of silicone grease will make it easier too, but is not necessary (never use oil to lube the tool shaft as oil will dissolve the rubber plug and cause a unexpected rapid blowdown of air pressure).

6. Insert a rubber mushroom plug into the insertion tool as shown in Fig. 14-4 tail end first and use the hollow nozzle tip to push the convex head of the mushroom plug down into the hole in the tool (See Fig. 14-5) so the rubber mushroom plug will not be protruding from the tool.

Tip: The rubber plug should be pushed down into the plug barrel until the plug's mushroom head is recessed and inverted down into the tool's shaft. Otherwise the rubber plug can jam inside the tool and refuse to be inserted all the way into the tire, making you think it is inserted all the way when it is not. You can use your finger tips, an Allen wrench, or the nozzle end of the tool to push the rubber plug's round mushroom head down into the plugger tool. See Fig. 14-5.

7. Place the insertion tool's nozzle tip on the sharp pointed "probe" tool. See Fig. 14-6 and screw it down onto the probe tool. It

need not be tightened very tightly, just screw the tip on to the tool all the way it will go. The head of the mushroom plug should not be protruding from the tool. Make sure it is inside the insertion tool's hollow cylinder or the cap may not screw on.

8. Insert the tip of the hollow insertion tool into the nail hole in the tire and push. See Fig. 14-7. This will insert the nozzle tip into the tire. Make sure the nozzle tip has gone all the way into the tire. Hold the nozzle end firmly, and unscrew the probe tool leaving the nozzle tip in the tire. Make sure the hollow nozzle tip's small shaft is sunk all the way down into the tire. If you can't insert it, lube the tool's exterior shaft with a few drops of water or silicone grease. It is okay to gently twist the tool to get it inside the tire, but do not rock it back and forth as the thin hollow shaft could be crushed or broken off.

Note: If your rubber plugs have dried a bit and need lubricant or you just want to use a bit more to make things easier, apply a thin layer of silicone grease. You can buy this grease at auto parts and electrical supply stores. Never use motor oil. It will corrode the plug and tire. Even saliva, water or soda pop is okay if that is all you have to lube the tool tip.

9. Install the plugger tool male threaded end the female threaded end on the insertion tip that is sunk into the tire by screwing it on snugly. It need not be tight. See Fig. 14-8. This is the portion of the tool that has the rubber plug installed into it.

10. Insert the Allen hex wrench into the plugger tool. Turn it clockwise until it stops. This action is pushing the rubber plug down into the nail hole in the tire. See Fig. 14-9. It will take a surprising amount of force, so do not fear applying torque. A good thing to do is to mark the Allen wrench with a piece of electrical tape where you know the mushroom head has exited the insertion nozzle. Do this with your testing to create your own depth gauge. This way you will know for certain that you have inserted the mushroom plug all the way inside the tires when you reach this mark. Then you can also know the tool will bottom out soon thereafter. There is a chance, due to friction, you may believe you have reached bottom as you turn the Allen wrench and stop before inserting the rubber plug all the way into the tire. The plug will not be properly inserted and will leak air if this happens. Try this procedure on your practice testing on a used tire. Don't wait to get a flat tire to learn how to use the flat tire repair tools.

Note: Due to the force required to insert the plug into the tire you may want to consider buying a 3/8" socket wrench, Allen socket with a very long reach. This will make using the tool and insertion very easy. When using Hex/Allen wrenches make certain the Hex wrench tip is fully inserted all the way down into the Allen bolt to avoid stripping the Allen head bolt. This is the secret to use Allen wrenches as they will certainly strip if the tool is not inserted all the way down.

11. Now that the rubber mushroom plug is installed into the tire turn the Allen hex wrench counterclockwise until the inner rod inside the plugger tool backs out and rises flush level to the top of the plugger tool then remove the Allen wrench. See Fig. 14-10.

12. Slowly pull the plugger and nozzle assembly clear of the tire. Pull straight out as shown in Fig. 14-11. You will now see the tail end of the rubber plug extending from the tire's nail hole. Watch as you pull as you should see the tail end of the rubber plug being stretched out as you slowly remove the tool. Don't yank on the tool or the tail of the rubber plug could stretch and break. If that happens remove and install a new plug.

13. Use pliers to pull the rubber plug's tail two inches. Don't pull more than this, or the plug could deform or slip out of the tire. This light tugging of the plug will insure that the mushroom head inside the tire is seated snugly against the inside surface of the tire. See Fig. 14-12.

14. Inflate the tire, then trim the rubber plug's tail flush to the tire tread surface if need be as shown in Fig. 14-13. If you test the plug with soapy water it may still be leaking tiny bubbles of air. This may stop or it may not giving you a very tiny slow air leak. You can still drive home on that. Just check air pressure often. If the leak is severe, deflate the tire or just push inward the plug into the wheel with the tool's probe tip and insert a new plug. This time don't pull the plug's tail 2" just pull it 1/2". See instructions below, "How to Remove a Leaking Rubber Plug".

15. Drive slowly. Avoid freeway speeds. Stay under 50 miles per hour. Get home or to a repair shop to have a new tire installed. This job is finished.

You can see from the diameter of the rubber plug that this system can fix a large nail or 1/4" bolt with ease. Some people on Internet chat rooms testify that this system is a permanent fix and has lasted for thousands of miles, even on street bikes. It is best to get home and replace the tire.

I have used the plug for thousands of miles but in my case I have found the plug will loosen up and leak air. I would wake up in the morning only to find the tire is flat. It is not a permanent fix for street motorcycles, but it does work and if it can get you home or pre-

How To Install Tires on Motorcycles

vent a trip interruption it is well worth having the StopnGo system with you. I do carry one in all my motorcycle flat tire repair kits.

PHOTOS USING MUSHROOM PLUG

Special thanks to Stop 'N Go® for donating these thirteen photos revealing how to use their rubber plug system.

Fig. 14-1 Using Pliers To Remove Nail In Tire

Fig. 14-2 Use Probe Tool To Clean Out Nail Hole

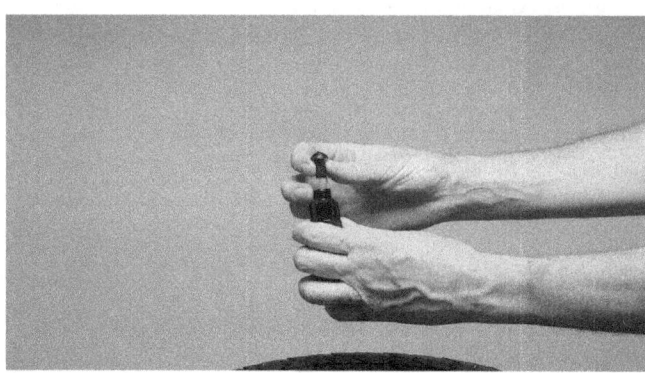

Fig. 14-4 Insert Mushroom Plug Into Insertion Tool

Fig. 14-3 Using Rasp Tool To Enlarge Hole In Tire (optional use)

Rubber mushroom plugs require no glue. Instead they are coated with a lubricant grease that is pre coated on the plug. This lubricant makes it easy for the plug to slide out of the tool and slip into the tire's nail hole.

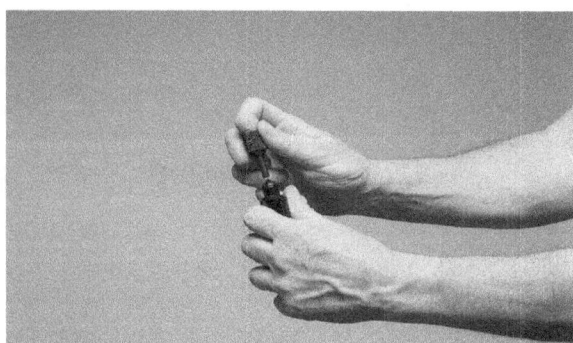

Fig. 14-5 Use Insertion Tip To Push Mushroom Down Into Tool

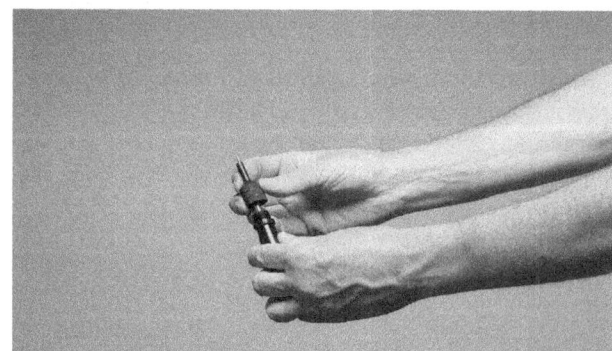

Fig. 14-6 Screw Hollow Insertion Tip To The Probe Tool

Note: We are now going to switch tool tips to different tool handles. Remove the hollow insertion tip from the insertion tool and screw it on the sharp pointed probe tool. See Fig. 6-9. We will use the probe tool to insert the hollow insertion tip into the tire.

And Fix Flat Tires

You may be wondering how you will be able to remember all of these specific steps. The device comes with instructions, but if you practice a few times and do this a couple times a year to refresh your memory you will remember. The instruction sheet will be handy to jog your memory.

Once you do this a couple times you will find the process so very easy. What I love about the product is that it works. It will repair a nail, bolt or screw hole in your tire (but not a long slice like from broken glass) and you will be down the road in just minutes as if nothing happened at all. Wonderful!

Note: If you get a slice in your tire the string rope may be able to fill that hole if it under an inch long.

Danger: Any slash type slice in a rubber tire really needs to be replaced. Too many internal cords may be broken especially if it is deep. Also, be careful when removing glass or flat metal as it will be sharp as a razor blade. A round plug will not fill a square hole? In this case of tire repair the plugs will fill a square hole, but a "slashed" hole in a tire can't be repaired. Sometimes, if the slash is narrow and not more than 1/2" inserting two "rope-type plugs" may get you home.

Fig. 14-7 Insert Hollow Insertion Tip All The Way Into Tire

Fig. 14-8 Screw Plugger Tool On The Insertion Tip

Fig. 14-9 Allen Wrench Driving Plug Into The Tire

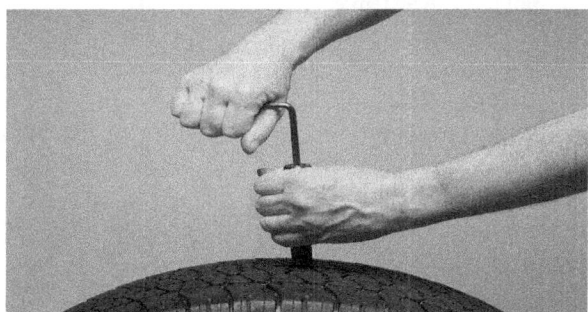

Fig. 14-10 Removing Allen Wrench From Tool

Fig. 14-11 Remove Tool From The Tire Fig.

Fig. 14-12 Pull Back On Plug's Tail To Seat Mushroom

Note: Before you perform the pulling of the plug's tail as shown in Fig. 14-12 I need to give you my two cent opinion. If you pull as hard as shown in the photo it causes a problem on motorcycle tires due to the thin rubber carcass. What happens is when you let go it may stay in place and reveal a long tail. Then when you cut the exposed end in Fig. 14-13 all appears well until after you ride a day you will find the end of the plug has contracted way back into the tire leaving a "hole" in the tire. I found the plug started a slow leak of air. When I replaced the plug and did not snug the end very hard the plug's tail stayed in place and did not leak air. The reason for "tugging" on the plug's tail is to help pull the mushroom head back against the tire to seal air.

This job of plugging the tire is now completed.

Important: It is now time to inflate the tire with air and test for leaks.

Fig. 14-13   Cut Exposed End Of Plug Flush To Tire Tread

Hook up your air compressor and inflate the tire to normal operating air pressure. If you do not know the pressure for your tires, then inflate tire to 35psi.

It is now time to leak test the plug. Get some water or any drinkable liquid and with a dab of soap (if you have it) apply it to the rubber plug and look for air bubbles. If you see micro bubbles it means the plug is leaking. You can ride a mile and retest to see if the plug has seated and the leaking has ceased. A micro air leak (tiny bubbles that are barely visible but create a foaming) will get you home even if the tire is losing air. You may be surprised to realize the air pressure will hold for many days. Just keep an eye on it.

Install the valve stem cap.

This job is done!

If the tire plug is still leaking badly? It's time to replace the plug. If it still leaks badly? Leak test the puncture area to see where the air bubbles are leaking from. It is possible you picked up two nails. It is also possible the tire's ability to hold air is compromised and the air is leaking past broken internal belts. That is rare. Most every time a flat tire occurs it can be fixed with a plug to get you home or to a shop to replace the tire.   Keep reading.

HOW TO REMOVE A LEAKING RUBBER PLUG

If for some reason the newly installed rubber plug leaks air, you can use the probe tool to push the rubber plug into the tire's air space in the rim, then insert another rubber plug in its place. If you pull hard enough on the rubber plug's tail with pliers you can remove the plug, but you also may snap the plug in two and have to push it back into the tire anyway. This could happen if the plug was not inserted deeply into the tire or some object was in the nail hole creating a leak.

Note: If the plug itself comes out of the tire it means the hole in the tire is too large for a mushroom plug of this size. Or, if the rubber mushroom plug keeps leaking air you need to switch to the string/rope system. Read Chapter 15. Belive me, it will fix the leak.

CAR & PICK UP TRUCK TIRES

Order from StopNGo.com the 1" long rubber plugs if you plan to use your Pocket Tire Plugger for your car. The motorcycle tire repair kit comes with the shorter 3/4" long plugs. The probe tool must be long enough to reach down past the exterior tread into the carcass of the tire into the air space so the tool will work with street car and standard summer tread pick-up truck tires, but are not long enough for deep all-season knobby tire treads. The motorcycle size tip will not be long enough for aggressive all-season or snow tires. Their deep tread blocks will stop the tool from reaching into the tire's carcass. It is okay for street tubeless motorcycle tires, but also remember that you can use the string/rope described below to fix tires on street and off road vehicles, including Trikes, because the insertion tool and the string/rope is very long in length.

CHAPTER 15

String Rope - Tubeless Tire Repair

PLUGGING THE TIRE WITH STRING ROPE

Why should you also carry a string rope tire repair kit with you? Because string rope can handle the bigger jobs along with the small. If you happen to pick up a huge 1/2" bolt you can use one, two, even three strings to fill that huge hole in your tubeless tire. Or you may have picked up a nail that has ripped into the tire a bit beyond the size a rubber plug can fix. You may be trying to fix a flat on car, truck, or snow tires and string rope has few limitations. I always carry string rope and a air compressor and tools with my motorcycle. Slime® brand products is my favorite choice.

Fig. 15-1 String-Type Rope Plugs for Tubeless Tire

Black string may be thinner or larger than red or brown string. You should carry small and large size string/rope with you. The string in Fig. 15-1 has no tube of glue because the glue is not needed. The black, red, brown or yellow color rope is saturated with vulcanizing agent that will bond the string to the rubber tire. It seals within seconds of insertion. The color can be ignored, just look for a small and large size to carry with you. Leave the product sealed in the package so it will not dry out.

How To Install Tires on Motorcycles

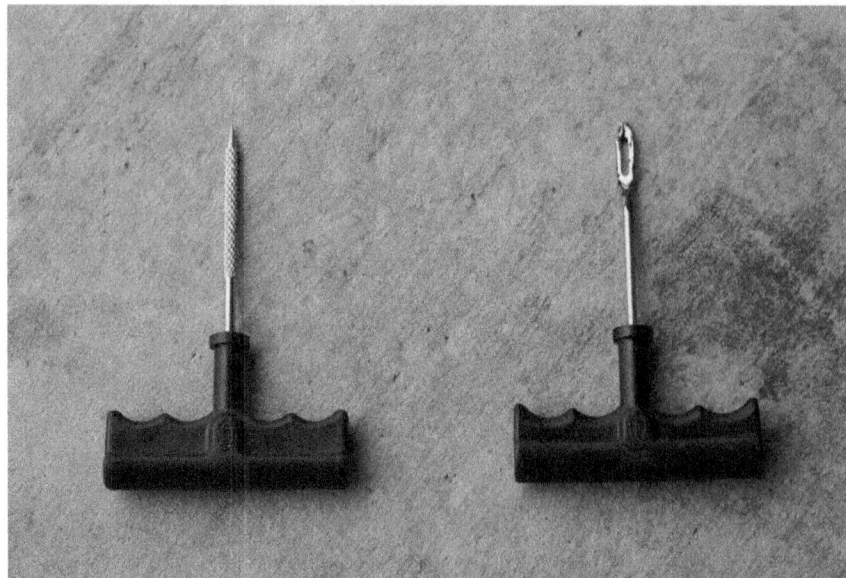
Fig. 15-2 Tire Tread Rasp Reamer & Rope Insertion Tool

Note: Before beginning this procedure you should use some white paint or chalk to draw a circle around the nail on the rubber tire because after you remove the nail the rubber closes up and can make it difficult to find where to insert the string plug. See Fig. 15-3 and 15-4.

Caution: String and rubber plugs are for tubeless tires only. You can not use these systems to fix a spoke wheel innertube.

1. A nail or bolt can be removed from the tubeless tire with pliers. Just grab and twist it out. It may require quite a bit of force if it is bent inside. A screw should be unscrewed (counterclockwise) with a flat blade or Phillips screwdriver. See Fig. 15-5, but if you must just pull the screw straight out. String/Rope has the ability to fill and flow into jagged holes in rubber tires.

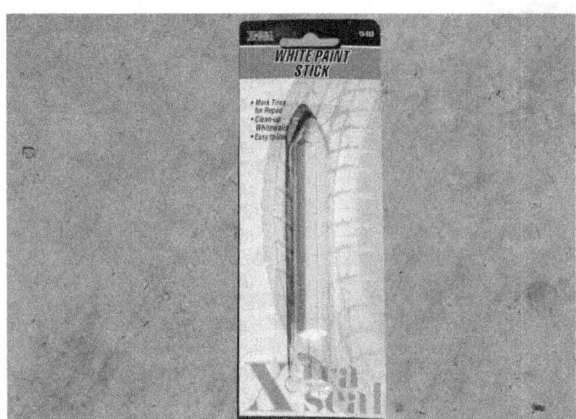
Fig. 15-3 Tire Marking Pencil

Fig. 15-4 Marking Nail Hole In Tire

2. Make sure you marked the nail hole with chalk, paint or some other means. See Fig. 15-4.

Tip: When you are testing the tire repair system on a old tire, go ahead and drill a hole in the tire, rotate the tire and try to find that nail hole. You will see how important it is to mark the tire's nail hole!

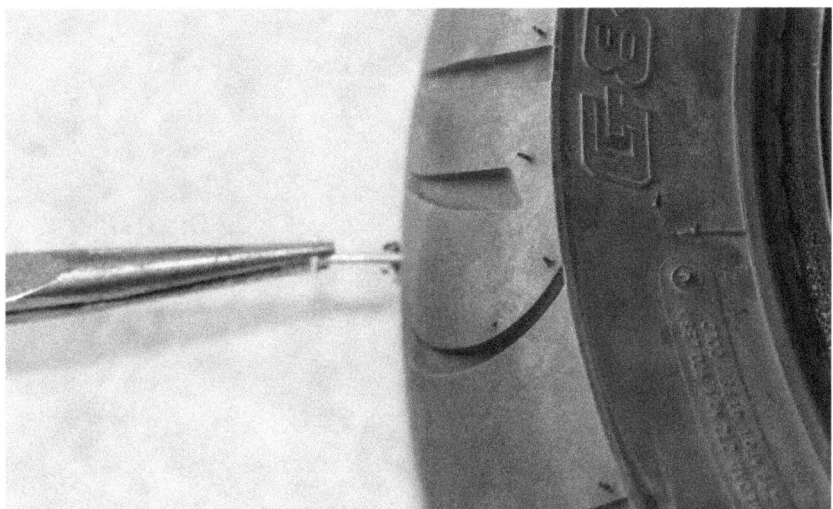

Fig. 15-5 Use Needle Nose Pliers to Remove Nail From Tire

If a screw is imbedded into the tire you may need to unscrew it turning the screw counterclockwise with the pliers or with a screwdriver or just pull it hard straight out of the tire if you do not have a screwdriver. Any damage done to the nail hole channel in the tire will be filled with the sting/rope repair plug.

3. Use the rasp file (the rod with rough edges) to ream out the hole. First, though, remove your wood twig marker if you inserted one from the tire, then insert the rasping tool and push it straight in and out three times without twisting it into the nail hole. Just enough to clean and roughen up the hole in the tire. The tool only needs to travel down about an inch or two, not all the way down to the handle. But it won't hurt anything if you do. See Fig. 15-6.

Note: String rope has rough surfaces so it will flow into irregularities and bite into these rasp serrations in the tire to make a tight fit. This is why you want to use the rasp tool when using string rope. The mushroom plug has a slippery, smooth rubber shaft that will not perfectly flow into the rasping serrations and therefore rasping can cause a loose fitting rubber plug that seeps air.

Fig. 15-6 Using The Rasp Tool - It Has A Serrated Surface

The rasp tool can also be used as a probe that when inserted into the tire it will push out any foreign objects or a broken nail. Each tire repair method has written instructions on how to use the tools and the plugs.

4. Insert one end of the rope into the looped hole in the smooth split-end hooped plug insertion tool as shown in Fig. 15-7, halfway into the tool so the tool tip is dead-center in the rope.

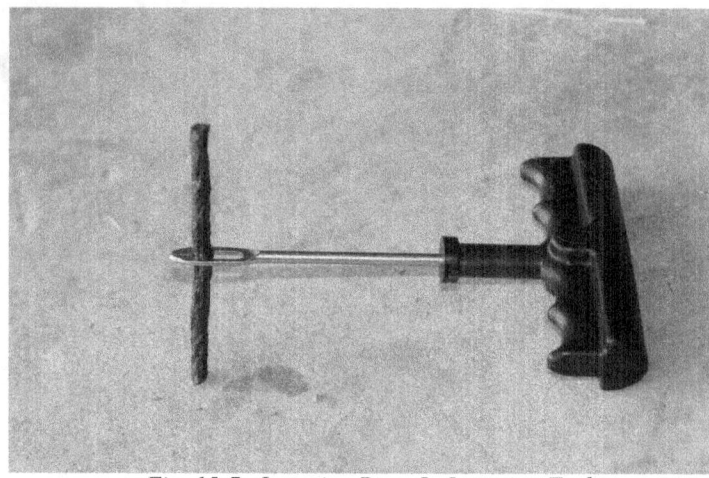

Fig. 15-7 Inserting Rope In Insertion Tool

5. Now coat the rope with glue. Use as much as you want, but make sure you cover the entire rope. No photo is shown. If you have no glue? Just insert the rope dry. Read why below.

Note: Some to most all string/rope systems today may not use added glue as the glue is impregnated into the rope already. Some may need activation such as dipping in water or some other instruction. Even kits that come with glue may not even need the glue as it is used as a lubricant to help inserting the rope easier and give an extra seal. Confusing? Yes. I tried using the Slime® brand rope without the glue and it worked just fine for thousands of miles. Never had the rope system fail me yet! It is by far the preferred method to fix street motorcycle tires at this writing. However, newer products are always being developed and I will note those that work on my Website: JamesRussellPublishing.com

Note: Sticky feeling rope is okay to use without glue because that sticky feel to the touch on your fingers is a vulcanizing agent impregnated into the rope. If you have the glue use it. If you find the glue tube has cracked and the glue has evaporated don't worry about it. Just plug the tire with the sticky rope without the glue. The glue dries rapidly so apply the glue and insert the rope plug right away. The glue is just a lubricant to help you insert the rope and adds a little stickiness to the rope when it dries, but you can plug a tire without the glue as long as the rope has a sticky feel to it. This is why you see rope sold in packages without the glue because the glue is not needed with rope coated with tacky vulcanizing agent.

6.   You can allow the two ends of the rope to touch each other as shown in Fig. 15-8. About 1/2" remaining is just fine. We can push the plug down a bit deeper so it looks like Fig. 15-10.

Fig. 15-8 Rope Ends Inserted With Insertion Tool

Quickly insert the rope insertion tool's tip into the tire's puncture hole and push it straight down all the way into the tire without twisting the tool until the remaining rope is about a half inch flush with the tire's surface tread. See Fig. 15-8.

And Fix Flat Tires

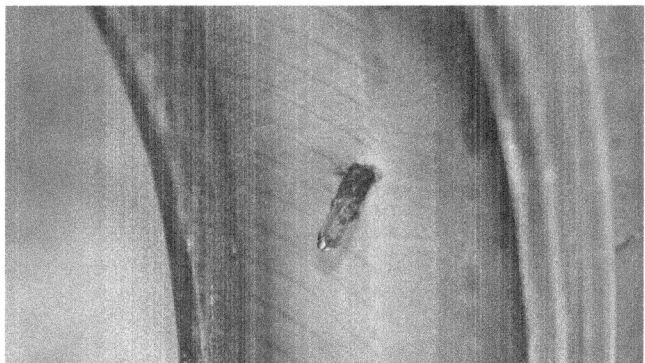
Fig. 15-9 Tool & Rope Viewed From Inside Tire

You won't be able to see what the plug looks like as shown in Fig. 15-9 but this is what it will look like. When the metal tool is removed the rope will flare out into a loop shape and will not fly out of the tire by centrifugal force as some people believe it will. When you practice on a tire you will see for yourself how well these plugs really do work.

Fig. 15-10 Rope Extended 1/2" - Pull Tool Away From Tire - Do Not Twist

Do not twist the tool when inserting the rope unless instructions call for it. Just push the tool into the tire, dragging the rope with it down into the nail hole. Before removing the tool, rotate the rope just a tad to the left and to the right and wiggle the rope around inside the hole to insure a nice tight fit of rope into the tire's casing (also called a carcass). See Fig. 15-8 and Fig. 15-10. Push slowly even if you feel resistance so the entire plug will not suddenly dive into the tire and be lost. If this happens just pull out the tool leaving the rope behind inside the tire's rim and start over with the rasp tool and then insert a new plug, or go to step #7.

7. If you pushed the rope down too far use your needle-nose pliers on the rope ends and just pull them both back up to where they should be. If this fails, remove the tool and insert new rope into the hole pushing the old rope all the way down into the wheel letting the new rope to take its place. You can use the rasp as a probe tool to push the old rope deep into the wheel rim. Old rope won't hurt anything as it will soon stick to the inner carcass of the tire and remain there.

8. To remove the tool after inserting the glued or unglued rope, just pull the tool straight out of the hole without twisting the tool unless the instructions say otherwise. This will release the rope plug, leaving the rope in the tire while letting the tool come out.

You may ask how does the tool release the plug? The rope ends inside the tire form a loop and are already stuck together and will not separate from each other. When you pull the insertion tool the looped ends of the rope are twice the size of the reamed hole in the tire so the rope will not be removed and the tool's split-end will open releasing the rope from the tool. Once you do this you will understand the process.

9. Let the glue dry for a minute or two if you used glue on the rope.

10. Inflate the tire, using an air compressor or hand pump to the psi you normally run in your tire. If you don't know, then run 32 psi in the tire for the time being. The job is nearly finished.

Fig. 15-11 Cut Excess Rope, but not flush with the tire.

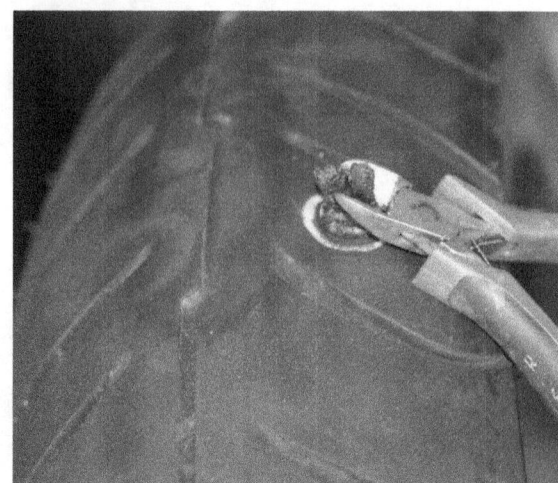
Fig. 15-12 Cut to Trim Rope Plug

11. Cut the exposed rope with a knife, razor blade or snip pliers close to even with the tread of the tire. See Fig. 15-11 and Fig. 15-12.

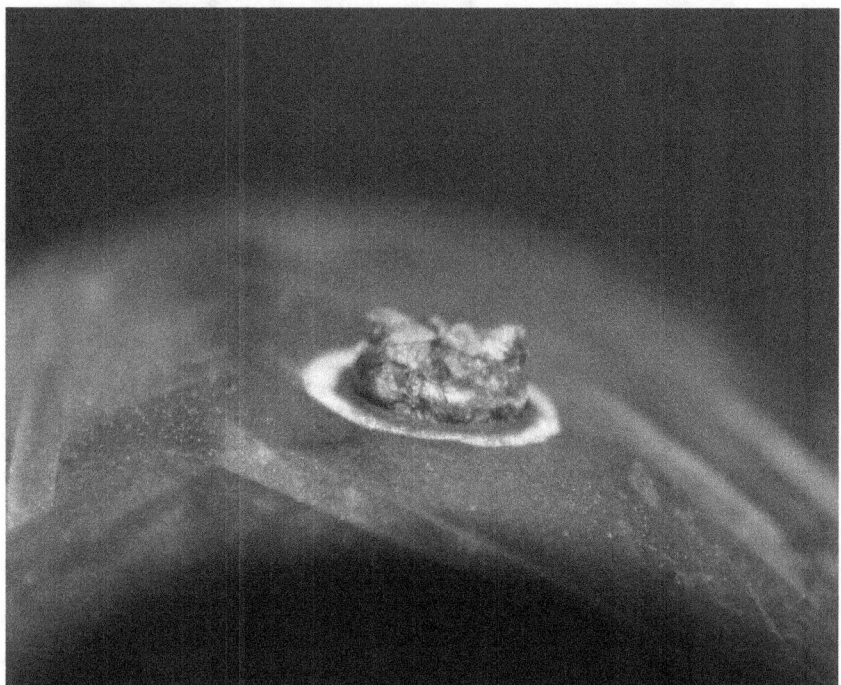
Fig. 15-13 Rope Cut 1/4" Beyond Flush To Tire Tread

The rope need not be cut flush with the tire, it can be raised as in Fig. 15-13 for the plug will wear down quickly from the rough road surface. Also, the plug may want to wiggle into final position and having a bit excess extended from the tire will allow for momentary shrinkage.

What if you don't have the sharp tool to cut the excess rope plug? Just drive away as it will be quickly worn down flush with the tire in no time at all.

And Fix Flat Tires

This excesses material is even more important when using a soft rubber plug as they will flex into a final position and pull itself down into the tire and with the excess material being available to fill the hole in the tire. This way, without sucking the rubber plug down into the tire that will create a concave hole where the tire's plug once appeared. If this hole develops beyond 1/8" deep remove the rubber plug and install a new one, but this time make sure you leave a bit more excess plug end exposed such as you see in Fig. 15-13.

12.   Drive slowly. Avoid freeway speeds. Stay under 50 miles per hour. Get home or to a repair shop to have a new tire installed.

Note: I have personally used rubber mushroom and rope type tire repair plugs and I have kept them in the tire for thousands of miles. However, I have found the rope plugs much more durable for such extended use because the material in the rope is stronger and even stronger than steel if Kevlar® rope is used. But as a reminder, using a tire plug for extended use on a motorcycle is never recommended by anyone.

CHAPTER 16

Tire Machine - Using Manual Machine

For this book we will use the manual tire changer, the No-Mar® brand Junior Professional model because that is the one I currently own. The operating procedure will be nearly identical no matter which type of rotary machine is used including the powerful electrical, air or hydraulic operated machines. Any differences in procedure between the machine brands will be minor.

Fig. 16-1   The No-Mar® Brand Manually Operated Machine

BASIC MODEL

No-Mar® has many different models you can choose from. You can buy the basic model and then add on later the optional tools you need. Here's what I suggest for the beginner.

1. Basic tire changer with bead breaker. Consider the No-Mar® portable trailer hitch unit.
2. Mount/demount bar.
3. Wheel Rim Clamps that can handle wide 16" wheels or larger.

4. Helping Hand tool.
5. Paste and liquid lubricant.
6. Wheel balancer stand.
7. 1/4 ounce strip of wheel weights.
8. Soap solution for leak test.
9. Tire irons (yes, you still need them).
10. Valve core removal tool.
11. Fexible air chuck with pressure gage.
12. Jack to lift bike.
13. Sizzor jack to lift wheels.

The above is the bare minimum. You may likely need to buy a tire bead starter strap from K&L or try using a nylon tie-down ratchet strap. You will need hand tools to remove the wheels from your bike.

TIRE MACHINE PROCEDURE - MANUALLY OPERATED

The tire changing machine comes with instructional owner manual and/or a video. Follow their instructions.

First thing to do is to lay the wheel and tire on top of the tire machine's rim clamps, but do not insert the clamps to the rim. Just use the clamp arms to support the wheel. You need to make sure the disk brake rotor is floating and not touching anything. Then you need to remove the Schrader valve from the valve stem completely. So "don't" insert the rim into the plastic spool grooves as shown in Fig. 16-2.

Fig. 16-2 Insert Lower Bead Edge of Rim Into Plastic Grooves and Tighten Snugly

Fig. 16-2 reveals the No-Mar® system of locking the rim to the tire machine. The machine has six plastic indented spools that grasp the rim and they can never scratch the rim surface and are perfect for expensive composite wheels. How tight should these clamps be? If they are too loose the rim will rotate, if too tight the rim could crack or break if you are changing a tire on a composite rim. On a pneumatic machine you can adjust the air pressure to 50 psi for perfect clamping pressure, but here you need to "discover" what works for you. You could use a torque wrench on the clamp bolts and when you find the right clamping force and log that foot-pound reading for future use. Now you will have the correct pressure every time. On metal wheels? Just increase tension on the clamps as needed. You can't scratch a rim using a No-Mar® tire machine. That is what makes their machine so desirable for motorcycle use and they work on composite wheels nicely.

I mention this procedure above for another reason. You may be using a machine that has metal clamps that grip the rim and even though you put a rag over the clamp ends you just can't afford to have the wrong clamping pressure and have the rim rotate, tear the shop rag and scratch the rim. Find a method where you can set the clamping force in a repeatable and reliable manner.

Fig. 16-3 Harley-Davidson Rim Secured at Three Points Ready to Mount Tire

Fig. 16-4 Tire 1/2 Mounted by Hand Ready For Tools to Finish the Job

Caution: Watch your eyes, wear eye protection, as the valve core can come flying out like a missile. Cup your hand over the valve stem to catch the core so it will not fly into your face.

Remove the valve stem cap and remove the valve core. Remember, the rim should only be resting on top of the rim clamps because we first need to break the bead on the tire.

When the air is out of the tire now you can use liquid tire lube on the tire where the tire meets the rim. This step is optional, but with lubricant it allows the tire to break from the rim bead area easier.

You may want to tie with a rope the wheel to the machine so the wheel will not flip or relocate itself or fall to the floor. See Fig. 16-5. You can't clamp the wheel to the tire machine rim locks yet because the tire's bead has not been broken. When you apply force on one end of the rim the wheel could flip suddenly so that is why I tie the wheel down as shown. Just wrap the wheel and tire with nylon rope and tie the opposite end down to the tire machine's frame.

Insert the bead breaker tip just beyond the rim as shown in Fig. 16-5 and pull down on the handle until the tire is broken away from the rim.

Caution: It will let go suddenly so watch for this sudden release so the bead breaker handle does not come crashing down violently or hit you in the head, shoulder or arm.

How To Install Tires on Motorcycles

Fig. 16-5 Tie Rim & Tire Down To Machine

Fig. 16-6   Reveals Bead Breaker Breaking Tire's Bead Away From Rim

You will have to rotate the wheel clockwise or counterclockwise and break the bead at various locations. When you see the entire top sidewall of the tire is broken away from the rim you can now turn the wheel over and break the bead on the opposite side.

The beads must be broken on both sides of the tire to remove it. You will know the job is done as the tire will be flopping around on the rim or appear by eye to be separated from the rim. See Fig. 16-6. Go ahead and break the tire's beads now.

And Fix Flat Tires

What is bead breaking? The rubber tire is amazingly stuck like a powerful glue to the rim and it requires a tremendous amount of force to "break the bond" and it is the smooth bead surfaces of the rim and tire that creates this sealing. A device is needed to push down on the edge of the tire near the rim to move the tire away from this tight sealing surface and that is why it is called breaking the bead. You may hear a loud pop when bead breaks. You may hear (or should hear) two separate "pops" as the lower bead seats to the rim and the top bead seats to the rim. Sometimes you only hear one pop noise so check to make sure both beads have seated. See Fig. 16-8.

Once you break the upper bead surface of the tire you can then flip the tire over and use the tire machine's rim locks to secure the rim to the machine, but I just use the rope as it is quicker and I don't have to flip the wheel over again later when removing the tire. In Fig. 16-5 this wheel has a chain sprocket and disk brake rotor. I want the disk brake rotor on the bottom so it does not impede progress. However, using a tire machine's rotary mount/demount bar does not cause interference problems on standard size tires. Then again, if you can't mount the tire and have to use a tire iron you may want the disk brake or rear wheel drive pulley facing down, but this is not an absolute requirement, just a preference. There is no need to remove any brake disk rotors from the wheel when changing the tire.

Fig. 16-7 Tie Rim & Tire Down To Machine

Fig. 16-7 shows one of three of the tire machine's rim clamps. You need to adjust them so the wheel rim will insert into the plastic protective clamp tips, the two round objects on top. These plastic tips grab the rim and will not scratch the wheel or mar it in any way. Once you adjust the three rim clamps you can now lower the wheel rim onto the machine's rim clamps and tighten the clamps so the wheel is snug and in some cases a bit tighter. As you remove and install a tire the wheel will want to spin in the rim clamps. If this happens just snug up on the rim clamp tension with a Box wrench that is shown in Fig. 16-7 left of my pointing finger.

Tip: Those numbers in Fig. 16-7 are for rim sizes for clamp location. You can move each clamp into the holes in the frame for a perfect fit to the rim size. I have a personal system I use. I label the three spoke arms differently; North, South or West and I put a number beside each that represents the hole numbered from the far end (where the box wrench is located) starting at #1. I can then instantly have a formula for my Harley-Davidson clamp set up to save time and a different formula for my Triumph motorcycle. It just saves time setting up the clamps. Example: Harley-Davidson 16" wheel, N-4 , S-3, E-3. I don't use the number on the support arm as shown in Fig. 16-7 as the other two arms are not numbered. Those numbers you see help you to set up the machine indicating rim diameter size.

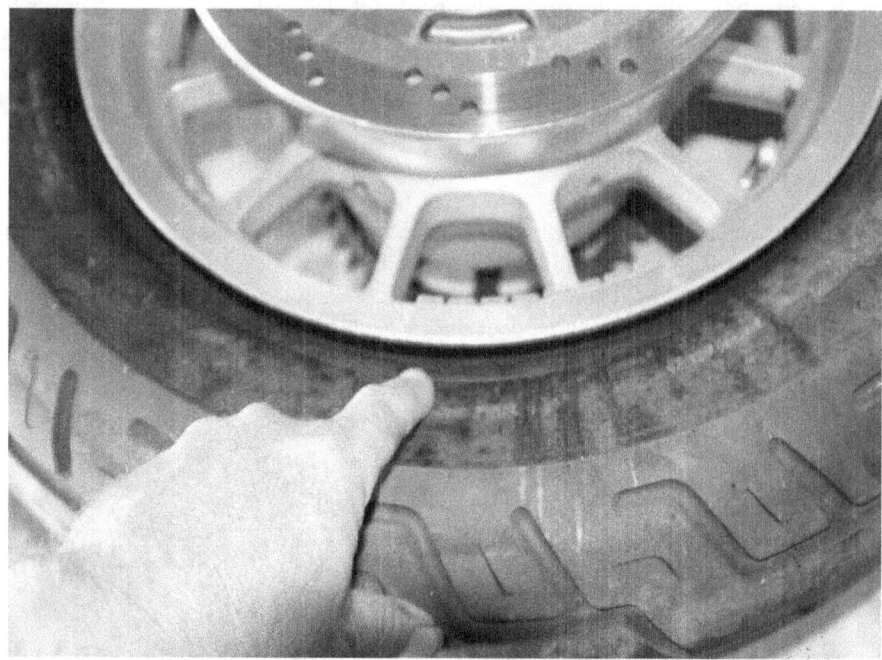

Fig. 16-8 Tire Bead Is Broken

On this side of the rim in Fig. 16-8 you can see the tire has fallen away from the rim indicating the bead has broken at this location. It must be broken free and clear of the rim all away around, top and bottom side of the wheel rim.

The edge of the rim fits into the machine's plastic tip's groove. Now lower the wheel down on to the rim clamps and locate the underside rim into all three of the rim clamps as shown in Fig. 16-2 and Fig. 16-9. Tighten the rim clamps with the Box wrench so the rim is snuggly fit. You often only need to tighten one rim clamp to make a nice tight fit.

Fig. 16-9 Rim Clamp Clamping On To The Wheel Rim

Fig. 16-9 shows the black rubber tips of the machine's non-marring wheel clamp tips centered on the lower rim. Notice also how the tire has easily moved away from the rim showing that the tire's bead is broken away from the rim. If the bead were not broken you could not lift the tire away from the rim with gentle hand pressure to insert the rim into the machine rim clamps. See Fig. 16-2 for a better view of how the rim is locked into position.

Fig. 16-10 Remove Sprocket & Rubber Cushion Shocks In The Wheel

You should remove the wheel sprocket and the rubber cushions if you feel they will fall out when you later turn the wheel over. If you do, take a photograph of the rubber cushions as shown in Fig. 16-10 to reveal the cushion elements orientation as they sometimes can be a puzzle to reinstall for the beginner. Some Harley-Davidson's do use these rubber cushions.

Tip: When you insert the mount/demount bar's single tip into the tire, insert it with the tip in the flat horizontal position then flip the tip so it is in a tall vertical position, then rotate the the bar to remove the tire.

Note: The wheel bearings are located in the center of the wheel just to the right of my finger in Fig. 16-10. They will not fall out. Or I should say, they should not fall out. If the wheel bearing falls out then something is wrong with the bearing and it needs to be replaced or the bearing was smashed into position by some butcher mechanic and ruined the bearing outer race surface in the wheel's hub and may have even destroyed your wheel. Another good reason why you should be changing your own tires!

If you only knew the "uneducated butchers" who are actually working on your bike (even at so-called respectable dealerships) you would be very alarmed and vow to do it yourself.

Fig. 16-11 Lifting Tire Off The Rim

Now that the wheel is locked into the machine's rim clamps you dive the single end of the No-Mar® mount/demount bar under the tire's edge as shown in Fig. 16-11 at about the 11 0'clock position, drop the machine's centering bar into the wheel's axle hole as shown. Pull the far right end in the photograph mount/demount bar clockwise. The centering bar will act as a pivot point to create the rotary motion. As you rotate the tire will lift away from the rim as shown.

Note: The above paragraph is how the mount/demount bar is inserted into the tire then pulled down to lift the tire over the rim, then the bar is rotated around the rim to remove the tire. When you dive and pull, the tire may be stubborn and the plastic tip on the mount/demount bar can be broken. I have broken two of them in the last three years. So, I now use a tire iron to do this initial lifting or I use the Coats® brand mount/demount bar for it is made of solid steel. Make sure you use a rim protector when using the tire iron or Coats® as they can scratch the wheel's rim. Coats® does sell rim protectors that fit on the ends of their bar. See Fig. 16-13.

Tip: Sometimes the tire reinstalls itself, so in Fig. 16-11 insert a tire iron or piece of wood in the gap to the left of the mount/demount bar to prevent the tire from falling back down into the rim.

Note: Notice the mount/demount bar is pivoting on the bearing housing in Fig. 16-11 and in Fig. 16-12. Do not do this. Lift the bar vertically and let it pivot on the centering bar otherwise you could crush, dent or crack the bearing housing. The correct procedure is shown in Fig. 16-14 where leverage is applied not on the wheel, but on the center pivot bar.

Fig. 16-12 Upper Side Of Tire Is Lifting Away From The Rim

Fig. 16-12 shows the mount/demount bar has now moved to the 1 o'clock position and the tire is being lifted off the rim. Keep going, it will soon be off the rim. It comes off the rim surprisingly easy. If you want, just use a tire iron to get in some practice using them.

Tip: Don't forget you do not have to use a tire changing machine to change tires on your motorcycle. The entire job can be performed with tire irons. This means if you are using a machine and run into trouble just reach for your tire irons to finish the job.

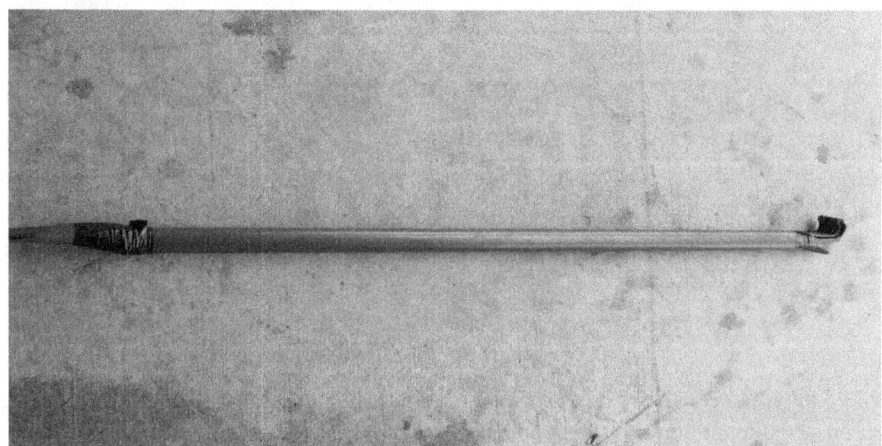

Fig. 16-13 Coats® Mount/Demount Bar With Plastic Non Scratching Tips

Fig. 16-13 shows the Coats® brand mount/demount bar. The flat point on the left is the "demount" end. The sharply curved side on the right is the "mount" end. I have electrical tape holding the plastic rim protectors on the bar as they tend to slip off when in use.

This bar is solid steel, yet even then, I have encountered tires that will bind up and make this rod of iron useless to the point I have to resort to using tire irons to get the tire on the rim.

   Note: Even fully powered automatic tire installers can have trouble with some tires that will pop the mount bar right off the rim. The installer must then use the "helping hand" and if that fails they must use tire irons. So don't think using an automatic machine you can discard your tire irons as that is wishful thinking.

   Tip: If you are having big trouble installing a tire it means you have left out a fundamental step like forgetting to lubricate the tire and rim sufficiently and/or not using a "helping hand" device to get the tire down into the rim's drop center. The method of pushing the tire down into the rim's drop-center applies to tire changing machines too.

Fig. 16-14 Taking First Bite Of Lower Edge Of Tire

   Look at Fig. 16-14. Do not turn the rim over in the machine. Use your left hand to lift up on the bottom of the tire and try to force it over the top lip of the upper rim, then insert your single (shallow end if using Coats®) under the tire's lower bead edge. You may want to use a tire iron to do this for it is easier and will not break the plastic end tip on the No-Mar® mount/demount bar, then insert the single tip of the mount demount bar in a horizontal position first, then flip the bar so the tip is now vertical. Drop the centering bar into position then rotate clockwise to remove the tire. The tire will come off with surprising ease.

   The Greatest Secret Tip: Many mechanics do not even bother to use the machine to remove the lower edge of the tire. Just lift the tire, insert a tire iron or two then grasp the tire and pull it off the rim with your hands. Do you know why the tire comes off so easily? Because both of the tire's bead edges are pigeon toed and sunk into the central drop center of the rim. The tire is so floppy loose when in the drop center and the tire can move deeper into the drop center so far as to allow the tire to just come off with hand pressure alone. Keep this in mind when installing the tire. It will go on easily when you use a "helping hand" device to push that tire down off the bead and shoulder area of the rim and get that tire to move downward into the rim's drop center. This is the greatest secret of installing tires! After you do a few tire installs you will better understand this procedure.

Fig. 16-15   Tire Removed From Rim

Here it is in Fig. 16-15 the tire is fully removed from the rim. Now it is time to install the new tire.

Clean the rim with Scotchbrite® brand non-scratch pads. Lubricate the new tire and the rim with paste lubricant. To review these steps return to Chapter 4 and Chapter 5. See Fig. 16-16.

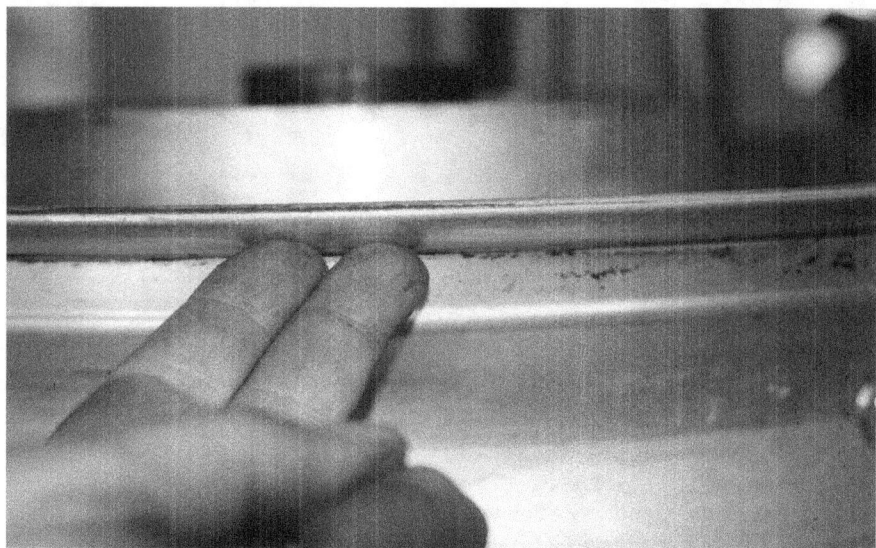

Fig. 16-16 Bead Surface - Upper Area of Rim

Clean the rim then lubricate it with paste lube. Fig. 16-16 shows bits of rubber bonded to the rim mostly on the rim's shoulder which must be clean to bare metal. We want to remove that rubber from the shoulder and the curved bead surface. The bits are tiny in size so you can leave them if you wish for they are on the shoulder of the rim and not on the actual curved bead surface, but a clean rim will make for a better bonding tire and will not develop a slow leak due to uncleanliness. Fig. 16-17 and Fig. 5-1 shows a shiny clean lower edge of the rim which is just the way it should be, clean.

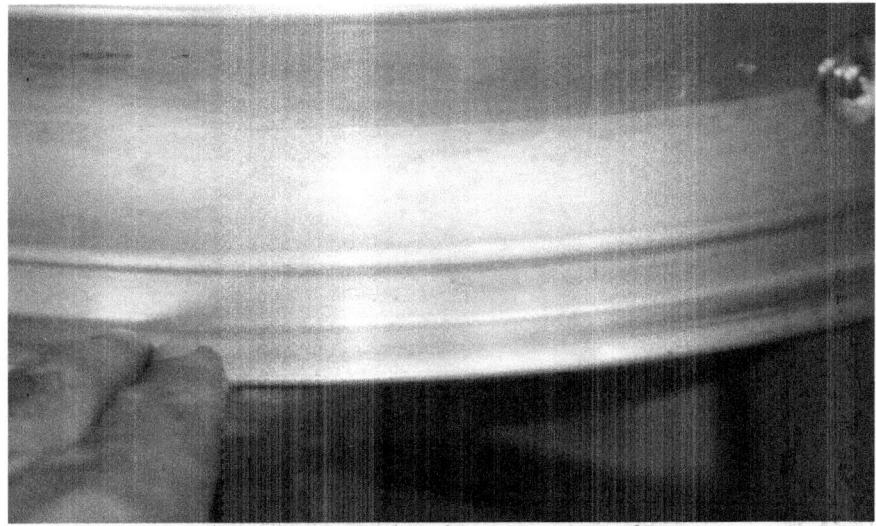
Fig. 16-17 Bead Surface Lower Area of Rim

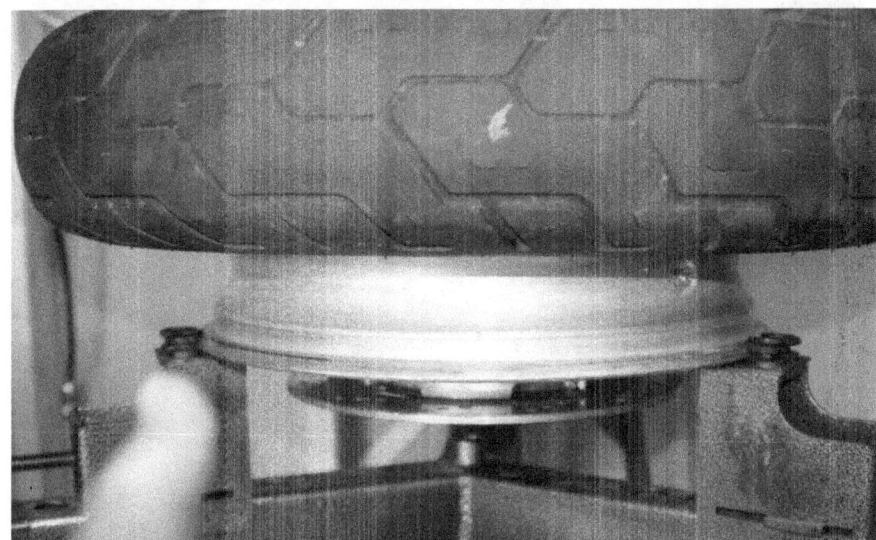
Fig. 16-18 Rim Locked To Machine & Tire Resting On Rim

Fig. 16-18 shows the rim is still locked into position. We have never removed the rim from the machine and we do not have to. The tire is just resting on the top of the rim. Here you want to make sure the tire will rotate in the proper direction on the rim and the balance paint mark on the tire is adjacent to the rim's valve stem.

Fig. 16-19 Dive Tire By Hand On The Rim

Fig. 16-19 shows the tire being pushed down hard by hand on the rim. Get as much as the tire as you can on this way. Look at the 2 o'clock position and you can see the bottom edge of the tire rising out of the lower drop center of the rim and now riding high over the rim. It is this lower section of the tire we need to fold or press over the top rim bead edge. This will require the use of tools.

Fig. 16-20 Installing Tire's Lower Side Over Upper Rim

Fig. 16-20 reveals the set up. Notice we are now using a "different" end of the mount/demount bar to install the tire. With the No-Mar® we are using the double forked end "mount" end of the bar. They will push the tire's lower bead down over the rim. Fig. 16-22 shows a better image of the fork end.

Note: I have run into problems using this end of the mount/demount bar on some stiff cruiser sidewall tires with shallow rims. The bar keeps popping out or in most cases I just can't move the bar any further for it is jammed tight. Fig. 16-21 (lower tire bead jam) reveals a jammed situation. You can try lifting the bottom of the tire 180 degrees away if tire is not in the drop-center at that location. There is too much rubber over the rim to fight with. To stop this nonsense you need to insert the helping hand at the 6 o'clock position and the tool should work okay. If not, don't fight it. Just use tire irons to get that tire over the rim. Believe me, tire irons will flip that tire over the rim with great ease and with delightful amazement!

Fig. 16-2 shows the lower edge of tire just won't go over the rim. The rubber has bound up and I do not have the strength to force the tire on with the mount/demount bar. Insert a couple tire irons here and the job is done. Do the same if the mounting bar gets jammed when installing a tire.

And Fix Flat Tires

Fig. 16-21 Lower Edge Almost On But Still Jammed

Fig. 16-22 Starting Top Side Of Tire Over The Rim

Fig. 16-22 shows the No-Mar® "mount" end of the bar inserted. Notice the "fork" end is used to mount the tire to the rim as shown. The tips are plastic so rims can't scratch.

How To Install Tires on Motorcycles

Fig. 16-23 Tire End Stage & Is Almost Over The Rim

Fig. 16-23 reveals the end stage of inserting the upper bead area of the tire over the rim for the final tire install. You can use the mount/demount bar, but this photo shows how to use the tire irons in case you have to use them to get a stubborn tire onto the rim. Some tires go on easy, others are very mean and uncooperative. Notice I am using the long tire irons and I am using the highly curved side to get the leverage I need. This tire is going on with just one more flip of a tire iron. This Triumph rim has a somewhat shallow drop-center and the tire is tougher to install than Harley-Davidson wheels.

One question to ask yourself if you run into a problem like in Fig. Fig. 16-23. Do you have a "helping hand" device installed to push the tire down into the wheel's drop center 180 degrees away from where the tire irons are working? Is the "helping hand" in proper position or did it pop out of position? Do you need to use a second or third "helping hand' to get the tire to relax from its bound up state?

Fig. 16-24 Balance Mark Out Of Alignment

Caution: The work area is clean in the photos with no dripping lubricants on the floor or on the wheels and tires. Keep your work area clean at all times or you will risk slips, falls and injuries. Make sure the tire's rubber is also not smeared with any tire lubricants or axle wheel bearing grease before inflating with air.

Fig. 16-24 shows the tire has rotated out of position due to the rotary motion of the mount/demount bar dragging the tire with it. You can grab the tire, while the rim is still in the machine's rim clamps and with great force rotate the tire to the right the balance dot aligns with the valve stem. If you find the tire won't budge and is stuck don't worry about it. When you balance the wheel with wheel weights this will all be forgiven. It is no big deal.

And Fix Flat Tires

Fig. 16-25 Try Filling Tire With Air Without Bead Starter Strap

Remove the wheel from the tire machine's rim clamps and rest the rim on top of the clamps to support the tire or the tire will not inflate. Insert the valve core into the rim's valve stem and try to fill the tire with air (See Fig. 16-25) without using the tire bead starter strap as shown in Fig. 16-26. Do not exceed 40 psi to seat the bead. Use short bursts of air to fill the tire. If you have trouble with air leaking around the rim try bouncing the tire on a concrete surface to help seat the rubber against the rim. Also lift and drop the tire on the rim numerous times when inflating the tire. If that does not work use the tire bead starter strap to seal the tire's shoulder edges down against the rim. This procedure is explained in detail in Chapter 7, see "Tire Bead Starter Strap - How to Use".

Danger: There are safety rules to follow so don't use a bead starter strap until you have read all of the rules.

Fig. 16-27 shows the shock absorbing cushions are reinstalled in their proper order. When they are new they often come with tabs as shown keeping the cushions in order, but over time the tabs break off and the cushions can tumble into a pile on the floor. Like a puzzle, you need to put them back into the proper order. This is why I told you to take a photograph of your wheel's cushions. Notice their is a pattern to follow. Each pair alternates like the others. Each pair can go anywhere in the hub as long as the pattern remains the same. If you can't install the sprocket/pulley the pattern is wrong. After installing and there is a large amount of back and forth slop in the sprocket/pulley the pattern is wrong. The sprocket/pulley must be snug. A tiny bit of rocking back and forth is okay. If the rocking is severe still look to see if the cushions are worn out. It may be time for a new set. Keep in mind they should last well over 100,000 miles or more (except racing use).

Fig. 16-26 Bead Seating Strap Must Be Dead-Center of Tire

When the tire inflates with air and the beads loudly "pop" into place the job is done. Deflate the tire and reinflate to the correct tire pressure. The correct pressure is stamped or stickered on the bike's frame and in the owner manual. The pressure indicated on the tire is not the correct tire pressure. It is only the minimum and maximum pressure the tire is capable of handling.

When the tire has inflated check for air leaks on the tire/rim and valve stem area with soapy water solution. Watch for tiny air bubbles indicating a leak. Install the valve stem cap.

How To Install Tires on Motorcycles

Danger: Before installing the wheel on the motorcycle make sure the wheel bearings on both side of the wheel are present. In Fig. 16-27 you can see the wheel bearing is clearly in dead center. You may want to tap the bearing surface very gently with the palm of your hand to make sure the bearing is snug sunk down and not floating loose. Do this on both sides. You don't want a wheel bearing to come out of the hub and you install the wheel with no wheel bearing! The wheel would wobble badly if this did happen, so check the bearings to see if they are still there. Do it now and do it later when you install the wheel on the bike.

Fig. 16-27 Install Rubber Cushions In The Wheel Hub

Believe it or not many mechanics fail to lubricate the axle and wheel bearing inner race. The internal bearings may be sealed with grease, but the axle and inner bearing race can not be run dry of lubrication or heat of friction can burn the bearings and axle or rust. Another good reason to do the job yourself. Fig. 16-27 and Fig. 16-28 reveals lubrication axle grease must be applied on the bearing face and spools sockets.

You must coat the interior roller bearing inner race surface with grease, but if you forget and you at least did grease the axle you will be okay. You will likely be fine even if you fail to grease both bearing race and axle as many repair shops totally neglect to do it and charge you money for the privilege. I have found dry axles too many times to count. When you do it yourself you know the job is being done right. You can lubricate again the next time you change tires.

Fig. 16-28 Grease Chain Sprocket Spools

Fig.16-28 shows the chain sprocket that needs to be installed into the wheel hub's rubber cushions. Also, my finger is pointed at a spool spacer that also must be greased and inserted into the sprocket.

Important: Pay attention to any spools/spacers that can fall out of the wheel, sprocket or drive pulley. If you look at Fig. 16-28 that spool looks like it would never fall out, but it can and it likely will when you turn the wheel over when changing tires. The sprocket is not bolted into place. It has metal splines (now shown) on the opposite side of the sprocket wheel that just sits in between the rubber cushions shown in Fig. 16-27.

Lubricate the axle with a light coat of axle grease before you reinstall the wheel to the motorcycle. This is so the wheel bearings will not get welded by rust or overheating/swelling/binding on the axle.

This job is finished. Now it is time for you to learn even more in Chapter 17 and Chapter 19

CHAPTER 17
Tire Information

TIRE TALK

We have more motorcycle related Questions & Answers on our website. And more photos of tire changing if they are needed will be posted.

Visit JamesRussellPublishing.com for a free guide on how to buy a cruiser motorcycle and many other free articles on several subjects to save you time, money and grief. From buying a car, motorcycle, or RV to consumer alerts, our website will help you in your life journey. Check it out.

AIR PRESSURE MONITORING

Checking air pressure in tires is often overlooked because you can check them with a pressure gauge each day and find nothing wrong and soon become complacent skipping the chore. I have used Accu-Pressure brand valve caps from AccuPressureCaps.com with no problems. However, I have used other external monitor brands that leak air over time. These inexpensive devices permanently open your tire's Schrader valve (valve core) in the valve stem to monitor air pressure. Of course that's just asking for a leak to occur due to leaking valve cap seals or a cracked sun-baked valve housing, but once you find a quality brand to use they can be reliable and make checking the air pressure just a glance to see the green flag. Install a new pair once each year. You can select a tire pressure range at or slightly higher than the tire pressure you normally set. When the air pressure in your tire drops below that point, a red flag appears, letting you know it is time to add air. Since you carry (or should be carrying) an air pump or compressor, you can add air whenever necessary. I find these caps work fine in summer and fail in cold winter months. The rubber seal tend to harden in the cold and leak air.

Caution: Some riders may ride too fast and wild to trust these valve cap monitoring systems. Others may simply not want to use them at all just for the fact they could fail at any moment and begin leaking air from the tire. I have found in cold weather transitions from summer to fall they require an extra twist to tighten down due to expansion and contraction. I have never had one fail with an abrupt release of air, only a tiny slow leak over the course of many days to reveal itself with a red flag.

There are internal pressure monitors that are trouble free and safer because they do not monitor air from an open Schrader valve. The in-tire pressure systems are expensive, but they will not cause a leak in your tires.

HOW TO SELECT TIRES FOR YOUR MOTORCYCLE

See, "Buying Tires For Your Motorcycle" in Chapter 2 for more advice and the "Question & Answer" section at the back of this book.
Front tires are different than rear tires, so do not mix and match tire sizes. When you order tires make sure you use the proper sizing data, such as 180/55/18 to determine tire size. You will find tire size data on your motorcycle's frame and stamped on the existing tires on your motorcycle. If there is a discrepancy, the tire size in your factory owner manual, service manual, or the sticker on the frame will settle the matter if the rims are factory stock.

First find out if your tires are bias ply or radial and jot it down here: _____.

Both tires must be bias installed or radial. Do not put a bias on front and a radial on the rear or vice versa. Both tires must be identical unless the manufacturer of your motorcycle says otherwise. That is the general rule to follow.

Front Tire Size (three sets of numbers): _____.
Rear Tire Size: (three sets of numbers): _____.

What you are looking for on sizing tires are three numbers such as: 180/55/18. There can be letters inserted such as: 180/55ZR/18.

How To Install Tires on Motorcycles

The number 180 means the tire's section width (180mm), and 55 is the aspect ratio rated as a percentage. It is the relationship between the section height and section width of a tire expressed as a percentage of section width. If the section height is one-half the section width, the aspect ratio is 50. Z is the manufacturer's speed rating for the tire, which is 149 miles per hour. R is the construction (radial or bias), and 18 is the wheel rim size in inches (18 inches).

Tire Load and Speed Rating: _____. You may see a code like this: 150/80/16 /77H. The 77H is the load and speed rating. You will need a chart to decipher the meaning. The manufacturer has this reference data on its Web site or should have.

Tire Size Problems - When you purchase a 150/80/16 size tire you would think that first number "150" millimeters tread width would be what it says it is. Don't bet on it! Some tires will match up with no problem and some other tires may be as much as 20 millimeters wider. This can cause problems as it will increase the size of the tire's width 10 millimeters on both sides of the tire. The tire, though selected to the proper size is now way too wide as it may hit the drive belt or be within 5 millimeters to it which is too close to be safe. A bit of underinflation with accelleration and braking and the tire could bulge and rub against the belt. The belt will be ruined or the belt will cut the sidewall of the tire causing a blow-out.

What you can do is before you buy or install the tire measure the maximum width of the tire with Vernier calipers to make sure that "150" millimeter width is what you are actually getting. Kenda Kruz® tires are very wide, so be careful with them. You will find that if you measure different tires all will be different in width despite that they all claim to be 150 millimeters. For most bikes it is not a problem, but Harley-Davidson motorcycles are more finicky as the drive belt can be wide in size and the stock tire already wide so there is not much room to install a wider tire than what came with the bike as stock.

The solution to the problem for the installer is to measure tires and buy those tires that fit. You don't have to buy OEM tires. You just need to make sure there will be 10 millimeters between the sidewall of the tire and the drive belt or any other item near the sidewall of the tire. If you do run into problems ask for advice and examine bikes like yours to see which size tire they are using.
What if you find a certain tire others brag of and you want one, but it is too wide for your bike? Go down one size 10 millimeter in width to a 140/80/16.

If you run into problems with tire size and hate returning the tires as an expense and hassle just buy OEM tires that came with the bike. You will pay more for those tires at a dealer, but at least they will fit and you will be on your way or buy tires "specifically" designed for your bike on the Internet.

Bias-ply - A type of tire construction utilizing plies that run diagonally from one bead to the other. One ply is set on a bias in one direction, and succeeding plies are set alternately in opposing directions crossing each other. Sometimes called a cross-ply tire. Go to any motorcycle tire manufacturer's website to learn more about tire construction.

Radial - The tire construction utilizing plies that run radially from bead to bead under the tread. This construction requires a belt to stabilize the tread and define the tire diameter. Go to any motorcycle tire manufacturer's website to learn more about tire construction. I have swapped out bias tires for radials with no problems. Some bikes may incur adverse handling, but most riders will actually see an enhancement.

Load-Carrying Capacity - Consider the total weight of your motorcycle, including the weight of any optional equipment, and whether you will be carrying a passenger. The load-carrying capability of your tires will be reduced by under-inflation. It is possible for you to overload a tire even though it is the size specified by the motorcycle manufacturer. Maximum loads and corresponding pressures are indicated on the sidewall of the tire. Do not exceed this load limit. Adding a trailer will add weight that can easily exceed the maximum tire load limit, so beware. A sidecar is okay as long as the tire is designed for such use, and your motorcycle user manual should call out the tire type and proper size to use.

Tire Vendors - It is easy to order tires and accessories online and get a good deal, but it can turn sour if you are not diligent. Consider these suggestions.

Restocking Fees - Let's not forget to deal with reputable companies with generous returns and shipping policies. Try to avoid firms that charge a restocking fee for they profit on your (and sometimes their mistakes). Nothing is more insulting is for the company to make a mistake to ship you the improper or defective tire and they bill you 25% restocking fee. Read their policies before you place the order. Restocking fees are hostile to consumers and permits theft by profiting at the consumer's expense. Avoid those companies!

Returns - Sometimes you need to return a product. What are the time limits? I have returned products a year later even when the policy claims returns must be in 30 days. How? The company treats its customers well. Tell them a truthful reason and the odds are good they will honor your request, but you may have to forward your initial refusals to upper layers of management. Some companies have a "no return" policy. Do not do business with them, ever! By contract law, if they mistakenly send you the wrong product they don't have to refund you.

Shipping Fees: Many Internet vendors offer free shipping on tires. Be aware of their shipping policies as they can come back to haunt you in a big way. Make sure if the company sends you the wrong tire or a defective tire they will send to you a prepaid shipping label so they pay the shipping to return the tire and reship the replacement tire at no charge to you. Did you know it can cost almost $100 to return a tire? That is the rising cost of shipping for individuals. Corporations get discounts we do not obtain. If you have to pay for shipping it will wipe out your tire purchase savings costing you more than if you purchased it from a retail store. Always use credit card so you obtain dispute protection.

Company Policy - Always read the company written policy before you pay a merchant a dime. Once you pay and later read the policy and find out you are being robbed it is too late... you are being robbed!

Visit: JamesRussellPublishing.com for more articles on motorcycles, tires, engines, etc.

EXPENSIVE TIRES ARE NOT BETTER

Do not believe that expensive tires are better than inexpensive tires for this rule of, "You get what you pay for" does not always apply in the case of purchasing new motorcycle tires. Just because a certain brand of tire from a certain country of origin has success in the marketplace does not mean it is the wise choice tire to use. The tire that is a successful brand is no indication of the tire's performance and economy. A $200 tire, or a tire that is way more expensive than competitors tires, may be unwise to purchase.

First, do not follow the crowd when selecting tires. Riders and dealers may say, "Buy this brand..., that's the one I use and most everybody else uses" may be just another rider being deceived by brand success.

Second, dealers sell tires to make money and they will tend to stock the branded few tires that have the most profit markup to them. That high profit margin is what drives the frenzy and proliferation of a certain brand.

Third, so when you see most everyone is using certain brands of tires you should be aware that somewhere out there is a set of tires that cost half the price and last nearly twice as long! At the time of this writing I found Kenda® and Mitchelin® cruiser brand tires fit this bill. Maybe when you read this in the future it may be another brand of tire. My Website may mention what tire this may be to save you a bunch of money so check it out at JamesRussellPublishing.com Price is not the only thing, these tires also ride with a absorbent soft shock effect, grip the road well, last a long time, are quiet, do not squirm on rain grooves and cost less than half in price even from tire discounters. You can pay twice as much from a local motorcycle dealer for a popular branded tire that is inferior.

Fourth, the successful branded tire may be a good tire after all and usually is, but you will pay too much money for them. You will find many custom bike builders using these successful tires. Now why is that? Could they be getting those tires for free for advertising exposure? It happens more than you know. Magazines get free tires for product reviews too and this keeps the publicity and popularity machine well oiled to continue the myth that one or two certain brands are the best money can buy. Don't you get caught up into this propaganda or it will drill a hole in your wallet!

Fifth, granted there are other bikes than just cruisers that do need a much higher quality performing tire than the street rider. Even then, if you shop around and give the inexpensive tires a try you will find the most expensive is not always the best. However, if you are racing this is another story. The branded tire will likely be better, but only for that "racing" tire. Just because they have a winning edge racing tire does not mean their street tires are better than everyone else.

Six, I know the peer pressure effect well for we have all fallen for it. If you install branded tires on your bike it makes your bike acceptable to everyone else who rides and sees your bike. We no longer should play those games In reality, nobody cares and neither should you. In fact, being different gives you the edge that draws attention to you and your bike anyway. I'd rather save money and have a better ride experience. Wouldn't you?

Seven, tires other riders use may not be the right tires for your bike. Going with the "flow" is not advisable as the majority are mostly wrong just like investing in the stock market the contrarian investor usually has the most consistent success. Dare to be different. Dare to try other brands. Find the right tire brand for your bike.

A FATTER TIRE

Many riders want to install a wide rear tire on their motorcycles. This is easy to do. First, measure to see how much clearance you have between the existing tire and the sides of the rear fender, belt, chain or swing arm, whichever is closest to the tire. Just take the measurement from one side of the tire to the fender, belt, chain or swing arm. Convert that measurement into millimeters. Second, add that figure to the first number of your existing tire. You may end up with a wider tire that still has clearance to not rub against the rear fender or swing arm if you do not exceed this tire width. The front tire can be measured the same way, but usually there is not as much clearance to work with. The fender rides close to the tire on the top and on the sides. Adequate clearance of fenders, swing arm, etc., must be maintained.

Example:
Existing tire width: 180mm (180/55ZR/18 size tire).
Tire to fender (or tire to swing arm which ever is closest to tire) clearance: 30mm.
Add both numbers above (210) then subtract 5mm = 205mm tire can be installed.
Look for this tire: 210/55ZR/18 because they do not make a 205mm wide tire.

The above formula allows a 20mm increased wide tire than what you currently have installed on your wheel, but depending on your bike you may find the general 10mm wide increase formula will be the maximum size anyway. It is the rule of thumb.

But when the new tire arrives, despite that it may be embossed on the tire as a 210mm wide tire you got to measure that tire with a ruler or calipers, remember that some tire companies fudge on their size numbers so you must verify the tire width before you mount the tire to the rim or install the wheel to the motorcycle. Read next section.

The tire height should be okay because the change here is not radically large. Just find a tire with the same aspect ratio or close to the original, around 5% or less. Otherwise the top of the tire will hit and rub on the fender when you hit a bump in the road and the motorcycle shock absorbers compress downward.

To install a huge fat tire will require an increase in rim width. When increasing tire size and/or rim width, rotate wheel and inspect closely for sufficient clearance to the sides of the swing arm and fender top and sides. You can purchase pre-engineered kits to do this for an easier installation.

Tip: To measure tire width and clearances to frame you can use a large size Vernier caliper. In most cases you can install a 10mm wider tire than what is stock on your motorcycle without any problems, but not in all cases.

Again, it is almost impossible to use a formula as I gave above with reliability due to the fact tire manufacturers actually are dishonest and lie when describing their actual tire sizes. With Harley-Davidson motorcycles you really do need to make sure the tires are sized to fit Harley-Davidson motorcycles. You just can't trust tire sizes otherwise stamped on the tire. It is my opinion false advertising is taking place and it is dangerous. Read the next paragraph.

TIRE SIZE NOT TRULY STATED

It is important to mention once again there is a problem in the tire industry as their tire sizes may not actually match the actual tire size usually in width. This makes it hard on all of us when the tire industry does not post truthful tire dimensions. You look in a tire catalog seeing many different brands of tires and they have similar tire sizes so you think they will fit on your bike. Most will fit, but Harley-Davidson is one brand of motorcycle that requires an "exact fit" or no more than a 10mm width wider than stock size in some cases. Harley-Davidson wheels have tight clearances and there is nothing wrong with this at all, its when the tire manufacturer sells a too wide tire way beyond its rated width size the belt drive could rip into the new tire or the fender can tear the new tire. This is not the fault of Harley-Davidson. So, when you purchase tires look in the catalog for "Tire For Harley-Davidson Motorcycles" and these tires should have correct and accurate sizes you can trust (if the catalog is not in error). When I tried the Mitchelin Commander II tires on my new Sportster 1200 custom their advertising was specific to fit Harley-Davidson's and it was a perfect fit match in heaven. Contact the manufacturer of the tire you want to purchase and ask about the dimensions and fitment for your specific brand of motorcycle.

If you purchased a tire that when measured by your ruler/calipers is wider than its stated size it is false and misleading advertising and on that basis you can get your money refunded, even if the tire was damaged.

Tip: When buying tires always use a credit card or PayPal® or some other system with a free dispute system that will go to bat for you to get your refund if something goes wrong. You may even get a new defective tire that will be out of round and will not inflate to the rim or bead-up concentrically. Most tire companies will not dispute, but dealers often will due to their ignorance that sometimes tires come out of the mold defective.

OVERSIZED REAR TIRE

Why you should not install those huge 250mm+ tires? They may look cool to some people, but the tire wears out really fast and they are terribly expensive to renew. The rear wheel is so wide that hitting even a tiny bump while turning will tend to throw the motorcycle down (even a tire 230mm wide will do this, but not as bad as the 250 and the humongous 330mm tire). The bike will not want to turn into corners. You will fight to make the bike lean in, and you will extend a lot of effort to come out of the lean. Your arms will tire on a winding road in no time at all. And if you cannot quickly maneuver (which you can't) to evade hazardous traffic situations you may not escape an accident. And one more thing. That big wide tire out back is a nail magnet. Bring a flat tire repair kit with you at all times because you will need it.

OVERSIZE FRONT WHEEL

The "fad" of installing 26" to 30" front wheels on motorcycles, mostly baggers (dressers), is actually ridiculous as it cants the frame to slope to the rear. You also get horrible handling and the danger increases as a loss of front wheel traction results from the reversed center of gravity and a much smaller tire/pavement contact patch. Don't get wrapped up in such styling fads for it may look cool to some, but anything that can increase a motorcycle's risk of crashing is plain senseless. But, if you still want to do it you can install 26" and taller tires using just tire irons. Just make sure the rim you buy has a deep drop-center so the tire will install easily. You should rake the tripple tree to lower the bike and regain handling and ride quality. You can buy raked trees so no welding is required. These low-profile tall size rims will have shallow drop-centers so the tires will install a bit more difficult, but you can put them on the rims using the procedures in this book.

EXTRA SET OF WHEELS

You are probably wondering why I bought an extra set of wheels for my Sportster. If you change your own tires you will save a tremendous amount of money each year especially if you ride a lot and go through three to fours sets of tires a year. Add it up. But it also takes time to remove and install the tire. If I buy a complete wheel set all I have to do it just swap out the wheels and I am finished. Later, when I am in the mood, I can install the new tires on the other rims. You'll need to install brake rotors and drive pulley or chain sprocket.

What about rotor and brake pad wear? The tires will normally wear out in six to twelve thousand miles so the differences between the old set and the new set will be minor. Yes, the rotor and brake pads do wear perfectly to the original wheel set and when you replace your spare wheel they will not match up. However, they do conform in about 100 miles as the pads are of a material that can adapt so no harm is done. Just bed in the new brakes as if they were brand new brake pads on a old brake rotor. When you install new brake pads you do not install a new rotor, right? So you have been doing this all along and didn't realize it. Only cars and trucks grind the rotors to fit the new pads because they last for tens of thousands of miles and motorcycle brake rotors wear out in just ten to thirty thousand miles on average so the wear differences are minor.

What about the drive sprocket/pulley wear? Yes, a chain sprocket will strive the most to find equilibrium once again, but you will never notice it. And if there is a bit more wear and tear on the chain and sprockets due to the minor mismatch you may still not notice it. Don't worry about it, just swap the wheels and go. The belt drive pulley will also adapt to the new (or slightly different wear pattern of the replacement) pulley much better and quicker than a metal chain. In both instances you will not notice any difference. Sometimes we worry about things too much or become too technical. Sometimes what works in the real world simply works.

You will read motorcycle articles not to replace a chain without replacing your two drive sprockets and this is true, even true with belt drive pulleys. What you need to do is keep a log of how much miles are put on your drive pulleys. This way if you drive 60,000 miles you will know just how much miles were put on each pulley. It will help you to determine when it is time to install new pulleys.

What if I have a shaft drive bike? You would have to purchase a wheel with the drive hub and that can be awfully expensive unless you can find a used one. Most riders do not have an extra set of wheels with new tires already installed in the garage waiting to swap out the wheels. Plus, it is very quick to remove a shaft drive wheel so I would not bother. Why not just have a spare front wheel? Well, you can, but the front wheel is the easiest and quickest to remove.

Granted, having two sets of complete wheels is not for everybody, is expensive and is not normal for street riders in general, but you will see this quick replacement system used in professional racing and dirt bike riders. The money you save installing your new tires yourself permits you to have these conveniences.

Important: This system have swapping out entire wheel assemblies works, but keep in mind you should start with new drive belt pulley/sprocket and chain on the engine, both rear wheels and new brake pads on "all" wheel rotors. When you do this the wear differences between wheel swaps will remain manageable and negligible. It does not work if the wear pattern differences are greater than 15,000 to 20,000 miles between the two wheel sets. I like to keep the differences within 6,000 to 12,000 miles. At about 30,000 miles the chain sprockets will be time for replacement. At 60,000 to 80,000 miles the belt and pullies will need to be replaced. When it eventually comes time to replace a drive belt or chain you need to replace both belt pulleys and chain sprocket and engine pully/sprocket as a new matching set.

Tip: If you want more fuel mileage, increased torque and lower engine rpm's for cruising you can increase 2 tooth size on the countershaft/engine pulley/sprocket or decrease 3 teeth on the wheel pulley/sprocket. Reversing this formula will increase engine rpm's, lower mileage and gain more acceleration. Yes, you can change tooth size on both sprockets for maximum benefit or you can just change one tooth size and leave the other pulley/sprocket stock size. It does not matter which sprocket/pulley you want to alter. It may be cheaper to replace the front or the rear so go with that. In all cases, you must install both pullies/sprockets as well as a new belt/chain to do it right.

TRACKING LOG CHART FOR SPARE WHEEL SETS

Just jot down the miles accrued on each item. It will also help you determine when to replace the items. You may need to also write in the miles on both left and right side brake pads and brake rotors. Generally, they should be the same in miles unless one was replace. If so, the rule is broken. Both rotors should have been replaced as the same time.

Example: Sportster, left front brake pads 12,000, rear pads 6,000, rotor front left 15,000, rear rotor 15,000, wheel pulley 18,000, front wheel bearings 18,000, rear wheel bearings 18,000.

Use pencil in this book or create a electronic data file to keep track of miles. The wheel set that came with the bike is usually Wheel Set #1.

Wheel Set #1_____

_____.

Wheel Set #2: _____

_____.

Engine Pulley/Sprocket: _____

_____.

Drive Belt/Chain Miles: _____

_____.

When you incorporate this wheel swap technique its only real purpose is to enable you to quickly replace the wheels without having to spend time mounting new tires to the rims. Its not for everyone, just for those who want to get back to riding in one hour instead of two or three hours.

There is another benefit, you will see your brake rotors, wheel bearings, sprocket/pulley last longer before needing replacement as the wear and tear is spread out between both sets of wheels. The drive belt or chain or engine pulley/sprocket and brake pads will not last longer. These items will wear out normally as they are not swapped out. Keep a log of the miles put on your drive belt or drive chain.

Don't forget to log the engine pulley or chain sprocket attached to the engine's transmission is not swapped out and it will be subject to constant wear regardless of wheel set swapping. It will always be the total of both wheel sets miles. Example: Wheel Set #1: 8,000 miles. Wheel Set #2: 8,500 miles = 16,500 miles on engine sprocket/pulley. Keep an eye on it for replacement due to wear.

Note: When it comes time to replace the engine drive pulley/sprocket due to wear you will need also replace the Wheel Sets #1 and #2 pulley/sprockets as a matched set including a new belt/chain.

Keeping an extra set of wheels is expensive to purchase and to maintain the extra sets, but for those who do not mind the expenditure of cash it is a rapid and less strenuous method to renuing tires on your motorcycle. If you ride every day or snowbird with your motorcycle in RV parks time can be of the essence. Elderly riders also benefit as the work load is split in half.

Snowbirding: Many riders head to the southern states in the winter, but they forget that they can greatly benefit by bringing along an extra set of wheels with new tires already mounted on them. This way they are not paying the high-prices for a new set of tires. Most snowbirds will use two sets of tires in the winter.

These predatory motorcycle dealers take advantage of snowbird riders. Also, since there's no oil to drip, many RV parks may let

And Fix Flat Tires

you swap out the tires on site. If not, off site will do just fine a few feet away from the property line. This advice alone will save you at least $400 to $800 or more each year in tire expenses! Add up the savings and you can see how an extra set of wheels will pay for themselves and pocket you money yearly.

MAGAZINE BIAS

I am amazed at the bias of magazines to withold important information in their articles from readers eyes. It has come to the point the truth is being covered up to protect companies from getting a black eye for selling inferior products. Even motorcycle test rides are incomplete and focus on areas that are ride eventful, but routine maintenance horrors are not being revealed. From oil filters that can't be changed without removing the exhaust system to air filters that require the bike to be disassembled just to access it. How about valve adjustments that require the engine be dropped out of the frame? And the list goes on as the rags rave on the bike and ignore the practical side us riders have to endure. This includes known engine defects and complexity of maintenance being ignored.

Magazines are terrified to print the real world brutal truth for fear advertisers will be upset and pull out and the magazine loses money. There is a reason to the madness after all, but we consumers get screwed and perish for lack of knowledge.

You can still get a lot of good information from the motorcycle magazines, and some of the V-Twin magazines are some of the best in honesty, fairness and notifying readers of the "problems" of owning a certain brand or model of bike.

I also have written articles for my Website that appease no advertisers. Visit: JamesRussellPublishing.com

CHAPTER 18
Quick Reference Guide

Use this Quick Reference to cut through the chatter and go right to the steps required. Table of Contents reveals the page number.

Break Tire Bead: Go to Chapter 4.

Remove Tire From Rim With Tire Irons: Go to Chapter 4.

Lubricate the Rim/Tire: Go to Chapter 5.

Install Tire With Tire Irons: Go to Chapter 5.

Using Manual Tire Changing Machine: Go to Chapter 16.

Install Tube & Tire on Wire (spoke) Wheel: Go to Chapter 11.

Inflating Tire/Bead Starting: Go to Chapter 7.

Balancing Wheel: Go to Chapter 8.

Fix Flat Tires: Go to Chapter 13 and 14.

CHAPTER 19
Questions & Answers

You will learn a lot here reading the answers to questions so do not skip this section.

1. Question: I fixed my flat inserting the plug, but I can't add air to the tire with my air compressor. What should I do?
Answer: If the weight of the motorcycle is strong enough and most of the air was lost in the tire, then it is possible the tire is broken loose. This is unlikely, but it can happen especially when riding with a passenger. Look at the tire. Do you see the tire separated from the side of the metal rim? If so, this is where the air is leaking from. Try rolling the bike forward two feet without sitting on the bike and adding air again. This hopefully will take the weight off that section of the tire to let the air expand the tire where the bead was broken. If it won't inflate, try this same procedure again two more times (also try with the wheel off the ground if you can). If these

attempts fail, call a tow truck. There is nothing more you can do to fix this tire on the spot. Again, this would be a very rare instance. A tire bead doesn't usually break away from the wheel's rim unless you rode it a long way without air—which is also unlikely as today's cruiser sidewalls are very strong. They're not so strong if riding with a passenger, though. That extra weight can break the tire's bead from the rim. Heavy cruiser motorcycles can cause tire beads to break if tires are run without air. This is why I like to use a tire pressure monitor to keep tabs on the air pressure in the tires. In most cases with tubeless tires, the air leak is slow and you can catch it right away before the tire runs completely flat so bead separation does not occur.

2. Question: I want to change my tube tires. How do I do that?

Answer: You use mostly the same procedures, but you keep a tiny bit of air in the tube so the tube remains "puffy" and the tire irons don't pinch and break the tube. You may also, if it is a dirt bike, have wheel rim locks. These simple devices press down and clamp the tire to the rim locking the tire to the rim. They are recommended for use on all off-road machines and any application using low tire pressure. You just have to loosen the rim lock to remove a tire, and tighten the rim lock last when you finish putting the new tire on. After you have inflated the tube to seat the tire bead, then you can tighten the rim lock. Always buy and install a new innertube and rim band when changing tube tires. Also, you will find that dirt bike tires are removed and installed much easier than street cruiser tires. Cruiser street tires are stronger and have thick rubber, so you need to use the large tire irons to get the job done. Install a tire designed for tube use.

3. Question: I ride hard on my bike with laced wheels, as I do like to drag race a bit on the street and on dyno-drags. I once blew a tube at the valve stem. Is there a device I can use to stop this?

Answer: A rim lock can be used on a cruiser motorcycle rear laced spoke wheel to prevent the tire from rotating on the rim and shearing the valve stem off. It's not a good idea if you ride fast on the street as the rim lock can create localized heat to weaken the tube. The best cure? Stop drag racing or install cast wheels.

4. Question: You say a dynamometer can ruin a tire. Please explain.

Answer: Laced or cast wheels placed on those wheel dynamometer that test horsepower and assist in tuning an engine can ruin a tire, breaking the cords inside. So, beware of anyone putting your bike on a wheel dyno. Most shops have dynos, where the rear wheel runs a controlled braked roller. The tire folds under the pressure, and the tire was never designed to survive such grueling forces being applied to it. Tire companies warn against putting their tires on wheel dynamometers, but few heed the advice, mostly by unawareness. Repair shops don't care if you break the tire cords, which causes the tire to run hot and then wear out quickly. They get to sell you another tire!

5. Question: Why can't I ride my plugged tire at normal speeds?

Answer: The centrifugal force and flexing of a motorcycle tire can work the plug loose, causing you another flat tire and a chance to crash. It may not happen, but it could. In my personal experience? I have had really good luck with plugging flat tubeless tires and I drive at highway speed 55 to 65 mph with no problems. Is this lucky? I think the tire plugging products are performing just fine and the string/rope plug in my opinion is the most secure of them all.

6. Question: Why must I install a new tire after I plug my flat tire?

Answer: The tire's strong inner cords can slowly grind away at the soft plug and cut it in half, allowing a blowout or at least a small leak. Safety is important to you. Get a new tire.

7. Question: What do I do if my plugged tire leaks again after fixing it?

Answer: If it is leaking from the rubber plug, you can insert a sting/rope to replace it. That is why I recommend you carry both types of plugs with you. If one won't work, the other likely will. If you can only carry one type then carry the string/rope repair kit.

8. Question: I installed my new tire, but I get a bumpy ride. Why?

Answer: You likely did not set the bead properly. Go back and read "Adding Air to the New Tire." Make sure you have the tire running in the proper rotation. There is an arrow on the tire. Inflate the tire to the correct pressure. Balance problems usually create vibration, but check your wheel balance with a static balance stand or computer wheel balancer to be sure this is not the problem. If you still have a bumpy ride, make sure the tire is not hitting the fender top or sides and your shock absorbers are not failing. It is rare, but you could have a defective, out-of-round tire that somehow became heated and deformed or was damaged in the shipping process. You may even be able to feel a flat spot in the tread are if the damage is severe. Spin the wheel off the ground and examine the tire to see if it is hopping. Worn or broken wheel bearings can cause a rough ride, usually a wobble or shaking. The same will occur if your wheel is out of true. If all was well until the tire was installed, then focus on the tire and mounting process to find the cure. You could also have a bad steering head bearing needing adjustment or replacement.

9. Question: Please explain how to use a motorcycle jack.

Answer: Read the manufacturer's instructions that came with your jack. There is only one way to use a traditional ATV/motorcycle lift, and that is to lift the entire bike level, with no tipping forward or back. Strap the bike down to the lift. However, the scissor jack is used three ways: (1) to lift the entire motorcycle by setting the jack perfectly centered under the bike, (2) to position the jack a bit forward and lift only the front wheel off the ground, or (3) to position the jack a bit to the rear to lift only the rear wheel off the ground. When tipping a bike, make sure it will not roll forward or backward. You should strap the bike down to the jack or to the floor (or motorcycle lift stand) so the bike and the jack (or lift stand) become one unit.

10. Question: Can I mix bias and radial tires on my bike?
Answer: Motorcycle radials and motorcycle bias-ply tires each give a motorcycle a definite type of handling characteristic. Mixing them on one motorcycle creates an insecure condition. You may receive a rough ride, jittering, and even wheel hop. It will lessen the bike's aptitude to corner well. You could do it, but where is the benefit?

11. Question: My bike came with bias tires. Can I switch to radial tires?
Answer: I have yet to find a good answer for this question. Most sources and motorcycle magazines say not to do it. Since radial tires are better than bias for handling heat and longevity of tire life, it would be a benefit to switch. It appears for liability issues everyone seems to fear making any recommendations. Even the tire companies and motorcycle manufactures are not being clear with us on this issue, at least at the time of writing this book. One day I will just try a set of radials and see what happens. For some bikes it may work out just fine, while others may develop handling problems. This is all we as consumers can do at the moment.

12. Question: I was told to overinflate my tubeless tire air pressure by 8 psi. Why?
Answer: The only time you should overinflate your tire is if you find the current tire pressure below what is indicated on the nameplate on the bike's frame. However, never inflate beyond the pressure stamped on the sidewall of the tire. Purchase the correct tires for your bike. Overinflating stresses the tire's casing in ways it was not designed to handle, including dangerous sudden deflation from tire failure and even picking up a small nail hole. It also reduces the tire's contact patch to the road, reducing handling and stopping distance. Plus it will give you a stiff, harsh ride, not being able to absorb road shock, and it makes for an excessive stiffness overpowering the rebound damping of the shock absorbers. Instead of taking the advice of just anybody, check on the Internet with the manufacturer for advice. They have "engineered" their products, and they know them best. Under inflated tires can result in imprecise cornering, higher running temperatures, irregular tread wear at the edge of the contact patch, fatigue cracking, overstressing, and failure of the tire casing. Overinflating tires does not increase load carrying capacity, but it will result in a very hard ride and rapid tire wear in the center of the contact patch.

13. Question: I was told that balancing motorcycle tires must be performed by motorcycle shops with dynamic tire balancers. Is this true?
Answer: No. You can static balance tires yourself, if you wish, for street and highway riding. Unless you are racing above highway speeds or on a closed track, dynamic balancing will give you little to no advantage. Many shops actually have dynamic balancers that are out of calibration and are operated incorrectly. Most shops never calibrate their computerized dynamic spin balancers, so the customer is getting poor balancing results and does not even realize it. Calibration needs to be performed on a regular basis, and most shops don't even bother to do it. This says much about paying for high-quality repair work and not getting it.

14. Question: Why do some tires last longer than others?
Answer: Soft tire compound is the major cause of tire wear. If you ride a cruiser and you purchase a duel sport tire, the softer rubber will wear out quickly. Cruisers need a harder rubber compound for best longevity. Pay attention to how you operate the throttle and clutch. Abrupt throttle and clutch transitions that cause micro-skidding of the tire can wear down the tire rapidly. If you smooth out these transitions, you can easily gain 3,000 miles or more tire longevity. Spoke wheels run hotter than cast wheels because cast wheels act as heat sinks, removing heat from the tire/rim quickly and lowering tire operating temperature. Riding with a passenger wears tires down faster. Research the new tires and find one designed for the type of riding you do. Also, a new tire with more tread depth than the competition can give you an edge in tire longevity, as long as the tire compounds are similar. New tire compounds are always arriving. Trial and error is the only sure way to find the perfect set of tires for your bike.

15. Question: I can't get my tire to balance except using over 60 grams of wheel weights. Is this okay?
Answer: I have seen wheels from the factory with over 100 grams of wheel weights on the rear wheel. I have had no trouble with that, except that it looks ugly with longs strips of weights on the rim. Generally you should be able to balance a tire with less than that, with 40 grams being good and 20 being excellent. But in reality it does not matter how many weights are required as long as the balance is perfect or close to perfect. The bottom line is, a balanced wheel is a balanced wheel. There is a balancing ink dot on the tire, and this dot is to be aligned with the valve stem in the rim. This is the starting point. The wheel weights take over after this. In some very rare cases you may need to move the tire around the rim away from the ink dot, but again this would be a very rare instance. Plus, you will discover that wheel balancing for street cruiser riding at normal highway speeds is not as critical as you are led to believe.

How To Install Tires on Motorcycles

Many riders are riding with out of balance tires, with no ill effects that they can detect, due to missing wheel weights that have fallen off the wheel. Bikes come into a dealership or independent repair shop like this all the time. Many leave in the same condition if they have come in for some non-tire-related repair, and nobody is the wiser. Sport bikes need more precise wheel balancing. They are lighter in weight and dive deeply into corners, and their riders ride faster than the rest of us. Static wheel balancing is still okay for any street bike. You could buy new aftermarket custom wheels as they are better balanced. Some economical tires like a Shinko® brand are well balanced and only require 1/4 or less while expensive brands may need a lot more weight than that.

16. Question: I got a flat tire and found no nail hole in the tire, but the tube was leaking. How did this happen?
Answer: Likely the tube was slightly pinched when being installed. When the tube is caught between the tire iron and the rim or tire pressure is too low, it can cause the tire to flex and rub against the tube, creating a "pinch-flat." Hitting an object in road can break a tube as can and old tube or a torn internal rim-band.

17. Question: My valve stem on my innertube was torn. How did this occur?
Answer: Under hard acceleration or braking or with low tire pressure, the tire can rotate on the rim, dragging the tube with it. Since the valve stem is bolted to the rim, the tube's stem tears.

18. Question: Is it true I will receive less longevity with tube tires?
Answer: Yes. Tube tires generate and fail to dissipate frictional heat, so they will wear out faster than tubeless tires. Tubes normally chafe constantly against the tire's interior surface, which generates a lot of heat and increases the tire's temperature. That chafing also wears down the tube, and that is why you must install a new tube when installing a new tire.

19. Question: Why do tubes blow out?
Answer: Rubber is naturally flexible. When heated from tire friction, it becomes even softer and can become so hot to actually deform and lose strength and pop like a balloon. A nail can rip the tube causing an internal explosion. As the tube fails, the tube rips a larger hole into the rubber as the force of air escapes, causing a sudden release of compressed air like a popped balloon. Because of this danger of blowout, tubeless tires were created to escape from the hazard. To ride on the street with spoke wheels is dangerous. Mostly the Harley-Davidson dealers sell to the unsuspecting rider big, heavy cruiser motorcycles with dangerous spoke wheels. The wheels cost less than cast wheels. I once bought a new Harley-Davidson with spoke wheels because the price was good, but I immediately replaced the laced wheel with chrome cast wheels. It is easy to do by yourself or to have it done for you, and now you can ride safely and fix flat tires quickly.

20. Question: Is it true if I slam on my brakes on my motorcycle I can earn a flat tire?
Answer: Yes, you can. If you have traditional laced spoke wheels the rubber tire will rotate on the rim when skidding on rough pavement. This rotation will drag the innertube along with it and rip the tube open. These forces can be so great that even rim locks won't stop the tire's rotation, especially on a big, heavy cruiser motorcycle riding with or without a passenger. Tubeless tires will not go flat unless the skid was so long and severe that it wore the rubber all the way through the tread, breaching the tire's casing.

21. Question: Should I check my tire pressures when hot or cold?
Answer: Cold. How cold is cold? After one hour of riding let the bike sit in a shaded area is sufficient. But lets not be too finicky here as you can check your tire pressure anytime you feel they are low of air. It may be better to check tires when cold, but it is safer to check tires pressure any time! What you want to avoid is checking air on a hot tire, add the recommended air pressure then ride off on hot pavement for this will only raise the air pressure in the tire due to heat expansion of the air over pressurizing the tire. So add 3-5 psi less air when checking the tire pressure when hot to allow for this extra air pressure to accumulate and not over pressurize the tire.

22. Question: Should I replace the valve stem and core on each tire change?
Answer: On cars and trucks this is common, but on motorcycles it is not normally performed on each tire change. The tires wear out faster on motorcycles. Examine the metal valve stem rubber seals, and if they appear cracked with age replace them. The Schrader valve cores last a long time. They are located inside the valve stem and can be reused, but it is very economical to replace them at your choosing. Once each year is fine or every fourth tire change, but sooner is fine if you prefer. Make sure you have a metal valve cap in place, as this is an extra safety feature to prevent air from escaping a leaking Schrader valve. However, if you have a pressure monitoring valve cap installed, that device will have to serve as your valve cap.

23. Question: My tire won't hold air, but I can't find an air leak from a hole in the tire.
Answer: You may have a leak at the bead surface, a Schrader valve or valve stem seal leak, or even damage to the casing of the tire which is leaking air, all with no visible nail hole. If your rim is not bent, buy a new tubeless tire or a new tire and tube. Dunk the wheel vertically under water (bath tub will work) and look for air bubbles. Don't submerge wheel bearings.

24. Question: What is the speed rating I must use when buying new tires?
Answer: Your motorcycle manufacturer or dealer or your owners manual and will tell you. If you drive at normal freeway speeds in the USA, which means around 70 miles per hour, you won't need speed ratings of 180 miles per hour.

25. Question: I installed new tires and my bike feels unstable. What is wrong?
Answer: I assume you have air inflated in your tires. New tires will have a different contact patch and lean-over edge. This can make the bike feel unstable at first until you become accustomed to the new tires. Installing one new tire and keeping your older worn tire can mix things up regarding handling and ride quality. You need to break in the tires anyway, so ride easy for the first 100 miles.

26. Question: When should I replace my tires?
Answer: There are shallow bumps called "wear bar" markings located at the bottom of the treads. When these wear bars are at the surface, it is time for a new tire. There will only be about 1/16" to 1/32" tread left on the tire. The majority of riders often do replace their tires before this point. Yet there are riders, due to economic reasons, who go beyond this point until no tread is left and the tire is bald of tread. Usually they will not be riding in the rain. The tire grooves (treads) are only for water to escape. Racing bike tires are completely bald. However, running a tire so low on tread on the street makes the tire vulnerable to any nail or sharp object to puncture the carcass due to less rubber protection. You will see some bikes with the tire's string-like cords showing. This is dangerous as the tire can now blow out at any moment, even with a tubeless tire. The quick test is to insert a Lincoln penny into the tread. If the top of Lincoln's head is level with the remaining tread, you need to replace the tire.

27. Question: I have used CO2 cartridges to inflate my tires with success, but you say not to rely on them. Please explain.
Answer: You are lucky. The hotter the weather or higher the elevation, the more the CO2 cartridge is prone to freeze, solidify, and block all gas flow into the tire. This can leave you stranded by the side of the road. You can also get a dangerous frost bite "freezer burn" if you are not careful. That can require amputation of a finger, so beware. They also will not fill the tire completely. This is why I say to carry a portable air compressor to be certain you can inflate your tire after fixing it.

28. Question: I read on Internet testimonials that the rubber and string plugs can be permanent repairs. Why do you say it is not?
Answer: Because tire manufacturers and the companies that make these rubber plugs and strings also say their products are not permanent repairs. It is a liability issue that nobody desires to go on record to claim the repair is permanent and then have a plug or string come loose. It is best anyway to just fix the flat and buy a new tire. The carcass of the tire has been compromised and its strength is weakened, and that nail hole is the weakest point to fail. StopnGo.com and other tire repair product companies do make a permanent tubeless tire repair kit called the Patch/Plug system. Even then, tire manufacturers are reluctant to call them permanent, even if the nail hole is less than 1/4" in diameter. Speed should not exceed 50 mph for the first 24 hours after the patch/plug repair, and the repaired tire should never be used over 75 mph.

29. Question: I installed new tires, and I now get a wobble when I let go of the handlebars. There is no wobble when I have my hands on the handlebars. Why is this happening?
Answer: This can happen if you change brands of tires. The good news is that a wobble like this usually does not call for expensive repairs. A lot of bikes will wobble when the front tire wears down. A shimmy begins when the handlebars are let go, and this shimmy can be violent. The same is true if saddlebags are loaded unevenly or cause air turbulant wind flow. Unless you damaged the wheel bearings when installing your wheels, which is highly unlikely unless you took a strong hammer to them when inserting an axle, just don't buy that brand of tire anymore. You could check the fall-away steeringhead bearing race adjustment, but it seems to me that the bike just does not like these tires. Make sure you have air in the tire. A flat tire will wobble like crazy. Do you have to replace the tire? No. Just keep your hands on the handlebars where they belong.

30. Question: I can't inflate the new tire no matter what I do. I'm rotating the tire bead starting strap to different positions, altering the tension of the straps, and it still will not inflate to seat the bead. What am I doing wrong?
Answer: Make sure there are no obstructions between the tire and rim, like a rim protector still in place, some other object, cloth—anything. Did you clean the rims before installing the tire? A dirty rim will prevent the tire from sealing to the rim and leak air. Did you lube the tire and rim? The tire can't seal air if it is stuck to the rim and cannot flex and move to the rim bead. Sometimes you really have to tighten the bead starting straps ridiculously tight to get the tire to seat against the rim before filling with air. Take the tire to a shop that has a higher air line capacity to initially expand the tire to inflate. If all these things were performed, you have a bad tire. Yes, it happens on occasion. A tire is just out of round and will not seal air to inflate to set the bead. The tire should be returned for warrantee replacement as defective. And if the replacement tire does the same thing, something else is wrong, like the wrong size tire being installed to that rim.

31. Question: What is the white colored dot for on the new tire?

Answer: The dot (white, yellow, blue, or some other color) is the lightest portion of the tire (on most tires these days, check with the manufacturer as it may be the heavy spot) and is to be aligned with the heavy spot on the rim where the valve stem is located. This helps begin the balancing process. Once I messed up and did not bother to balance the tire. I also found the white paint dot moved to the opposite side of the valve stem after installing the tire on the bike. I wanted to see what would happen, and nothing did. Always do the job right and put the white dot where it belongs. But if you are just cruising on the street at legal highway speeds, you likely will not know otherwise. Bikers who like to burn rubber with tubeless tires can tell you that the white dot will walk around the rim and they ride on without a care. Wheel balance is most critical at high speeds over 90 miles per hour. Below that speed, you may or may not see a bit more tire wear than normal. Sometimes we are just too technically touchy about wheel balancing, as if it is a mysterious black art. Unless you get obvious handling issues or severe uneven tire wear, do not worry about perfect wheel balance for normal street use. Modern wheels and tires are better balanced from the start than anything available yesteryear.

32. Question: Will modern tires fit vintage rims?
Answer: Not always. The tire may slip or lose air when mounted to the rim. Consult with the tire manufacturer to see if the tires will fit your rim properly. They still do make vintage tires for old bikes.

33. Question: What happens if I install a tire backwards?
Answer: You must remove and reinstall the tire. This is an unforgivable error because it can tear the motorcycle tire in two at high speed, causing you to crash. It has to do with the engineering and final construction of the tire joints, including the layering of plies and the rubber overlay as they are wrapped and vulcanized together. Also the tread pattern is designed to shed water and if installed in reverse this shedding of water may not function. Tire treads will also wear out quickly. Just reinstall the tire so the directional rotation of the wheel coincides with the arrow on the tire.

34. Question: I hit a brick on the freeway, but my tire is okay. Must I replace the tire?
Answer: You could still have internal tire damage, so take it easy or just replace the tire to be safe. If you see that your rim is bent or cracked, have the wheel fixed or replaced immediately. Bent rims may cause wheel wobble, bead unseating and, for tubeless tires, gradual air loss. Sudden wheel failure may result from the use of cracked wheel.

35. Question: I was told it is okay to use tire shine and UV protecting products on my tires.
Answer: Not a good idea. As you ride, these products can break down the rubber and actually increase ozone cracking. But worst of all, some of these products can make your tires slick as ice and cause a crash. Just use soap and water and rinse to clean your tires.

36. Question: How can I tell my tires are too old?
Answer: Manufacturers advise that tires over three years old are too old, even if sheltered from the sun and weather. Humidity or dry air can weaken the tire. If you store your bike and tires near electric motors, the ozone produced from the motors can age your tires quickly. Look for tiny cracks in the rubber sidewalls and replace the tire if you see them.

37. Question: Why must needle-nose or Vise-Grip® pliers have teeth?
Answer: Pliers without teeth will not grip or pull anything. Only pliers with serrated teeth will. The needle-nose pliers have a slight edge over the narrow Vise-Grip. The needle-nose can dive deeply into a puncture to remove a screw or nail embedded into the tire with a worn or broken head. The Vise-Grip will remove a large bolt from a tire. You don't have to carry both styles of pliers if you don't want to. Just the needle-nose is fine, and it need not be very long. Small 5" pliers will do, as most punctures will be small nails and screws.

38. Question: Must I stay with the same brand of tire that came with the bike?
Answer: No, but make certain the new brand of tire matches identically the characteristics of the stock tire you are replacing. Load capacity, speed rating, exact rim size, intended use (a street cruising tire is better for mileage than a sport bike tire). Aspect ratio can change along with width, but not too much or the new tire will rub against swing arm or fender. Manufacturers offer a cross-reference to match tires from brand to brand. Some parts catalogs do the same.

39. Question: Are there other flat tire fixes not mentioned in this book?
Answer: Yes. New products are surfacing all the time. One such new product is the "Cargol Turn & Go" emergency tire repair system by Gryyp. Visit Ventura-MCA.com. It looks like a hard nylon screw with a large paddle on one end. You remove the nail from the tire, twist the Turn & Go into the tire's nail home, snap the paddle clean off, and inflate the tire. Flat tire fixed. I have not tried it yet. It appears the device is limited to small holes in the tire due to the ridged size of the device. It comes with CO_2 cartridges (which are not relieable and trustworthy) and only 4 inserts and it cost about $50. Check motorcycle magazines and the Internet for all the newest devices. However, the rubber mushroom plug and string/rope systems will be around for a very long time because they work and have proven themselves over the period of many years with satisfied customers and the string/rope are affordable and can fix small and large

holes in a tire. The patch/plug system is not covered in this book and they are the best money can buy and they are too expensive. If you need to save a new tire with a flat the patch/plug system will save your tire, but it is not a side-of-the-road fix.

40. Question: Are professionals installing tires at dealerships?
Answer: No. You will often discover young kids operating the tire changing machine. The dealer won't usually pull a mechanic off his work schedule. And that is just one reason they don't want you to see what is going on in the shop. They want you to believe a professional is changing your tires when in fact the parts counter guy is likely doing it. And that is one reason why tires are installed improperly, not balanced, and even put on backwards and are under or overinflated, etc.

41. Question: My dealer recommends I pay extra for nitrogen instead of air. Should I?
Answer: No. The atmosphere is mostly nitrogen and other inert gases anyway. Only about 25% is oxygen. Dealers may tell you that the oxygen will corrode the interior of the tire, that oxygen will leak out of the tire, and that your tire will last longer if you use nitrogen instead. All the statements are true, but you will not need pure nitrogen to deal with it. Your tire will wear out way before oxygen will dissolve a rubber tire. Oxygen will leak from the tire slowly over time because its molecule is smaller than nitrogen. That's why we have air compressors to check and add air to the tire. Nitrogen will in principle run cooler than air, so your tire may run truer and last longer, but by how much longer will it last? Nobody knows for certain if there is a real-world benefit for street riders. It won't hurt to fill your tires with nitrogen as race cars and motorcycles do, but for the street rider it is not necessary. I wouldn't pay extra money for the nitrogen service from your dealer or repair shop.

42. Question: I installed a new tire, and at 3,000 miles I noticed a bulge in the sidewall. What caused this?
Answer: I don't know. You could have hit something in the road or a curb. It may even be a manufacturer's defect and that will be covered under warranty. Fill out a warranty claim, and you may get a new tire. This holds true if the tire will no longer hold air. Read the warranty that comes with your new tire, or go online to locate one. Flat tires generally are not under warranty unless otherwise stated as a road hazard warranty.

43. Question: How can I tell which tire is front or a rear tire?
Answer: The tire will have a stamping mark indicating which tire is which. Generally, the wide tire is the rear and the thin tire is the front.

44. Question: Can I install a fat tire on the front and a thin tire on the rear?
Answer: You can customize your motorcycle any way you want, but it may not be the wise thing to do. The bike will not handle worth a darn, but it may give you the visual effect you desire.

45. Question: My tire has three different colored dots on the tire. Which one is the balancing dot?
Answer: The colored dot system marking is not universal among tire manufacturers. It could be a blue, red, white, yellow, or some other color—or none at all. Contact the tire manufacturer to find out which scheme it is using.

46. Question: I saw tire installers at the garage use liquid, not paste lubricant. Why must I use paste lubricant if they don't?
Answer: Liquid tire lubricant is designed to evaporate rapidly and is used on tire mounting machines because the machine mounts the tire to the rim very quickly. With tire irons the installation process is slower. Before you are finished, the liquid lubricant has dried, and mounting the tire becomes highly frictional and difficult. The paste lubricant dries more slowly, keeping the surfaces slippery for a long time. And the paste lube is way more slippery than the liquid lubricant, and you need this extreme greasiness to get the tire mounted onto the rim when using tire irons. It is one of many "trade secret" tire mounting tips revealed in this book. That is why using liquid lube is okay for removing the motorcycle tire from the rim with tire irons. The process is quick and easy. Installing is always slower especially when you are learning.

47. Question: Where do I put these flat tire tools? My saddle bags are full.
Answer: Use a fork bag as shown in Fig. 1-1. The fork bag should be small in height so it will not prevent the forks from compressing and striking the bag. You could use a swingarm bag or mount a bag behind windshield or use a sissybar bag. You could even make your own bag and zip-tie or tape it to the motorcycle frame. Someplace there is a place.

48. Question: How can I tell if my dealer balanced my tires?
Answer: Look for brand-new wheel weights on the rim or wire spoke. If you did not change the brand of tire, there may not be any new weights installed.

49. Question: I balanced my wheels when I installed my new tires, and my wheel balance was way off when I checked before replacing the tires. Why?

Answer: The moment you begin to wear down the tire, the wheel falls out of balance. This is normal. As you can see, keeping a wheel perfectly balanced throughout the tire's life would require balancing the tire multiple times, perhaps every two thousand miles on a cruiser and less for a sport bike. So the next time anybody says that tire balancing is super critical for street riding, ask, "How come you're riding with out-of-balance wheels?"

50. Question: I have wire spoke wheels but no balance weights. What can I use?
Answer: You can still use stick-on wheel weights directly on the rim, but some riders, especially dirt bike riders, find the wheel weights will still fly off. If so, wrap soft wire solder around the spoke above the spoke nipple instead.

51. Question: I tried three tire irons, but I find I need four. Why is this?
Answer: You can get most every tire on with three irons, but once in a while a tire will give you a tough time. I installed two new Kenda Kruz® street tires on my Triumph. The tires were so perfectly fitted that there was no loose fit when placing onto the rim. The tire would not move down into the shallow drop center and would only stick to the bead area of the rim as the tire was being installed. I tried to install the tire with my tire mounting machine, and the mount bar just kept popping up, refusing to mount the tire. I had to use tire irons, and the last eight inches were really tough to flip over the rim on the tire. I did eventually need to use four tire irons. I used two to tie the tire down on both top sides, to the left and to the right, where I was working. Then the tire stayed put and didn't walk out of the rim. The other two took incredibly tiny bites of rubber to get the tire to flip onto the rim to mount. Of all the tires I have changed over the years, this one brand of tire was unusually difficult due to the sizing of the tire. The thickness and stiffness of the rubber tire itself just made it a bear of a job. However, the tire still went on. You have to work slowly to allow time for the rubber to stretch into place before taking the next bite with your tire iron. If you did not lube the tire and rim, the tire will not drop downward and will get stuck, tightening the rubber. You will need to use more tire irons. You should back up and try again when things get tough unless you have a tire like the Kenda® (or shallow rims) that simply cannot drop down past the rim's bead area. These Kenda® tires are great, but this particular model of tire gave me a very difficult time when combined with a shallow drop-center rim. This could happen to any tire if the manufacturer changes dimensions or rubber consistency or the wheel rim is too shallow. When you find a tire that installs with ease, it can be best to stay with that brand of tire. Yes, some tires install easier than others. See Question 52.

52. Question: I have a very tough tire that refuses to mount and I can hear rubber cracking. I am overstretching, so I have to back off. What do I do now?
Answer: Insert a tire iron 180 degrees away from where you are working (opposite side), flip the tire iron down, and tie it down. This will force the rubber off the bead, allowing the rubber to flex just enough to help you. It should install now. The rubber can't move if it is already set into the bead or hung up on the rim's internal shoulder below the rim's bead area, which is what happened to me in question 51 above. That means you may need 5 tire irons to install abnormally difficult tires. The fifth iron is usually a helping hand 90 degrees from where you are working.

53. Question: My tire irons sometimes flip out violently when installing tires. What am I doing wrong?
Answer: This usually happens when you insert the tire iron under the tire's rubber edge. You don't get a good bite-grip of rubber and the tip of the rim, and the tire iron slips from the rim and flips out of your hand. Another reason is that the bites of tire you are taking too large. The rubber becomes so resistant that your hand slips and the tire iron flips forward. Just be a bit more careful. It will happen occasionally.

54. Question: What about the new "run flat" tires with stiff sidewalls? Can they be removed and mounted with tire irons?
Answer: Yes. Just tie down a couple tire irons to the left and right of where you are working. They'll hold down the stiff sidewall so the bead will not walk and lift out of the rim bead as you work. Then take small bites of rubber—and work slowly to allow time for the rubber to flex and fold over the rim. You do this only at the last few inches of mounting the tire on the final segment when mounting the upper bead where installation is the most difficult. Don't forget to use the helping hand. Fig. 5-23.

55. Question: I read this book, but I want to learn more. Where can I go?
Answer: To the Internet. A video site like YouTube.com has videos of large commercial tire changing machines, and you can see the process. The machines "push" the tire's bead over the rim, while manual tire irons "fold" the bead over the rim, tire irons "flip". These machines use immense brute force to get the job done. However, you can see the technique is somewhat similar as to how the tire is removed and installed from a rim. This book focuses on manually installing tires. Even with using machines, eventually you will need to learn how to use a tire iron on motorcycle tires. Motorcycle machines can't use the brute force of a automotive tire changing machine and must be "toned down" to 50psi air pressure otherwise the force will be so great when turning the wheel that spokes can snap and the cast and composite wheels can crack and snap in two! There is a torque safety feature to prevent this. But this also means that when a tire binds, the machine's tire-mounting bar will lift "pop" out of position stopping the installation. You then must finish by using tire irons. This is why the occasional do-it-yourself tire changer does not need an automatic tire changing machine for motorcycle tires. A manually operated tire machine is just fine to use. If you have no machine, just do it on the floor with the wheel supported by

56. Question: Can I mount a rear tire on the front of the motorcycle?

Answer: Mount only tires marked "front wheel" on front wheel and only tires marked "rear wheel" on rear wheel. You will see crazy things when it comes to custom-built bikes. They break the rules because the bikes are generally show bikes. For street and racing use don't reverse tires. You would have to reverse the rotation of the tire on the rim so the tire arrow is backwards to the wheel rotation to maintain the internal structural integrity of the tire. I would not do these sorts of things. Why not do it the right way?

57. Question: Should I be aware of mold release on a new tire? What is that?

Answer: Mold release is a slippery lubricant sprayed into the tire mold to keep the melted rubber tire from sticking to the steel mold. This lubricant is slippery and the tire falls out of the mold with great ease. The problem is that this lubricant is melted into the tire and remains slippery when installed on your bike. Some tire manufacturing companies do not use mold release, but even then the tire is new, slippery and the rubber is stiff on a cold tire and can lose traction. Some riders abrade the tire with sandpaper or ride on a gravel road to scuff up the new tire. You just need to ride more slowly with brand new tires, without leaning or accelerating hard and being extra careful on smooth concrete like at fueling stations. Avoid painted lines and arrows on roadways.

58. Question: My friend tells me it is critical to have proper wheel alignment on my new tires. Are the notches on the swing arm sufficient to align the wheels?

Answer: Be sure to align the wheels each time the rear wheel is removed or the chain or belt is adjusted. Each revolution of an incorrectly aligned wheel can scuff off tread rubber, reduce tire mileage, and impair steering and cornering. For street use the alignment marks on your swing arms are fine. For racing use some use laser beams, straight edge, string or some other measurement tool for a super-precise alignment. I just use the swing arm marks. I do not race or ride fast and hard. I have not had problems, but if you do then consider using another method. The Internet will show you how. In most cases you don't need to perform a precise wheel alignment on street bikes. When you change tires you align the rear wheel using the rear wheel alignment marks on the swing arm making sure the axle is equalized on each side. It is possible to obtain a more precise alignment using a laser beam or a long straight edge, or string, but most street bikes just don't need to be that precise.

59. Question: I installed a new tire. Once I installed it on the rim, I could not rotate the tire. So the tire balance mark lines up with the valve stem. It is way off by over twelve inches. I remounted the tire, but could I have ridden my bike with that mark being so far out of alignment?

Answer: For street use on a cruiser motorcycle, you sure could have just ridden off with that mark being out of alignment. I once tested this by intentionally mounting the tires on my bike 180 degrees out of alignment. I felt no adverse effects. I always line up the marks, but if I make a mistake or notice the tire is out of alignment to the valve stem I am likely to just forget about it. High-speed riding above highway speeds is a different story. I wouldn't worry about it for normal highway riding speeds.

60. Question: How many spokes can be broken before I have to have them replaced?

Answer: Three is too many. Some may even say one broken spoke is one too many. The danger is that once a spoke snaps, it loads up the other nearby spokes making them fail. A snowball effect takes place, and failures keep coming. You should rap your spokes gently each week to hear a nice "ping" noise from each spoke. A "clunk" noise is a loose or broken spoke. When you are home, not on the road, tighten the loose spoke until the "ping" noise is identical in pitch to the adjacent spokes and you should be okay. Yes, alignment of the rim is likely out, but at least you will have a tight rim for integrity and strength. Loose spokes are dangerous. They can suddenly cause spoke and wheel failure when accelerating, carrying a passenger, or braking. Wheel trueing is not hard to do or difficult to learn. With practice you can do your own wheel lacing and trueing.

61. Question: I was told not to buy a wheel balancer with ball bearings.

Answer: Static balancer comes with ball bearings or knife-edge grooves that act as bearings. Both types work perfectly. You don't grease the static balancer's ball bearings. You can use a dry lubricant such as silicone spray. Once you grease the ball bearings too much friction prevents accurate wheel balancing. Keep those bearings rust-free, clean and dry.

62. Question: Should we install a new valve core when changing tires?

Answer: Yes, you can and should replace the valve stem and core. If you have metal valve stems you don't have to replace those of course unless five years has passed you should at least replace the valve stem's rubber seal. If you have a plastic or rubber valve stem replace it with a new one. If you have an innertube, replace it at each tire change along with a new rubber rim-band liner. However, it is most important to perform a soapy water leak test after installing a new valve core in the valve stem. Apply the soap and water solution and look for tiny air bubbles. Let it fully dry and then cap the valve stem. That cap prevents air from escaping if the valve leaks. You don't want the tire to deflate when you are riding as it can cause a loss of control and a crash. Check the cap for tightness periodically and leak test it too!

63. Question: Can I tell by looking at the tire if the tire has sufficient air?

Answer: No. A tire can lose as much as 50% of its air before it begins to show signs it is low on air. You have to check the air with an air pressure gauge or with a tire monitoring pressure system. Inflation pressure in a tire goes up in hot weather or down in cold weather 1-2 pounds for every 10 degrees of temperature change. When inflating a tire, make sure the tire is cool, not hot. Do not remove air from a hot tire.

64. Question: When should I replace my tires?

Answer: When the tread is worn down to 1/16". Just stick a penny into the tread. If part of President Lincoln's head is covered by the tread, you're driving with the proper amount. The tire also has tread wear indicator bars, small bumps of rubber at the bottom of the tread. When they come to the surface, the time to change the tire is now, or every 3 years.

65. Question: How important is wheel alignment on a motorcycle?

Answer: Amazingly, not as important as you may think. Close is good. That's why the chain or belt tension adjusters have gradation marks—so you can align the rear wheel. Balancing these rear wheel marks does not necessarily perfectly align the rear wheel to the front wheel. For racing bikes alignment is crucial, but for street bikes close is usually good enough. Unless you have poor handling, wobbling, vibration, or abnormal tire wear patterns, I would not worry about using a straight edge or plumb line string for alignment. By the way, a cruiser bike with a large windshield and saddle bags will wobble at high speeds. This is due to wind turbulence and is not a wheel alignment problem.

66. Question: Can I install tubeless tires on my spoke wheels?

Answer: No, but you can purchase new spoked tubeless wheels that have the spoke appearance but are in reality tubeless rims. They are expensive.

67. Question: I have an 18" tubeless rim on my bike, and I need to save money on tires. Can I install a 16" tire?

Answer: No. Your rim is 18" wide. If your tire can't fit snugly to that dimension, it will leak air. However, the tire's width can be decreased this way. Let's say your bike came with a 180/55/18 tire. The first number, "180," is in millimeters, and this dimension can be reduced by 10mm to a 170mm tire. So, a 170/60/18 tire can save you money. However, check with the tire manufacturer and the motorcycle dealer for further advice. Every bike is different and technology is changing rapidly. This old formula may be becoming outdated or not allowed on some wheels.

68. Question: I want my dealer to install Dunlop® tires on my bike, but he says they will not fit. True?

Answer: Go to the Dunlop tire website and look in their fitment guide and find the tires that will fit. It could be that your dealer does not want to bother ordering tires for you and he only wants to sell the tires he already has in stock. Or he may be right, and the tires you want will not fit on your wheels. Dunlop® tires are made in the USA so consider that when you buy tires for it helps Americans.

69. Question: I come across tires 180/55/18 on websites, but they say they are for Harley-Davidson's not Victory motorcycles. Can I use them on my Victory?

Answer: Yes you can use those tires on your motorcycle if your rim is 18" and the tire is 180 mm wide. The aspect ratio of 55 says it is a perfect match regarding the height of the tire, so you can buy and use those tires. There is no huge difference between cruiser motorcycles. Tires made for a Honda cruiser will be fine on a Victory. The key is to get the numbers right. In this case, for your Victory, any 180/55/18 tire will fit your bike. Make sure you buy tubeless tires for tubeless rims or tube tires for tube rims. The sizes will be the same, but you shouldn't interchange them. Install the right type of tire on your bike's wheels.

70. Question: Will cold and hot weather damage my tires?

Answer: Yes being exposed to extreme hot or cold weather can ruin them, especially when stored in a garage or storage shed over the winter or summer. Most people will not notice a problem, but damage can occur to rubber and the laminated belts.

71. Question: I have seen bikes with a car tire on the rear wheel. Is this safe?

Answer: Not safe at all. The profile for car tires is flat. When cornering, the rear wheel will cause the tire to ride off the flat tread and ride precariously on the sharp edge. The bike can suddenly lose grip and fall down. Tread surfaces are flat all across car tires. A motorcycle tire tread is rounded so that the bike can roll over and still maintain full traction. This same effect can arise in a motorcycle tire. As it wears, a wide flat spot wears in the center of the tire. When you corner, the bike's tire rides onto the sharp edge, losing about 1/3 of its contact patch. So if you like to ride the twisties on a sport bike at high speed, do it on new tires or you risk sliding out the rear wheel. A cruiser at low speed should not have a problem, but be aware that the wider the rear tire, the worse that flat spot will be and the less contact patch with the roadway.

72. Question: Why must we use valve caps on the tubeless rim?
Answer: The main purpose is to keep air in the tire. But you ask, how can air get out of the valve? When the wheel is rotating at very high speed, or if the spring in the valve is weak, the valve core can be pulled downward from centrifugal force opening the valve to let the air out of the tire. To avoid this, install a 90-degree-angle valve stem and keep a valve cap cover in place with rubber seal in good condition.

73. Question: Should I change out the valve core each time I change my tires?
Answer: You can if you want to. I don't. For street use, it is not critical to install a new valve core each time you change your tires. Replacing them once a year or two is fine. They really will last for many years.

74. Question: How come you do not use a Handy-Lift® in your book?
Answer: Handy-Lift® is a brand of motorcycle lift table. Those large lifts create problems of their own for the occasional do-it-yourself mechanic. The bike can fall off the lift, securing the bike is a balancing act, and the large lift takes up a lot of space in the garage. They are not practical for most riders. However, if you plan to work on bikes a lot, there are many fine lifts you can buy including the Handy-Lift®. Don't expect it to make installing tires on your bike easier, though. It can actually be more work setting and resetting up the lift for each wheel to be changed out. Motorcycle shops use them because stooping down all day long to work on motorcycles every day is not practical. I believe the average rider only needs two lifts: an ATV/motorcycle lift for the bike and one broad-faced scissor jack to lift the wheel into position. If you can afford the price of a table lift and have the room for it, this is okay.

75. Question: What other tools must I have to fix flat tires?
Answer: Whatever tool you need to remove the front and rear axle of your motorcycle. You may get a flat that can't be fixed. A new tire needs to be installed, but nobody has that special tool to remove your wheel. Example: Go try to find a 16mm or 24mm Allen socket, and you will become a believer. Such oddball tools are not easy to find. Get the tool you need and carry it with you. There are repair shops that do not have the special tool for your bike.

76. Question: Is it true that some dealers sell unsafe tires?
Answer: Yes. They may be selling a tire that has exceeded its shelf life. They do this when buying up others' old inventory and then sell the goods to their own customers. The date the tire is made is on the tire usually in a coded format. Contact the tire manufacturer on how to interpret the code. Example: 0304 can mean the tire was made in the third month of March or the third week of January of 2004. Each manufacturer may use its own coding or may use the DOT method. The dealer may even install the wrong tires on your bike. Just because a dealer is a dealer does not mean you will always get quality workmanship.

77. Question: How do I use the hair dryer when installing my tires?
Answer: On cold days when the rubber tire is cooled, the rubber will not flex easily over the rim. Using a hair dryer to warm up the tire will make installing the tire easier, especially at the end point when the last few inches of rubber have to flip over the rim with the most resistance. Heat that end point and all around the entire tire to get the rubber nice and warm. You can't overheat the tire with a hand-held hair dryer. The tire should feel a warm 80 degrees. Do not use a heat gun. That will melt and overheat the tire. Don't stand in water when using the hair dryer or allow the dryer to contact the metal rim to avoid electric shock.

78. Question: How many miles should I get on my tires?
Answer: An acquaintance may tell you he gets over 14,000 miles on his tires. It can be true, but most often it is because he never rides the freeways much. Most of his riding is in the city and solo. Remember, heat kills tires and causes them to wear out. Riding a heavy cruiser with a passenger will cause tires to run hotter. Your friend's bike may even have reduced backlash in the drive chain, causing less scuffing of the tire when shifting. He may transition the shifts smoothly with clutch and gas, causing even more tire longevity. It is often how you ride your bike and the bike itself that determines what is normal. You should aim at getting at least 6,000 miles on your tires for a cruiser. I had a Harley-Davidson with solid alloy wheels, and I got over 15,000 miles on my tires. Why didn't the heavy bike eat up the tires? Those solid wheels acted as heat sinks, soaking up the heat from the tires and causing them to last a long time. I miss those wheels! Spoke wheels are the worst for tire longevity. Their innertubes act as an insulator, preventing frictional tire heat from reaching the steel rim and heating up the tire instead. Hot, soft rubber wears quickly. Carbon fiber composite wheels run hotter, so you will obtain less tire longevity. Look for tires that have long-wearing compounds. Eventually you will find the tire that lasts the longest for your bike. I would like to see motorcycle magazines perform real-world tire longevity testing and give us readers the results.

79. Question: Can I mix tire brands on my bike?
Answer: Generally it is not recommended to mix up brands, like putting a Bridgestone on the front and a Dunlop tire on the rear. However, if you are not driving like a maniac you would likely not run into major safety problems. Nobody wants to tell you otherwise, but it is like putting radial tires on a bike designed for bias belted tires. If you drive normal highway speeds and are not hot-rod-

ding, you will not run into trouble. There is only one way to really find out, and that is to try it. If it doesn't work, then it doesn't work for your specific bike. Odds are you will be just fine. If you can save money and the bike handles predictably and stops with stability, you win the price/performance game. My new Victory® motorcycle came stock with Dunlop® tires, but two different types were mixed up on the bike. If you are looking for maximum proven performance, then stay with what came with your bike from the manufacturer as they already did the testing. The only problem is that configuration may be expensive to replace. I like to save money, so I try different brands until I find the right combination. I generally buy a matched set instead of mixing them up with different brands or models. I have never found a motorcycle tire yet that was dangerous to use or so troublesome I had to remove them.

80. Question: I was told to buy a tire that has the deepest tread for the best in tire longevity.
Answer: This was true, but not anymore. Today tire technology is really advancing, developing long-wearing compounds and hard-wearing compounds in the center of the tire. Also, tires with more tread depth to begin with will be more prone to cup, make noise, and vibrate and can even wear out faster than the newer tires being made today.

81. Question: How can I find the best tire for my bike? There are too many brands to choose from.
Answer: I know the frustration. If you are seeking tire longevity and low price, shop around different brands and tire dealers for the best price. To find the best tire for my bike, talking to riders just does not work. They tend to exaggerate, lie, or just try to deceive me with their great knowledge of tires. Soon I find out that they know little to nothing. Try to find somebody who changes their own tires. They will have more knowledge than some rider who just pays others to do the work. Don't listen to salespersons or order clerks selling parts behind a counter. What do they know? Nothing! The simple formula I use is to research cruiser tires first (if you are riding a cruiser) among the different brands, then shop for the lowest price you can get those tires. I may have Mitchelin®, Pirelli®, Dunlop®, Bridgestone®, Avon® and others stockpiled in my garage ready for installation when needed. For a cruiser, what is most important is finding a tire that lasts the longest at the lowest price. Although they may last a few thousand miles longer, the best tires may still cost too much. Finding the best tire for your bike is not easy to do because compromise is always in the mix. Performance of the tire versus price and wear is the issue. The best tires may wear out too fast, or they may last but cost too much to buy. Try to find a happy medium. If a manufacturer advertises its tire to last a long time, try it. Chances are it is not false advertising.

82. Question: Will a wide rear tire make handling a problem?
Answer: It sure will if it is too wide. The fat look may be cool, but it will create trouble even if the wide tire is factory installed as stock. Any tire larger than 180 millimeters wide will begin to create problems. (1) Slight differences in pavement height at low speed will tend to flip the bike over on its side. Without firm footing you can find yourself lying under the bike, especially during parking lot maneuvering. (2) A fat tire is asking for a flat tire. It is like a wide vacuum, picking up nails, screws, and any sharp object a skinny tire would easily have missed. (3) The wide tire does not let the bike lean into and out of turns. You will need to use a bit of muscle, and this will wear you out quickly. Eventually, you will find yourself not wanting to ride on long curving roads. (4) These fat tires do not last long at all. They run hot and the rubber is often of a soft compound, so don't expect the tire to last. A wide tire will quickly develop a center flat spot. When that happens, the tire will rapidly wear out at an impressive rate. (5) The cost to replace a fat tire can be ridiculous, even if you change the tire yourself. The cost of the tire can run into hundreds of dollars. Is it really worth it? (6) You can use a wide tire if it has a low-profile design. This will allow the bike to roll over into the turns and will help a great deal, but only up to a limit. The fat tire will still require you to work the bike a lot when turning in the city or on country roads. What you want to stay away from is putting a wider or thinner tire on your rims that did not come with the bike by the manufacturer. Ten millimeters won't hurt, but more than that can upset the handling of the motorcycle and cause the chain or frame to hit the tire, causing a crash. Many people make alterations to their motorcycle and risk making unsafe changes.

83. Question: When do I use the tire C-clamps?
You don't have to use them. I have installed tires for years without using C-clamps, but when you get a tough tire you can use the clamps to make the job easier. I have photos in this book showing how to apply the clamps to the tire or to the tire and rim together. At the end point, apply the clamp there with one portion of the clamp on the center tread of the tire and the opposite end on the rim. This will squeeze the center of the tire, causing the edges to fold. That way the tire irons need not use brute force to resist the tire folding over the rim. At the same time, you can apply the clamp at the opposite end, squeezing the tire down into the drop center. You can use a combination of the techniques at any location you desire. Whatever works best for you works fine. The clamps can help take the load off the tire iron and the rim so you won't dent or crack the rim. The C-clamp and ratchet clamps are the two styles I have used in this book.

84. Question: How do I use heat to install a cold tire?
Answer: Warm rubber will be more pliable and flex to flip over the rim when installing the tire, so letting the tire sit in the sun for an hour before installing will be a great help on warm days. On cool days you can keep the new tire in your home, but this is often not enough for some tough tires being mounted onto a rim in a cold garage. Heat the tire with a hair dryer. Usually at the end point where the tire resists being flipped over the rim, apply heat there and directly opposite and push down on the tire at that point to get the tire to

move down into the drop center of the rim. Don't use an industrial heat gun. It gets too hot and will melt rubber or internal belts in the tire.

85. Question: What about roadside assistance? Can't I rely on this instead of traveling with a flat tire repair kit?
Answer: You can, but there are problems. Unlike a car, truck or motor home, roadside assistance won't fix your motorcycle flat tire at the point of breakdown. They will only tow you to the closest motorcycle repair shop, which may be closed for the weekend (usually Sunday and Monday) or a holiday. That will run up motel and meals expenses for you that may or may not be a covered item in your towing roadside assistance contract. Then when the repair shop opens, they may not be able to fix your motorcycle. They may be overbooked and can't do it today, tomorrow, or the next day. Now a week can pass by before you ever get your flat tire fixed. These things can easily happen. I have roadside assistance, but I carry a flat repair kit and air compressor. I'd rather fix the flat and be on my merry way in fifteen minutes rather than suffer the grief of waiting for a tow and waiting to get a tire fixed. Plus, you will get an expensive bill from a repair shop for labor and a brand new tire. You could have fixed the tire and replaced the tire yourself when you got home.

86. Question: What is the most important tool I should carry with me at all times?
Answer: A flat tire repair kit. Few riders even bother to carry one, but they wish they had one when they do get a flat tire. But there is one tool more important, and that is the socket required to remove wheel axles. Usually the front wheel axle requires a large, special-size socket bit. Believe it or not, some motorcycle repair shops (not to mention other shops) will not have that size socket for your motorcycle. So they can't help you if you need to have the wheel removed to install a new tire when you are traveling for any reason. A dealership could be hundreds of miles away. Auto parts stores don't even sell sockets in that size. If you don't believe me, go try to buy a large 19 or 24 mm metric Allen socket or bit. You'll need to buy it from Motion Pro or another specialty tool company online or at a local motorcycle specialty shop, if they stock those sockets. Take the time and find the socket tool bit now before you need one in an emergency and discover none are available.

87. Question: How come motorcycle magazines do not explain motorcycle mechanics?
Answer: I am not really certain why. It may be a lack of quality writers knowledgeable about fixing motorcycles on staff. Maybe they aren't interested in paying writers for such articles. Another reason may be that today's riders are not interested in repairing their own motorcycles as they were in years past and prefer to pay for the privilege. Of course, they are told by dealers and repair shops that everything on a motorcycle is too complex to fix it yourself and attempting to even install new tires will void your warranty. Amazing but true. There are a few motorcycle mechanics magazines still being published in England, and they can be purchased in major bookstore magazine racks. I see more repair articles surfacing so the trend looks promising it will continue. Problem is, even those extensive repair articles leave out many techniques and procedures, but it is better than nothing at all.

88. Question: Explain the difference between a static and dynamic wheel balance.
Answer: The dynamic balancer is a machine that spins the wheel and automatically calculates the placement and size of the balancing wheel weight. The static balance does not rely on spinning the wheel. It relies on gravity to determine the heavy spot on the wheel. You reposition the wheel on the balance stand and see where it stops. That heavy spot is at the six o'clock position. The wheel weight is placed 180 degrees, directly opposite, from the heavy spot at 12 o'clock high.

89. Question: I hit a large bump in the road. Now my front tire makes a funny noise. How can I inspect the tire for damage?
Answer: You can't see internal cord separation damage, and it is dangerous to use the tire. The cords can squirm and cause loss of control or permit an instantaneous release of air (blowout). Just get rid of the tire.

90. Question: Which system do you like the best for fixing flat motorcycle tires?
Answer: All of the systems work, but one product stands out and that is the Pocket Tire Plugger®. It is easy to use. I like the way the mushroom head seals air from entering the plug repair area. The mushroom also locks the plug in place so it cannot flex to work itself out or blow out of the plug hole from compressed air in the tire. The rubber plug is soft and fills the hole in the tire perfectly. It requires no lubricant, glue or vulcanizing agent. I trust the string/rope system. I carry both type systems with me.

91. Question: The bead was tearing so I stopped. Now what do I do to continue to get the tire on?
Answer: You need to push the tire down all around the rim to try to get the tire to move into the drop center of the rim and keep it down. Just doing this alone frees up the rubber to flex over the rim the next time you try to install with your tire irons. Add liquid lubricant around the tire and rim area so the tire can slip and flex when using the tire irons. Take smaller bites of rubber with the tire irons. Rock the tire back and forth using two tire irons like a seesaw. This will flex the rubber to loosen it up, and the tire should begin to slip over the rim. Some tires are really tough to get on, and even tire machines won't put them on. Learn which tires install best on your bike, and use that brand and style of tire. You will always have trouble with the last six inches of tire, so stop, rest, push the tire downward, take small bites, lube the tire, stop, rest, push the tire downward, lube the tire again, seesaw the tire irons, and do it all very slowly so the rubber has time to catch up. Going too fast just rips the bead. Using C-clamps on the tire can compress the tire and force

it down into the rim's drop center. You can also try heating the tire with a hair dryer. Some tires are just plain difficult to get on the rim.

92. Question: I may have destroyed the bead of the tire. What should I do now?
Answer: You may not have destroyed the bead. A tiny tear (1/4") will not be a problem. The actual bead of the tire is not the edge of the tire where the tire irons are working. The bead is the smooth half-moon shape near the edge of the tire. As long as that portion is not ripped, you are good to go. Just because you hear a little rubber tearing noise does not mean you have ripped the bead. However, hearing tearing noise is a warning for you to stop applying force, back off, and try again in a different location or try a different approach.

93. Question: I still have a tough time getting the last bead at the ending point to flip over the rim. I used all your methods, but still struggle. Any more tips you can give me?
Answer: Yes, there is one more tip. I don't need to use it, but for a real tough tire you can apply a couple of C-clamps to the tire near or opposite where you are working and squeeze to "pinch" the tire down with them. Keep the ends of the clamps on the rubber tire only, not on the rim. The clamps don't need to be excessively tight. You can use the newer ratcheting clamps or the old screw C-clamps. This clamping will compress the rubber and will force the tire's edge to enter the drop center in the rim. Then more rubber can move over the rim as you use your tire irons. Use this if all your efforts fail or if you find it just works easier for you. It's one of the tricks I have learned over time. You can also use these clamps to stop a tire's bead from lifting back out of the rim (walking) instead of using tire irons.

94. Question: I accidently bent my disk brake rotor by not supporting the rim so the disk was floating. Is there any way to fix the rotor?
Answer: Yes, you can send it out to have the rotor straightened. You can find frame straightening companies on the Internet. I have some posted on my motorcycle links page. Make sure the rotor touches nothing the next time you change tires. Support the wheel on wood blocks so the rotor is floating in the air. Some guys use an old motorcycle rubber tire. I don't like the old rubber tire as the tire flexes and the job keeps wobbling around. A firm surface is best. A large car or truck tire will have better support.

95. Question: What should I look for when buying a tire changing machine?
Answer: Shop around for the best features and price. For a manual tire changer, just make sure it has a bead breaker, accepts motorcycle tires/rims sizes, and has a heavy-duty tire mount/demount bar. The machine may have all of the above but still need other features, like a method that allows odd-size rims and tires to be fitted, or a method to prevent scratches to the rims. The No-Mar tire changer is a good choice for no scratching of rims. A bare-bones tire changing machine will work too. Just use rags or apply tape or a thin rubber coating on your tool tips so they won't scratch rims. And one more thing, you do not need a tire changing machine to change tires on your motorcycle. You can do it all by using tire irons and build your own stand.

96. Question: How can I practice fixing flat tires before doing it for real?
Answer: Just go get your supplies and go to a tire store. Ask them if you can practice on their old tires. Keep in mind you should do this on motorcycle tires, not on car tires. The motorcycle tire's casing is thinner than a car tire, and the plug you are using may not fit a car tire. This is true with the Pocket Tire Plugger—the 1/2" plugs you have are for motorcycle tires, not car tires (unless you purchased the 3/4" longer plugs, and even they won't work on deep-tread truck tires). Ask them to drill some 1/8" holes in the tire, or bring your own portable drill with you. Or ask them for a tire you can take home and you can practice whenever you need to. It is a good idea to practice once a year in the beginning of riding season so you don't have to figure out how to fix a flat when it does happen.

97. Question: What is the most common mistake you see with riders?
Answer: They do not carry a flat tire repair kit with them. And those that do often fail to bring along with them a means to inflate the tire after they fix the flat. The biggest mistake I see is people still riding motorcycles with spoke wheels. You can't fix their flat tires for them. Another problem is I see riders carrying CO2 cylinders believing they will work, when they can freeze up and not discharge the gas or not carrying enough of them to actually inflate the tire. I also see people with a bicycle air pump that will not reach to the valve stem and can't pump air easily so it is near useless. You should have a 12-volt air compressor or a manual air pump that will work. But the worst offenders are the ones who don't bother to carry a flat tire repair kit, saying, "I've never had a flat tire before." One day they will wish they had. These people can't be relied on to help another biker in distress. Carry an extra string/rope repair kit to use or to give as a gift to a rider in distress with a flat tire.

98. Question: Do I have to remove one disk on a dual-disk front wheel to change my tire?
Answer: No. But if you must for some reason, go ahead and remove one disk. When removing a rotor disk's bolts, make sure you have the correct size bit; the bolts are tight. If the tool is slightly undersized, it will strip the bolt head. The disk's wheel hub is not ruined. You will need to drill the bolt head out. Also, these disk brake rotor bolts use heavy-duty thread-locking compound on them, so heat the bolts first to break the thread-locking bond. Then you can remove them. The bolts need not be heated cherry red, but get the

bolt hot. Coat the Allen tool tip with valve grinding compound as this will create a tighter fit and prevent stripping the Allen bolt.

99. Question: What is the purpose of tire mounting lubricant?
Answer: It serves two purposes. The solid lubricant does not dry out quickly, and it allows the rubber to slip and slide upon the rim. That way the tire does not lock up and bind, preventing the tire from moving freely over the rim. The liquid tire lubricant is used to add more lubricant when installing the tire. It will be messy and coat the tire's bead, which actually helps bead sealing. Many tire installers use machines and fail to lubricate the tire, and this lack of liquid lubricant does not enhance tire bead sealing. This is why sometimes a brand new tire will not hold air and a customer has to tow the bike back to the shop. If you want the job done right, do it yourself. The lube also seals the tire bead to the rim.

100. Question: I removed a nail from my tire, but I could not insert the reamer or plug to fix the leak. Why?
Answer: A nail can bend. What appears to be a straight line hole may actually be a bent hole, so when you try to insert the straight reamer it will not go into the tire. Another reason I like the Pocket Tire Plugger® is that it has a pointed probe tool you can use to follow the curvature of the nail hole to locate and trace its path in the tire. This tool also can clear out any broken nail from the tire. Other systems do not permit this.

101. Question: What if I have a tiny hole in my tire, creating a slow air leak? I found a small metal staple in the tire. Which system should I use to fix that tiny little hole?
Answer: There is a plug system made by Dynaplug.com that works with much smaller holes. It is so simple and easy to use it is comical. You wet and insert a tiny rope plug without glue into the tool, push the tool into the tire's nail hole, and pull the tool out. There is no need to use a reamer to enlarge the nail hole. But all systems will still fix these tiny air leaks from tiny brad nails. You just have to enlarge the hole until the plug fits. However, a large screw or massive size nail it will not repair as the rope plug is tiny in size at about 1/8" diameter. Make sure you carry a thick string/rope plug kit in case you need them.

102. Question: I used the rope plug, but it goes all the way inside the tire. What am I doing wrong?
Answer: When using the rope plug there is a lot of resistance to get the rope inserted. You normally push so hard, not being prepared, that suddenly the rope will give way and the rope ends up being inserted too deeply or all the way inside the tire. This is a good reason why everyone needs to practice fixing flat tires before having to do it for real on the side of the road on a hot or cold day or night. Also, carry more spare plugs than you think you need.

103. Question: I inserted a Pocket Tire Plug® in my tire, but it still leaks air. How do I remove the plug and fix this leak?
Answer: First, use the end of the insertion tool and just push the rubber plug back into the tire all the way in. It will fall into the rim, where it will do no harm. Use the reamer again to gently polish the nail hole in the tire and insert a new plug. There could have been an obstruction letting air escape on the first try. The internal carcass of the tire may be distorted preventing the mushroom plug to seat correctly. If this fails use the string/rope plug system.

104. Question: How many CO_2 cylinders will I need to inflate my tire?
Answer: Do not use them. They can freeze up and also give you instant frostbite requiring amputation of a finger. They can even (rarely) explode in your saddlebag on very hot days or discharge. Also, to get a 180mm cruiser motorcycle tire to partially inflate, you will need to carry 17 to 20 16-gram CO_2 cylinders, not just the 3 or 4 sold in typical repair packages. And you only get one shot at filling the tire. If you run out of CO_2 gas, you're stranded. Instead, buy a hand- or foot-operated air pump or a 12-volt powered air compressor or both types. Just forget about those CO_2 cartridges for street motorcycle use. Off-road vehicles can get by with low air pressure, so they can use them. Street motorcycles should not rely on them at all for any reason. Also, due to the design of these CO_2 inflating devices and the angle and clearance of your wheel, many riders were astonished to discover that the device could not even access the valve stem to inflate the tire. These things are practically useless. Just because bike shops sell them does not mean they work.

105. Question: I tried balancing my tire with 1/4-ounce wheel weights, but I need a 1/8-ounce weight. Can I cut it in half?
Answer: Yes. Just use some dykes to cut the weight.

106. Question: I was told that sport bikes must have dynamic tire balancing. Is this true?
Answer: False. Believe it or not, static balancing is very accurate. Even at motorcycle race tracks, most of the balancing is done statically. Don't let tire installation shops fool you with their hype. You do not need to use a dynamic balancer to balance your tires.

107. Question: How come I found a nail in my tire and it did not go flat, but when I removed the nail it went flat?
Answer: It depends on how deep the nail went into the tire. The nail could also have sealed up the air leak so that the air escaped when you removed the nail. Tubeless tires also have a sticky compound in the tire to leak air slowly. A nail can enter a tire and bend so it has not punctured into the air space or tube. That is one reason why you removed a nail and no flat tire occurred. Should you ride

with a known nail in your tire? It depends on the situation and how far away you are from services. I have ridden on a rear tubeless tire 30 miles with a nail in it to get home. Just ride slow and be prepared in case the tire goes flat. A tube tire is too dangerous to ignore. Go get it fixed right away. If you do ride on it, be prepared for a blowout. Ride very slowly on side roads or call a tow truck. Some riders suggest inserting a can of Fix-A-Flat® with a tube type tire. You can, but it may void a road hazard tire warranty, if you have such a warranty to collect from. Most people I know don't have tire protection warranty on motorcycle tires, so go ahead and use the stop leak fluid designed for motorcycle use. It makes a mess of the inside of the rims, but who cares about that if it gets you home.

108. Question: Who makes and sells those 12-volt air compressors?
Answer: Aerostich.com, Slime.com, StopnGo.com and a few other companies sell them. You can find portable compressors in motorcycle magazines, on the Internet, and at automotive parts and tool supply stores. When you buy one, make certain you obtain the proper electrical connections so that the compressor will work when you need it. Whoever sells 12-volt heated motorcycle clothing will have the connecting wires you need. I use the same connector that powers my heated clothing to the battery to power my air compressor. A 12-volt female coax cable does the trick for the battery side. The compressor may need a male adapter. Store any adapters with the air compressor. Make certain the power line and air hose will reach to fill both front and rear tire with air.

109. Question: I was told to put the white dot on the tire opposite from the valve stem on the rim. You say to put the white dot beside the valve stem. Who is right?
Answer: Both can be right. Dunlop says to put the dot beside the valve stem because their dot indicates it is the lightest spot on the tire. But this rule can change from tire to tire. Another tire manufacturer may want their dot to be placed opposite, denoting it as the heavy spot on the tire. Find out which location method is right for your tire. I also intentionally tested this out by putting the dot opposite where it should be and I did not bother to balance the tire. I did this to both front and rear tires. What did I find? I found nothing has changed. I could not tell the tires were out of balance. The tires lasted just as long. No handling problems occurred. I am not saying for you to do it the wrong way. I am just proving my point that for street cruising use, tire balance is not as critical as you are led to believe. Like I said before, many riders have lost wheel weights on their rims, have worn tires and do not even realize they are riding on unbalanced wheels. Unless you are racing beyond normal highway speeds, don't be too concerned about wheel balancing. If you do run into problems, just slap on some wheel weights to balance your tires. No big deal.

110. Question: I inflated the new tire to 40 psi and heard no "pop" sound of the bead seating into place. What do I do now?
Answer: Some tires, like those with thick sidewalls, will not pop into place because they are essentially a tight fit when mounted to the rim. Look closely around the perimeter of the tire near the rim, and you may see a ridge on the tire. This ridge distance should be consistent all around the rim. If not, deflate the tire and inflate it again to 40 psi. If this still does not work, deflate and lightly or firmly rap the tire with a rubber hammer all around the rim to loosen up any binding. Do not exceed 40 psi or the tire could explode. If this still fails, demount the tire and reinstall it. If it still will not seat properly, the tire is defective. Send it back for a refund, and try to buy a different brand of tire that will not give you these troubles. If it is concentric and holding air it is good to go.

111. Question: Please explain the procedure to balance a tire one more time.
Answer: Place the wheel on an axle and give the wheel a slight spin until the wheel stops. Do this a few times. The bottom 6 o'clock position will be the heavy spot. Put a piece of duct tape at this heavy spot on the tire's sidewall. Temporarily attach two 1/4-ounce wheel weights to the rim or tire at the 12 o'clock position with some duct tape. This is the opposite side of the heavy spot, which should counter-balance the heavy spot. Turn the wheel a quarter turn, so it is level to the axle, and let it go. See if the wheel sinks or rises. If it sinks, remove some weight. If it rises, add some weight. You want to let the wheel go and have it stay put. Then try randomly positioning the wheel at different locations. If it stays put, it's spot-on balanced. It really is that simple and easy to do. If the wheel very slowly sinks or rises, it can be close enough in balance for most street riders. Let's be practical. There's no reason to spend more of your time to get it perfectly perfect. But to get it spot on perfect you may need to move the wheel weight's location a bit to compensate to fine tune the balance. If you had to add more than 1/2 ounce of weights you should split them evenly on either side of the wheel. To apply the weights, remove the sticky backing and apply them to the rim as close to the center line of the rim as possible. Go to a motorcycle showroom and look at the wheels and see how they distribute the weights. Some wheels have many ounces of weights, while some only have a fraction applied. It depends on whether the casting of the wheel is naturally balanced. To prevent the wheel weights from falling off, coat them with a layer of silicone rubber to the rim and let dry overnight. Some riders use a piece of duct tape to keep the weights from falling off. Usually it is cleaning fluids and high pressure washing that dissolves the glue.

112. Question: Have you tried using wheel balancing beads?
Answer: No. I hear they do work, but I do not want a mess of anything coming out of my tire when I am I changing it. Who needs the extra work to gather and clean up a bunch of beads rolling all over the place? I go through three to four tire changes a year, so for me it would not be fun. However, for the average rider it may be okay. But since it is so easy to balance a tire, why not just stick with the old wheel weights? You can make your own wheel balancer stand or buy one inexpensively. You could even just put a spare old axle in a strong vise and put the wheel on the axle to spin it. It is no mystery. If you do not have any wheel weights, then go ahead and use tire

balancing beads or fluid. It may work just fine for your purposes.

113. Question: The tires a dealer sold me and installed developed cracks in the rubber soon after they were installed. What caused this?
Answer: They sold you old tires as brand new! Tires sold in the United States have a date stamped on the sidewall. The date code follows the DOT serial number located on one side of the tire. Tires built before the year 2000 use a three digit code. The first two numbers refer to the week and the last number the year the tire was manufactured. A sideways triangle at the end of the serial number tells you the tire was made in the 1990's. Starting in the year 2000, four numbers are used. The first two numbers identify the week and the last two the year the tire was manufactured. The future may even have more changes. Contact your tire manufacturer to find out how they are dating their tires. It always pays to change your own tires. Old tires crack unless new tires were subjected to a solvent eroding environment. Cracked tires should be replaced. The shelf life of new uninstalled tires is six years, so don't buy any tires older than that and don't ride on tires that are eight years old.

114. Question: How large an air compressor in my garage should I have for mounting new tires?
Answer: You can use a 1/4-horsepower, 3-gallon, 100 psi compressor with no problem. Even smaller can work, but 3 gallons means lots of air capacity to inflate stubborn tires leaking around the rim.

115. Question: Should I install radial tires on my bike?
Answer: If your bike was designed for bias fitment, you may or may not not gain anything by switching to radial tires. You can install radial tires if you find they are cheaper to buy. You may need to select a different size tire regarding the width and height. The radial may not come in the exact size your bias tires are. Just make sure you don't go too wide or too tall tire size. You need a tire that will fit and not rub against the swing arm or fenders. Also, some bikes may not handle as well with radial tires. Others may handle better. It is a cloudy issue. However, I have not read anything warning that putting radial tires on a bike designed for bias-ply tires is outright dangerous. If it were incredibly dangerous the motorcycle magazines and tire manufacturers would be screaming loudly not to do it ever. I have had no problem putting a radial tire on a motorcycle designed for bias tires. If you do run into a problem just don't do it. You can never go wrong by following your bike's owner manual recommendations. Modern bias tires are still good tires.

116. Question: What is your opinion on using a digital tire gauge?
Answer: They work, but will they work when you need them? The display may not be easily read in blinding sunlight or in the dark and the battery may go dead on you when needed most. The old slim and compact pressure gauge is what I stuff in my saddle bags. I use a dial gauge in my garage. A digital gauge is okay to use in the garage, but I would not trust its reliability while traveling on the road.

117. Question: Why should I bother to change my own tires?
Answer: I know most riders today do not, but they should. It gives you more confidence in riding a motorcycle when you can fix it and not just ride it. Prices are rising to terrible levels, threatening our standard of living as income is not keeping pace. Servicing your own motorcycle keeps the hobby viable and affordable. It is enjoyable to take the time to remove the wheel, rip off that old tire, put a new tire on, install the wheel, and ride away, knowing that the job was done right and that you saved a bunch of money to buy other things you want in life. More riders should simply make up their mind to do it themselves. Others who are lacking confidence only need good instruction and practice. That's why I write motorcycle maintenance books. See my book on how to change oil on Harley-Davidson motorcycles. It also covers spark plugs, air cleaner, lubricants and engine longevity secrets. There are dealers and repair shops intentionally not filling the primary and transmission cases with the proper oil level or filling the engine with inferior oil to wear out components faster than normal to create repair business. You really need to learn to do it yourself if you want it done right. I also have free articles on my Website exposing scams.

118. Question: Do all spoke tires require a rim lock?
Answer: No, just bikes that are subject to spinning the wheel a lot, like dirt and drag racing bikes. If you do burnouts on your heavy cruiser, you will rotate the tire and tube and that will shear the valve stem clean in two. Rim locks can be installed if you want to install them. They are not expensive. They just lock the tire down tight to the rim. They can increase heating and wear of the tire, so they are not recommended for todays high-speed sustained highway use. The wheel then must be rebalanced once you install rim locks.

119. Question: I experience strange handling after installing my new front tire. What is wrong?
Answer: If you followed the instructions in this book, making sure the tire bead is concentrically seated around the rim, and inflated the tire to specifications, there is no problem with the tire unless the tire is defective. When you installed the wheel onto the front forks and inserted the axle, you likely did not bounce the front forks to center the forks to the axle before tightening the axle and pinch bolts. This will cause strange handling. If front tire has a center rain groove it will cause the bike to wander on highway rain grooves.

120. Question: I just fixed a flat tire, and when I ride it feels like there is a flat spot with a thumping action. What is wrong?
Answer: The deflated tire broke the cords inside the tire and created this flat section. You must replace the tire.

121. Question: What is the right way to mark a front wheel with dual disk rotors?
Answer: Mark the right side hub or rotor spoke with the letter R and an arrow mark indicating the direction of wheel travel. Since I always use the right side I don't use the R mark, but in your case go ahead and use the right or left side of your choosing and mark the arrow R or L accordingly. You should engrave these markings permanently, with a prick punch or hand-held engraver. It is difficult to determine which side of the wheel goes where and which direction the wheel is rotating to mount the new tire on it without these markings. You can also use chalk, Magic Marker, or electrical tape. The right way is the way that works best for you.

122. Question: I read your book on changing motorcycle tires, but I still have some questions.
Answer: I cover all the major items in this book, but there could always be for some readers a few unanswered questions. I suggest you begin by actually doing the tire change job. In the process you will often have your question answered as you are performing the task. You can also watch some videos on the Internet may address your specific concerns.

123. Question: I watched videos on the Internet, and I failed to install a cruiser motorcycle tire successfully. Why?
Answer: The brief videos just do not really cover heavy street cruiser tires. You will notice that the tires they use are mostly thin-walled tires, like dirt bike and sport bike tires. They don't like to use cruiser tires because there are really a lot more steps to take for those tires to mount on to a rim. There are more procedures and tricks of the trade required, or you will fail to get the job done. Years ago, tires were all thin-walled, but cruiser tires are mostly heavier and with tougher cord material construction too. All this means that the rubber will not stretch over the rim. That is where people fail. My book reveals the tricks of the trade and tricks you have never heard of before in magazines or in instructional videos.

124. Question: I have very expensive carbon fiber rims. Can I use tire irons to install tires on these rims?
Answer: You can if you know what you are doing, but because the rims are very expensive I would use the rotary method of using a mounting bar with the rim locked to a tire changing machine. Composite materials can be very brittle and can crack easily when using steel or even plastic tire irons. For these wheels just go out and buy a manual tire changing machine at a discount tool store. They are inexpensive. This book shows photos of the machine, see Fig. 2-7. Contrary to public wisdom, they are not expensive, are simple to use, and will break the bead, remove, and install tires with ease. Once you buy a machine like this you'll never have to pay anybody to change tires on your motorcycle. And they even remove and install car and light truck tires too. Try using C-clamps to break the beads so there's no stress on the wheel.

125. Question: I saw a video showing a method of mounting tires using window cleaning fluid. Is this okay?
Answer: In a pinch you can, but these products evaporate quickly. You have to work fast or use a lot of it. Some products may have adverse chemicals that can corrode metal rims and rubber, weaken carbon fiber rims, or stain wheels. Tire mounting lube is cheap to buy and use and helps seal the bead. Why not use the proper product? Ammonia is corrosive to rims and to rubber so why use it?

126. Question: You did not show us how to use a hot patch or permanent tire repair patch in this book. Why?
Answer: I felt it is not necessary. The patches are easy to use. Just follow the manufacturer's instructions. Also, I don't believe in fixing a street motorcycle tire with a large hole in it. It is safer to just replace the tire. Some shops will fix your tire and charge you $100. Is that a bad deal? It sure is. You should have installed a new tire. Most of the cost was for labor anyway.

127. Question: Why can't I just carry a can of Fix-A-Flat® with me?
Answer: They don't always work. If you have spoke wheels with tube tires this can be your only option. Don't forget to look for more than one nail in your tire and remove all of the nails before using your one can of Fix-A-Flat®. You could have picked up a couple of nails. Large holes may or may not seal a torn innertube. Yes, a nail can rip a longitudinal hole in the tube so large it can not be sealed.

128. Question: I find that using the reamer was hard to do on my bike. Am I doing it wrong?
Answer: If the tire is flat and the weight of the motorcycle is crunching down on the tire and folding it, the reamer will have a tough time. Expect it to be a bit of work. You can try rolling the motorcycle forward or backward a bit to get a better position to work in. It may be a chore, but so is pushing the bike off the road and waiting for a tow truck to come get you in the middle of nowhere. Take your pick.

129. Question: I was told the rope plug could spit out of the tire. Can this happen?
Answer: It likely will not.

130. Question: A lot of people laugh at me when I tell them you don't have to balance motorcycle tires. How can I convince them?

Answer: Some people will never be convinced due to lack of experience. Most of these scoffers never change their own tires because they hire others to do the job for them. Tell them if they lose a wheel weight or ride into a mud puddle and mud sticks to the rim the wheels are totally out of balance. Do they notice the difference? If they have 4,000 miles on the tires, do they notice vibration? Of course not, they just ride on none the wiser. When your tires are worn down, they are out of balance. Do you stop to have them balanced at half-life? Of course not. I balance my wheels, but if I am replacing the same brand of tire I often will just skip the process because I don't see a change in handling, vibration, tire wear, or fuel mileage. With experience you'll understand. Some bikes need a closely set wheel balance, but most street bikes do not. If you want to balance the wheels go ahead. That's why I put the instructions in the book.

131. Question: What can be repaired on a tire and what should not be repaired?

Answer: You can fix nail holes in the tread area of the tubeless tire. Thankfully, this is where most all flat tires occur. You cannot fix a tube tire using tubeless tire repair kits. You can try using Fix-A-Flat®. If that fails, you must call a tow truck to get you home or to a dealer to replace the tire. You can't fix a blowout or holes or slices in the sidewall of the tire. So don't run over glass or shards of metal if you can avoid it. Don't fix a flat tire with tread less than 1/16 of an inch except to get you home to replace the worn-out tire. Any hole not round in shape can't be repaired or can't reliably be repaired.

132. Question: My tire went flat, and I can't find the nail or the nail hole. How do I locate the leak?

Answer: The head of the nail has likely broken off. There must be some air in the tire for this to work, so add some air with your air pump. You might be able to hear air escaping from the hole. When you are cruising you may have some water or soda you can mix with shaving cream or soap to create a soapy solution. Apply the solution to the tire and watch for tiny bubbles. Then use the probe tool (or if you have no such tool use the reamer tool) to bore out that hole in the tire to remove or push out that tiny nail. Then insert the rope plug with glue, cut off the end, and you are good to go. Don't worry, if you have no glue you can still insert the sticky rope plug without glue for the glue is actually a lubricant and glue mixture to make insertion of the rope plug easier. You can use the rope plug without glue. You will notice the rope plug is very sticky to the touch. That is vulcanizing compound and it alone will seal the air leak and bond the rope to the rubber tire.

133. Question: I am new at this. How many tire irons should I buy to get started?

Answer: Three long, highly curved tire irons are required. A fourth will come in handy to stop tire walking if you come upon a thick sidewall tire. This fourth tire iron can be a short one, but I use the long one.

134. Question: I found labels on my new tires so I removed them. I found two stuck on the bead surface. Why do they do this, and would the tire bead leak if I somehow forgot to remove them?

Answer: I have seen this too, and I have no idea why some tire companies permit placing sticky labels on the tire bead itself. I believe a slow air leak could form if the sticker is not removed, but it should not create a catastrophic, sudden deflation.

135. Question: How do I determine the speed rating of a tire?

Answer: Speed rating is stamped on the tire in a code format expressed with a letter. Example: you may see a number like 58/W. In that number, 58 is the load rating in code format and W is the speed rating. There are charts you can use to decipher the codes. In this case 58 is a load rating of 520 pounds. W stands for 168 miles per hour. Tire dealers and tire manufacturers and websites reveal these charts. The chart isn't in this book because the codes may change in the future, outdating the book and making the information improper. A tire manufacturer will have the data on their Website.

136. Question: I just bought new tires, and there are two dots of different colors on the tire. Which one do I use to balance the tire?

Answer: Each manufacturer has its own color scheme. The yellow dot may be the lightest spot, and it is suggested to mount this adjacent to the valve stem—usually where the heavy spot on the wheel is. The red dot may be the heavy point of the tire and recommended to be mounted at 180 degrees opposite the valve stem or, if applicable, adjacent to a wheel low point notched on the rim. This is only a suggestion of the explanation. You need to contact the tire vendor or manufacturer and ask them which color scheme they use to denote the heavy or light spot on the tire and which color dot to mount next to the valve stem. Unless you are racing don't fret if you can't get the information quickly enough, just put the tire on and ride and find out later for next time you install tires. Like I mentioned earlier, when I didn't align the color dot to the valve stem there was no noticeable ill effect to handling or high speed imbalance problems below 90 miles per hour (which is above freeway speeds in the USA; Germany is a different story of course where there are no speed limits). I don't put the color schemes in this book because they can change on a whim and date the book. Also, tire balance engineering is complex and I do not want to delve into it. Let's just be down to earth practical and realistic. We ride in the real world and are not engineering motorcycles. Let the magazines cover those subjects.

137. Question: What do I do when I see no color dot at all on my new tires?

Answer: Do nothing. Just mount the tires and balance the wheel. Some, but not all tire manufacturers put balance marks on the lightest part of the tire, which should be installed next to the heaviest part of the rim – usually the valve stem. However, if you see a heavy weld on a steel rim that could be the heaviest part of the rim so put the balance mark there. Balancing weights will balance the wheel.

138. Question: I have had to put four ounces of weights on my rim to balance the tire. Is this excessive?
Answer: If you run into trouble balancing the tire putting on more than two ounces you can rotate the tire on the rim a few times to find the right spot that will require less weight. It is not a disaster if you have to use a lot of weights to get a rim and tire in balance. It just looks strange and yet few will notice. Sometimes the tire is a reject from the vulcanizing process (lumping) and the tire will be difficult to balance. In this case exchange the tire for a new one under warranty.

139. Question: How often should we change the valve stems on wheels?
Answer: Automobiles have rubber valve stems and they are changed each time new tires are installed because the rubber stems are exposed to weathering elements including sunlight ozone degradation. Motorcycles normally use metal valve stems with a rubber seal located internally. Just visually inspect the condition of the rubber seal inside the rim each time you change tires. They normally last for five years or more. Eventually the rubber seal will need replacing. However, if you are using tire balancing or flat tire sealant additives it is possible they could deteriate the rubber seal causing an air leak. If so, it won't hurt if you renew the rubber seal at each tire change.

140. Question: There is not much instruction on installing tube tires on cruiser motorcycles. Why?
Answer: I touch on the subject, but the installation is much the same as installing tubeless tires. On cruisers there are no rim locks unless the bike is drag racing. Just loosen or remove the rim lock nuts before removing the tire. Remove the old and install a new rubber liner on the rim. Inflate the new tube just a bit so it is soft and puffy to the touch, but round in shape and insert it inside the rim. The proper amount of air is to inflate the tube and let it hand off your finger. The tube should bend over your finger and sag yet still not lie flat over the top of your finger. Just a little bit of air to keep the tube from laying down flat when installed inside the tire. Install the tire on the lower side of the rim. Make sure when you install the tube into the tire it will be sitting on top of any rim lock pads not under so the tube will not be pinched. When installing the top bead of the tire to the rim be extra vigilant not to pinch the tube with the tire iron or mounting bar. Use a finger or carpenter's shim as a wedge to push the tube away from the tire mounting tool if need be so there is no pinching of the tube. When the tire is installed inflate the tire to seat the beads then tighten the rim locks down snug. It is the same procedure as installing a dirt bike tire. If you pinch a tube join the club. It happens. Replace it with a new tube and learn not to do it again.

141. Question: Please give us advice on portable air compressors.
Answer: There are electrical and mechanical and compressed gas types. The compressed gas types, those that have carbon dioxide (CO_2) which is a refrigerant gas have frozen up on me and have proven to be quite useless and they can burn your fingers with severe frostbite that can require amputation of fingers if you are not very careful. They are sold in many bicycle and motorcycle stores and should be avoided. The electrical air compressor is nice. Just start your motorcycle engine so the air compressor will not draw down your motorcycle battery and plug the compressor power socket it into your motorcycle battery (after you have installed the adapter cables to your battery to be the power source or use the jumper cables if you can find room to attach them to your battery) affix the air hose to the Schrader air valve on the rim, turn the compressor on and fill the tire with air. Open the throttle just a bit past idle and turn off your high beam headlight so the bike's alternator can power up everything. The only drawback is the compressor motor could burn out, blow fuses or just fail. In this case use a mechanical air compressor designed for bicycles. Get a model that has a flexible rubber air hose so you can put the fill valve on the valve Schrader stem so you can have room to use the air pump away from the motorcycle exhaust pipes, fender, saddle bags, etc. Also, make sure the air fill valve is of the Schrader type used for cars and motorcycles, not bicycles which often use Presta and different styles of valve cores. I carry the electric air pump on my motorcycle. A mechanical air pump that has "lever action" pump handle is way better than most other mechanical air pumps. Get one with a visible air pressure gage and a long flexible air hose line. These mechanical pumps do pump small amounts of air, even the dual-acting types which pumps more air than the single-acting piston pump, so expect to have to pump the handle a hundred times or more to inflate a motorcycle tire. The mechanical air pump may be slow, but it will work to inflate your tire so you can ride on your way, but be aware they will tire you out. You can mount one onto your bike's frame down tube or under the rear luggage rack.

142. Question: Have you actually used the Tire Pocket Plugger® in an emergency situation?
Answer: Yes, I have. I have used it twice and twice it has worked with great ease. I have run into a minor problem though on my cruiser motorcycle. The plug eventually, after 1,300 miles developed a very tiny slow leak then leaked air and needed replacing every 300 miles. This is not a huge problem by any means, but it proved to me not to be a "permanent" flat tire fix. I found the air was low overnight and I checked the air pressure and there was still air in the tire to ride, but I removed the plug and installed another one. In any case, the Pocket Tire Plugger® worked as advertised. What I like about it is the ease of use. It is so quick to fix a flat tire. Ten minutes is all it takes. The device comes with about a dozen plugs so let's say you were on a cross-country trip and the plug developed

a slow leak? You could use three plugs to get you across country! The plug never blew out it only developed a miniscule air leak producing very tiny air bubbles of about one tiny bubble per minute. Just use the device to fix your flat tire and put a new tire on the next chance you get. That's how to use these flat tire fix devices anyway. They are actually only for emergency use to get you down the road to obtain a permanent repair.

143. Question: Can I plug a tire with a hole in the sidewall?
Answer: No, that is the one area a plug will not work as the sidewall must flex and the plug will work itself loose. However, if I had just a nail puncture, not a deep slice in the sidewall and I was stuck in a remote area with nobody to call for help I would then at least try to plug the nail hole and ride slowly away under 30 miles per hour with great caution. Being exposed to hot desert or cold mountain environments is dangerous. Generally, the sidewall of a tire should not be plugged or patched and just replaced whenever practical to do so. In no case shall the bead (the portion of the tire that is in contact with the rim) and the shoulder area of the tire be repaired. The answer is no, but maybe in an "emergency" you can try.

144. Question: I have a brand new tire on my bike and I picked up a nail. Can I salvage this tire?
Answer: Yes, there is a permanent repair patch/plug device you can buy that is a permanent fix acceptable by tire manufacturers. Problem is, you have to remove the tire from the rim to insert the plug/patch on the interior surface of the tire and you may need special equipment to vulcanize the patch. The patch can only be used in and behind the tread area of the tire, not the shoulder or sidewall. Motorcycle shops do not sell these patches. You have to buy them from a tire repair wholesaler or a tire repair shop. Maybe an auto parts supply in your town may have them, but they often are expensive. Why? They come with a metal core and most come in a box of 24 count and each box has its own size to fix certain size nail holes in the tire. Once the patch/plug is installed you can ride as you normally would with a new tire (I still recommend you just buy a new tire than use these patch/plug devices). The other option, if you are not inclined to wait for a specialized patch/plug device to arrive in the mail, is to install a new tire, permanent patch/plug the old tire and use the patched tire as a spare backup tire in your garage. Also to consider a proper permanent repair is normally vulcanized with heat and pressure bonding that this book does not explore using special tools. Your best bet is to just replace the damaged tire with a new one.

145. Question: I used all the advice in your book and I still had a tough time mounting my tires. Why?
Answer: The rims on your motorcycle may not have deep drop-centers so no matter what trick you use the tire will have to be slowly muscled onto the rim. Make sure you keep pushing down often the tire into the drop center. Use a tire iron, even two or three of them if need be to hold the tire down so the tire can slip onto the rim. Another reason may be lack of lubrication on the rim and on the tire and inexperience changing tires. If you have shallow drop centers just work very slowly with the tire irons to allow time for the tire to fold and stretch onto the rim. Speed is your enemy. Many cruiser rims do have deep drop centers and you will have no trouble putting on new tires as long as you push the tire down into that drop center opposite and to the sides where you are working. Let's say you are working at the 6 o'clock position to get the last few inches of tire onto the rim, but it will not go on. Push the tire down at the 9, 12 and 3 o'clock position with a free hand or use tire irons tied down with a rope to hold the tire down and the tire should slip right on the rim.

146. Question: I was told not to use the string/rope type plugs to repair a tire as they will fall out from centrifugal force. Is this true?
Answer: That won't happen if the string/rope is installed properly. If you install the string/rope deeply, at least 2/3 of the string/rope into the tire with only 1/3 protruding, the string/rope plug can't come out from centrifugal force because the string/rope plug makes a large loop mushroom inside the air space of the tire and it is saturated with glue or vulcanizing compound on top of that making it just about impossible for it to just blow or work itself out of the tire. That vulcanizing compound actually melts when the tire heats up to bond the string/rope plug to the tire. I could not remove a cured plug with large pliars when I tried.

147. Question: Explain what is considered a permanent repair.
Answer: Using the Tire Pocket Plugger® and the string/rope type plugs are not permanent repairs despite what riders may tell you or post on the Internet. These devices repair the tire while the tire is still on the rim and that is the difference which makes them only temporary repairs to get you down the road instead of being stranded. You should replace the tire or have it permanently repaired. A permanent repair is performed with the tire removed from the rim, the nail hole drilled out to make sure the hole is not intruded with steel belts and the plug/patch is applied from the inside of the tire. Check out the Rubber Manufacturers Association and most tire manufacturing websites for more information about making permanent tire repairs. This book does not cover making permanent tire repairs, only emergency repairs to get you down the road to your home. After plugging the tire you should replace the tire for a new one. I know a lot of people and even manufacturers of tire repair products say their external tire plugging devices are permanent repairs. They might be and then again they may not be. Until the tire associations and the tire manufacturers approve these devices we need to remain on the safe side and not use them for permanent repair. I know that liability is an issue and they may never be declared as permanent repair even if the products do in fact behave as a permanent repair. When in doubt always choose the safest route and that is to buy a new tire.

148. Question: My tire is sliced and does not have a hole in the tread area. What patch can I use?

Answer: No patch. A slice anywhere on the tire is generally not considered repairable. Even a permanent internal plug/patch may not work as the integral strength of the tire has been weakened and the tire could fly apart from internal air pressure and centrifugal force. Replace the tire with a new one.

149. Question: I was told I do not need to use a reamer to insert a plug in a tire. Is this true?

Answer: Yes, it is true you don't need to ream out the hole for the sake of just opening the hole larger in size. However, reamer is multipurpose. It removes any impurities, foreign objects and even a broken nail hiding inside the tread area. It will also roughen up the nail hole in the rubber tread so the plug will get a stronger grip. What your friend may be saying is you don't use the reamer if when you insert the reamer you come upon strong resistance hitting steel belts. In that case you would not use the reamer and just throw away the tire, but that won't do you any good if you are stranded on the side of the road. In the emergency you would just use the reamer and insert the rope type plug. If you are using the Pocket Tire Plugger® device you would just insert the plug without reaming the hole or just ream the hole just deep enough to get the insertion tool into the tire. Let's keep this simple as tire repair procedures can be complex. We are just covering emergency use not permanent repair techniques which requires special tools.

130. Question: I want to start a motorcycle tire repair shop. Can you share advice?

Answer: Don't bother. The liability on you if something goes wrong and a rider dies or is denied the enjoyment of life from a debilitating accident will be hard to defend in a court of law requiring expert witnesses and a law firm that can bankrupt you in a minute even with liability insurance. Another reason to stay clear is most people are just going to not fix their tires permanently. They just want to get a quick fix then put a new tire on the bike. Let's face it the average bike may get 6,000 to 12,000 miles on a set of tires anyway on a new set so what you would have to charge to fix a tire with materials and labor would make repairing the tire a waste of time and money. It would be cost effective to just buy a new set of tires. Better yet, go into the tire installation business for motorcycles along with oil changes, brakes, chain and sprocket replacements. A light maintenance business installing accessories could be worthwhile. That would be a good starting place and you can expand your services from there.

149. Question: What about the new tires not using steel belts but instead use Aramid® or Kevlar®® fibers. Can I fix flat tires with these new tires?

Answer: Absolutely yes. You will use the same procedure as a steel belted tire. Also, it makes no difference between a bias ply tire and a radial tire the procedures are identical to fix the flat tire. Now, we don't yet have "run-flat" tires for motorcycles (at this writing) but they may or may not be able to be plugged or will need a different type of plug or patch along with a specialized procedure. It that does happen I will post on my Web site the repair procedure until a future revision of this book permits its inclusion.

150. Question: I often see new tire repair products on the Internet and in magazine ads. How can I know if they are any good or not?

Answer: Just try it out and see what happens if the product is safe for motorcycle use. But keep the tried and true and proven products in your saddlebags. I have the Pocket Tire Plugger® and the rope/string plugs. Yes, two systems, but I know for a fact both work just fine. I also have two air compressors in my saddlebags; a 12 volt air compressor and a mechanical bicycle tire inflator. I do not want to be stranded especially out west where I live near hot deserts and the high mountains of Nevada Arizona, Oregon and California where cell phones do not work in such remote locations. I also do not want my day to end waiting for a tow truck and waiting for a dealer to put a new tire on the bike. Worse, they may not even be open and I will have to find a motel and hang around playing the waiting game. I rather carry the tire repair equipment, fix the flat and be on my way in fifteen minutes.

151. Question: I found the rope type plugs but motorcycles are not mentioned on the package for repair. Where can I find motorcycle specific plugs?

Answer: I know what you are up against. The package shows a car, truck, ATV but no motorcycle. That does not mean you can't use the rope plug to fix your motorcycle tire. The company just does not want to deal with high speed two-wheel vehicles so they don't put a motorcycle on the package. If it can fix a car or truck tire it certainly can repair a motorcycle tire.

152. Question: Can I use a flat tire sealant in my motorcycle?

Answer: You can, but it is not recommended for reasons of corrosion. It depends on the sealant ingredients and the composition of your rims and the valve core. Ammonia can corrode certain metals quickly. You don't want some chemical eating a hole in your rims or boring out your valve stem. If you have a tube tire you can use the product, but it must be authorized to use with rubber tubes. Let's say there are no nasty chemical and your rims and valve stem or tube is okay to use the sealant. You could use the product. The fluid may even act as a dynamic wheel balancer. As of this writing I don't use the sealants in my motorcycles as I don't want to deal with the cleaning up the product and it is a waste of money if I wear out a set of tires (I do this three times a year) and I never got a flat tire. If a product comes out that really works and is economical I may one day use them. The products work sometimes, but I have seen them fail on bicycle tires not sealing the air leak too many times.

153. Question: Can I install a tubeless tire on my spoke rim?
Answer: Generally, yes. As long as the tire and tube is the proper size for the rim (and the tire is not wider for clearance of frame, belt or chain drive issues) and the tire is not a radial tire. For best results, check with the tire manufacturer as they may allow conversions and alternatives. Yes, if you do go with a wider tire you do need to increase the size of the innertube.

154. Question: People on the Internet raved about a tire. I found it was a bad tire. Why?
Answer: Sometimes the chat rooms carry a conversation thread for a specific type of bike for a special purpose and when you try the tire it wears fast or causes handling problems. I have found many raving reviews for tires that I know are inferior. I assume many riders do not know what they are talking about. What they feel is good isn't compared to other brands of tires. Not everybody can be right and not everybody is wrong. Internet searching will help you find consistent reviews and the perfect tire for your bike.

155. Question: I am having a tough time trying to find the correct size tire for my motorcycle. When I search on the Internet they seem to be using strange codes for tire size. Help!
Answer: Harley-Davidson I have found does this to confound us riders so we will not easily switch away from the Harley-Davidson brand tire. They leave the tire width size out and use a code such as BT 90B/16. Just measure the tire width on your bike in millimeters from shoulder to shoulder near the tread to replace that BT code and the B after 90 and you will have your tire size, unless they change the other numbers to code to confuse us even more. Example: Replace BT with 140/90/16 would be the tire size to use to do your shopping. Some manufactures will have a cross-reference chart. Check out some Web forums and even some motorcycle tire supply stores on the Internet. You may find the correct size tire in very small print on the tire. But be aware there are often so many codes it will confuse you to find the correct numbers. Once you do find the size you can buy tires cheap on the Internet saving over $100 each tire with great ease. You really can save thousands of dollars installing your own tires. It is not unusual to pay a dealer $175 just to install a rear tire, but you could have bought a good tire that will last longer for only $87.

156. Question: What is your opinion on Metzler, Dunlop and Avon tires?
Answer: They are excellent tires. However, they are expensive tires. You may find better deals with Bridgestone®, Kenda®, Continental®, Pirelli®, Mitchelin®, Shinko® and other tire companies. My advice is to shop around on the Internet and read the customer reviews. Some economically priced tires just wear out too quickly at 3,000 miles while others can last equal to or longer than name brand tires. However, sometimes you find a tire that wears exceptionally slow and though it is more expensive it is better because it will last twice as long as the cheaper brand of tire. I like to use the tire that gives me the most miles at the lowest cost and I am always experimenting with different brands of tires to find the best for my purposes.

157. Question: I read I could use brake cleaner to force a tire to seat when inflating it. How do I do this?
Answer: What is going on is instead of buying a bead-setting (or starting) strap to wrap around the tire so air can inflate the tubeless tire the idiot is filling the tire with a burst of explosive mixture, lights it with a flame and "bang!" the explosion forces the tire to suddenly expand onto the rim. This is not only dangerous as the tire can explode, the rim can rip apart like a hand grenade or both and the tire can catch fire and hidden internal damage to the tire can occur. I don't recommend it. I use a bead-starting strap. Now even the bead-starting strap you have to be very careful as all of the above can happen except for catching fire, the rim and tire can explode. You have to release the bead-starter's tension the moment the tire begins to fill with air and expand and remove it right away. It is meant to only use it to seat the tire's bead onto the rim so it will not leak air preventing the tire from inflating. It is not used to actually seat the tire's bead section to the bead section on the rim in the tire's normal mounted position on the rim, air does that. When inflating tires use short bursts of air and check the pressure gage on the fill valve. You shouldn't need to exceed 20 psi to start an air seal with a bead-starting strap. The moment the tire moves outward toward the rim, loosen the bead-starting strap. According to the Rubber Manufacturers Association a rubber donut (another name and design for a tire bead starter) should not be used. However, these products exist to solve a problem of the newly installed tire not conforming to the rim allowing air to leak. Most people do not have large enough compressed air blast capacity to expand the tire rapidly and that is why these products were developed. Like anything else, if you do use the bead starting device with diligence and care you will have no problems.

158. Question: I would like to change my own tires but I lack the courage and the knowledge. Any advice?
Answer: How about going to a motorcycle or automotive shop that installs tires and ask them if they need a "volunteer" to help out. Tell them you want to learn how to change and balance tires. That's one great way to get on the job training at no cost to you except your time. You can also find some shops where you can observe the tire mounting process. Most shops use machines, but small motorcycle shops use tire irons. Some shops are secretive. They want to keep the tire changing process a mystery so you won't get any training from those repair shops. You could buy an old motorcycle tire and wheel at a swap meet and use it for practice.

159. Question: It is true a dealer can void your warranty if you change your own tires?

Answer: That is illegal. Search the Internet for the Magnuson-Moss Warranty Act to learn more. Dealers and repair shops have been lying to customers to incite fear into the consumer in order to obtain unjust profits. I was recently in a Harley-Davidson dealership where a salesperson told me, "The (drive) belt is made of Kevlar®® so you will never have to change the belt." We all know that statement is false! There's no end to the misinformation taking place. You need to read books on vehicle repairs to obtain the truth. Even the vehicle's owner's manual is a good place to begin.

160. Question: Can I use vegetable oil as a tire lubricant?
Answer: Yes, you can. However, using a specialized tire lube is always best. The vegetable oil takes a long time to be absorbed and evaporate and on a motorcycle wheel that can become problematic if the tire slips around the rim. Not so much on a tubeless tire, but on a tube tire the tire can rip the tube's valve stem off causing a blow-out condition.

161. Question: Is it okay to use aerosol flat tire fix in a can devices to fix a flat tire?
Answer: You can in an emergency, but be careful as the aerosol can have flammable mixtures that can explode. Special care must be taken to purge these gases out of the tire before removing the tire by inflating and deflating the tire numerous times. One spark from a tool can cause the tire and rim to explode. The best way to fix a flat tire while on the road for emergency purposes is described in this book using the rubber plug and rope/string plugs. You just have to carry an air compressor device to fill the tire with air after it is plugged.

162. Question: How do I test my air pressure gage?
Answer: Usually by having two air pressure gages you can simply test each one. They both should read nearly the same give or take a couple pounds pressure. There are gage testing devices industry uses, but this is not required for the home mechanic. Hint: Never trust any pressure gage is telling the truth. If you retain doubts you will always be working safer than someone who trusts everything they see. If you are filling your tire and it seems like it is taking longer than normal you are likely over pressurizing the tire and the pressure gage is giving you false readings. Work slowly, pay attention to details. Use a spare air gage to verify pressure accuracy.

163. Question: Shouldn't we be replacing the valve core each time we change tires?
Answer: Yes, you should as they are economical to replace.

164. Question: I do not have the confidence to change tires on my bike. Please help.
Answer: This is easy. Get a junkyard tire and wheel to practice on and this will build your confidence. You will learn a lot this way and not have to worry about ruining expensive rims. You may want to obtain a spoke wheel and a cast wheel. I may add that if you rip a junkyard tire with a tire iron it is likely the tire is dry, brittel and old and not your error. A rim that is severely square from an accident won't do. Small dents are okay. You need a round rim. You can get a good used tire for free at most small motorcycle repair shops to fit your junkyard rims for practice.

165. Question: Your book describes using paste lubricant while Websites only describe using liquids. Why?
Answer: They other guys are not familiar with the solid paste lubricants. The solid paste does not evaporate as fast as liquids do so when installing the tire to the rim it makes the job much easier to do especially when using tire irons. You can use liquid if you want to. I use the liquid to demount tires and I use the paste to mount them. Sometimes I use both to mount the tire if the tire becomes stubborn to install.

166. Question: I saw a dealer install an innertube into a tire but he put a white powder on the tube. What was that powder and why did you use it?
Answer: It is talcum powder and it acts as a lubricant so the tube does not stick to the rubber tire or rim strap. It makes installing the tube easier. You don't have to use it if you do not want to.

167. Question: How much tire lubricant should I use?
Answer: Most people use too much when learning. Using too much liquid will allow too much fluid to accumulate inside the tire which can cause havoc trying to maintain tire pressure as the liquid when hot evaporates creating higher pressures and when cooler condenses and creates lower pressure. That is why I like to use the paste lubricants as they don't make as much of a mess as liquids do. After you have become proficient changing tires you will learn where to apply and how little to use. An added benefit of using paste is the lubricant will not run onto the tire treads and the floor where you are working. When learning you should use a good smear of solid paste lubricant. You can buy the paste from No-Mar® on the Internet. One jar will last for dozens of tire changes.

168. Question: Can I use a screwdriver to mount tires?
Answer: No. A tire iron has a wide spoon on its end and will not rip the tire's bead as quickly and easily as a screwdriver will. Use the proper tools to do the job. When I was young many of us riders did use screwdrivers with diligent care and we were successful,

but we did make many tiny tears in the rubber no matter how careful we were. It's just not wise to use screwdrivers especially with the high power and speed along with the heavy weight motorcycle in use today. Use tire irons. This book shows you which type of tire irons to use.

169. Question: I read that tires should be inflated in a safety cage.
Answer: Yes, it is true just in case the tire explodes. However, if you look around nobody is using them. You can tie a couple ropes around the tire and rim to create a weak safety net, but the ropes must be loose to allow the tire to expand. The ropes should prevent the tire from hitting you or others nearby if it did explode. You won't have tire explosions if you inflate slowly in short bursts and have an accurate pressure gage and never exceed 40 psi to seat the tire's beads. Obviously, if you are inflating a tire onto an old rusty rim you are looking for trouble.

170. Question: Why do you tell us to inflate and deflate the tire to seat the beads?
Answer: Just to make sure all is well and bead is seated. Also, if you get into this habit you will never have to remember to do it when installing tubes in a tire so the tube will not become folded or wrinkled inside.

171. Question: When I inflated my tire I heard a loud bang. It scared me.
Answer: It sometimes startles professionals too when caught off guard. As the tire expands as you fill it with air the tire "pops" into position seating into the rim's bead channel with a loud "bang" that sounds like the tire has exploded. Once you hear that bang you need to stop inflating the tire. You use a pressure gage when inflating and you check the pressure as you approach 40 psi. If you do not hear that loud seating noise, STOP ADDING AIR and deflate the tire and try again. Something may have hung up the tire on the rim. That's why I use paste lubricant as it allows the tire to slide into position at lower air pressures.

172. Question: I am still having trouble installing my tire to the rim. What am I doing wrong?
Answer: Inexperience is a problem and we all have to get past this stage. The number one problem is allowing the tire opposite where you are working not being set low below the rim's shoulder so the tire can flow into the drop center when using the tire irons or mounting bar to get the last amount of rubber over the rim. Use a tire iron and tie it down so it is pushing the tire down into the rim's drop center well. This is the trick to mounting tires on rims. If you do this the tire, even if it is 40 degrees cold, will easily go on the rim. Of course, you need to lubricate the tire or even this trick will become tricky as the rubber will not slip and slide over the rim. If you follow the instructions in this book you should have few problems.

173. Question: When checking air pressure in tires should it be warm or hot?
Answer: Cold ambient air temperature. Ambient means the temperature of the atmosphere at the time you are filling the tire with air. If you inflate your tires in the cold winter atmosphere by spring time the air pressure will rise in your tires. If you inflate your tires on a hot day in summer, in winter the air pressure will drop inside the tire. Check tire pressure often and adjust pressure as needed.

174. Question: How should I store my spare tires?
Answer: Keep them in the house not a cold, hot, dry or damp environment subject to temperature extremes. Also do not store them near any electric motors as the ozone emitted from the motors will attack the rubber tires causing them to crack.

175. Question: Can I ride with tires with the arrow indicators facing backwards?
Answer: No. You need to remount the tires so the arrow permits the tire to rotate in the proper direction. The tire can actually come apart if you don't. Rare to happen, but it can occur especially when driving at freeway speeds. If you were driving only in the city at less than 40 mph you could get away with it. You won't make this mistake if you mark the wheel's rim or disk brake rotor with an arrow showing the direction of wheel rotation. It is now a simple task to check tire rotation direction before installing the tire.

176. Question: I was told the painted dot is to be positioned opposite the valve stem. Is this true?
Answer: Only if the tire manufacturer tells you so. The standard in the tire industry is to align the painted dot adjacent the valve stem. Standards can change and be updated with different color dots being positioned in other positions. Check with the tire manufacturer for advice regarding your tire model. I have made mistakes on my tires failing to align the dot to the valve stem and I did not experience any problems with tire balance. Unless you are racing or driving over 80 mph much of the time I would not be concerned about making this mistake.

177. Question: I heard using silicone lubricant is best for tire mounting. Can I use this?
Answer: No. Silicone will deteriate the rubber. Whoever advised you of this is mistaken. Don't use anything other than an approved tire lubricant designed to lubricate tires when mounting tires to rims. Petroleum based products will also rot your tires so do not use them to mount tires.

178. Question: What is a donut? I overheard mechanics speaking of it when installing tires.
Answer: It is circular hose strap that when filled with compressed air squeezes the tire to the rim when inflating it. It is like a tire bead starting strap. You have to be careful using these products so you do not prevent the tire from inflating causing an explosion of the tire or rim or both. This is why we use a working pressure gage and short bursts of air when inflating a tire so pressure will not rise and things get away from us. The donut must be removed once the tire begins to inflate in less than 20 psi on the pressure gage.

179. Question: Can I install a set of tube-type tires to my cast alloy rims?
Answer: No. Unless the tire specifically says it can be used on tubeless rims then it will be okay. A tube tire relies on the innertube to seal air. The tubeless tire relies on the tire's bead profile to match the rim's profile to seal air.

180. Question: Can I obtain discounts on new tires?
Answer: Yes, if you buy them out of state by way of the Internet and motorcycle mail order tire warehouses. The prices are lower and you may save money on local, state and federal sales taxes. Many firms also offer free shipping. See our section in this book, "Free Tires" how you can get tires for free. Many times if you simply ask a local merchant for a discount you can often get one. Most people are too prideful to ask, but those who do request a discount will save some money. I would not buy tires from on-line auction sites for one reason. Once in a while you get a tire that is slightly out of round and will not set the bead to seal air. You can't return it. Most all mail order and Internet tire warehouses allow returns from defective tires.

181. Question: I saw a product that used engine compression to inflate tires. What is your opinion on this?
Answer: I have not used the product. I do not like the idea that a volatile gasoline and air mixture could be introduced into the tire, do you?

182. Question: I saw a manually operated air pump that also uses CO2 cartridges. Do they work?
Answer: I have used CO2 cartridges and I do not recommend them as they tend to freeze up upon gas release, can burn your fingers or take out your eye with frostbite and it takes too many cartridges to fill a tire and you only get one chance to fill the tire. What if your plug leaks and you need to reinsert another plug? You will be stranded. The manual function is nice, but it must have an extended flexible hose otherwise it is useless. Any air pump with no flexible extension hose may only work on the front tire. The rear tire has brake rotor, saddlebags, sprocket/pulley and chain/belt guard so there is no way you can attach the device to the wheel's valve stem and pump the air pump piston. There are a lot of useless products being sold to motorcyclists in motorcycle shops and mail order catalogs. This book tells you what works and what doesn't! Check our Website for updates to new products: JamesRussellPublishing.com

183. Question: You did not teach us how to plug and patch a tire. Why?
Answer: After reading this book you could easily have attained the familiarity to purchase a patch/plug and follow the manufacturer's instructions to do the job yourself. However, this permanent tire repair also requires special tools. After considering the cost of the tools and the patch/plugs must be purchased in bulk (and are not cheap in price) it is not worth the investment for a one time repair. You could take the tire to a tire repair shop and have those professionals patch/plug your tire at less cost. Another option is to just scrap your flat tire and buy a new one. Sometimes the time and expense is not practical to save a tire.

184. Question: I am almost done mounting the tire to the rim, but the tire is so tight lying on top of the rim I can't get my tire iron to slip between the tire's bead and the rim to mount the tire. What do I do?
Answer: In the last few inches the tire will get wound up against the top of the rim. What you need to do is back off just a bit on one tire iron and that will release the tension so you can slip the next tire iron inside, then use both of those tire irons as needed to finish the job along with the third tire iron that you may also have inserted nearby. Take small bites of rubber, very small bites and make absolutely certain 180 degrees opposite you insert a tire iron or use some other device to hold down the tire's bead down and away from the rim's shoulder so the tire can easily move down into the rim well (drop center) and you will hardly need to use any force to mount the tire. This is the great secret to mounting tires.

185. Question: Can I use paste and liquid tire lubricants to mount tires?
Answer: Yes, you can if you want to. I use liquid to remove the old tire and paste to mount the new tire. But if you want to reverse the process you can. If you only have liquid you can use that to demount and mount tires.

186. Question: I think I applied too much paste lubricant to the bead and rim. Should I demount the tire and wipe it down to reduce the lubricant?
Answer: No, you don't need to remove the tire and wipe the tire and rim down. I intentionally smeared a great amount of sticky paste tire lubricant onto the rim and even the bead of the tire just to see what would happen. Nothing happened. When the tire is

inflated it will squeeze the excess lubricant out of the bead area. Likewise, if you used too little tire lubricant for some reason it won't bother anything. Now I am talking cruiser motorcycle here, not drag, road or street racing conditions. You don't use much lubricant under those demanding circumstances. Too much lubricant and the tire can slip around the rim. A tubeless tire will just rotate around the rim, but a tube type tire will rip the tube's valve right off causing a blow-out unless rim locks are used to lock the tire to the rim. You don't need lubricant for drag or professional track racing or use very little when mounting tires.

187. Question: Why do some riders get better tire mileage than others?
Answer: Let's assume we are comparing the exact same bike. One rider may be more abrupt with his clutch when shifting gears (upshift and downshift) that causes the rear wheel to scuff against the pavement causing rapid wear. He may also have a loose belt, chain or worn shaft drive bearings causing more backlash effects on the tire creating even more scuffing. Each scuff is a tiny patch of burnt rubber removed from the tire tread and this wears a tire out quicker. One rider may be riding with a passenger or with heavy items in the luggage compartments, ride with low tire pressure or rides more aggressively in the corners or accelerates like a mad man evading the police. Some motorcycles are harder on tires so when evaluating tires try to read user reviews with a bike like yours, but keep in mind riding habits mentioned above determine how fast a certain tire will wear out. Even under ideal conditions the tire is constantly scuffing against the road making friction that make heat and that wears out the tire naturally. Some roads are rough and scrub tires aggressively.

188. Question: I am having a hard time removing the lower tire bead. Top side is easy, just the lower bead is giving me grief.
Answer: This is because you have forgotten to break the bead on the lower side. You have to break the beads on both sides of the tire near the rim. Break the bead on the upper surface, flip the tire over and break that bead right away so you will not forget. Once you do this you will be able to just pull the tire off the rim with your bare hands. Don't forget to spray liquid tire lubricant on the beads and rim when removing the tire. Also lube the tire and rim after you break the beads. If you have a tough time breaking beads? Go ahead and spray or wipe some liquid lube by the tire and rim area. One more thing, make absolutely certain you have removed the valve core so you have evacuated all of the compressed air from the tire. Do not put the valve core back inside the valve stem until after you have broken both tire beads. Also, when breaking the bead on one side of the tire you may have to rotate the wheel or move the bead breaker to three or four sections to fully release the tire's bead from sticking to the rim. Sometimes you can get so distracted you can actually forget to let the air out of the tire and you can't break the tire's bead that way for sure. It will be helpful for you to keep a list of procedures to follow nearby or keep this book readily available by your side.

189. Question: I saw professionals mounting tires and they do not lubricate the entire rim as you suggest. Why?
Answer: This book if for beginners, people who are learning and by lubricating the entire rim and tire sections the student can have plenty of time to get the job done. Often, the tire will move out of position and the student will not realize it. If he mounts the tire with partial lubricant on the rim he may not be able to rotate the tire back to position by hand to align the color dot to the valve stem. Learning can be baffling to the beginner and lubricating the rim and tire a lot will be of great help to the student. Once you have gained experience you can revert to only lubricating 70% or less of the tire and rim. However, it is best to lube the entire tire and rim so you will gain the air sealing benefits of the tire lubricant. I use a lot of lubricant even though I have experience because I just like the get the job done with less fuss.

190. Question: I need to put a tire on without lubricant. What should I do?
Answer: Follow the instructions in this book except omit the lubricant. The tire will not go on easily. You have to make sure the tire floats down into the rim well when mounting or you will end up having a terrible time. It will not be fun and you will need three to four long curved tire irons and take very tiny bites of rubber to get the tire on. You need to move in slow-motion to allow the rubber to stretch and flow into position. If you move too fast you will hear the rubber rip as you work. You don't want that, so make sure the tire never rides up onto the rim's shoulder. I have done it dry many times. It can be done, just use patience and pay attention as tire irons will want to fling backwards and hit you. If they slip they will fly in the air.

191. Question: Why do my tires wear unevenly?
Answer: I can't get into that in this book as it has to do with the roads ridden, the rider, condition of the roads, suspension system design, alignment, frame geometry, balance, fork rake and so much more. However, I can at least say that some tires will wear horribly while other brands will wear nicely so just changing brands can often solve the problem with cupping of the tread and strange wear patterns and the annoying howling noise that makes. Same is true if your tires are wearing out quickly, try another brand of tires for it may solve the problem. My two new Kawasaki Vulcan 2000 motorcycles wore out the front tire in horrible noisy cupping fashion with vibration with the stock Bridgestone® tires. I switched to a different brand of cruiser tire and the problem went away. The Bridgestone® tire had a hard rubber composition. When I switched to Avon® and Metzeler® tires which are softer the cupping, noise and vibration vanished and I even got better miles on the latter tires and a much smoother ride too. Just because a bike comes with a certain tire does not mean that tire is best.

192. Question: My rear tire gets a flat spot in the center when it wears. Is this normal?
Answer: Yes, the flat spot forms because the tire is wide and most riding is on a straight line. The flat spot also is bad for tire wear for it increases the contact patch (good for straight line traction in dry weather and bad in wet weather if the flat spot is bald with no tread sipes) and this increases heat friction and the tire begins to wear down at an accelerated pace. Going to a narrower tire will solve the flat spot problem and give you better miles so the tire will last longer. However, this is usually not practical as the motorcycle has a wide wheel rim that needs a wide tire for best handling. You could find an aftermarket wheel that is narrower but I would not bother with it. Just buy tires at discount and change them yourself when they wear out.

193. Question: When inserting a rope plug to fix a flat tire I was told to rotate the tool 180 degrees when removing the tool. What is the correct procedure?
Answer: The correct procedure is the one the manufacturer of the rope tells you to do. Just follow their procedure. Some ropes are designed to be rotated to prevent rope unraveling and others do not have those problems due to the weave and impregnated vulcanizing capabilities of the rope.

194. Question: Most Harley riders I know use Dunlop or H-D brand tires. Can they use other brands?
Answer: Yes they can and yes, they should! Those tires can be expensive to buy. I have used many other brands on my Harley's and on my 19 other motorcycles I have owned as of this date. I have found many low cost brands to be actually superior in price and performance than the big name brand tires. I have also found tires that are so smooth riding and bump absorbing it was like putting on a new progressive suspension system. You will be amazed how good things can get at much lower cost. Don't be stuck doing what the monkey's do, you got to do your own thing. Be a trailblazer, be different, break the habits. Consider that if you find a new rear tire for $70 compared to a new name brand $220 tires don't assume the more expensive tire is the better deal. I have seen the $70 tire outperform and outlast the more expensive tire. Not in every case, so you need to experiment and shop around and try them out. Remember, DOT tires sold in the USA are safe to put on your motorcycle, even if the brand name sounds funny to you and nobody you know has those tires on their bike. Just buy them and find out what the other guys may be missing out on, usually a "great deal" can be had. I know, you are going against the grain, but take the plunge and be different. For me, it has paid off big time in tire savings and ride quality.

195. Question: I went to a Harley-Davidson dealer and I noticed the motorcycles with spoke wheels do not have rim locks. Why is this?
Answer: Two reasons. First, the rims may actually be "tubeless tire compatible" meaning they require no innertubes and no rim lock would be necessary. Second, just because a rim has spokes and an innertube does not mean a rim lock is required to hold the tire to the rim so the innertube will not be rotated and broken. Only drag and dirt bike racing generally require rim locks on tube-type rims. Drag racing bikes with cast wheels and slicks do not have rim locks to hold the tire to the rim. The bond between a tubeless tire and rim is extremely strong so for street use, even hard street riding, rim locks are not required on tubeless rims, and that is why stock street bikes are not equipped with rim locks.

196. Question: What is the purpose of that tall spacer installed on the rim lock?
Answer: On tube type tires the rim lock stem is held to the rim with a simple square threaded nut. If you look close the bottom flat side of the nut contacts the rim, but not squarely due to the rim being a round surface. The rim lock on a motorcycle can use these oval spacers so the nut can rest on a flat surface. This permits an accurate torque of the nut as the washer evenly spreads the load over the width of the rim where the rim lock is located. This reduces stress that can lead to rim flattening and stress cracking and prevents the rim lock from being twisted out of position. It is just an improvement, but many dirt bike riders do not use them unless they have a rim lock or rim failure.

197. Question: Why must I use an air pump that has a flexible hose to inflate my motorcycle tire?
Answer: The problem is if you place an air pump on the valve stem you will need to exert force to pump the pump and that force is going to slam hard against a very soft and hollow brass (or steel) tube (which is what the valve stem is) and the valve stem will bend, crack or snap off. Get an air pump with a flexible hose and no sideways forces will be applied to the valve stem so it can not snap. Imagine the mess you will be in using a bicycle air pump to fix a flat tire and you snap the valve stem in half. Time to call the tow truck.

198. Question: I was told tire irons are not strong enough to replace tires on modern motorcycles.
Answer: Yes, you were told wrong. Tire irons are strong enough to even change big-rig 18-wheel truck tires! Many truck tire irons are longer in length for ease of use, but the point is a "machine" is not required. And if you search the Internet you will find companies selling "hand tools" just for this heavy duty industry tire changing. Don't be fooled, you can change your tires yourself using simple tire irons.

199. Question: Can I use compressed air to burst the new tire to start the bead?
Answer: Yes, you can, but it is not recommended. You have to be careful and just give the tire a very brief burst of air. You have to remove the valve stem core to get the large volume of air to flow and you need a quick opening ball valve to get the strong burst of air along with at least a ¼" internal diameter air hose with 40 psi pressure. The fast burst and large volume of air acts like an small explosion forcing the tire outwards from its pigeon-toed configuration. It overwhelms those tiny small air leaks and it works, but I use the bead starting straps. Both are not recommended by the Rubber Manufactures Association and they give no advice otherwise what to use to start the bead on tires that are leaking air and will not inflate normally.

200. Question: I want to learn more about tires. Where can I go to learn?
Answer: Check out our Web site: JamesRussellPublishing.com as we will have motorcycle links and advice on the site. Search the Internet for more advice. I don't know of any book, except this one, that is dedicated to motorcycle tires. I admit this book does not have all the knowledge needed to be a tire professional regarding tire engineering, wear and tear and racing. I am focusing only on how to change tires and fix flat tires on motorcycles.

201. Question: I need a tire changing stand. Do they make any?
Answer: Yes. Do an Internet search under, "Tire Changing Tools" and you will find many tools.

202. Question: What is a tire bar?
Answer: Just another name for tire iron.

203. Question: Can I use soap and water as a tire lube?
Answer: Many installers do use it, but any product with water will be trapped in the air space and corrode the rim and play games with tire pressure due to temperature changes the water vapor changes state from liquid to gas. You will also find using soap and water is very messy as it runs all over the place. Water and your soap can have a low (acid) ph (percent of hydrogen) or high ph which is alkaline and both are wickedly corrosive not to mention the oxidation rusting from oxygen in the water corroding your rims. You will get all sort of advice from people from using hair spray to window cleaner as a tire/rim lubricant. Best to use a tire changing lubricant that is not water based and non-corrosive to metal and composite rims. The proper lubricant is "engineered" to do the job correctly and will also create a tighter bead between the tire and the rim. It will allow the tire to be removed from the rim without leaving a transfer of rubber to the rim which you will have to "work hard" to remove to avoid rim and tire bead leaks when you install your new tire. Just follow the advice in this book for best results all around.

204. Question: I have a slow air leak in a tire but I can't find it. What can I do?
Answer: Inflate the tire to at least 20psi or inflate to no more than what the tire is rated for. Make a soapy mix of water and dishwasher detergent and spray it on the tire and look for a steam of tiny bubbles. If you can dunk the tire and rim into a wide tub of clean water (no soap needed) you can check for a stream of air bubble leaks that way too. If you have no deep and wide tub just take your wheel to any tire installation garage and they can dunk it in their tank for you. If you still can't find the leak you may have a temperature sensitive leak that only leaks at a certain temperature range that is warm or cool. Odds are you have a valve stem air leak. Replace the entire valve stem on a cast wheel or replace the rubber washer seal with a new one that seals air inside the rim. Then again, you could have a pinhole leak in the rim itself too!

205. Question: The tire I have has two color dots on it. Which one do I use to align with the valve stem?
Answer: You likely have a red or yellow dot. Check with the tire manufacturer to discover if the red dot is in fact the light spot on the tire. If so, put the red dot near the valve stem. The yellow dot, if it is the heavy spot of the tire, can be placed at the point where the rim has a lighter spot. It is a bit more complicated than this, but for this book's purposes we need not delve into the duel balancing of the rim first, then the tire last, which is a two step process. We use a simple one step process in this book. Just find the light spot on the tire by asking the tire manufacture which color dot you should use and put that dot by the valve stem then static balance the wheel with the tire mounted to the rim and inflated with air with the valve stem cap installed. Generally, the red dot will be placed adjacent to the valve stem.

206. Question: I had my dealer install new tires and when I got the bike the front tire has a bump to the point I can feel it at most all speeds, but is worse at 50 mph. The dealer says they can't find anything wrong. What can I do?
Answer: The dealer may have damaged your tire or rim, most likely the tire when putting it on bending the internal bead wire so violently that it bent or broke. You may not be able to see the internal damage. Another problem can be the tire itself was damaged by a forklift blade ramming into it during the shipping and handling of the tire and again you may not be able to see the internal damage. The tire could be out of round due to a defective mold process direct from the factory. The tire and rim could be way out of balance. This often occurs when a different type of tire is installed than what you had before so the tire and rim must be balanced together

for the new configuration. It is possible you have a bad wheel bearing creating a hop. That is easy to check, just lift the bike, rotate the wheel and look for axial (up and down) run out. Take your bike back to the dealer and tell them of these things and ask them to replace the bad tire under the tire manufacturer's warranty if the wheel bearings are okay. If they refuse, then it is highly likely the dealer broke the tire when installing it improperly and they know the tire manufacturer will deny the warranty claim and they are trying to pass the grief to you. Yes, a tire changing machine can rip the tire bead like knife carving a turkey due to its high angle of circular ripping force. Learn to change tires and you will not have incompetent installation problems. And yes, there are many dishonest dealers and repair shops who will adamantly pretend there is no problem saying, "We can't duplicate the problem." They make you feel like an idiot all along they are the thieves ripping you off. That is one good reason why you should learn to work on your own bike as much as you possibly can. Also read Question #8.

207. Question: I am not certain I can change my own tires because I am getting old and I do not have the strength.
Answer: Yes, you still can. If you use a motorcycle lift or ATV/Motorcycle jack you will expend no muscle energy. If you place a scissor or other jack under the wheel you will expend no muscles energy lifting or lowering the heavy wheel. Removing and installing the tire requires little muscular energy if you use long tire irons and follow the procedures given in my book. The tire will slip right onto the rim with ease! Give it a try and you will see how easy it can be. A word of advice, work very slowly and be happy and relaxed and the job will be much easier than you expected. It can be fun.

208. Question: I heard bikers talking about if you try to change tires on modern motorcycles you will break the rims and the tire could even fall off because a tire machine must be used to glue the tire to the rim. This is confusing to me.
Answer: It is to me too how so many well-meaning people can be so ignorant and spread their unholy wisdom among the ranks of riders. If you get a chance, go to a motorcycle shop that has no tire changing machine and ask if you can watch them change a tire and you can see how easy it is. I assure you, once you put a tire on with or without a machine the tire will not fall off of the rim. How silly people can be! If the tire is too small or too large for the rim that can happen.

209. Question: I put on a set of tires that are not the same as what came with the bike and I even changed the rim and tire sizes so I can't use the tire pressures on the motorcycle frame's label. What pressure should I use?
Answer: You still can use the tire pressures recommended that is on the frame label and see how the bike handles and how the tires wear. You can also go to the tire manufacturer's Web site and look for any air pressure charts they may have to match your customizing, but if that fails to reveal anything you can run the air pressure recommended embossed on the tire itself. It will not harm anything if you run maximum cold tire pressure allowed as stated on the tire, but ride quality may be hard. Some manufacturers recommend that you do just that for their tires. If you do not feel comfortable with this then run 3 psi lower than the maximum and all should be well and softer ride. If you have fits with handling problems? Try a different brand of tire next time and see if things get better or worse. You mentioned new rims. You also need to make sure those new rims can handle the air pressure your tire can take or the rim can actually detonate like a bomb due to overpressure. Over inflation and under inflation of a tire will cause handling and wear problems. In your case, you need to experiment a bit to find what is right for your bike, but you will be close following the advice I just gave you.

210. Question: Can I install two different tires from two different manufacturers on my bike?
Answer: Yes, you can as long as the motorcycle tire sizes match the size of the rims. However, you will find the front and rear tire have a different contact patch profile and ride quality so there in no guarantee you will be happy with the ride and for that reason most mechanics will tell you not to do it. As far as safety is concerned the bike could wobble or you could lose control when diving around corners leaning hard, but the tires will not fall of the rim or explode or do wild things like you will hear on some Web sites and social gatherings. This situation usually arises when a rider gets a flat tire and has to replace it and the only tire available is of a different brand. You could pay to buy two tires of the same brand (which every dealer will insist that you do so with scare tactics and ghost stories) or you can just install the tire and see how it works out for you. Sports bikes are more sensitive to tire mismatch and generally is avoided, but for cruisers you can mix up the tires and you will likely not know the difference. Avoid buying a front tire with a solid straight line rain groove in the dead center of the tread as these tires wobble like mad on grooved concrete roadways. Some riders do and blame the tire mismatch as the problem when it is that center rain groove causing the problem. Don't buy those tires if you can avoid them.

211. Question: How do I realign the front wheel to the forks after a tire change?
Answer: On most bikes you simply install the wheel with the new tire on the rim by inserting the axle but do not tighten the axle nut and with the front brake on bounce the front end up and down about three times and that bouncing centers the axle to the forks and it should get the alignment very close to perfection. However, for absolute perfection for sport bikes generally need a more precise alignment you can buy an inexpensive tool from Motion Pro called the ForkTru® tool. You only need to strap the tool against the fork tube and it shows the misalignment then loosen the top triple tree clamp, place the loose front wheel between your knees and twist the handlebars until the tool indicates all is true then tighten the triple clamp, axle nut and pinch bolts and you are done. Most cruisers

won't need the tool so you can just bounce the wheel then tighten the axle and pinch bolts. This is very easy to do. Of course, if your cruiser's fork tubes are out of alignment you can use the ForkTrue® tool too to get things back to normal. Now don't be overly concerned. A lot of dealers and repair shops who install tires totally forget to bounce the forks and front wheel and you never knew your forks were actually out of alignment did you? Of course not! They may not have even balanced your wheel and you did not realize it. Just because you pay somebody else to do the work does not mean a good job is being performed. Consult a service manual for your bike.

212. Question: How can I tell if a repair shop is proficient?
Answer: Amazingly, I find the repair shop that actually washes and cleans your bike after a repair has done the job right. If you go to a dealer for tire repair and get your bike back and the wheels are dirty you can just about bet on it the repair job was also shoddy. Now this bike cleaning is not proof positive the job is performed correctly, but it sure does say a lot about how the dealer cares about you and your bike. If they go the extra mile to clean the bike they may just also be more professional in their repairs. But one must be aware that there are a lot of incompetent mechanics wrenching on bikes and some of them even have factory certifications and are still incompetent (bottom of the class rejects) and charge you good money for their inferior workmanship. All the more reason to learn to repair your own motorcycle!

213. Question: I see custom bikes with mismatch tires. Please explain.
Answer: Many custom bikes are built for show and tell not to ride so they can mismatch tires. On your street bike you can also mismatch tires if you want to. You can do anything you want whether it is correct or not that is what we call freedom of choice. There are reasons for mix or matching tires. You can put on a different brand front tire and a different brand rear tire, but you should not put on a radial and a bias tire on the motorcycle. That is the general rule. You can try it and see if you like it. If you are just putting around in town it may work just fine for you. If you are touring you may find mixing up tire brands will upset handling or are noisy. Whatever works for you will end up just fine for you and your specific bike. Experimentation is not always evil for it can be a good thing if you discover a tire combination that is superior to anything else. One thing I have found is that mixing up tire brands on a motorcycle will not cause the tire to come off the rim or blow out as some people will say to scare you. You may get a high speed wobble or feel squirms in a deep lean, get bad mileage and faster wear. As long as the tire size is proper for the rim size just go ahead and test the waters. Now, let's assume one more thing that technologies advance after I write this book and special tires, like run-flat tires, etc., are made that can't be mismatched then don't do it. Just do what the tire manufacture recommends for your bike. Rules are made for breaking some say, but if you do you should at least know that it is not a recommended procedure. Then again, a chopper is not a recommended design. The whole concept is outlaw in nature and much of what is done never makes sense and they are dangerous to ride, but they look and sound cool right? Do whatever you want at your own risk. If you don't want grief then follow the tire manufactures advice.

214. Question: Can I run spoke wheel on the front of my bike and a cast wheel on the rear or vice versa?
Answer: Yes, as long as the rim size is not changed. If you change the rim size to a wider or taller version you need to watch out for clearance problems. If that occurs you can make the changes required so the wheel and tire will not strike anything when running straight, cornering or hitting bumps in the road.

215. Question: Can I install racing tires on my street bike?
Answer: You should not as racing tires are dangerous to use on streets because they are "slick" with no rain grooves and they have no treads which means there is no grip if you come upon light coating of grit or sand on the road. The tires are expensive and very soft so they will not last long wasting your money. The rubber compound will lose tackiness on a damp road surface and if it rains the tire will hydroplane throwing you down on the pavement to crash and they are illegal, (not street legal) in most states if not all. You can install a street/race tire because it has rain grooves in the tread area, but don't expect the tire to last as the rubber compound is very soft.

216. Question: Can I install a tube with a straight valve stem into a rim with an angled valve stem hole?
Answer: No. The normal stress and strain on the innertube with a center valve will eventually tear the rubber near the hardened rubber, plastic or metal valve stem creating a sudden deflation of the tire and you could lose control of the bike and crash. Use the proper tube size and valve angle for the rim. In this case you need a tube with a side valve not a center valve tube. The valve can be of metal or rubber on the tube and the choice is yours which material you wish to install because both work just fine. If you review a motorcycle parts catalog they will show you many different valve stem configurations. Some cores are made of metal and others of rubber. Both work fine, but try to get the one that always has a threaded stem and lock nut that holds the valve stem to the rim.

217. Question: My front tire wears more on the left than on the right side. One dealer told me I may need front end work. I aligned the wheel and my forks are true. What gives?
Answer: In America the roads are convex in shape and if you ride in the right lane most of the time you will be every so slightly

steering your bike and leaning to the left. This creates a tad bit more wear on the left side of the tire than the right side. If you ride in the left lane on the freeway you may be able to counteract some of the wear. But overall, don't worry about it. The tire wear you experience is normal. The front tire shows this wear more than the rear tire due to constant steering inputs and some bikes just show this wear better than others.

218. Question: My friends get better mileage wear from their tires than I do. I ride with due care and I can't seem to figure it out and some have the same bike and even the same tires as I have. What can cause this?
Answer: I can bet the roads you travel are rougher in texture and that is why your tires wear out faster. Look into this and I believe you will find this to be the case.

219. Question: Why are motorcycle and automotive tire rope plugs black in color and some are orange or red? I see them in stores and I often wonder if I am buying the right plugs.
Answer: Some people want to see the plug in the tire making routine inspections easier and others do not want to see the plug. The composition of the rope plugs are identical and in function. Both will fix your flat tubeless tire. That is, unless the manufacturer has come out with a new color code that does not agree with what I just wrote.

220. Question: Can I put a rear tire on the front of my motorcycle?
Answer: Yes you can if you have the vertical and horizontal clearance so it is not hitting the fender or fork tubes and if you mount the tire in reverse so the arrow on the tire is rotating in the reverse direction. Why? Because the plies in the tire overlap and are designed for acceleration forces on the rear so the plies will not separate when you apply the front brake creating decelerating force if the tire is mounted on the front instead of the rear. I don't recommend doing this if you can afford to buy a front tire, but technically you can do it.

221. Question: If my pressure gage is broken or I lost it how do I inflate the tire if I get a flat?
Answer: Go check the air in your tires right now and feel the stiffness of the sidewall with your hand and fingers. When you get a flat tire and the air pressure is below 20 psi the tire sidewalls and center of the tread will flex with hand pressure applied. Add compressed air until the tire begins to feel strong resistance to your hand pressure then ride along at reduced speed to buy a pressure gage and fill the tire to the recommended pressure. I had to do this as my pressure gauge was broken and I just felt the tire pressure by hand and that got me home just fine even though the tire was underinflated. Of course, when I got home the air pressure in the tire was only a low 20 psi despite the tire feeling hard as a rock by hand. This "feel by hand" technique works to at least get you to a place where you can purchase a pressure gage.

222. Question: Which is the best rim protector to buy?
Answer: The rim saver I use are made of nylon. They resist breaking down under pressure and they last. The plastic ones crack and break easily.

223. Question: There are many tubeless tire repair devices on the market. Which one is the best as I only have room to carry one in my luggage compartment?
Answer: You can't beat the rope type as it will repair small and large size tire tread flats. The size that cars and small trucks use is the size you should carry with you along with the rasp and rope insertion tool. It seems there are many companies trying to make a better mouse trap, but the rope type plug has and will be the product to beat.

224. Question: Somebody slashed my tire with a knife. What can I use to fix the tire?
Answer: If the slice is the width of a nail you can fix it with the rope type of plug, but a long slice like glass rips a tire beyond repair and the tire must be replaced. This holds true with even a tiny hole in the sidewall area the tire can't be repaired. Usually, a knife slice to a tire is fatal to the tire. Don't even try to repair it. The tire repair systems are designed to fix "round or square shape" nail, screw and small bolt penetrations in a tire. An "oblong shape" penetration in a tire can't be repaired not even temporarily. However, let's assume you pick up a large bolt and it has made a huge hole in the tread area where inserting one rope is not enough to seal the leak, you can insert another rope plug beside it and that should work to fill up the large hole then get home right away and replace the tire.

225. Question: I have wire wheels and I want to purchase cast wheels. Where do I find them?
Answer: Check with the dealer first to see if they can help. If they can't help you check with custom wheel aftermarket suppliers and catalogs to see if they can. There may even be a service that can seal your wire rim to make it fit tubeless tires if you can't find cast wheels for your bike. If you ride a Harley-Davidson you are in luck as there are many firms that make and sell cast wheels for H-D's.

226. Question: What is your opinion on the turn and go flat tire fix?

227. Question: Should I use those liquid tire sealers?
Answer: I believe they have a purpose. The problem is the cost can be high to protect a tire from a flat tire. I ride daily and I have picked up nails only three times in ten years. I can remove the nail, use a rope plug and I am on my way. However, by filling the new tubeless tire, or innertube, with this sealant you could pick up a nail and it would seal itself around that nail and you would never know you have a flat tire. Only later when you examine your tire would you see the nail. You could then remove the nail when you get home and fix the flat tire with a rope plug or replace the tire at that time. This sealant can prevent a trip interruption or loss of air pressure at an inopportune time. The insurance factor here for added tire protection I believe is a plus. As long as the product will not corrode or degrade your fiber, steel or aluminum alloy rims and will not solidify into a huge mess when changing a tire then why not use it? If you have tube tires I say yes to use sealant.

228. Question: So I do not need to use glue when using the rope plug?
Answer: This is true. If you remove the rope plug from its package and it has a terribly sticky feeling you can just insert the rope without using any glue as the vulcanizing glue is already impregnated in the rope. So, if you can't find the glue or the glue tube has punctured (they do this a lot) and the glue has solidified or evaporated do not panic. Just insert the rope plug without the glue. One more thing about those tiny tubes of glue, they never seem to be usable when you need them anyway. The tubes leak in transit and the glue solidifies unless heavily protected. I would not worry about not using the glue as long as the rope is very sticky to the touch. Keep the rope in a air sealed package until needed so the vulcanizing glue will not dry out. These ropes are so economical you can buy new ones each spring at the beginning of riding season.

229. Question: I was told modern tires do not need to be broken in like old tires. Is this true?
Answer: Yes, it is somewhat true. Modern tires do not really need to be broken in that you must lower your forward speed for the first 50 miles or more. Some modern tires also do not have slippery "mold release" agents on the tires so you can just ride away. However, it is still best to ride slow and not accelerate or brake harshly on new tires due to the tire lubricant has not dried to a tackiness phase yet and the wheel can slip on the rim. If this happens on a tube tire the tube's valve stem can sheer right off creating a blow-out. Another reason to corner easy is to scuff up the smooth tire surface so you do not slip, slide or fall down. So, the tire still needs a 100 mile break in period even if the tire itself structurally can handle the high speed.

230. Question: Why would a tire's bead break? Please explain?
Answer: Generally, when air is low in a tire the tire's bead separates and folds away from the rim. The bead is not actually broken at this point. This usually happens to the bike's rear tire when getting a flat tire and more so when riding with a passenger the extra weight on the tire causes it to squish down hard and fold away from the rim. You can still remove the nail and plug the tire, but using a tiny air compressor will not provide a great burst of air to seat the bead to the rim so the tire can be inflated. It is time to call a tow truck or remove the wheel and take it to a shop to affix the bead to the rim by filling the tire with air using a bead setting strap then reinstall the tire to the bike.

231. Question: What can I use to avoid flat tires when I have a tube type tire and rim?
Answer: Install stop leak fluid when you install a new tire and tube. If you pick up a nail the stop leak fluid should fix the flat as it happens. If you happen to notice a nail in your tire should you remove the nail or drive away to get home? I would leave the nail in the tire if it is driven down flush with the treads and drive slowly home as long as the tire is holding air pressure. Some may not agree with this and tell you to move the nail to the 7 o'clock position, remove the nail and let the stop leak fluid seal the leak. Problem is, removing the nail could be a rusty or bent nail that may rip the innertube beyond the ability of the stop leak fluid to seal the leak. Now you do have a flat tire.

232. Question: What happens if I rasp the nail hole too much when plugging a tire?
Answer: If you rasp the hole excessively all you are doing is making the nail hole much larger in the tire and that can allow for a looser fitting plug or rope fitment. It won't hurt to plunge the rasp tool once in and out, but to keep rasping is like a file that removes too much rubber. The rasp tool does have a cleaning effect removing rust and metal chips from the nail hole. You don't have to use the rasp tool at all in some cases. Also, rasping the hole does make insertion of the rope plug much easier. If the nail was a brad in size you may have to rasp that tiny hole so you can enlarge the hole to get a plug inside of the tire. You can over-rasp using a mushroom plug, but it would be difficult to over-rasp a nail hole using those thick rope plugs. Carry large car size rope plugs with you.

233. Question: What tire pressure should I use when I know I will be riding through high and low terrain?
Answer: It can drive you crazy to keep adjusting tire pressures in anticipation of elevation changes and there's no way you can practically do it manually. Just adjust your tire pressure when tires are cold in a lower elevation and go on your trip. Even then under perfect weather conditions ambient air temperature, road surface temperature, speed, road surface texture and changes in elevation will constantly be changing the air temperature inside your tires. Tire air pressure will never be constant so don't be overly concerned about it.

234. Question: What drawbacks is there to fitting oversize tires on my motorcycle?
Answer: There can be many problems and the worse will be if you go too wide the tire will be pinched together at the rim making for a tire that can come off the rim unexpectedly. At best you will get sloppy handling and run into frame, chain, belt, fender clearance issues and it changes the chassis attitude making for unpredictable handling. Yes, it can even change rake and trail of the front forks. Even changing tire brands with the same size can do this. Ten millimeter wider than stock is generally considered okay on rear wheel. Narrow fender and forks prevents wide tire up front.

235. Question: Will changing speed and/or weight rating of my tires upset the handling of my motorcycle?
Answer: Yes, if you are riding a sport bike and maybe if you are riding a heavy cruiser. Tires that are thicker to handle high speed and weight will create numb-like handling.

236. Question: What is your opinion on steel belt tires verses nylon and rayon?
Answer: That is a complex question. Avoiding the engineering materials and focusing on tire behavior steel belt tires are heavy in weight and do not flex easily, but are good for preventing nail punctures. Kevlar® belts are even better as they flex and are stronger than steel so try them out. Nylon belts are flexible and may be too flexible for some riders. Rayon belts are smooth running tires and may give the best ride for the money for a sport bike but are usually more expensive. Kevlar® is my pick for a cruiser. Rayon for a sport bike.

237. Question: Will inserting a cold flat tire rope plug in a cold tire be troublesome?
Answer: I have inserted rope in my motorcycle tires in below freezing weather conditions, around 20 degrees and I have not had any trouble. In fact, the tire rubber is so stiff the plug went into the tire will less restriction than when warm. It seals the air leak in the tubeless tire flawlessly. You will like using the rope plug system. Make sure you practice on an old tire so you can get the hang of it. They are easy to use. Practice with glue and without glue each year.

238. Question: When I check my tire pressure it is a pain to get the tire pressure gage on the valve stem or even to fit the valve stem on the air hose. Is there a cure for this trouble?
Answer: Sounds like you have a straight valve stem and that makes it hard to reach. Next time you change tires install a 90 degree valve stem to the rim and this problem will cease.

239. Question: What is a divot in a tire?
Answer: A divot is a dent in the tire or a slice of rubber removed to produce a depression. This happens when you strike a object in the road. They can't be repaired. Just because a tire has a slight dent in it does not mean it must be replaced, but since there is no way to know for certain if the underlying cords have been damaged you have to replace the tire. For your safety there is no getting around this expense.

240. Question: Are there other methods to preventing tire irons from scratching rims?
Answer: You can experiment with placing a rubber hose over the tire iron about one inch from the tip, but I find the hose can get in the way on some tires and rims. Try wrapping the tire iron end with electrical tape or dip it in liquid rubber and let it dry. There is nothing wrong with using rim protectors that slide along the rim as you work.

241. Question: I saw videos on the Internet how easy it is to change tires on a motorcycle, but when I tried, it did not work for my Harley-Davidson. I could not get the new tire on the rim at all. What did I do wrong?
Answer: You did nothing wrong. What you saw was somebody changing a dirt bike or a sport bike tire or a thin diameter tire to a rim. Those tires go on the rim with great ease because the tires are thinner than cruiser tires and the rims has a deep well (drop center). This book specifically tackles those tough to install cruiser tires giving all the tricks needed to remove and install them with ease using simple tire irons. And if you have a sport bike these techniques make the job all the easier. You do not need to invest in an expensive tire changing machine using the instructions in this book. When you try this book your tires will install easily on your Harley-Davidson rims, no problem!

242. Question: I can't believe it. I bought a new tire and it has no balancing paint mark dots on it. Now what do I do?

243. Question: I would like to purchase a tire changer machine. Which do you recommend?

Answer: I recommend using tire irons for light personal use, but for heavy commercial use a machine is best. There are many systems not mentioned in this book so do an Internet search on "Motorcycle Tire Changing Machines" and find the one you like best that will not scratch rims. I mention the No-Mar® brand machine in my book because I have one. It works, but I still often have to use tire irons on the last phase of installing heavy cruiser size tires with shallow rims. Coats makes more expensive automatic tire changing machines and you will see other brands listed in motorcycle tool supply catalogs. Make sure they sell rim protection devices that fit their machine designed for motorcycles.

244. Question: What is a square-bead tire?

Answer: Beneath the flat edge of the tire bead where the tire irons do their work there is a metal band of metal just under that area that supports the rubber bead making that portion of the tire stiffer and stronger than just thick rubber. The metal ring is a round shape wire, but now a square wire is being used in some tires for it gives the tire additional stability and flexes a bit more to permit easier installation on the rim. Keep your eyes peeled as technology is moving forward at a fast clip and many new developments are in the works. However, rest assured this book will not be outdated as tire installation will likely remain the same unless split-rim designs come into favor a different mounting technique will be required and no tire irons or mount/demount bars will be needed, just a couple wrenches.

245. Question: What does the rasp tool do when fixing a flat tire?

Answer: It will enlarge the hole to insert a wide tire repair plug into the rubber tire. A nail hole is very tiny and the rubber tire closes up on it when the nail is removed so you can't even get the plug inserted. The rasp tool is a file that enlarges the hole and it can also act as a probe tool to push out any debris in the nail hole channel in the tire and push aside metal and fabric cords to make room for the tire repair plug. Normally, you only need to insert and remove the rasp tool two or three times. You don't want to keep filing away to bore a huge hole in the tire. Just make a tight pathway so the repair plug will go into the tire. Yes, the repair plug should have resistance to install os when set in position it makes for a tight fit.

246. Question: Can I install a smaller tire on my motorcycle?

Answer: Yes, but not more than 10mm thinner or wider than what the original manufacturer recommends. You can't make your determination based on the tire already installed on the motorcycle for you don't know if the tire size has already been changed from stock. The wheels may even be different too. Tires must fit the rims and rims must fit the tires. If you go too small or too large at the bead area the tire will be installed in a "relaxed" or "pinched" pigeon-toed condition in the rim and the tire can come off the rim unexpectedly. If you check your rim size you can match tires to the rim for a proper fit.

247. Question: How can I remove the slipperiness on new tires?

Answer: That slippery slick feel is due to mold release agents to help get the tire out of the hot steel mold so a mold release agent is sprayed into the metal mold prior to inserting the uncured carcass into the mold. After the heating vulcanizing process is performed the tire comes out of the mold with a slick lubricant and it is like an oiled tire and can be dangerous to ride on it. Some riders use sandpaper to scuff up the tire tread surface. Others ride in gravel or do some mild burn-outs in sand (not advised as grit can get into belt and chain drive components) while others just drive slowly to wear the lubricant off. Many new tires are now being made without that slippery mold release while other brands still use it.

248. Question: Why should I install my own tires? I know a lot of riders who will not do it.

Answer: Because the quality of workmanship today is horrific and price of labor and marked-up price of tires are terribly expensive. C'mon, is what you are paying for new tires truly worth hundreds of dollars? Riders are being robbed. They believe they are getting quality workmanship when in fact some kid with little mechanical knowledge is changing their tires behind the scene. I see this at many large and small dealerships! Some of these uneducated tire and accessory installers are idiots actually ripping tire beads and telling nobody about their sins. You could be riding on these damaged tires! You can insure the job is being performed properly and at half the cost or more by doing it yourself. That is why I wrote this book so more riders can learn how to change their own tires. To remove the mystery, to give knowledge, do the job right and save them money!

244. Question: I don't have time to bother changing tires? Can I buy them off the Internet and have somebody else install them?

Answer: Yes, you can if you can find a repair shop or knowledgable friend to install them for you. But there is a way I often use. I just do the rear tire on one day and the next day I do the front tire. By breaking the job down into smaller segments you will find time and realize it is easier to do. You can elongate the job further by removing the rear wheel on Monday. Tuesday remove and install tire to rim and balance wheel. Wednesday install rear wheel to bike. You get the idea. Nobody says you have to do it all at one time. Try this method and you will find the time. It is more relaxing!

245. Question: My dealership, and others, only recommend a certain brand of motorcycle tire. Everybody in town has those tires on their bikes. What is your opinion on this?
Answer: I will tell you the dealers and tire installers that only recommend certain brands of tires to customers is a farce scam to rob you of your money. Granted, the tires they sell may even be good tires and used by custom bike builders and other reputable firms, but it is still a money-making scam being played on you. Those dealers are making huge amounts of money for selling a brand of tire that is expensive, but their profit per tire is also much higher than normal. The tire may also be of the same reputable manufacturer, but of a different wear characteristic model that wears out quicker so they get increased repeat business from YOU! Again, you are being cheated. Success of a brand is no assurance of superior performance! Imagine this, you can often get a better handling tire, a longer lasting tire, a smoother riding tire at a hundred dollars less cost on each tire! Just by not following the "herd mentality" you will save hundreds of dollars on your very first tire purchase! Example: I used Metzler® and Dunlop® brand tires on my bike which are excellent tires. Then I tried a Kenda® Cruiser brand street tire and I got twice the mileage at $75 savings on each Dunlop® tire and a $130 savings per tire on the Metzeler® brand. It's just an example of how you can save serious money changing your own tires.

246. Question: I have a dealer that offers free tires for life. Is this a good deal?
Answer: Yes and no. I was shopping for a new Harley-Davidson Sportster 1200 Custom and I was offered the free tires for life. I turned it down. It certainly sounded good until I read the fine print and instantly discovered the scam that it is. Yes, the tires are given to you a no cost, but you will pay dearly for those free tires! You must pay installation labor fees, so the deal is not free and the installation fee can be more expensive than normal. But the real theft of your money comes with a "catch" that you must agree to have your bike serviced routinely at that dealership. Those tires will likely cost you a thousand dollars (or way more) before they wear out. My advice? Run for the exit!

247. Question: Why did you write this book?
Answer: I despise dishonesty. I see riders, many who live on tight budgets, being robbed by dealers and repair shops. Hundreds of dollars they charge to change tires on motorcycles. I see sport bike riders and dirt bike riders and especially street cruiser riders being lied to "in their face" being told they can't do the job themselves. That it takes special machinery or the wheel will be broken, etc. These lies have become so prolific in the power sports industry they have become the new truth, but it is still a lie. You can change tires. You don't need a tire changing machine. All you need is someone to show you how to do it. That's what my book does! People who are in the tire repair and replacement industry are fearful of liability so they won't write a instructional book like this. Factory and aftermarket service manuals often avoid the subject keeping more riders in the dark. You certainly won't see a book like this in motorcycle repair shops and new bike dealerships because they don't want you to learn how to do it yourself as they will lose picking your pocket. When I grew up we riders all changed our own tires. As I grew up over the years I saw this trend revert to the dealers and repair shops until it has become "usual and customary" not to change your own tires. Many stupid excuses are created like you will bend your rims and/or the tire sidewalls are too strong these days to use tire irons. What a crock of lies being sold to the public to perpetuate a scam on motorcycle riders. Use this book, change your own tires and you'll have hundreds of dollars in your bank account. Tell other riders too what is going on! The Bible says, "My people perish due to lack of knowledge." Do you believe?

248. Question: How do I align my rear wheel after installing it?
Answer: Most bikes with belt and chain drives have indicators showing where the axle is located. You count these "line" markings and make sure they are both equal in distance. You find them on the chain/belt tension adjusters on each swing arm. H-D Sportsters, believe it or not, have no axle indicators standard to the industry. In this case you can use is a set of calipers to make the measurement at each exposed axle slot in the swing arm. See a service manual or talk to a mechanic about this. Fortunately, in most cases when removing a rear wheel you do not have to alter the belt/chain adjustment. You just remove the axle nut and slide the axle out and remove the rear wheel. When both indicator lines are equal on each side of the swing arm the wheel is aligned. Now, some will argue against this, but I don't want to get overly technical in this book. Yes, you can do better using a plumb line or laser beam from rear to front wheel, but let's stay in the real world for the average street rider. Believe me, dealers and repair shops just use the swing arm lines. It's good enough. Serious sport bike riders may want to use the laser beam for competition use. The lines on the swing arm must be equal so the brake disk and rotor will be centered and will not bind the brakes when applied. It also increases gas mileage, gives you better handling and tire wear. If you momentarily take your hands off the handlebars and the bike pulls hard left or right it can be the rear wheel is not aligned. It could also be saddlebag and tail rack loading causing this too.

249. Question: Over inflating or under inflating a tire. Which is worse?
Answer: Both. Low pressure self-destructs the tire from excessive heat generation and the tire will wear down quicker along with a

risk the tire could actually fly off the rim when cornering. Low pressure generates terrible internal heat in the tire due to the flexing of the tire. That flexing and heat actually damages internal cords. Low pressure will cause miles per gallon of gasoline to increase costing you money. High pressure can cause a tire to burst on a hot day or if climbing a tall mountain. At best you will get a rough ride as the tires are critical components to the shock absorber system. Many other problems can develop if the tires are not set with the correct air pressure. You will never get the tire pressure spot on due to ambient air, road surface temperature and barometric air pressure changes, but you can get it close. Check tire pressure when the tires are cold or have not been ridden in one hour.

250. Question: Should I use those tire pressure monitors that attach to the valve stem?
Answer: Yes, you can, but you will find that they are functional but can be unreliable. Why? They tend to leak air slowly from the rubber seal in the device. I have used them. I really do like looking at my tires when stopped and seeing I have air in the tires. I don't like suddenly seeing the red flag showing and having to add air due to the device itself not sealing well on the valve stem. Some brands are better than others. Some leak air, some don't leak as much, but in a few months time and less than a year they leak air. Maybe improvements are made by the time you read this. Overall, I do like them even if they play games on you once in awhile because I carry an air compressor I can add air at any time or place. However, many times I do not use them at all. Believe it or not, when you are traveling you can give the sidewalls of your tires a quick squeeze by hand to see if your tires are not going flat. This is better than using a pressure gage each time you gas up because nobody uses a pressure gage at each filling of their gas tank to check their tires! Maybe once a day some riders do. Most riders hardly do it at all. At least squeezing by hand is a safety check anybody can do at any time. It's not the best, but it does work and can keep you out of trouble. If you feel a flexing sidewall by your hand you are losing air! This method is better than the guy who is not checking the tires at all. But be aware some tires are so stiff you can't squeeze them at all. You can rap the rubber with a solid stick of wood like truckers do to determine if air is in the tire. Be careful as the stick may bounce back and hit you.

251. Question: What is your opinion on tire monitoring devices?
Answer: The internal devices will not leak air. I wish all motorcycles had them!

252. Question: Which side of the rear wheel should be facing down when I am using tire irons to remove and install a new tire?
Answer: If you have a front tire with just one brake rotor face the rotor down. On the rear tire you will have a brake rotor and a sprocket or pulley. You can remove the pulley or sprocket if it gets in the way. You could even remove the brake rotor if you want instead. If your pulley is bolted on to the wheel hub? Leave it be. Just place the pulley side down and you should be able to use your tire irons on the brake rotor side facing up at you. If the brake rotor gets in the way? Remove the brake rotor. Every bike is different. In most cases you won't have to remove anything to use your tire irons. To replace a brake rotor just install it in the same direction, paint blue thread locker on the bolts and torque them to specifications in a cross-hatch pattern. Red thread locker can be used, but are harder to remove. You may have to heat up bolt heads with a propane torch to remove rotor bolts. The heat melts the thread locker so they release the bolt's threads. Don't over do it with heat. Nothing should be glowing hot or even close to that temperature. Don't use acetylene torch as it will melt aluminum.

253. Question: What torque wrench do you recommend?
Answer: I use the click type. But the dial or (digital crystal display) type is great. The cheaper beam types are also great to use. Why? Because using a click type requires some experience when working with steel bolts and soft aluminum threads. You can still strip them using a click type torque wrench if you are not careful. The beam or dial types are more sensitive and are often cheaper in price too. All torque wrenches are better than no torque wrench.

254. Question: You mention in this book expensive tires are not better, but I beg to differ with you. Everybody I know uses _____ brand tire. How can they all be wrong?
Answer: They are not wrong, they are just paying too much money for those tires! The successful branded tires that are most popular are good tires, but they may still not be the best tire. I have found this to be true so much I rarely purchase those expensive branded tires. Price is not everything. The tire I use must also be soft riding comfortable, quiet, not grabbing rain grooves, last a long time, give great fuel mileage, handle good, grip and brake well and be about half the price or less (or at least 30% less in price) of the branded tire.

255. Question: Is it possible the frame on my motorcycle could have incorrect information?
Answer: Yes, it can happen a misprinted label has been applied to your motorcycle. Usually this is a recall issue so check with a dealer to see if your motorcycle has the correct label. I have seen recalls on this issue and it can cause you problems when trying to find the correct size of tires and the air pressure to use.

256. Question: When is the best time to buy tires?
Answer: When you get the best price! While it is true prices tend to fall in the winter months you can often do very well when the

season is heating up in the spring and in full swing in the summer. Watch for sales. The tire companies are always competing for business. Amazingly, even in the best of sales I can usually find a less known brand of tire at lower cost of the deep discounted branded tire. I like Mitchelin® and Dunlop® which is a successful brand with some expensive tires, but they also have inexpensive models of tires that are economical. Keep in mind this recommendation can change over time. Check my Website for any updates and new developments: JamesRussellPublishing.com

257. Question: How come you don't show dirt bike tire photos?
Answer: Changing dirt bike tires are so easy they practically install themselves. You can actually push them onto the rims with your bare hands or at least with a tiny spoon tire iron. I have included basic instructions regarding installing cruiser innertube in tires which are much more difficult to install then dirt bike tires. Just follow the instructions in this book and you will have no problems. Just don't pinch the innertube. That is really the only thing you need to watch out for when using tire iron or the rotary mount bar. Keep the tools clear of the tube and all will be fine.

258. Question: I was told by my dealer dynamic wheel balancing must be performed on motorcycles. Is this true?
Answer: Just more dealer hype being told to you. I just recently was in a Harley-Davidson dealership and met a automotive mechanic who was afraid to change the oil on his Harley and feared to change the tires on his Harley motorcycle. I listened to all the fears this rider had and it all came down to dealers everywhere acting in collusion to spread lies into the motorcycle community to get you so fearful to perform your own routine maintenance work. Dynamic wheel balancing is not required on motorcycles. If you go to a professional motorcycle race you will see they "static balance" their tires which only proves that static balancing is all that is truly needed for motorcycles, even high speed suspension sensitive motorcycle. Don't let ignorant riders tell you the same thing. I belonged to the Harley Rider's Club (HOG) a few times in my life and I can tell you most of these riders have bought into the misinformation being presented to them by dealers. Many of them will not change their own oil or change their own tires out of fears implanted inside of them. Don't be one of them! Don't get me wrong, it is not only Harley-Davidson dealers doing this it is "All Motorcycle Dealers and Repair Shops" creating this problem for riders. Look at the old motorcycles. The old riders changed their own tires and changed their own oil. Today, look at the engine and wheels and nothing has fundamentally changed in these oil and tire routines except a great fear to maintain your own bike has taken over the masses. You can change the oil and tires on your motorcycle and you will save a ton of money too. And you can change the chain and sprockets and brake pads too! Check our Website for these repair books: JamesRussellPublishing.com

259. Question: I have a very stiff sidewall tire that just does not want to go on the rim. What do I do?
Answer: Some tire brands or models do have rigid sidewalls. Example: Kenda Kruz tires (as of this writing, but may have changed when you read this) have heavy sidewalls that will not easily dive down into the rim's drop center especially if that drop center is shallow. This makes the tire difficult to install, but it will install with three to four tire irons. The rubber at the end point of installation will lay tightly flat against the rim, even making inserting the tire irons difficult. Drive a wedge of wood (even a rubber wedge door stoop is fine) between the tire and rim, insert the tire irons, and then go back to work. Don't forget to use the carpenter C-clamps if this sort of tire gives you a hard time. When you have a tough tire make certain you are using a helping hand tool to drive the tire's top bead down into the rim's drop center. Use two helping hands if need be and the tire will then install much easier. Of course, make certain the tire is not too small to properly fit the rim otherwise the tire will not install. Warm up the rubber tire with sunshine or hair-blow dryer so the rubber will be soft and flexible. Be aggressive to push the tire down into the rim's drop-center. Work slowly to give time for the rubber to stretch. See Question #297.

260. Question: Is there more to learn about tires and if so what books can you recommend?
Answer: This book is written only to instruct riders on how to install tires on their motorcycles. There is much more to learn about tires if you wish to race or design tires and these matters are terribly complex engineering tasks. I find sport rider motorcycle magazines often have tire design and function articles for the layman to decipher. Contacting the tire manufacture will be your best bet for technical details. I am certain a college library engineering section will turn up technical books on tire technology.

261. Question: Please help me to select tires for my motorcycle.
Answer: Your owner manual is a good place to begin as for sizing information. From there you can dare to branch out and contact tire manufacturers to get tires for your brand of bike. I find that friends and other riders are not a reliable source of getting tire recommendations as 90% of them are dead wrong. Example: Most Harley-Davidson riders stick with Dunlop tires because their dealer tells them to. Harley-Davidson repair shops recommend Avon or Metzler brands and they are good tires too. However, when I put on a pair of Mitchelin Commander II® tires (as of this writing) on my new Sportster 1200 Custom I found these tires were way superior in handling, heavenly ride softness, quiet, great feel, brisk handling and wide tread footprint makes braking strong road grip in wet weather and the tires wear like iron. All this with an incredibly low price. At 8,000 miles the tires were only half-worn down. I never saw tires wear this well. It means the tires on this bike will go 16,000 miles before replacement! The point is you should try different tires. You may get some tires that are duds in your opinion, but in the end you will find a great tire combination that will reward you.

And Fix Flat Tires

I like magazine reviews on tires as they do help me determine the next tire to try. The Mitchelin Commander series tires has a square-bead design which makes installing the tires on the rim easier and gives the tire additional stability. I like these cruiser tires. Check my Website for more information as I will report if a better tire is found and no doubt as technology progresses a better tire will be created.

262. Question: I got a flat tire so I have a new innertube. Can I salvage the tire?
Answer: Probably not in most cases because the innertube rides against the smooth underside of the tire. At the nail hole even if burnished smooth will soon become frayed and chaff the innertube. However, if you apply a internal tire patch over the nail hole you can salvage the tire. Problem is, if you can purchase a patch. Most dealers don't have them and tire repair firms may not sell one to you. Dirt bike retailers may be your best bet. You can buy them, but they are often sold by the dozen and they are not cheap in price.

263. Question: Please explain the rim's drop center as it relates to tire installation again for I am still confused.
See Fig. 5-1. The deep canyon in the wheel's center and sides allows the installing tire's rim bead to be pushed down into this depression which then gives "slack" to the tire so it can be flipped over the rim. If one end of the tire did not enter this deep well the tire will "bind" up and the tire refuses to flex, flow and flip over the rim. When you are installing the last bead of the tire this is the most crucial time to get that portion of the tire opposite of where you are working with your tire irons pushed down deeply into the rim's drop-center. When you do this the tire will miraculously flip over the rim with great ease. Not knowing this trick of the trade will stop you from installing the tire, tear and break the tire's bead from excessive force and bending a rim.

264. Question: What complexity is involved with removing/installing a wheel with anti-lock brakes?
Answer: It should not create problems. However, be careful not to bend the reluctor gear on the wheel. You can wrap it with a towel to protect it. You need to read your owner or shop manual or ask your mechanic about any special procedures you need to follow to insure calibration of the anti-lock system is not going to occur.

265. Question: In Fig. 15-1 the string/rope package shows no car or truck. Can it be used on a Trike?
Answer: You can use the product for cars, trucks, Trikes and all motorcycles with tubeless tires.

266. Question: I only heard one "pop" when seating the bead to the rim. Why?
Answer: Listen to hear the top and the bottom beads "pop" when they seat. You should hear two pops, one for each bead. If you do not hear two distinct "pops" deflate the tire and reinflate again. However, sometimes the lower bead silently slips into place and you only see and hear the top bead "pop" into place. If the tire is concentric on both sides of the rim then hearing only one "pop" is just fine. It is rare, but sometimes happens, you hear no "pops" yet still the tire is installed correctly. Low inflating air volume and low air pressure will do this "silent" install.

267. Question: Can't I just use my hand or knee to hold down the tire deep into the rim's drop-center to install the tire?
Answer: You can, but it is a total pain and some tires can be so tough to install due to a shallow drop-center and a cold or rigid tire composition you will be glad to have a "helping hand" tool to hold the tire's bead down deeply into the rim's drop-center for you.

268. Question: Can I rotate tires as I do on my car?
Answer: No. Even if the wheels were identical in size from front to rear the disk brakes and drive mechanism and tire direction rotation just makes it impractical as motorcycle tires just don't last 30,000+ miles like car tires do.

269. Question: What about rims with tire pressure monitors when mounting tires?
Answer: Generally you would work no where near them with your tire irons or rotary bead mounting bar. Another method is to just remove them by loosening the locknut and push the valve stem so the device drops into the rim so it will be out of the way of your tire dismounting tools. Installing the tire you just work around the device. Make sure you install new rubber air seal washers to the valve stem. Read the tire pressure monitor instruction manual or go online to find them.

270. Question: I believe a "composite" is a soft or brittle material. Is this correct?
Answer: Composite generally refers to "brittle" ceramic or space age fibers such as Kevlar®® and Carbon Fiber, but composite can also mean a mixed alloy of different metals. Composite brake rotors can be made of a blended alloy of steels. Ceramic brake pads and rotors are considered a composite too.

271. Question: I saw a video of a tire's bead being seated and they did it without the valve core. Can we do this too?
Answer: Yes, if you can get an air connection that will fit on the valve stem and fill air into the tire. Often with this device the bursts of air are strong enough to not require a Tire Bead Starting Strap, but not in all cases. You need to use very short bursts of air when doing this so you will not over pressurize the tire and rim and set your air compressor regulator not to exceed 40psi.

272. Question: Is there a portable bead breaker to fit in saddlebags?
Answer: Yes, MotionPro® BeadPro brand is one such device. I am not certain if it works on big cruiser motorcycles with the wheel still on the bike. You may need to remove the wheel, perform the tube patch. I just don't know. I would carry a can of aerosol fix a flat in a can just in case the tool won't work. Years ago we removed the wheel and patched the tube on the side of the road. You still can if the bike is light in weight. Most every Harley-Davidson or other brand of cruiser is just too heavy.

273. Question: What tools do I need to fix a leaking tube?
Answer: Needle nose pliers to remove nail, chalk to mark nail hole, valve core removal tool, tire bead breaker, two tire irons minimum, tube patch kit, air compressor, small tube or jar of tire lubricant. You may or may not need to remove the wheel from the bike. If you must remove the wheel you will need those tools, but be aware you need a method of jacking up the bike or blocking it and I would not want to do this on a roadside or parking lot. Make the investment and get rid of spoke wheels that require innertubes and you eliminate this grief.

274. Question: Can I plug a flat tire in the rain?
Answer: Yes. Rain water will not obstruct or ruin anything. The string/rope plug is saturated with vulcanizing compound that is waterproof. The rubber plug will expand and squeeze out any water in the tire. Rain, snow or shine these products work.

275. Question: Should I banlance my new wheel first then install my new tire?
Answer: You do not have to balance the rim first then rebalance the rim again after installing a new tire, at least not for street use. Just purchase your new wheel, install your new tire then balance both at the same instance as a paired assembly. Expect to use more wheel weights using this assembled method due to the increase in mass needing to be balanced.

276. Question: Can I use a tube-type tire on my tubeless rims?
Answer: No. But where the confusion originates is that some tubeless tires are rated/stamped to be installed on tube-type rims. But a pure tube-type tire is not designed to fit a tubeless rim for it is not designed to seal hold air against a rim.

277. Question: How do I remove a spoke wheel weight?
Answer: These weights are tapered in shape with a split end that hugs a spoke nipple adjustment nut. To remove, gently tap it away from the spoke adjustment nut and remove. To install just tap the new weight down over the spoke adjustment nut.

278. Question: Can I obtain better handling with a smaller rear tire?
Answer: Generally, yes. Motorcycle manufacturers test tire sizes that will work best, but sometimes they select tires for a fashion statement instead of sheer performance, think Harley-Davidson for example. Fitting different size tires to a rim will create tire countour changes affecting the tire tread shape and that affects how the motorcycle will lean into turns for better or for worse. Just changing tire brands alone will do this. If you had a 180mm wide rear tire and replaced it with a smaller width 160mm tire the bike will be more nimble in turning while at the same time a reduction of traction occurs due to the smaller footprint contact patch with the road. Generally, staying with the stock tire size can be the wise option and experiment with different brands of tires can give you the results you desire.

279. Question: I notice a slight pounding from my front wheel. What causes this?
Answer: A tire with internal damage or a bent rim. You may have lost wheel weights causing a "thumping" imbalance and when riding you can tell if you see the front forks fluttering, responding to this hammering effect. Bad wheel bearings or too much fall-away slack adjustment in the tripletree bearings can do this too.

280. Question: What is a split rim?
Answer: A rim where no tire irons or tire changing machine is needed to renue tires. The tire is deflated and the rim bolts apart. The rim is made in two sections a lower and top section. When you pull away the top side of the rim from the lower side the rim is split into two peices. The tire is pinched between these two rims that makes up the wheel. Some big-rig trucks still use them. Mostly ATV's and industrial equipment use these wheels.

281. Question: If I change the tires on my motorcycle will it upset the speedometer?
Answer: It can, but in most cases will be neglible less than (+ or -) 5 miles per hour. Drastic tire size changes can be corrected with software download or hardware. SpeedoHealer.com makes a corrective product that will correct the odometer and speedometer.

282. Question: Can I install tall 30" tires on rims without a tire changing machine?
Answer: Yes. These tall size low-profile front tires usually have shallow drop-center rims, but there is much less rubber on these tires

to obstruct installing them. You can use tire irons or a manual tire changer. If you run into trouble just make sure you use the helping hand devices to push that tire down deeply into the rim's drop-center.

283. Question: Do I have to move the tire forward into the rim when using the helping hand tools?
Answer: You don't always have to, but yes, you can. Automatic tire changing machines that have a helping hand ram device don't do this as they just push the tire downward. Most installers use their knee to drive the tire forward so the tire will give up slack at the end point of install. If you push the tire way down, even as far as below the rim's drop center, the tire irons (or rotary mounting bar) will pull the tire forward anyway.

284. Question: I saw installers use a tire iron when using a powered tire installation machine. Why?
Answer: The bead head needs to be started by lifting the tire off the rim with a tire iron to get the bead head into position under the tire's bead edge/shoulder. Once the bead head is in position the machine rotates the tire off the rim. So, it just goes to prove you do not need a tire changing machine to remove tires on motorcycles or ATV's. The entire job can be performed with tire irons.

285. Question: Can you tell me largest size tire I can use on the front of my bagger motorcycle?
Answer: The rule of thumb for baggers is to not exceed a 23" front wheel. You'll get the tall look without sacrificing good handling. Larger wheels will require a raked tripple tree package, but don't expect handling will not suffer for it will. It is a trade-off. Kewl-metal is a company that can help you in this regards.

286. Question: Will a new different brand of tire stop the wobbling in my front end?
Answer: It can. I have had new bikes that wobbled and when installing a different (no center line sipe) tread pattern and a more rounded profile tire solved the problem. But be aware a cupped tire, warped brake rotor, grabbing brake pads, worn chain/sprockets, imbalanced wheels, bent rim, worn or loose swingarm bushings, deviant wheel alignment, bent fork or no fork oil, worn parts in shocks (front or rear), failed wheel bearings, wrong tire air pressure, loose or missing spokes, improper tire bead seating to rim due to a dirty interior rim surface and worn steering head bearings can also create a wobble. And that includes air turbulance from fairings, windshields, saddlebags and any other accessory exposed to the wind.

287. Question: I see bikes with scratched rims. Are dealers doing this?
Answer: The answer is yes they are. Some installers that have machines do not use the tire iron to lift the tire to get the machine's bead head in proper positioning and they scratch the rims. Others do not make the correct bead head to rim adjustment and the bead head crashes down on the rim. Others use no plastic bead head protection. Some use automotive machines to change motorcycle tires which is wrong to do. Others are just not well trained mechanics while some are just plain incompetent, untrustworthy and don't care about the customers. I have seen people using metal tire irons without using rim protectors scratching rims. Why pay for this grief? You may as well do it yourself and be certain the job is done right.

288. Question: I did not see in this book specific tire recommendations. Why?
Answer: Each tire company has dozens of tire types within their brand and that fitment on all the different motorcycles in use would require a huge catalog. Parts supply companies have these catalogs and so do dealers and repair shops.

289. Question: I notice you do not like spoke wheels. Are you being too severe in their criticism?
Answer: Those traditional spoke wheels for street bikes requiring an innertube are dangerous, unreliable, untrustworthy and you can't fix a flat tire on the side of the road with any degree of certainty. Spokes crack then snap, corrode and break and constantly need truing and people have suddenly crashed and become maimed and lost their life due to spoke wheel failure. Also, changing tires on them takes longer and cost more due to the cost of rim-band and innertube. Tube tires run hot and they do not last as long as tubeless tires. They clearly are nothing but trouble and the cast wheel was developed to address these problems. They have a place with dirt bike racing as the wheels are light in weight and nails, broken glass and metal are not on the racetrack as found on our highways.

290. Question: I can't mix radial and bias tires on my bike even though I have cast wheels?
Answer: You can mix those tires on your bike and it can be a bit tricky on some bikes especially when at racing speeds, and nobody wants to go on record saying that you can. Motorcycle magazines generally forbid it, but the fact remains some manufacturers actually do mix these tires on their bikes. They won't even recommend putting radial tires on a bike that comes with bias tires. I have done the latter with no problems at all and I even gained a better ride on cruiser motorcycles. You can try installing radials on your bike and ride slow and gradually test the waters especially at high speeds, cornering and braking. Be sensible. When you do extreme things you need to factor in more caution into your testing evaluation. You may run into handling instability problems, so be prepared. Then again, you may find that particular brand and style of radial tires work just fine on your bike.

291. Question: Can install a tire that has a smaller or larger aspect ratio, but the tire fits the rim?

Answer: The aspect ratio is a determination of the height of the sidewall. A low-profile tire will generate a harsh ride on bumps, but you can put them on your bike if it fits the rim and it will not hit any parts on the motorcycle. Low-profile tires are often found on large diameter wheels. These large diameter tires do not last long as they heat up and do not cool as a tire with more mass do. You may get the look you want, but the price you pay will be high.

292. Question: Can I install radial tires on my bike?
Answer: If you have cast tubeless wheels, yes. Sometimes radial tires are not a good idea. When I switch from bias to radials on my heavy cruiser motorcycles I find I get a better ride. But radial tires have less sidewall and can be rough-riding, wear faster and cost more. It is an individual choice and depending on the bike and how you ride it may or may not work for you. Bias-belt tires are really great tires, cost less than radials, last longer, run cool and they have strong sidewalls. Sometimes you just have to try and see what works better for you and if it does not work chalk it up to experience. One hint I can share is when you buy a motorcycle and you see big tires find out what those tires will cost to replace them. People are shocked to discover that the rear tire alone can cost over $200 retail price and last less than 10,000 miles. And that goes for radial or bias tires.

293. Which wheel is stronger, Kevlar or Carbon Fiber?
Answer: Carbon fiber. Both are extremely expensive and not affordable for most street riders. They have huge limitations so you need to contact the manufacturer before you buy. You may not even be able to ride with a passenger with these wheels.

294. There seems to be a lot more advice than in this book on buying new tires. Right?
Answer: Yes. I have only given basic advice on buying tires for this is a tire changing book not a tire buyer's guide. I can't possibly cover all the dozens of variations in sport, vintage, cruiser, dirt and hill climb, road race, drag race, touring, trail, sport-touring, duel-sport or adventure type tires. I need to leave this to the motorcycle magazine for new tires are coming on line that are outdating tires like new computers do to old computers. Things are changing rapidly in tire development.

295. What is your opinion of digital tire pressure gages?
Answer: The analog dial gage is best when traveling for there are no batteries to drain and fail to work when you need it most. Even accuracy is not an issue for the digital is more accurate, but tire pressures change with temperature and speed 5-10 psi plus or minus a couple pounds. The analog gage is best for reliability and less sensitive to shock and vibration on motorcycles.

296. Why is the cost of this book so high?
Answer: Would you pay $50, even $100 to have a mechanic come to your home and show you how you can save thousaands of dollars on how to change tires on your motorcycle? Or, how to change the oil on your motorcycle? Or change brake pads, chains an sprockets? When you think just how much money the book can save you'll see $1,000 saved is $1,000 earned and, that can be for just one year for many riders. Add up how much money you have paid dealers to perform routine maintenance and you will see just how low a price these how-to motorcycle books truly are.

297. Can I use two No-Mar Helping Hand devices as shown in Fig. 5-23 and Fig. 5-24 and if so, how?
Answer: You can use two and this will help you install larger size tires with greater ease. Assuming the end-point is at 12 o'clock put the helping hand at 4 o'clock and the other at 7 o'clock. I have found as the tire is almost finished going over the rim a second helping hand can prevent the rubber from releasing and jams up the works, so at that time remove one helping hand device residing at the 7 o'clock position. Assuming even this is not working, insert a tire iron where the 4 o'clock helping hand resides and that should give the slack needed to get the tire to flip over the rim. When using a rotary mount bar using two helping hands may or may not work and using only one may be your better option locating it at the 6 o'clock position. You normally don't move one helping hand around the rim, but there is no rule that you can't.

298. How can I find a portable a tire changer machine?
Answer: No-Mar makes one that attaches to a vehicle tow ball hitch and I recommend it. Search the Internet under "motorcycle tire changing stand" and many will be found. Keep in mind a lot of these machines use the rotary mount/demount method and you must to bolt or tie it down so the machine will not rotate. All of the stands can be used to hold the tire so you can use tire irons which is one good reason alone to buy one.

299. I have used tires on my rims and sometimes they leak air and the bead just won't seat. Is there a fix for this?
Answer: Sometimes used tires have deformed beads from being in contact with a different shape rim-bead. ATV's also have this problem even with brand new tires because they use very low air pressure in the tire. There is a product you can use called X-Tra Seal, Bead Sealer. It is a tire sealant designed to seal up the rubber tire's bead to the metal rim.

300. Where can I purchase tire repair products?

Answer: BellAutomotive.com has a lot of tire repair products (click on the Monkey Grip® link). Gemplers.com has even more goodies. Amazon.com has parts, tools and machines.

301. Can I use automotive tire irons on motorcycle wheels?
Answer: No. They don't have the countour required to install the tire without denting or cracking the rim.

302. My friend uses a hammer and chisel to break the bead on the tire. Is this okay?
Answer: Actually, it is okay. There is a special tool you can buy that looks like a big chisel that is hit with a hammer to break the bead on a tire. Why I do not use it in the book is because you can get hurt badly if you make a mistake and if you miss your aim with the hammer or bead breaking tool say goodby to your rim. I like to use slowly applied pressure to force the tire from the rim.

End of Questions and Answers.

LAST WORD

I enjoyed writing this book so riders can save money installing their own tires on their motorcycle. It also gives readers greater pleasure by not being ripped-off by uncaring dealers and repair shops overcharging customers just to install new tires. When I was young almost everybody changed their own tires on their motorcycles then, riders lost confidence as more and more mechanics and salespersons made up horror stories that tire irons can no longer be used on modern rims and tires. It was all a lie to drum up more business for the shops. It still is a lie. After you learn how to install tires on your motorcycle using this book... tell your friends about it too!

Thank you, James Russell/Author

The End

PHOTOGRAPH INDEX

(Begins On Next Page)

How To Install Tires on Motorcycles

Photograph Index

Fig. 1-1 Harley-Davidson Sportster Used In This Book - Location: Frenchman's Lake, California   9

Fig. 1-2 Tire Resting On Wood Blocks.   10

Fig. 1-3 Portable Tire Changing Stand With Bead Breaker   11

Fig. 1-4 Reveals Trick of the Trade   15

Fig. 2-1 No-Mar Machine & Helping Hand Clamped To Rim   17

Fig. 2-2 No-Mar Manual Tire Changer System   17

Fig. 2-3 No-Mar® Mount/Demount Bar With Side Handle   18

Fig. 2-4 Coats® Brand Mount/Demount Bar   18

Fig. 2-5 Gel Type Tyre Lube® Brand Is Super Slippery   19

Fig. 2-6 RuGlyde® Liquid Tire Mounting Lubricant   19

Fig. 2-7 Chicago Tools Manual Tire Changer   21

Fig. 2-8 Harbor Freight Tools® Brand Tire Bead Breaker   21

Fig. 2-9 16" Long-Reach Tire Iron & Rim Protectors   22

Fig. 2-10 Motor Sports® Brand Portable Tire Installer With Bead Breaker   22

Fig. 2-11 Slime® Brand Flat Tire Sealant Repair   25

Fig. 2-12 Cast Metal Rim Wheel Showing Tire Bead Being Broke Loose   25

Fig. 2-13 Axle Wrench Multi-Size Socket For Front Wheel   26

Fig. 2-14 ATV/Motorcycle Hydraulic Frame Lift   26

Fig. 2-15 Harbor Freight Tools® Brand ATV/Motorcycle Lift   27

Fig. 2-16 ATV/Motorcycle Lift Arms Supporting Frame   28

Fig. 2-17 ATV/Motorcycle Lifting Entire Bike - Don't Forget To Tie Bike Down   28

Fig. 2-18 K&L® Brand Motorcycle Specific Scissor Jack   30

Fig. 2-19 Air Compressor 3-Gallon 100 psi   30

Fig. 2-20 Large Metal Carpenter's C-Clamp   31

Fig. 2-21 Large 8" Metal Screw Carpenter's C-Clamp - Use With Gentle Care   32

Fig. 2-22 Shows Four 16" Motion Pro® Tire Irons   32

Fig. 2-23 Photo of Schrader Valve Core & Tool   35

Fig. 2-24 Rotation Arrows Marked on Rim   36

Fig. 3-1 Torque Wrenches - Click Type 3/8" & 1/2" Sizes   37

Fig. 3-2	Pinch Bolts To Loosen On Front Fork	38
Fig. 3-3	Loosening Front Axle Nut	39
Fig. 3-4	Wood or Plastic Blocks Supports Under Wheel	40
Fig. 3-5	Carpenter's Wood Shim used to Spread Caliper Brake Pads	41
Fig. 3-6	Valve Stem With Valve Cap, Bolt-In Type	42
Fig. 4-1	Wood Blocks To Support Wheel	43
Fig. 4-2	Wood Blocks Floating Tire Reveals Blocks Are Long Enough to Use	43
Fig. 4-3	Harley-Davidson Wheel Floating on Two 4"x4" Wood Blocks	44
Fig. 4-4	Valve Core Removal Tool Slotted End On Top - Multi-Purpose Tool	45
Fig. 4-5	Using Tool To Remove Valve Core	45
Fig. 4-6	Valve Core Is Often Called A Schrader Core or American Valve	45
Fig. 4-7	Tying Down Rim With Rope & Setting The Bead Breaker On Tire.	47
Fig. 4-8	Bead Breaker For Tire - Powerful, Portable & Inexpensive	47
Fig. 4-9	Carpenter's C-Clamp - 8" Size - Cast Iron or Steel	48
Fig. 4-10	Bead Breaker Breaking A Tire Bead - No-Mar® Tire Changer	48
Fig. 4-11	Rim Protectors Made of Nylon Are Very Strong	49
Fig. 4-12	Rim Protectors With Rope - Use On Metal Rims	49
Fig. 4-13	Paste Lubricant No-Mar Brand Works Very Nicely	50
Fig. 4-14	Tyre Lube® Brand Gel Lubricant Is Very Slippery	51
Fig. 4-15	Rim Protectors - Inserting Two To Four	52
Fig. 4-16	Inserting First Tire Iron	52
Fig. 4-17	Both Tire Irons Inserted Over Rim Protectors	53
Fig. 4-18	Starting To Remove Upper Bead on Tire	54
Fig. 4-19	Lifting Lower Tire Bead Over Upper Rim Removes Tire From Rim	54
Fig. 5-1	Cleaning Lower Bead Edge of Rim	56
Fig. 5-2	Lube The Cleaned Lower Rim Bead Surface	56
Fig. 5-3	Lubricating Curved Bead Section of Tire	57
Fig. 5-4	Lube the Flat Inside Edge of Tire's Bead	58
Fig. 5-5	Tire Bead's Face - Lubrication Are.	58
Fig. 5-6	Tire Irons - Highly Curved 16" Long.	60

Fig. 5-7 Lube the Rim's Two Bead Edges   62

Fig. 5-8 Lubricating Drop Center Of Rim With Paste Lube   62

Fig. 5-9 Wheel Rotation Mark   63

Fig. 5-10 Tire Rotation Indicator Embossed by Tire Manufacturer   64

Fig. 5-11 Tire Position Prior to Mounting to Rim   64

Fig. 5-12 Yellow Dot   65

Fig. 5-13 Place Tire on Rim as Shown Tilted Downward at 6 O'clock Position   66

Fig. 5-14 Installing Tire By Hand - Lower Edge Of Tire - Side View   66

Fig 5-15 shows the bottom installed and the top of the tire now resting on the rim. It's just dying to go on.   67

Fig. 5-16 Bottom Edge of New Tire Folding Over Upper Rim on Harley-Davidson Wheel   68

Fig. 5-17 Harley-Davidson Rim with White Nylon Rim Protectors Snapped Onto Upper Rim Edge   68

Fig. 5-18 Bottom Lip of Tire Going Over Top of Rim   69

Fig. 5-19 Harley-Davidson 16" Wheel Tire 1/2 Way Installed by Hand   69

Fig. 5-20 Bottom Edge of New Tire Folding Over Upper Rim on Harley-Davidson Wheel   70

Fig. 5-21 End Stage of Mounting Tire to Rim   71

Fig. 5-22 Shows Harley-Davidson Wheel & Mitchelin Commander II Tire   71

Fig. 5-23   No-Mar ® Helping Hand Tool   72

Fig. 5-24   No-Mar ® Helping Hand Tool Installed on Victory® Kingpin Wheel   72

Fig. 5-25 Drop-Center Enforcement - Tire Irons Tied Down Forces Tire Into Rim's Drop-Center   73

Fig. 5-26 Just Starting To Install Upper Bead of Tire On The Rim   74

Fig. 5-27 Installing Tire With One Tire Iron   74

Fig. 5-28 Walking Tire Uninstalling Itself   75

Fig. 5-29   End Point - Tire Overlaps Rim   75

Fig. 5-30 Helping Hand Tire Iron   76

Fig. 5-31 Helping Hand Tire Irons   76

Fig. 6-1   End Point Problems Begins Here   78

Fig. 6-2 Steel Ratcheting C-Clamp   79

Fig. 6-3   Steel Screw 8" C-Clamp Compressing Tire Away From Rim   80

Fig. 6-4 C-Clamp Compressing Out Tire Bulge   80

Fig. 6-5 Inserting Two Helping Hands Tire Irons.   82

Fig. 7-1 Dial Pressure Gage With Trigger & Lock-On Fill Connector 83

Fig. 7-2 Tire Balance Mark by Valve Stem 83

Fig. 7-3 Installing Valve Core 84

Fig. 7-4 K&L® Brand Tire Bead Starter Strap 86

Fig. 7-5 Reveals a Common Ratchet Tie-Down Strap Used to Seat Tire Bead to Rim 86

Fig. 7-6 C-Clamp Used to Help Seat Tire Bead For Tire Inflation 87

Fig. 8-1 Harley-Davidson Rim on Static Balance Stand 90

Fig. 8-2 No-Mar® Brand Static Balancing Stand 91

Fig. 8-3 Wheel Mounted On Low Friction Static Balance Stand 92

Fig. 8-4 Affixing Temporary Wheel Weight With Duct Tape 93

Fig. 8-5 Weight Placed On The Wheel Rim 95

Fig. 8-6 Gluing Weights To Rim or Caulking Edges 96

Fig. 8-7 Strip of 12- 1/4 Ounce Weights. 97

Fig. 9-1 Harley-Davidson 16" Fat Tire Installed on Rim - Job Well Done! 97

Fig. 9-2 Lubing The Axle With Axle Grease 98

Fig. 9-3 Lube Added to Wheel Hub Bearing Chamber 98

Fig. 9-4 Lubing Axle Grease To Speedometer Hub 99

Fig. 9-5 Insert Spool Spacer In Opposite Side Of Wheel Hub 99

Fig. 9-6 Spool (Spacer) Inserted Into the Wheel 100

Fig. 9-7 Wheel Insertion Between Forks 101

Fig. 9-8 K&L® Brand Scissor Jack Lifting Bike By The Frame 102

Fig. 9-9 Axle End Nut Screws Into Axle On Triumph 103

Fig. 9-10 Holding The Front Axle With Special Tool 103

Fig. 9-11 Using Torque Wrench To Tighten Front Fork Pinch Bolts 104

Fig. 9-12 Torque Wrench Tightening Fork Pinch Bolt 104

Fig. 10-1 View of Triumph Rear Wheel Removed 106

Fig. 10-2 Swing Arm Frame Brake Caliper Tab 106

Fig. 10-3 Brake Caliper Inserted Into Swing Arm Tab 106

Fig. 10-4 Axle Sliding Into Left Swing Arm 107

Fig. 11-1 Rim Lock Clamp For Tube Type Tire 108

Fig. 12-1 Slime® Brand 12-Volt Portable Air Compressor — *111*

Fig. 12-2 Slime® System — *112*

Fig. 12-3 Fix-A-Flat® Aerosol Can Is Portable & Needs No Tools — *112*

Fig. 12-4 Flat Tire Repair Kit With Electric SAE to Coax Adapter — *113*

Fig. 12-5 Screw In Sidewall Condemns Tire To Trash Heap — *114*

Fig. 13-1. Compressed CO2 Gas Systems Are Unreliable — *115*

Fig. 13-2 StopnGo® Brand Mushroom Plug Insertion Tool — *116*

Fig. 13-3 StopnGo® Brand Mushroom Plug Insertion Kit — *116*

Fig. 13-4 String/Rope Tire Repair Kit With Rubber Cement Glue — *118*

Fig. 13-5 Headlamp LED Flashlight Is Needed At Night — *119*

Fig. 14-1 Using Pliers To Remove Nail In Tire   *Fig. 14-2 Use Probe Tool To Clean Out Nail Hole* — *122*

Fig. 14-4 Insert Mushroom Plug Into Insertion Tool   *Fig. 14-3 Using Rasp Tool To Enlarge Hole In Tire (optional use)* — *122*

Fig. 14-5 Use Insertion Tip To Push Mushroom Down Into Tool   *Fig. 14-6 Screw Hollow Insertion Tip To The Probe Tool* — *122*

Fig. 14-7 Insert Hollow Insertion Tip All The Way Into Tire   *Fig. 14-8 Screw Plugger Tool On The Insertion Tip* — *123*

Fig. 14-9 Allen Wrench Driving Plug Into The Tire   *Fig. 14-10 Removing Allen Wrench From Tool* — *123*

Fig. 14-11 Remove Tool From The Tire Fig.   *Fig. 14-12 Pull Back On Plug's Tail To Seat Mushroom* — *123*

Fig. 14-13 Cut Exposed End Of Plug Flush To Tire Tread — *124*

Fig. 15-1 String-Type Rope Plugs for Tubeless Tire — *125*

Fig. 15-2 Tire Tread Rasp Reamer & Rope Insertion Tool — *126*

Fig. 15-3 Tire Marking Pencil   *Fig. 15-4 Marking Nail Hole In Tire* — *126*

Fig. 15-5 Use Needle Nose Pliers to Remove Nail From Tire — *127*

Fig. 15-6 Using The Rasp Tool - It Has A Serrated Surface — *127*

Fig. 15-7 Inserting Rope In Insertion Tool — *128*

Fig. 15-8 Rope Ends Inserted With Insertion Tool — *128*

Fig. 15-9 Tool & Rope Viewed From Inside Tire — *129*

Fig. 15-10 Rope Extended 1/2" - Pull Tool Away From Tire - Do Not Twist — *129*

Fig. 15-11 Cut Excess Rope, but not flush with the tire.   *Fig. 15-12 Cut to Trim Rope Plug* — *130*

Fig. 15-13	Rope Cut 1/4" Beyond Flush To Tire Tread	130
Fig. 16-1	The No-Mar® Brand Manually Operated Machine	131
Fig. 16-2	Insert Lower Bead Edge of Rim Into Plastic Grooves and Tighten Snugly	132
Fig. 16-3	Harley-Davidson Rim Secured at Three Points Ready to Mount Tire	133
Fig. 16-4	Tire 1/2 Mounted by Hand Ready For Tools to Finish the Job	133
Fig. 16-5	Tie Rim & Tire Down To Machine	134
Fig. 16-6	Reveals Bead Breaker Breaking Tire's Bead Away From Rim	134
Fig. 16-7	Tie Rim & Tire Down To Machine	135
Fig. 16-8	Tire Bead Is Broken	136
Fig. 16-9	Rim Clamp Clamping On To The Wheel Rim	136
Fig. 16-10	Remove Sprocket & Rubber Cushion Shocks In The Wheel	137
Fig. 16-11	Lifting Tire Off The Rim	137
Fig. 16-12	Upper Side Of Tire Is Lifting Away From The Rim	138
Fig. 16-13	Coats® Mount/Demount Bar With Plastic Non Scratching Tips	138
Fig. 16-14	Taking First Bite Of Lower Edge Of Tire	139
Fig. 16-15	Tire Removed From Rim	140
Fig. 16-16	Bead Surface - Upper Area of Rim	140
Fig. 16-17	Bead Surface Lower Area of Rim	141
Fig. 16-18	Rim Locked To Machine & Tire Resting On Rim	141
Fig. 16-19	Dive Tire By Hand On The Rim	142
Fig. 16-20	Installing Tire's Lower Side Over Upper Rim	142
Fig. 16-21	Lower Edge Almost On But Still Jammed	143
Fig. 16-22	Starting Top Side Of Tire Over The Rim	143
Fig. 16-23	Tire End Stage & Is Almost Over The Rim	144
Fig. 16-24	Balance Mark Out Of Alignment	144
Fig. 16-25	Try Filling Tire With Air Without Bead Starter Strap	145
Fig. 16-26	Bead Seating Strap Must Be Dead-Center of Tire	145
Fig. 16-27	Install Rubber Cushions In The Wheel Hub	146
Fig. 16-28	Grease Chain Sprocket Spools	146

Book Catalog

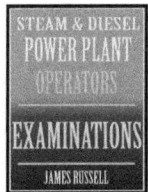

STEAM & DIESEL POWER PLANT OPERATORS EXAMINATIONS
ISBN-10: 0-916367-08-8 ISBN-13: 978-0-916367-08-4
117 pp., 8x11, illustrated, $34.95 Over 1,400 multiple-choice test questions & answers (with explanations) helps stationary engineer power plant operators pass steam boiler licensing and pre-employment exams. This book has the answers to the exams!

TRAP SHOOTING SECRETS
ISBN-10: 0-916367-09-6 ISBN-13: 978-0-916367-09-1
18-3 pp., 8x11, 85 illustrations, $34.95. There has never been a book like this, ever! *TSS* is like having a shooting coach telling you precisely what to do to hit the targets. It is the first book ever to be endorsed by professional trap shooters!

PRECISION SHOOTING - THE TRAPSHOOTER'S BIBLE
ISBN-10: 0-916367-10-X ISBN-13: 978-0-916367-10-7
230 pp., 8x11, 145 illustrations, $34.95. The *only* trap shooting book with ATA & Olympic Double-Trap technical instructions. The *only* professional advanced-level trapshooting book in the world. Has hundreds of answers to competition shooting questions in great detail to help you understand precisely what professional shooters know.

SCREEN & STAGE MARKETING SECRETS
ISBN-10: 0-916367-11-8 ISBN-13: 978-0-916367-11-4
177 pp., 8x11, 60 illustrations $34.95. The only book specifically written for writers to sell television and feature film movie screenplays and theatrical stage plays to literary agents and production companies. Many books explain how to write scripts, but this one tells how to get them sold! Insider industry secrets of marketing scritps are revealed.

INTERNET ADDRESS BOOK WITH COMPUTER BACK UP FILES
ISBN-10: 0-916367-12-6 ISBN-13: 978-0-916367-12-1
116 pp., 8x11, $19.95 Never lose another important password, ID number, e-mail or Internet contact. Log them here in this book. Also, enter your computer data files so you can recover from computer failure, theft, fire, flood, or just making a file deletion error.

AN EVENING OF COMEDY SKITS – 11 TEN MINUTE THEATRICAL PLAYS
ISBN-10: 0-916367-32-0 ISBN-13: 978-0-916367-32-9
117 pp., 8x11, $34.95. A collection of 11 ten minute comedy sketches. Plays are low budget with common household props and focusing on the funny relationships between men and women. Two parodies included of two TV shows: "Cops" and "The Dating Game. Suitable for general audiences.

James Russell Publishing.com

STAGE PLAY – A COMEDY THEATRICAL PLAY
ISBN-10: 0-916367-34-7 ISBN-13: 978-0-916367-34-3
132 pp., 8x11, $12.95 Two women must get married at all cost and they pick two goofy actors using every trick in the book to get the "I do". A fast-pace, low-budget, full-length comedy play focusing on the courtship ritual. No harsh offensive dialog. Common household props. Strong emotional acting.

TRUE BUMS - A COMEDY SCREENPLAY
ISBN-10: 0-916367-26-6 ISBN-13: 978-0-916367-26-8
118 pp., 8x11, $12.95. Three movie executives burned out on life escape the good life of Hollywood to become bobos on a California railroad. Here they discover other rich men doing the same, living the high-life in lavish Disneyland-like fantasy whistle stops, until the wives find out, steal a freight train and the great train chase is on. The bums must save Christmas at all costs from the wives who are determined to capture and return them home, forever!

REVENGE OF THE GRANNIES - A COMEDY SCREENPLAY
ISBN-10: 0-916367-25-8 ISBN-13: 978-0-916367-25-1
124 pp., 8x11, $12.95 Rich grandmothers fed up with crime and a corrupt mayor form a military assault team, MEBOM, to wage full-scale war against the city of Lost Angus street gangs and city hall. Military fireworks and destruction is severe, though nobody is killed in this comedy screenplay. Grandma is the hero!

WALKING WITH THE LORD A CHRISTIAN DEVOTIONAL – DAILY INSPIRATIONAL & WITNESSING INSTRUCTIONS
ISBN-10: 0-916367-19-3 ISBN-13: 978-0-916367-19-0
140 pp., 8x11, $12.95. A powerful daily devotional focusing on what a believer can do for the Lord with hundreds of instructions on how to prepare for God's service. Become a positive and effective witnesses to the Lord. Written for those who believe the Bible to bear good fruit.

HOW TO CHANGE THE OIL IN YOUR TWIN CAM HARLEY-DAVIDSON MOTORCYCLE
ISBN-10: 0-916367-75-6 ISBN-13: 978-0-916367-75-6
144 pp., 5.5x8.5, $34.95 A guide on how to change the three oil compartments on the motorcycle. Also replacing the air filter and spark plugs with valuable engine longevity advice. Written for the rider who wants to learn how to do it himself. This book makes it easy to learn with 80 photographs and highly detailed step-by-step instructions.

THE OATMAN ARIZONA HOLY LAND TOUR
ISBN-10: 0-916367-17-7 ISBN-13: 978-0-916367-17-6
104 pp., 5.5x8.5, 60 photographs, $19.95 A Self-guided 60 mile automobile and motorcycle tour of Arizona rock formations resembling Biblical scenes near Oatman, Arizona. A new tourist attraction near Laughlin, Nevada. The tour is on Route 66 and entirely accessible by paved roads. No other tourist attraction in the USA has more Biblical rock formations than in Oatman, Arizona. The tour is on old Route 66.

Book Catalog

THE LOST GOSPEL OF JOHN
ISBN-13: 978-0-916367-57-2
306 pp., 6.x9 $24.95 Discover a different, more powerful and entertaining Jesus you never knew existed. Experience strange and unusual parables, incredibly wild miracles, intense wisdom and fabulous sermons that will lift you to heavenly realms. Relive John's eye-witness commentaries never before published until now. A novel that will educate and enlighten with a very serious message.

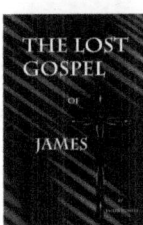

THE LOST GOSPEL OF JAMES
ISBN-13: 978-0-916367-59-6
320 pp., 6x9 $24.95 A continuation of *The Lost Gospel of John* this book advances the series with Saint James version of the gospel. A bonus feature of gospels from unknown saints of old are now included. James exposes apostate teachers and warns of the dangers of being too productive for the Lord and takes you to see the beauty of heaven, the fires and pains of hell and whisks you away to exciting pagan festivals around the world.

PROFESSIONAL TARGET SHOOTER'S DIARY & JOURNAL
ISBN-13: 978-0-916367-60-2
236 pp., 6x9 $24.95 A *combined* diary and journal specific to the target shooting sports to log competitive event pre-conditions to jog the memory of unfavorable environments, to record score, conditions, ammo, equipment modifications, etc. There are 108 shooting club (or event) listings, so there is ample room for attending and logging entries into many competitive events and practice sessions. Never be taken by surprise again forgetting what you should have remembered.

PROFESSIONAL SPORTSMAN'S EXPENSE LOG BOOK
ISBN-13: 978-0-916367-61-9
230 pp., 6x9 $24.95 Take a full tax deduction on all your sporting equipment! That's right, you can. This is the book that gets you started into the professional arena even if you are still in training and not a professional. So easy to begin you can start deducting the moment you buy the book, including practice and competitive event fees, gasoline, clothing, and dozens more deductions. It's like getting a huge pay raise! And there are no license or business fees whatsoever. Save money now!

APOSTASY DEVOTIONAL BOOK
ISBN-13: 978-0-916367-62-6
160 pp., 6x9 $24.95 This is the first published daily Christian devotional book giving remarkable insight every day of the year exposing false shepherd pastors ruling in the church today. You will learn the secrets pastors use to control and manipulate their congregations and peel back the disguise deceiving millions of churchgoers. Discover how pastors get believers to obey them... yet disobey Jesus and do it without being caught. You're in for one wild ride. Get the Biblical truth teaching you how to escape the great falling away. Stop being duped! Get the book.

James Russell Publishing.com

HOW TO INSTALL TIRES ON MOTORCYCLES & FIX FLAT TIRES
ISBN-13: 978-0-916367-77-0
202 pp., 8x11, 187 photos $34.95 for riders who want to save big money installing their own tires. Written for a novice. Tricks of the trade make it easy to install and balance all brands including Harley-Davidson, sport, dirt, touring bikes. Tire irons and machines are covered with 300 Q&A. Also learn how to fix flat tires in ten minutes. No more tow trucks! If you ride a motorcycle you will benefit from this book... I guarantee it! Stop paying dealers, save your money!

Book Catalog

BOOK ORDER FORM

QUANTITY   TITLE   RETAIL PRICE

___Steam & Diesel Power Plant Examinations $34.95
___Trap Shooting Secrets $34.95
___Precision Shooting - The Trapshooters Bible $34.95
___Screen & Stage Marketing Secrets $34.95
___Internet Address Book $12.95
___An Evening of Comedy Skits $34.95
___Walking With The Lord Christian Devotional $12.95
___True Bums $12.95
___Revenge of the Grannies $12.95
___Stage Play $12.95
___How to Change the Oil in Your Twin Cam Harley-Davidson Motorcycle - $34.95
___The Oatman Arizona Holy Land Tour $19.95
___The Lost Gospel of John $24.95
___The Lost Gospel of James $24.95
___ Professional Target Shooter's Diary & Journal $24.95
___ Professional Sportsman's Expense Log Book $24.95
___ Apostasy Devotional Book $24.95
___ How to Install Tires on Motorcycles & Fix Flat Tires $34.95

Shipping: $6 first book. Add $2 for each additional book. _____
Nevada business: Sales/Use Tax resale number # _____
TOTAL: Shipping Charge and Purchase Price of Books $ _____
Send order and payment to the mailing address listed on our Web site.

BOOKSTORES: PLEASE PURCHASE OUR BOOKS FROM OUR WHOLESALERS
For Print on Demand books contact Lightning Source listed here.

Baker & Taylor: www.btol.com Phone 908-218-3950

Ingram: www.ingrambookgroup.com Phone 800-937-8000

Lightning Source USA www.lightningsource.com Phone 615-213-5815

Brodart Company: www.brodart.com Phone 800-233-8467
Spring Arbor also wholesales our Christian books. Phone 800-395-4340

QR Code: Snap Above
Image With Cell Phone

James Russell, SAN 295-852X. Web site: JamesRussellPublishing.com
E-mail: Jrpub2002@yahoo.com

www.ingramcontent.com/pod-product-compliance
Lightning Source LLC
Chambersburg PA
CBHW060250240426
43673CB00047B/1904